Dealing with Dying, Death, and Grief during Adolescence

For some, life's introduction to death and grief comes early, and when it does it can take many forms. Not only does *Dealing with Dying, Death, and Grief during Adolescence* tackle them all, it does so with David E. Balk's remarkable sensitivity to and deep knowledge of the pressures and opportunities adolescents face in their transition from childhood to adulthood. In seamless, jargon-free language, Balk brings readers up to date with what we know about adolescent development, because over time such changes form the backstory we need to comprehend the impact of death and bereavement in an adolescent's life. The book's later chapters break down the recent findings in the study of life-threatening illness and bereavement during adolescence. And, crucially, these chapters also examine interventions that assist adolescents coping with these difficulties. Clinicians will come away from this book with both a grounded understanding of adolescent development and the adolescent experience of death, and they'll also gain specific tools for helping adolescents cope with death and grief on their own terms. For any clinician committed to supporting adolescents facing some of life's most difficult experiences, this integrated, up-to-date, and deeply insightful text is simply *the* book to have.

David E. Balk is professor in the department of health and nutrition sciences at Brooklyn College, City University of New York, where he directs the graduate program in thanatology. He is the author of *Adolescent Development: Early Through Late Adolescence, Helping the Bereaved College Student,* and several other books on death and bereavement. He is also co-editor of the second edition of the *Handbook of Thanatology* (Routledge, 2013).

THE SERIES IN DEATH, DYING, AND BEREAVEMENT

ROBERT A. NEIMEYER, CONSULTING EDITOR

FORMERLY THE SERIES IN DEATH EDUCATION, AGING, AND HEALTH CARE

HANNELORE WASS, CONSULTING EDITOR

Dealing with Dying, Death, and Grief during Adolescence

David E. Balk

Routledge
Taylor & Francis Group

NEW YORK AND LONDON

First published 2014
by Routledge
711 Third Avenue, New York, NY 10017

and by Routledge
27 Church Road, Hove, East Sussex BN3 2FA

Routledge is an imprint of the Taylor & Francis Group, an informa business

© 2014 Taylor & Francis

The right of David E. Balk to be identified as author of this work has been asserted by him in accordance with sections 77 and 78 of the Copyright, Designs and Patents Act 1988.

Library of Congress Cataloging-in-Publication Data
Balk, David E., 1943–
   Dealing with dying, death, and grief during adolescence / by David E. Balk. — 1st Edition.
      pages cm. — (The series in death, dying, and bereavement)
   Includes bibliographical references and index.
   1. Teenagers and death.   2. Grief in adolescence.   3. Bereavement in adolescence.
4. Teenagers—Counseling of.   I. Title.
   BF724.3.D43B35 2014
   155.9′370835—dc23
   2013035465

ISBN: 978-0-415-53449-9 (hbk)
ISBN: 978-0-415-53450-5 (pbk)
ISBN: 978-0-203-11335-6 (ebk)

Typeset in Minion
by Apex CoVantage, LLC

Printed and bound in the United States of America by Sheridan Books, Inc. (a Sheridan Group Company).

This book is dedicated to

Nancy S. Hogan, Irwin N. Sandler,
Phyllis R. Silverman, and J. William Worden,
for their pioneering research into the multifaceted phenomena
of children, adolescents, and loss.

To
Dennis Klass,
scholarly gadfly, incisive mind, and inspiring conversationalist,
whose intelligent discussions and challenging writings
taught me much about thanatology.

And to
David Fajgenbaum,
cofounder and Board Chair of National Students of AMF,
for his groundbreaking efforts to assist college students
who are coping with a dying parent or
grieving the death of a loved one.

Contents

Figures

Tables

Contributors

Corinne Cavuoti, MA, graduated with a master's degree in community health with a concentration in thanatology from Brooklyn College in Brooklyn, New York. She previously worked as a patient facilitator, counseling patients experiencing loss at a women's clinic in New York City. In addition to facilitating bereavement groups and developing an online support program for adolescents dealing with loss and bereavement, she is currently teaching thanatology courses at Ramapo College of New Jersey and Brooklyn College of The City University of New York (CUNY).

Anne M. Smith, MA, received her master's degree in community health, thanatology from Brooklyn College, CUNY. She has been working in the field of hospice and bereavement for the past 15 years. In addition to her work as a bereavement counselor at an inpatient hospice, she is currently facilitating bereavement groups at a local hospital and teaching a thanatology course at Ramapo College of New Jersey. She also works with her husband, a veterinarian, to support and educate clients regarding end-of-life issues for pets and pet bereavement.

Series Editor's Foreword

For millennia humans gazed at the sky and saw the sun, moon, and stars wheeling across the heavens, describing them in variegated terms as the movements of gods, the migration of heavenly bodies, or the rotation of celestial spheres. What these diverse accounts had in common was the assumption that it was the firmament that was in motion, and the earth on which we stood as the center of the universe that was at rest. Finally, in 1543, in an act of scientific (and religious) hubris, Nicolaus Copernicus turned this conception on its head, sifting through careful calculations to support a dramatically different and ultimately more useful model. As a result, the notion of a geocentric universe was overturned, the rotation of our small globe recognized, and its orbit around the sun "seen" as if for the first time. With this paradigm shift, the field of astronomy grew suddenly larger, and the eccentricities of earlier cosmologies were accommodated in a broader frame.

In these pages, author David E. Balk accomplishes a similar Copernican shift in the study of adolescents who, at too early an age, are confronted by human finitude in the form of pending death or actual loss. Paralleling his scientific predecessor in astronomy, Balk boldly reviewed and revised a subfield of developmental psychology that had long seen teens as inherently in motion, engaging in all manner of maturational, social, and identity transformations, while the word in which they lived was presumed to be a relatively static backdrop. In contrast, Balk drew attention to pivotal shifts in the adolescent's world occasioned by the introduction of death and loss, to which its occupants necessarily responded in light of the personal, social, and developmental resources available to them. The resulting recognition of the associated challenges is in a sense no less significant than the shift from a pre-Copernican cosmology introduced by the noted astronomer, as Balk challenges contemporary clinicians and scholars to bring to bear the substantial research on adolescents as they contend with a world made smaller and more vulnerable by loss.

Balk first began studying adolescent bereavement in the early 1980s when he wrote a dissertation on sibling death during the high school years—at the time virtually an unknown field of study. In the decades since, he has written and edited a series of articles and books exploring adolescent experiences of grief, and introduced us to the surprising incidence of bereavement among traditional-age college undergraduates as well as the practical interventions that might best support them. And in keeping with his own predilection, so evident in the pages that follow, he has emerged as a leading voice in thanatology intoning the need to span the gap separating bereavement researchers and clinicians.

What some may not realize is how deeply Balk's thinking about adolescence and thanatology has been influenced by thinkers in theology, philosophy, and psychology. The present volume, with its refreshingly vast scholarship made accessible by Balk's practical prose, reflects the holistic framework advocated by hospice as well as the public health model of primary, secondary, and tertiary interventions that characterizes community mental health. Balk's exploration of palliative care for adolescents acquainted him with the realities experienced by teens facing life-threatening illnesses, just as his long contact with and study of grieving college students marinated him in the realities faced by other emerging adults contending with the death of a family member. Integrating the voices of these young people into an astonishingly comprehensive survey of developmental, ecological, psychological, and systemic factors that shape who they are and how they grieve, Balk places both their struggles and their adaptation in context, and in so doing provides a greatly clarified framework for those who would offer them support or therapeutic assistance.

In short, whether the reader is interested in the latest actuarial data on causes of death in adolescence; the prevalence of disease, suicide, and bereavement among young people; a consideration of the relevant social niches in which they seek adaptation to loss (e.g., family, school, peer networks, and gangs); a consideration of their responses to illness, tragedy, and trauma; a contemporary conceptualization of grief that integrates features of several leading models; or specific educational, medical, and psychosocial interventions, Balk delivers. Remarkably, the volume accomplishes a vast survey of relevant, but typically neglected literature, and does so without neglecting depth. The result is a compendium that is as practical as it is authoritative.

A decade ago, Steve Jobs heralded the announcement of the iPhone with the immodest claim, "This changes everything," and it did. In a scholarly work that may prove to be as revolutionary to studies of adolescent grief as Apple's invention was in the field of personal technology, Balk, like Copernicus nearly five centuries before him, might stake a similar claim.

Robert A. Neimeyer, PhD
Series Editor
November 2013

Preface

I am indebted to several persons for numerous conversations on thanatology I've had over the last nearly 40 years. While my intent is to herald a few individuals in my field of professional work, first place in these conversations goes to Mary Ann Balk, whose intelligence, humanity, and love have been at the core of my development as an adult and as a scholar. Her encouragement supported my desire to apply to doctoral studies and to complete a marvelous PhD experience at that wondrously challenging campus, the University of Illinois at Urbana-Champaign. She and I have talked about other books I've written, and she has given me invaluable advice on editing and challenged me to rethink some of my positions.

My thinking and writing about adolescent development began with independent reading projects that Professor Garth J. Blackham guided when I was completing a Master's of Counseling degree at Arizona State University. Garth stands out for me as the epitome of a mentoring professor grounded deeply in his own subject matter and desirous for the growth of students. Whenever I showed up at his office, he had time for me. And when I mentioned an interest in studying adolescent development, Garth told me the titles of some books to start reading.

Writing a dissertation at the University of Illinois led me to the next conversations about adolescence, but this time with a particular focus: the responses of adolescents to sibling death. The graduate faculty in my doctoral program introduced me to life-span developmental psychology, a conceptual framework I found congenial and intellectually stimulating. A conversation with Julian Rappaport, a professor in the Psychology Department at the University of Illinois, was instrumental in righting my sinking dissertation ship: I had been getting fairly universal negative assessments about the prospects of pulling off research with bereaved adolescents. One serendipitous moment Julian was in his office when I had come to talk with him about dissertation alternatives other than one on sibling death during adolescence. After listening to me for a few minutes, Julian simply stated, "I don't usually get this direct" and then asked me, "David, why don't you do your dissertation on bereaved adolescents since it is what matters to you?"

Work on my dissertation led to meeting Dennis Klass. Some of the most challenging and stimulating conversations about bereavement, grief, and mourning have been with Denny. These conversations have occurred in diverse places: a diner in Columbia, Missouri; the grassy lawn of an Oxford University college; a dorm room at King's College in London, Ontario; a hotel in Sydney, Australia; planning meetings of the Center for the Advancement of Health; a bed and breakfast in Brookline, Massachusetts; subway trains in New York City. Denny got me thinking about alternative points of view, and I remember vividly his evocative description of what writing books provides readers: "an authorial voice."

Between completing my doctorate and beginning work on a college faculty, I met Nancy Hogan, who was thinking of writing a dissertation on adolescent sibling bereavement. Nancy was going to be visiting Tucson, where she knew I was living, and she arranged to meet me one fine spring day in the mid-1980s. That conversation about dissertation work and adolescent sibling bereavement led to other discussions, one in particular at an annual conference of Association for Death Education and Counseling (ADEC) when we skipped out on a keynote address and spent over two hours talking about trends in thanatology, about some old ideas being traipsed out as new, and some fundamental needs for thanatology research to advance.

Eventually I became a new assistant professor at Kansas State University, where Joan McNeil, at one time a President of the ADEC, invited me to survey the hundreds of undergraduate students in her course on life-span human development; Joan was interested particularly about her students' experiences with death and bereavement. From that conversation began a nearly 30-year examination of college student bereavement. That first survey certainly uncovered the hidden fact that bereavement is more prevalent among college students than had been realized.

In the early 1990s I traveled to Boston to an annual conference of the American Psychological Association (APA), where I was to present the research I had begun on testing the efficacy of a social support intervention with bereaved college students. Looking through the conference brochure, I found only two presentations on bereavement: mine and one about a longitudinal study on children's responses to the deaths of parents. For some unexpected providential luck, APA had not scheduled these two presentations to compete in the same time slots. I went to several presentations at the conference, but it was not until sitting in the session run by Bill Worden and Phyllis Silverman that I felt at home. Following their presentation I stuck around to chat and to my surprise and delight was invited to join them for brunch. And we talked about many things, some about our different research examinations of bereavement, grief, and mourning. It was my introduction to Phyllis's strong advocacy of qualitative methods and to Bill's early rethinking of his tasks of mourning as he reflected on the phenomena of what later came to be called continuing bonds.

Three years before I began doctoral studies at the University of Illinois, I was working in the Research Department of Phoenix South Community Mental Health Center. One afternoon a young man about my age showed up to drop off the latest findings from his research into mental health needs of children in the Phoenix South Catchment Area. The young man—named Irwin Sandler—was an assistant professor in the Department of Psychology at Arizona State University. Irwin and I have worked since that encounter on numerous projects, and his substantial research program into developing evidence-based interventions with bereaved children and adolescents impresses me. Irwin and I have talked about dissemination of randomized control trials, written together about the research-practice gap, and lobbied strongly (and I think reasonably and gently) for ADEC's Board of Directors to commission a Scientific Advisory Committee.

In 2005 or 2006 a young man named David Fajgenbaum phoned me to solicit my membership on the Mental Health Advisory Board for a fledgling group calling itself

National Students of AMF. I had been honing my skills to say "No" and was going to decline this opportunity being extended my way. Partly my resistance stemmed from several recent encounters long-distance with college students who said they were interested in college student bereavement and would like to do research in the area. And then they said something along the lines of "Tell me everything I need to know." But David Fajgenbaum was not like these other students. He was enthused, and he had done his homework. He knew a lot about the literature posted on college students and bereavement. He listened to my questions and answered them clearly and succinctly. He won me over, and working with him, the other members of National Students of AMF, and the persons on the Mental Health Advisory Board, has been a rewarding experience.

This book brings into play my reading, thinking, education, writing, teaching, and conversations over the past 40-plus years. Its immediate genesis stems from a conversation from Anna Moore, an editor at Routledge, who in 2011 saw I was giving a half-day workshop at ADEC on adolescent bereavement and asked me whether I would be interested to write a book on that topic for her publishing house. I had just had the privilege of giving a two-day conference at Helen DeVos Children's Hospital in Grand Rapids, Michigan, on life-threatening illness and bereavement during adolescence and suggested to Anna that we broaden the focus of the proposed book. As you can tell, Anna said "Okay."

David E. Balk
Brooklyn College
August 13, 2013

Acknowledgments

Some material in this book appears with the express permission of the following publishers:

- The Association for Death Education and Counseling for material from *The Forum: The Quarterly Publication of the Association for Death Education and Counseling,* 2011, 37(4), 24.
- Cambridge University Press for material from Burnett, P., Middleton, W., Raphael, B., & Martinek, N. (1997). Measuring core bereavement phenomena. *Psychological Medicine,* 27(1), 49–56. Reprinted with the permission of Cambridge University Press.
- Springer Publishing Company for material from *Helping the Bereaved College Student,* David E. Balk, PhD. (2011). Reproduced with the permission of Springer Publishing Company, LLC ISBN: 9780826108784.
- National Students of AMF for material from its website (www.studdentsofamf.org).
- Integrated Research Services, Inc. for material from *The Prevention Researcher,* 2011, 18(3), 3–9.
- R. Kelly Crace for material from the Life Values Inventory (www.lifevaluesinventory. org/).
- Taylor & Francis for material from Balk, D. E., Tyson-Rawson, K., & Colletti-Wetzel, J. (1993). Social support as an intervention with bereaved college students. *Death Studies,* 17(5), 427–458; Balk, D. E. & Vesta, L. (1998). Psychological development during four years of bereavement. *Death Studies,* 22(1), 23–41; Balk, D. E. (2004). Recovery following bereavement: An examination of the concept. *Death Studies,* 28(4), 361–374. Stroebe, M. & Schut, H. (1999). The dual process model of coping with bereavement: Rationale and description. *Death Studies,* 23(3), 197–224. Reprinted by permission of the publisher (Taylor & Francis Ltd, www.tandf.co.uk/ journals).
- The World Health Organization for material from *50 facts: Global health situation and trends 1955–2025.*

1 Adolescent Development and Serious Life Crises[1]

Good quale

Adolescence is a perplexing time, mainly to adults but also at times to adolescents themselves. Adults for the most part (particularly parents) realize the dynamism and energy of adolescents, yet see them at times lethargic and bored and at other times restless and agitated. Adolescents can find their lives perplexing given the many changes occurring to them and the multiple demands on their attention. The many changes include physical, cognitive, interpersonal, and self-awareness issues; the multiple demands on their attention include family matters, peer expectations, school work, electronic media bombardment, and interpersonal questions about identity, belonging, and life direction.

The Myth of Inevitable Storm and Stress   *— Great pt.*

A myth about adolescence is that it is a time of constant turmoil, conflict, distress, and confusion. To paraphrase Anna Freud, one of the proponents of this myth, the one thing we can expect to be normal about adolescents is they will be abnormal. G. Stanley Hall, a singularly influential American psychologist in the early 20th century, asserted that the adolescent years recapitulate the human species' struggles to overcome savagery and applied the phrase "storm and stress" to adolescence.

Parents accept wholesale that the adolescent years inevitably involve personal chaos and interpersonal confrontation. Parents express astonishment when informed that cross-cultural, longitudinal research indicates that relative calm and peace mark adolescent development. There seems a willingness (a) to accept that something dreadful occurs when puberty ensues and (b) to expect inevitable conflict. It is as though parents consider the adolescent years the werewolf stage of human development.   *— ✓B*

National and international research studies about adolescent identity formation tell a different story than the plot line of endemic turmoil, conflict, distress, and confusion. Adolescents in many nations indicate satisfaction with their family life, appreciation for their parents, a sense of self-direction, acceptance of self, and good relationships with their peers. It is not that adolescents and parents never clash, but rather that these interpersonal conflicts do not produce self-doubt in the youth, resentment toward parents, or antagonism toward society. Adolescents, in short, on the whole describe their lives as primarily calm and satisfying.

A minority, around 20%, depict their lives as filled with personal chaos and interpersonal struggles. The minority of youth whose lives are filled with inner turmoil and acting out behavior come to the attention of the larger public, even at times to the attention

Findings

of authorities. It has been hypothesized that, based on adults' experiences with troubled teens, sweeping generalizations are drawn about the adolescent years being inherently problematic and conflict-ridden. The reality is that adolescents on the whole cope well with daily life. They impress researchers and school counselors with their resiliency in the face of life crises such as a death to a family member or a serious, even life-threatening, illness to the adolescent.

This book looks at the impact on adolescents of two challenging life events: (1) becoming seriously ill, even terminally ill; (2) grieving the death of someone cared for. We are learning more and more that the adolescent years are not protected from the onslaught of wrenching incidents that challenge coping. The prevalence of adolescents dealing with a life-threatening illness is relatively slight compared to the many youth whose lives are spared from being turned upside down by dreadful maladies. The prevalence of adolescents grieving the death of someone loved is higher than many persons realize; we know, for instance, that every year around 25% of all college undergraduates are in the first 12 months of bereavement due to the death of a family member or friend.

Development and Life Crises

Much of adolescent growth and development occurs as interplay with various internal and environmental demands—at times with serious life crises—and most adolescents meet these demands successfully. Influential models of human development emphasize the central place coping with life crises plays in growth and transformation for adolescents. Life crises present catalysts for growth and transformation, and a life-threatening illness and bereavement over the death of a loved one contain the structural features of any life crisis: fundamental challenges to well-being, coping, and assumptions about the world.

The influence of development during adolescence forms the back story when an adolescent copes with life crises due to a life-threatening illness or to the death of someone who mattered to the youth. In order to provide such adolescents the best support possible, counselors, clinicians, and others should understand adolescent development and how youth respond to the life crises of life-threatening illness and bereavement.

Phases to Adolescent Development

It has become useful in the past several decades to adopt the idea that adolescent development occurs in three phases: early adolescence, middle adolescence, and later adolescence (an idea introduced by Peter Blos in 1979). Distinctions between early, middle, and later adolescence have been instrumental in such practical outcomes as the creation of middle schools to ease students' transitions from the elementary grades to high school. More recently the span of years called later adolescence is being termed "young adulthood" and "emerging adulthood."

Early adolescence is considered to extend from approximately the ages of 10 to 14, and is marked by the onset of puberty. Middle adolescence extends from the ages of 15 to 17, and later adolescence extends from the ages 18 to 22. Of course, these age ranges are likely conditioned by Western cultural biases in developed countries. In some cultures, coming of age has no three-part phase of adolescent development; instead, boys and girls pass from childhood into adulthood when they reach puberty and can perform the tasks expected of an adult.

From the early through later adolescent years, it is expected that individuals will gain increased skill and competency to make career choices, enter into and maintain intimate relationships, and form an autonomous identity. In short, the developmental tasks adolescents are expected to master involve responsibility, interpersonal intimacy, and individuality. Underlying these developmental tasks lies a central question about coherent identity as a physical, emotional, sexual being. Of course, reaching the age of 22 does not propel one automatically out of the phase of later adolescence and into conscientious adulthood. Some persons throughout their adult years remain ambivalent about accepting responsibility, sustaining interpersonal intimacy, and forging a separate identity.

Tasks and Conflicts as Part of Development

In the mid 1980s, Stephen Fleming and Rheba Adolph developed a model that identifies linkage between developmental markers and issues that bereaved adolescents face. I have extended their model to include adolescents faced with a life-threatening illness. As Fleming and Adolph put it, "What is needed . . . is *a model of grieving for adolescents* that reflects the distinct and differing maturational levels of adolescence, one that offers insight into what happens to adolescent development when the conflicts of grieving collide with those of ego development" (Fleming & Adolph, 1986, pp. 102–103, italics in original). In this model, they identified tasks and conflicts all adolescents face.

Movement toward greater maturity can be measured by charting how well adolescents cope with tasks and conflicts endemic to each phase of adolescent development. These tasks and conflicts are discussed directly following.

- Early adolescents face the task of separating emotionally from parents and managing the conflict of leaving their family's secure surroundings. They need to manage the tension created by the allure of remaining safe and the fear of being abandoned.
- Middle adolescents increasingly face the desire of achieving personal autonomy, self-efficacy, and individual control. Dependence on parents abuts against the adolescent's interest to achieve independence. Thus, the task for middle adolescents is gaining a sense of mastery, and the conflict lies in the tension created over the press to be independent while in the push and pull of continuing dependence.
- Later adolescents' level of success in mastering earlier maturational conflicts influences their struggles to achieve interpersonal intimacy and commitment. Coping with intimacy and commitment involves managing tensions over interpersonal closeness versus distance. Some individuals fear losing the independence they have achieved should they become overwhelmed by the demands of intimate, close relationships. Some remain ambivalent about the demands and expectations of intimacy and oscillate between commitment and running away.

Fleming and Adolph proposed that bereavement requires adolescents to cope behaviorally, cognitively, and affectively with five core issues. These five core issues are predictability of events, mastery/control, belonging, fairness/justice, and self-image. Additionally, the content of these behavioral, cognitive, and affective responses change according to the adolescent's current maturational phase. All adolescents face these core issues. The death of a family member or friend or the actual threat of one's own dying gives the issues special poignancy.

Adolescents dealing with the severe life crises of dying and of bereavement face not only the ambiguity and confusion of their situation but also the ambivalence stimulated by the push and pull of maturing or remaining immature. Resolution of this ambivalence occurs within the context of dealing with five core issues while also coping with the multiple manifestations of dread, anxiety, and fear. Directly following is a concise overview of how these five core issues play out for life-threatened and for bereaved adolescents in the early, middle, and later phases of adolescence. The author assumes that readers understand that the specifics within a particular adolescent's life bring variation to this overall general template of behavioral, cognitive, and affective responses to each core issue. To help readers sort out the complexities of developmental phases and coping with the life crises of dying and of grieving, Tables 1.1, 1.2, and 1.3 summarize the central matters of cognitive, behavioral, and affective responses, respectively, to the five core issues.

Core Issues during Early Adolescence (10–14)

Cognitive responses. The early adolescent normally has a sense of being different from others, and this sense of being different is heightened when the adolescent is grieving a death or facing his or her own death. The crisis has shaken if not shattered the adolescent's assumptions about the predictability of the world. The affected early adolescent looks to peers for acceptance and belonging, and asks questions about the fairness and justice of his or her situation (for instance, "Why was I singled out for this illness?" or "Why did that drunk driver escape unharmed but my sister died?"). The core issue of personal mastery and control may manifest for the bereaved youth in idealizing the

Table 1.1 Cognitive Responses to the Core Issues When Bereaved or Dealing with a Life-Threatening Illness

	Early Adolescence	Middle Adolescence	Later Adolescence
Predictability of Events	Shaken assumptions about the world	The world is dangerous	The world can be unsafe and unpredictable
Mastery/Control	Idealize the person who died	Unrealistic expectations vs learned helplessness	Risk intimacy in the face of possibly losing someone else
Belonging	Look to peers for acceptance and understanding	Sense of belonging is fleeting at best	Others need to be able to rely on me A spiritual quest emerges
Fairness/Justice	Questions about why the crisis had to occur	Existence seems arbitrary	Existence may be absurd
Self-Image	I am different from others and I am more mature than my peers	I am vulnerable and I am more mature than my peers	I am trustworthy and I am more mature than my peers

Table 1.2 Behavioral Responses to the Core Issues When Bereaved or Dealing with a Life-Threatening Illness

	Early Adolescence	Middle Adolescence	Later Adolescence
Predictability of Events	Undue risks vs excessive caution	Aggressive risk-taking vs losing spontaneity	Gain support against the unpredictable world
Mastery/Control	Become more like the person who died or like others with my illness or minimize the importance of that death or of my illness	Greater commitment to school vs losing interest Nonconformity Insure others don't die as well	Reach out to assist others vs withdraw into self to avoid risks
Belonging	Seek peers or avoid them	Seek peers or isolate oneself	Fidelity and loyalty vs overdependent, clinging behavior
Fairness/Justice	Self-protection vs self-destruction	Protest the indifference of the universe	Act on behalf of the larger community
Self-Image	Altruistic	On one's own vs totally dependent	Committed to others vs vacillation

Table 1.3 Affective Responses to the Core Issues When Bereaved or Dealing with a Life-Threatening Illness

	Early Adolescence	Middle Adolescence	Later Adolescence
Predictability of Events	I am afraid and angry	Unpredictability of life scares me	Fear others close to me will die
Mastery/Control	My situation seems overwhelming to me	I am angry and resentful	I have hope vs I feel hopeless
Belonging	I am angry at being misunderstood and at fake friendliness	Others have no clue what I am experiencing I need to camouflage my grief	I am accepted vs I am afraid of being vulnerable
Fairness/Justice	I am afraid, especially that someone else will die	I am angry at the indifference of the universe	I am angry at many things and accept that evil is in the world
Self-Image	I feel ineffective	I am afraid and angry	I am accepted and worthwhile vs I am rejected and unlovable

person who died, and the life-threatened adolescent may find a sense of self-efficacy has disappeared.

Behavioral responses. The early adolescent's behavioral responses oscillate between seeking and fearing separation from parents. This tension becomes more pronounced when the adolescent is grieving the death of a parent or facing his or her own death.

Dealing with the core issue of the predictability of events, life-threatened and bereaved early adolescents may engage in undue risks or insulate themselves in excessive caution. Altruistic behavior, unlike the actions of nonaffected early adolescents, marks their sense of self-image. As an example, I have yet to find a bereaved early adolescent who is fearful to be in the presence of someone who is in emotional pain, particularly grief, whereas nonbereaved early adolescents typically flee such an encounter.[2] The issue of belonging plays itself out in dichotomous ways: seeking peers or avoiding them. At times the matter reveals itself in finding out who one's real friends are. The core issue of fairness and justice manifests in behaviors that also can be dichotomous: for some, the behaviors are self-protective, whereas for others they are self-destructive. Examples from bereaved high school students included self-protective behaviors of refusing to get in a car with an intoxicated driver and self-destructive behaviors such as driving while under the influence of alcohol. The core issue of personal mastery can lead the bereaved early adolescent to take on characteristics of the person who died as a means of coping, such as becoming more studious like one's sister had been prior to her death; in other cases, adolescents work to master the confusion of their bereavement by denying the importance of the person who died.

Affective responses. Life-threatened and bereaved early adolescents' affective responses revolve around concerns over separation. Their dire situations have produced fear and anger at the unpredictability of events. Because their emotions are deflated, they may judge themselves as helpless. Their sense of belonging becomes marked by anger and alienation when friends reject them or when peers they hardly know try to ameliorate their anxiety or distress by fake shows of being upbeat and caring. Their emotional response to the core issue of fairness and justice is tinged for bereaved youth with fear, primarily the fear of someone else's death, perhaps their own. For life-threatened youth, the menace of their own dying is a foremost possibility. Anxiety may overwhelm these adolescents, and they feel incapable of exerting mastery over how they feel.

Core Issues during Middle Adolescence (15–17)

Cognitive responses. Life-threatened and bereaved middle adolescents' principal cognitive response is to see the world as dangerous, making one vulnerable. While wanting to believe "I can handle this misfortune," in reality the adolescent realizes how brittle and unsure are responses to his or her distress. A sense of belonging is fleeting, and for the life-threatened and the bereaved middle adolescents their more common perception is one of not belonging. Fairness and justice are handled by speculating on how arbitrary existence seems. Unrealistic expectations about being able to master their situation may transform into the extreme of learned helplessness.

Behavioral responses. Life-threatened and bereaved middle adolescents' behavioral responses are part of the conflict endemic to this phase of adolescent maturation, namely, achieving independence versus remaining dependent. Some middle adolescents engage in aggressive risk taking as a defiance of unpredictability, and others submerge any spontaneity by adopting highly controlled, rigid behaviors to impose predictability. The desire for belonging can stimulate dichotomous actions: while some life-threatened or bereaved middle adolescents go to practically any lengths to gain peer approval, others isolate themselves from peer contact. A rich and moving illustration of a bereaved middle adolescent's effort to isolate himself from peers is portrayed in the remarkable novel and movie *Ordinary People*.[3] The unfairness of their own terminal illness or the death of someone they loved leads some adolescents to protest the indifference of the universe. Mastery and control are manifest in various ways, stretching from increased academic involvement to its opposite, total loss of care about school work; acting out by refusing to conform to rules and flouting the norms and conventions of peers as well as adults; and becoming preoccupied with insuring others won't die as well.

Affective responses. Life-threatened and bereaved middle adolescents' affective responses are disjointed and unpredictable, perhaps lacking any sense of coherency for the adolescent and persons who care for him or her. Anger and fear predominate. The prospect of dying for the life-threatened middle adolescent and the death of a loved one for the bereaved group has made clear that existence is unpredictable, eliciting fear in the adolescent and also anger at being afraid. Fear also marks the core issue of self-image, as the adolescent in distress fears losing competency or fears appearing incompetent; in addition, life-threatened and bereaved middle adolescents are acutely aware that others have no clue what they are going through. It is not uncommon to hear bereaved adolescents consider themselves more mature than their peers because of what coping with bereavement has taught them. This sense of feeling different from their unaffected peers can manifest in many ways in terms of the core issue of belonging: feeling misunderstood, as just noted; fear of belonging and then being abandoned; and a concerted effort to camouflage grief in order not to lose acquaintances and friends. The core issue of fairness and justice gets mingled with anger at the indifference of the universe. Mastery and control seem to be insurmountable obstacles, and some life-threatened and some bereaved middle adolescents succumb to anger and resentment; however, resilience marks the lives of other adolescents as they deal successfully with the dread and confusion of their existential predicament.

Core Issues during Later Adolescence (18–22)

Cognitive responses. Life-threatened and bereaved later adolescents' cognitive responses center on trust. Because the world has shown itself to be unsafe and unpredictable, the adolescent recognizes the salience of being able to rely on someone else and of others' being able to count on him or her. Being trustworthy marks their idealized sense of self, but so does the recognition that the prospect of dying and the reality of bereavement have set them apart from others. Finding others who are enduring similar crises gives a lifeline and renewed hope. As one bereaved college student said, "When I am able to tell people what has happened in my life so far, it has led to me being brought closer to them. Many have become like family and I am able to rely upon them. One of my friends I now consider a big brother. I feel that he took on this role to provide me with a male figure of support" (Balk, 2011b, p. 129). Another student said, "I know that those who are my true friends will not leave me, and without actually knowing it I have surrounded myself with others who have lost loved ones. It has brought some of us together like my boyfriend and me, but it has also made others leave" (p. 128). A significant component of cognitive responses to the core issue of belonging involves a spiritual quest for connectedness and meaning, and such an issue is no less prominent for life-threatened and bereaved individuals in the later phase of adolescent development. The impacted later adolescent faces the core issue of fairness and justice with questions about the apparent absurdity of existence. The core issue of mastery and control centers on risking intimacy and commitment in the face of the possibility of losing someone.

Behavioral responses. Life-threatened and bereaved later adolescents' behavioral responses are focused on the overall developmental task of achieving interpersonal intimacy and commitment. Extremes of overinvestment in other persons may occur as a means to gain support against the unpredictability of the world. Behavioral responses to the core issue of self-image may vacillate between commitment to and withdrawal from others. The core issue of belonging may be fulfilled in fidelity and loyalty to someone else; however, there are possibilities of becoming overdependent on and clinging to others. Responding behaviorally to the core issue of fairness and justice may emerge in acts on behalf of the larger community, as evidenced in the many campus chapters of a national support network of bereaved college students (www.studentsofamf.org/) that engage in public service, such as completing 10K walks to promote breast cancer research and working as camp counselors for bereaved and ill children. The core issue of mastery and control may see dichotomous responses: some persons reach out to assist others, whereas others withdraw into themselves in order to avoid challenges that involve risk.

Affective responses. Life-threatened and bereaved later adolescents' affective responses are influenced noticeably by others' acceptance or rejection. Their coping with the predictability of events zeroes in on fears that others close to them, such as parents or siblings, will die; or on the very prominent fear that their illness will kill them. Their self-image is either one of being accepted, loved, and worthwhile or, due to rejection, of being unloved and unlovable. The core issue of belonging is fulfilled if others accept and understand the adolescent; this core issue is tested should fear of being vulnerable due to attachments to others dominate the adolescent. One can see the emotional significance of belonging for bereaved later adolescents in what an undergraduate whose father had died said when talking about the individuality of coping with bereavement: "Why do I have to do this alone?" (personal communication, October 12, 1997). The core issue of fairness and justice emerges as "generalized anger" (Fleming & Adolph, 1986, p. 108) and an emotional acceptance that the world contains evil. The core issue of mastery and control is fulfilled when a life-threatened or bereaved adolescent regains hope but is constrained when the dominant affect is despair.

Concluding Comments

My purpose with this chapter was to examine some central matters that are germane to understanding issues adolescents face when coping with life-threatening illnesses and with bereavement. Appreciating the interface between these life crises and adolescent development is a matter with both practical and theoretical implications.

[handwritten annotation: + long-term impact on lived experience.]

'Lived experience'

The thesis of this book is that adolescent coping with the demands of a life-threatening illness or with bereavement occurs within the context of multiple demands society places on youth to mature and become responsible, autonomous adults. The plan of this book is to situate adolescent development as the back story for comprehending the impacts of dying and bereavement in an adolescent's life. I believe that coping with these formidable life crises influences identity formation, interpersonal relationships, and life direction. I also believe that the fundamental matters at stake in all adolescent development—identity formation, relationships with others, and life direction—influence coping with dying and bereavement.

The book's structure enables me to examine this thesis and to look at empirical data regarding life-threatening illness and bereavement in the lives of adolescents. More than anything, my intent is to depict how adolescents cope with these events, to identify some interventions that are helpful, and to engage the reader in an intellectual journey about the emotionally demanding experiences that some adolescents face, often without empathic and informed adults and peers at their side.

This book makes use of developmental systems theory. Developmental systems theory is the guiding framework to understand, examine, explain, and intervene when faced with adolescent dying and grieving. Developmental systems theory orients the scholar to many disciplinary approaches, though the scholar may not be an expert in all. For example, there is a need to integrate into discussions of bereavement and its outcomes knowledge of scientific findings from cognitive neuroscience, counseling psychology, social learning theory, and developmental psychology. This book is replete with concepts and findings from those disciplines and from others, including psychodynamic psychotherapy, existential phenomenology, and social psychiatry.

The concept of triangulation has gained a prominent place in many research methodologies and, I hasten to add, of nuanced interventions from clinical practitioners. Each chapter in this book employs the idea of triangulation. The goal throughout is application. This book is an effort to bridge the gap separating practitioners and researchers. My tacit and at times explicit tack is toward making connections across varying disciplines offering help for persons coping with difficult life circumstances.

The bulk of my scholarly writings are replete with textual citations, typically following APA style rules. Recently I completed a book titled *Helping the Bereaved College Student*, and in that volume left out all citations within the text, placing at the end of each chapter titles readers can consult regarding the matters under discussion. The approach met with very favorable responses from readers, and I have continued that practice here.

Notes

1. Portions of this chapter appeared originally in *The Prevention Researcher*, 2011, **18**(3), 3–9 and are used with explicit permission from *The Prevention Researcher*.
2. Actually, it seems that fleeing the emotional turmoil of someone else's bereavement is common to many persons, but not to people who have coped with the distress of bereavement. Such anxiety is found when people—adolescents in particular—are in the presence of someone who has a life-threatening illness.
3. *Ordinary People* illustrates, in fact, all the core issues, tasks, and conflicts in the life of Conrad, a middle-adolescent boy grieving the death of his older brother, as he struggles to regain himself in the midst of what we would now consider an enduring grief trajectory.

Sources

Arnett, J. J. (2000). Emerging adulthood: A theory of development from the late teens through the twenties. *American Psychologist, 55*(5), 469–480.

Balk, D. E. (1981). *Sibling death during adolescence: Grief reactions and self concept perceptions.* Unpublished doctoral dissertation, University of Illinois at Urbana-Champaign.

Balk, D. E. (1995). *Adolescent development: Early through late adolescence.* Pacific Grove, CA: Brooks/Cole.

Balk, D. E. (1996). Models for understanding adolescent coping with bereavement. *Death Studies, 20,* 367–387.

Balk, D. E. (2011a). Adolescent development and bereavement: An introduction. *The Prevention Researcher, 18*(3), 3–9.

Balk, D. E. (2011b). *Helping the bereaved college student.* New York: Springer.

Balk, D. E. & Corr, C. A. (Editors). (2009). *Adolescent encounters with death, bereavement, and coping.* New York: Springer .

Balk, D. E., Walker, A. C., & Baker, A. (2010). Prevalence and severity of college student bereavement examined in a randomly selected sample. *Death Studies, 35,* 459–468.

Bandura, A. (1980). The stormy decade: Fact or fiction? In R. E. Muuss (Ed.), *Adolescent behavior and society: A book of readings* (3rd ed.) (pp. 23–31). New York: Random House.

Blos, P. A. (1979). *The adolescent passage: Developmental issues.* New York: International Universities Press.

Bonanno, G. A. (2009). *The other side of sadness: What the new science of bereavement tells us about life after loss.* New York: Basic Books.

Buchanan, C. M. & Hughes, J. L. (2009). Construction of social reality during adolescence: Can expecting storm and stress increase real or perceived storm and stress? *Journal of Research on Adolescence, 19,* 261–285.

Cobb, N. J. (2010). *Adolescence* (7th ed.). Sunderland, MA: Sinauer.

Coleman, J. C. (1978). Current contradictions in adolescent theory. *Journal of Youth and Adolescence, 7,* 1–11.

Corr, C. A. & Balk, D. E. (Editors). (1996). *Handbook of adolescent death and bereavement.* New York: Springer.

Corr, C. A., Nabe, C. M., & Corr, D. M. (2008). *Death & dying, life & living* (6th ed.). Belmont, CA: Wadsworth.

Damon, W. & Lerner, R. M. (Editors). (2008). *Child and adolescent development: An advanced course.* Hoboken, NJ: John Wiley and Sons.

Erikson, E. (1968). *Identity: Youth and crisis.* New York: Norton.

Fleming, S. J. & Adolph, R. (1986). Helping bereaved adolescents: Needs and responses. In C.A. Corr & J. N. McNeil (Eds.), *Adolescence and death* (pp. 97–118). New York: Springer.

Freud, A. (1969). Adolescence. In *The writings of Anna Freud* (Vol. V, pp. 136–166). New York: International Universities Press.

Garrod, A. C., Smulyan. L., Powers, S. I., & Kilkenny, R. (2011). *Adolescent portraits: Identity, relationships, and challenges* (6th ed.). Boston: Allyn & Bacon.

Guest, J. (1976). *Ordinary people.* New York: Viking Press.

Hall, G. S. (1904). *Adolescence: Its psychology and its relations to physiology, anthropology, sociology, sex, crime, religion, and education.* (Vol. 1). New York: D. Appleton.

Hines, A. R. & Paulson, S. C. (2006). Parents' and teachers' perceptions of adolescent storm and stress: Relations with parenting and teaching styles. *Adolescence, 41,* 59–0614.

Hornbeck, G. N. & Hill, J. P. (1988). Storm and stress beliefs about adolescence; Prevalence, self-reported antecedents, and effects of an undergraduate course. *Journal of Youth and Adolescence, 17,* 285–306.

Josselson, R. (1987). *Finding herself: Pathways to identity development in women.* San Francisco: Jossey-Bass.

Lerner, R. M. (2007). *The good teen: Rescuing adolescence from the myths of the storm and stress years.* New York: Crown.

Lindholm, J. A. (2007). Spirituality in the academy: Reintegrating our lives and the lives of our students. *About Campus, 12*(4), 10–17. Retrieved October 12, 2010, from www.interscience. wiley.com.

Manning. M. L. (2000). A brief history of the middle school. *Clearing House, 73,* 192.

Moos, R. H. (2002). Life stressors, social resources, and coping skills in youth: Applications to adolescents with chronic disorders. *Journal of Adolescent Health, 30,* 22–29.

National Middle School Association (NMSA). (1982). *This we believe: Developmentally appropriate middle schools.* Columbus, OH: NMSA.

Offer, D. (1969). *The psychological world of the teenager.* New York: Basic Books.

Offer, D., Offer, M. K., & Ostrov, E. (2004). *Regular guys: 34 years beyond adolescence.* New York: Plenum.

Offer, D., Ostrov, E., Howard, K. I., & Atkinson, R. (1988). *The teenage world; Adolescents' self-image in ten countries.* New York: Plenum.

Redford, R. (Director). (1980). *Ordinary people.* Hollywood, CA: Paramount Pictures.

2 Adolescent Development
Physical, Cognitive, and Personal Changes

Radical changes over time—physical, cognitive, and personal—occur during adolescence, and Chapter 2 examines these changes. These changes manifest in such observed ways as adolescents' physical development, interests in body image, sexuality, identity, interpersonal relationships, social reasoning, awareness of possibilities, shifts in abstract thinking, and challenges to become more engaged in critical thinking. Psychological neuroscience provides some of the fundamental data identifying changes in brain functioning and activity during adolescence.

Indisputable Evidence: Physical Changes in Ever-Living Color

Reaching reproductive maturity is a definitive physical event during adolescence, and it occurs within a concatenation of social and cognitive changes that move an individual toward greater maturity. Reproductive maturity refers to the completion of sexual development, when females can conceive a child and males can impregnate a female. It is self-evident that reaching reproductive maturity does not invoke adulthood with its defining criteria of establishing functional autonomy, forming a clear career direction, and committing oneself in stable, intimate relationships.

Sexual development does not necessarily coincide with chronological age. Thus, children the same age may be at different points of sexual maturity. Different levels of development have been identified to chart progress of an adolescent toward sexual maturity. The levels are rated according to the presence of secondary sex characteristics: in females, the onset of menstruation and breast and pubic hair development; in males, genital and pubic hair development. For both boys and girls, peak height velocity is also charted: peak height velocity denotes that point during the adolescent growth spurt when the maximum annual increase in stature occurs. This framework for rating sexual maturity is primarily the work of James Tanner, a British pediatrician.

Tanner's system uses five grades to identify growth into sexual maturity:

1. The absence of any secondary sex characteristics
2. The first appearance of a secondary sex characteristic
3. The further development of a secondary sex characteristic
4. More mature stages of a secondary sex characteristic
5. Full adult development of a secondary sex characteristic

Variance marks the completion for both genders of the various secondary sex characteristics. Thus, a female who has begun to menstruate by age 13 may have reached Grade 5 peak height velocity by age 12, but still be in Grade 3 breast development at age 16. Boys' development shows comparable variation. A boy typically reaches peak height velocity between the ages of 14 and 15, but Grade 5 pubic hair development may not occur until age 17 or 18.

There are more than physical changes to consider here, and we must also consider psychosocial issues for variance of sexual maturity during adolescence. For instance, girls who are 14 but look older are treated differently by their peers and by older adolescents than 14-year-old girls who have yet to develop any secondary sex characteristics and other 14-year-olds who are developing at what is considered an on-time pace. Girls who mature early sexually must learn to cope with new social circumstances (for instance, dating older boys), which place greater pressures on them than on peers who are the same age chronologically but not biologically.

Reactions to the onset of puberty and its tell-tale signs, namely, secondary sex characteristics, vary by gender.

- Early maturing girls initially experience distress and self-consciousness, whereas early maturing boys show increased confidence and heightened prestige from peers and adults. By later adolescence, early-maturing girls develop sophisticated social skills and more self-confidence. Early-maturing boys, strangely enough, by later adolescence seem to become less spontaneous and less open to considering alternatives than boys who are maturing on time or who are late in maturing.
- On-time girls have more positive images of their bodies and feel more socially attractive than do early- or late-maturing girls. Maturing late has some negative sequelae for girls: they are less popular, less sophisticated, and less self-directed than their early- and on-time counterparts.[1]
- On-time boys feel less attractive than early-maturing boys but more attractive than late-maturing boys. Late-maturing boys develop problem-solving flexibility not seen in early-maturing boys and seen less often in on-time maturing boys. Late-maturing boys are less submissive to authority than are early maturers.

Cognitive Changes, New Perspective Taking, and a Look at the Adolescent Brain

As adolescents develop, their cognitive skills become more complex and sophisticated than the cognitive operations available to children. Some of the notable signs of this cognitive growth during adolescence include (a) considering competing points of view, (b) keeping competing points of view in mind when examining issues, and (c) thinking systematically. All in all, the gains are matters of using abstract concepts and engaging in critical thinking. Generations of developmental psychologists have described these gains as the product of formal operations, which was part of the signal achievement of Jean Piaget in his study of cognitive growth in children, adolescents, and adults. While Piaget's approach is a renowned, well-received model for discussing adolescent cognitive development, I have decided to spend more time with the information processing framework.

Information Processing Providing a Lens on Adolescent Growth in Cognition

Information processing coined several terms useful for understanding human cognition. Some of these terms are short-term memory, sometimes called working memory; executive control processes; long-term memory; metacomponents, performance components, acquisition components, retention components, and transfer components. Here is a brief look at each term.

- Short-term memory (STM) holds information temporarily and carries out (i.e., executes) operations on information. Short-term memory has limited capacity and limited duration (approximately seven chunks of information retained for several seconds at best). Learning to use rehearsal strategies allows a person to retain information, such as remembering a phone number.
- Executive control processes plan and run each phase of information processing. They regulate attention, select appropriate memory processes and problem-solving strategies, and monitor the quality of answers and solutions. Unless executive control processes focus on STM content, the information is soon forgotten.
- Long-term memory is a relatively permanent and unlimited storehouse of knowledge and information-processing strategies acquired from experience. STM content that is transferred to long-term memory (LTM) becomes available for retrieval when needed.
- Metacomponents are higher order cognitive processes whereby decision-making and problem-solving occur. These processes involve problem identification, strategy selection, and goal accomplishment. They control and regulate the other components.
- Performance components carry out the overall plans and decisions established by the metacomponents by encoding problem elements, combining elements, and assessing the applicability of a solution.
- Acquisition components enable a person to learn new information.
- Retention components enable a person to retrieve stored information.
- Transfer components enable a person to apply stored information to new situations.

Information processing emphasizes involvement and activity and puzzle-solving. Human intelligence develops as the five components interact; they activate one another and offer feedback. In several ways, significant changes in human intelligence differentiating adolescents from children—and later adolescents from early—have been identified in the information processing model.

More Sophisticated Control Strategies. Executive control processes gain greater use during adolescence. For example, in comparison to children, early adolescents use rehearsal strategies to remember information. Seventeen-year-olds have greater skill than younger adolescents and children in retrieving information. Greater experience in using information processing enables persons as they grow to attend to relevant information and ignore irrelevant.

More Exhaustive Processing of Information. Adolescents process information more thoroughly than do children. Adolescents learn better encoding procedures and evaluation strategies, and they use these processes more exhaustively. In comparison to children, adolescents when reading make more thorough attempts to extract the main idea of what they are reading, to scan the text more completely while they read, and to retrieve information about what they have read.

Greater Ability to Comprehend Successively Higher-Order Relationships. The adolescent's ability to comprehend relations of a successively higher order is due to increasing skill in abstract reasoning. For instance, understanding analogies such as "a horse is to a rider as a car is to a driver" is a second-order relational skill that emerges in early adolescence. A more difficult order of abstract reasoning, called third-order relations, emerges during adolescence; third-order relations are illustrated in comprehending how separate analogies are analogous to each other. An example of a third-order relation is found in "(Happy: Sad::Red: Courage) :: (Tall: Short :: Yellow: Cowardice)" (Sternberg & Downing, 1982, p. 214). To translate, happiness is the opposite of sadness and red symbolizes courage just as tall is the opposite of short and yellow symbolizes cowardice. The parallelism in the structure is critical: both happy/sad and tall/short present opposites, and colors are used to represent opposite emotional states.

Increased Flexibility and Wisdom in Using Information. As adolescents mature, they extend their repertoire for obtaining information and their strategies for applying information, particularly in novel situations. Partly this growth in flexibility and wisdom emerges from learning to look for alternative approaches. Chemistry puzzle solving differentiating 10th grade high school students from college undergraduates helps to illustrate the idea. A type of puzzle posed was to explain what accounted for the color reaction when two or more chemicals were combined.

The high school students had not taken chemistry, and the college students did not have substantial experience with chemistry. In all cases, the 10th graders were less flexible than the college students. The 10th graders developed poorly stated hypotheses and poorly stated definitions of the problems to be solved. They demonstrated difficulty synthesizing and organizing dissimilar information, and their planning to answer the problems was haphazard, a matter of trial-and-error. The college students, however, performed much better in all these areas of problem solving, particularly knowing when to change strategies when an approach was not working.

Four overarching conclusions about human growth in intelligence are possible to draw based on information processing. Here is a brief overview of these conclusions.

1. Changes in strategies mark intellectual development of adolescents over children. Changes in use of intellectual strategy are associated with increasing age, and these changes give us insights into the developments of the human mind. As adolescents develop, they tend to use more information to solve problems, and they integrate the information more successfully than do children.
2. As a person's LTM content increases, self-awareness of this growth—a function of what information processing would call metacognition—influences further acquisition of the knowledge base.
3. Changes in how information is represented and transformed, that is encoded and connected, occur as persons age and gain more experience.

4. Cognitive processes become increasingly more available as persons enter adolescence. Access to processes has been shown to be faster for middle and later adolescents than for children and early adolescents. Experimental social studies curricula have been shown to be able to teach early and middle adolescents to develop and use more cognitive processes. These processes included such skills as identifying, retrieving, organizing, and evaluating information needed to solve social studies problems.

Engaging in Reflective Judgment

Both cross-sectional and longitudinal research studies have demonstrated that later adolescents who attend college increase their use of reflective judgment, as well as grow in using writing skills, reasoning at a formal operational level, thinking critically, and handling conceptual complexity. The young college student typically enters with an inflexible understanding of knowledge and grows to understand that reality is much more complex than he or she had appreciated when beginning undergraduate studies.

One model of cognitive development during college indicates that students perceive knowledge and learning in one of three divergent ways, and that growth toward greater flexibility occurs as the student comes into more and more contact with alternative points of view. This model talks of dualists, relativists, and committed relativists.

William G. Perry, a psychologist at Harvard, first presented this development in reflective judgment in his book *Forms of Intellectual and Ethical Development during the College Years*. He gained his perspective into these changes in students' lives with in-depth, rich interviews with Harvard and Radcliffe students over the 4 years of their undergraduate work.

Dualists are interested in facts, do not consider that shades of meaning exist, believe that facts are true or false, and understand answers to be correct or incorrect. Rather than a changing, evolving body of understanding, knowledge for dualists is stable, unchanging, and true. Authorities know the correct answers, and the student's job is to unearth what those correct answers are. Connections between ideas are difficult for dualists to comprehend, and synthesizing information to form theories is beyond their capacity.

Relativists have reached more advanced intellectual development than dualists. Relativists engage in a more critical, skeptical approach to claims about truth and to claims based on authority. They expect that evidence will support claims. They appreciate that several sides can exist to a story and that alternative points of view compete for allegiance. Relativists appreciate that some ideas explain reality more adequately than other ideas. But they also accept that all ideas are open to revision. Relativists can synthesize information to form theories, and they do more than engage in rote memorization of unconnected facts. They apply and analyze the connections between ideas and facts. They see no basis for choosing one position over another; however, they are convinced that relativism is correct, can show the subtlety of arguments for and against an issue, can compare competing points of view, but make no commitment to a position other than relativism.

Committed relativists have achieved a level of cognitive development beyond that of relativism. They can reason abstractly and can compare competing points of view. They choose positions based upon evidence and reasoning. Unlike dualists, committed relativists see the ambiguity in knowledge and the need to remain open to new information.

Unlike relativists, committed relativists weigh evidence and choose a position. They take provisional stands and remain open to revising their views should new information enter the picture.

The stark dichotomy of utter dualism has inadequate resources to withstand the various, multiple perspectives encountered in the pluralistic milieu of a university. A shift from utter dualism occurs in surges rather than in some progressive, linear manner.

Although there are three overarching perspectives regarding knowledge—dualism, relativism, and committed relativism—within each are three positions of increasing complexity. The first shift, the individual's progression out of dualism, is termed the Modifying of Dualism. The second shift is termed the Realizing of Relativism. The third shift is termed the Evolving of Commitments. Perry identified three distinct aspects, which he called positions, to these three shifts in perspective.

The Modifying of Dualism encompasses these three positions:

- Position 1—The person's basic assumptions are that knowledge and moral values are dualistic and that authorities are in possession of all knowledge. It seemed inconceivable to Perry that a person could remain in Position 1 and remain in a college that challenged him or her to think.
- Position 2—The person realizes that a plurality of answers on similar topics exists, but remains convinced that ideas contrary to what is the truth have no legitimacy, even when held by a person deemed to be an authority. Position 2 begins the movement from utter dualism into multiplicity.
- Position 3—The person begins to reflect on the implications of multiplism and comprehends that authorities are fallible.

The Realizing of Relativism encompasses these three positions:

- Position 4—Realizing that authorities hold different points of view leads to the recognition that some knowledge eludes even the best minds. Differences in points of view get explained loosely as "Everyone has a right to his own opinions."
- Position 5—Relativism becomes more pronounced in the person's evaluation of knowledge. In some areas of knowledge, such as physics, the student thinks clear, definite answers override relativism, but in many other cases, such as literature and history and philosophy, there are no definite, clear answers. Persons who have reached Position 5 do not reflect on the implication that moral values may be as relative as is knowledge.
- Position 6—The person grasps that relativism is all pervasive and realizes he or she will need to make choices. Making such choices is delayed.

The Evolving of Commitments encompasses these three positions:

- Position 7—The individual makes some initial choices about what seems most probably true.
- Position 8—The individual reflects further on being required to make choices in a world characterized fundamentally by relativism in knowledge and in moral values.
- Position 9—The individual expands his or her commitments and recognizes that the choices influence the very style whereby he or she engages in the larger world.

Within Perry's dynamic model of movement from dualism to committed relativism one can see wisps of three formidable thinkers about human reasoning and about how persons actually think. First, in his essays about uses of logic within particular contexts, about the dangers of demanding certainty, and about the evolution of human understanding, Stephen Toulmin argued the same constructivist framework that Perry says marks intellectual growth in a pluralistic society. Second, in his writings on intelligent judgments and understanding, what he calls tacit knowledge, Michael Polanyi asserted the whole person—not just a mind constrained by logic—becomes engaged in judging what is true and what is right. Third, the great Victorian thinker, John Henry Newman, who opposed the encroachments of relativism, argued forcibly that a succession of converging probabilities forms the foundation of all human thought and action; Newman argued for what he called "the illative sense of judgment," a form of reasoning more recently noted present in experts' use of intuition when they make judgments based on a recognition of patterns that escape reasoned explanation. All these formidable thinkers—Toulmin, Polanyi, and Newman—present arguments that conform to what Perry said (a) occurs naturally in the thinking of college students and (b) leads not only to increased self-confidence but influences achieving the developmental task of forming a stable identity as the young adult begins questioning authority and taking informed stands.[2]

Changes in Perspective Taking

The increasing capacity to engage in reflective thinking manifests itself in the adolescent's growing awareness of other points of view. In short, the adolescent becomes increasingly capable of holding in mind alternative perspectives. Such perspective taking emerges not only from changes in cognition but also from experience, in particular, encounters outside one's frame of reference that cause a person to change his or her social perspective.

Persons alter their social perspective for one of two reasons: either the individual comes across external evidence that contradicts personal understanding of social reality, or the person becomes aware that his or her values or beliefs are deficient. Here are four stories adolescents told me about events that led them to change their social perspectives.

- A girl changed her sweeping belief that all teachers are to be trusted when a teacher began singling her out for criticism and ridicule in front of her classmates after she had dared to express opinions the teacher disliked.
- After his sister died in an accident, a boy learned who his real friends were when several classmates stopped talking to him while other individuals offered him their support and attentive listening.
- A girl learned the importance of being careful when confiding in other people when someone she thought was her friend began to gossip about some very private information she had told the other girl in confidence.
- A boy who firmly believed that poor and homeless people are at fault for their troubles did some wrenching reappraisals when his family became homeless after his parents lost their jobs in the aerospace industry and could not find other work to pay their bills.

For changes in perspective to occur, however, one other element is needed: the conceptual conflict cannot require thinking far above the person's current level of interpersonal understanding. Five qualitatively distinct levels of understanding interpersonal relations—from least complex to very complex—comprise such perspective taking. The first three levels occur in childhood, and involve an increasing awareness that physical appearances and psychological realities need not match. As examples, consider (a) the 4-year-old child who might not understand that a smiling stranger could intend harm, (b) the 8-year-old child who understands that other persons have their own inner thoughts and feelings but does not appreciate that a toy he likes may not be something other children also like, and (c) the 11-year-old child who can engage in meta-perspective taking and realizes she and other persons can put themselves in someone else's shoes, though with some imprecision.

The final two levels in perspective taking occur during adolescence. The first involves coordinated reciprocity; that is, middle adolescents can mentally step outside interpersonal interactions, take into consideration not only their viewpoint about someone else but someone else's viewpoint about them, and see that to get along these different perspectives need to be managed. At the last and most complicated level of perspective taking, individuals understand that they and other persons are more complex than what is always understood or understandable. People have unconscious motives. Persons in this level of perspective taking appreciate that relationships involve the superficial and the intimate. In addition, persons at this level of perspective taking recognize that multiple factors such as politics, the legal system, the economy, and cultural customs influence their social worlds.

A Look at the Adolescent Brain

Metacognitive skill emerges during adolescence, and this ability to reflect on one's own thinking is seen to be "a hallmark of cognitive development in the second decade of life" (Kuhn & Franklin, 2008, p. 518). Metacognition clearly indicates executive functions that enable persons to select how to respond, to restrain initial impulses, and to permit sequestering one's own perspectives in the effort to understand points of view different from one's own. The umbrella example of this use of metacognition is found in the move from dualist through relativist to committed relativist perspectives.

How to account for the increasing use of executive functions during adolescence and for the amplified differences that mark individual adolescents? Empirical evidence points to marked changes in the brain, particularly in the prefrontal cortex, which occur during adolescence. In short, magnetic resonance imaging has shown that, starting in early adolescence, "a sequence of overproduction and pruning of neuronal connections occurs. This pruning of unused connections is guided by the activities in which the young teen engages . . . (leading over time) to an increasingly firm sense of personal identity" (Kuhn & Franklin, 2008, p. 543). But what marks the changes in adolescent brains from the brains of children?

Magnetic resonance imaging has documented two fundamental changes that mark adolescent brain development. One involves what is called grey matter, and the other change involves white matter. Here is a brief overview of these two changes.

Changes in Grey Matter. During puberty an overproduction of grey matter (GM) takes place. Grey matter refers to brain tissue such as dendrites and dendritic processes, as well as glia, axons, blood vessels, and extracellular space. The pattern in GM overproduction is for a peak initially in the primary sensorimotor areas and later in brain areas that involve higher order associations and integrate the primary functions. One location for such GM development is in the prefrontal cortex. Gender differences have been identified in GM developments, such that peak cortical GM volume occurs for early adolescent girls around 9.3 years of age and for boys around 10.5. Researchers do not yet well understand GM developments that occur in the amygdala and the hippocampus, but descriptive data indicate marked changes involved in emotions, language, and memory occur between the early and later adolescent years.

Following the pattern of GM overproduction, a reduction in GM volume actually begins; this reduction is related to synaptic pruning; that is, a reduction in the number of synaptic connections that occurs as the individual engages more regularly in some mental activities and stops doing others.

Changes in White Matter. White matter (WM) increases in the brain during childhood and adolescence. WM denotes the color of myelin, a substance that permits electrical signals to move exponentially faster than for axons lacking myelinated sheathing. The increase in WM characteristic of adolescent brains means increased connectivity between synapses that "allows for greater integration of disparate neural circuitry" (Giedd, Stockman, Weddle et al., 2012, p. 21).

WM plays a central role in the brain's fine-tuning during the adolescent years. WM is a necessary ingredient providing the foundation for learning, and it "encodes the basics for thought, consciousness, and meaning" (p. 21). This increase in WM produces connections between different parts of the brain and presents the main signal of several developmental differentiations occurring in brain functioning. Increased connectivity during adolescence is the main idea when researchers discuss brain development during adolescence. A metaphor using examples from language depicts what these increases in brain connectivity due to WM mean: ". . . consider the maturational changes not so much as adding new letters to the alphabet (but rather) as combining existing letters into words, those words into sentences, and the sentences into paragraphs" (p. 28).

The Relentless Personal Journey

The search for personal identity has become a chief construct influencing our understanding of development during the adolescent years. The scholar most associated with this point of view is Erik Erikson, who considered the primary developmental task of adolescence is to obtain a clear sense of self. Erikson viewed identity formation as a journey that continues throughout the human life cycle, and this metaphor permeates his writings about children, adolescents, and adults.

The Formative Views of Erik Erikson

Erikson maintained that identity formation throughout one's life is a process of facing crises endemic to certain life stages (or "ages" as he called them) and making choices (or "commitments" as he called them). These crises present a fork in the journey where we must make decisions. These crises impel growth and development. In choosing which way to turn on the journey, we make commitments that have enduring influence. Thus, for Erikson, the lifelong journey of identity formation involves confronting crises and making commitments.

The crisis endemic to adolescence centers on the process of self-discovery, with the ultimate stake being either the formation of a clear identity or the malformation of a vague sense of self, that is a confused identity. Two pitfalls endanger identity formation for adolescents. One, the adolescent may settle too quickly on a path approved by others, but not one that the adolescent has examined and then chosen. Erikson named this pitfall identify foreclosure, a premature resolution to the crisis over finding one's self. Adolescents in identity foreclosure no longer experiment with possible roles, and thus forego experiences that facilitate making personal commitments to the self they want to be.

The second pitfall that endangers adolescent identity formation is identity confusion, sometimes called identity diffusion. Adolescents who stumble into this pitfall avoid making decisions about identity and fail to make lasting commitments to anyone or to any values. They have no core set of beliefs. Adolescents in identity confusion do not experiment with potential roles because they shy away from making extended commitments. They are typically self-centered, emotionally immature, and lack any roots of friendship.

Erikson argued that the adolescent needs extended time to experiment with possible roles without the pressure to fulfill excessive obligations. He called this extended time a psychological moratorium. He saw it as adaptive and something that society should support. In short, Erikson maintained that a psychological moratorium enables the adolescent to explore options and gain the foundation for a fulfilled identity.

Adolescents who successfully traverse their moratorium attain a sense of purpose and a sense of continuity in their lives. Erikson called this sense of purpose and continuity fidelity; that is, faithfulness to the person one was, is now, and will become. The physical, cognitive, emotional, and social changes that adolescents experience present serious threats to attain purpose and continuity.

Adolescents whose journeys toward identity result in a clear sense of self become achieved identities. These persons possess several important traits. They are confident about their values, they have a core set of beliefs, and they live autonomous lives connected with other persons, some in intimate friendships. Unlike persons with identities that are foreclosed, confused, or in moratorium, individuals with achieved identities have come to terms with several domains of social life, such as choosing a career and making commitments about religion and politics. Adolescents with achieved identities gain the skills and composure to manage the next developmental crisis in Erikson's schema, namely, the crisis over intimacy with others versus isolation from others.

Erikson had a profound influence on scholars investigating adolescent identity formation. Two of these scholars are James Marcia and Ruthellen Josselson.

The Research of James Marcia

This Canadian psychologist is deeply tied to Erikson's framework. He accepted the important place of crisis and commitment in identity formation and the four distinct identity statuses: foreclosed, diffused, moratorium, and achieved. He developed reliable research instruments to determine which identity status best depicted a person's self-understanding. One of the research instruments was a series of phrases that research participants were asked to make into sentences. Three examples are "When I consider my goals in the light of my family's goals _____," "I am really convinced that _____," and " Ten years from now I _____" (Marcia, 1964, pp. 157–159). Marcia's other research instrument was an interview that takes about 30 minutes to complete. The interview focuses on three topics: career, politics, and religion. In his work with 86 college students who formed his research sample, Marcia said the completed sentences and the interview responses led to the determination that his sample contained 24 foreclosed identities (28%), 21 diffused (24.4%), 23 moratorium (26.7%), and 18 achieved (20.9%).

Marcia's work has had a seminal impact on research into adolescent identity formation. He established a systematic research procedure to investigate Erikson's concepts of identity, and he demonstrated a reliable means to differentiate the various outcomes of handling the crises and commitment integral to identity formation during adolescence. The ramifications of such an achievement have not escaped other researchers who have built on Marcia's work. Ruthellen Josselson, for example, has uncovered patterns to identity formation in females.

The Research of Ruthellen Josselson

An American psychologist named Ruthellen Josselson embarked on an extensive longitudinal project focused solely on identity formation in females. The study used the template of the four identity statuses and obtained data over 20 years at three different points in time: later adolescence with the women in their early twenties, 10 years later when the women were in their early thirties, and 10 years later when the women were in their early forties. Forty-eight participants started in the study, with equal numbers in each identity status. The notion is not that these identity statuses are equally distributed among women, but rather the study used a design that required equal numbers of participants in each identity status. Josselson still had 30 women in her study 20 years after her dissertation and subsequent first book, *Finding Herself.*

Diffuse Women. In the beginning phase of the study, 12 of the women were in the diffused identity status. These individuals were difficult to comprehend. They shied away from making commitments and would not make decisions. Four subgroups emerged: two women severely disturbed psychologically; three women traumatized due to extreme neglect in childhood; three women who oscillated between moratorium and diffusion; and four women who vacillated between foreclosure and diffusion. None of these women had personal integration, any sense of core beliefs, and existed primarily from moment to moment.

At the end of their college years, these diffuse women were fearful that making choices would lead to loss of identity. They were captured by fantasy, such as relationships with celebrities they had never met, rather than real life events. Their response to challenges and difficulties was to escape, and thus they had not mastered how to cope with events. They led lives marked by fear, fantasy, and flight.

At the first follow-up the diffuse women showed variant patterns. Some remained diffuse despite efforts to gain a more definite identity. Two of the women had died before the age of 30. Some had entered a form of foreclosed identity, living their lives around goals chosen by someone else for them. The trajectory of these women's lives since college had led most to function in mentally healthy ways. For half of these women, their lives remained unsettled. Settling into a diffused identity during late adolescence marked persons in serious psychological distress.

Ten years later in their early 40s the diffuse women still participating in the study had been pared to seven. Josselson now called them Drifters rather than sticking with Marcia's term "diffuse." Josselson noted that these women always surprised her every time she encountered them. She wrote that in their forties they reflected with regret on their missed opportunities and "were saved by their capacity not to ponder too much" (Josselson, 1996, p. 144). At best they had jumbled connections to their past, and their "capacity to forget the past" (p. 144) alarmed Josselson. The major developmental tasks of adolescence (intimacy, life direction, and autonomous identity) had frightened them, they had side-stepped all commitments, and by adulthood "these women lacked internal structure" (p. 148) and remained unformed.

Foreclosed Women. At the beginning of the study, 12 women were in the foreclosed identity status. The central theme in the lives of these women was the closeness and security their families had provided during childhood. The main criterion for self-esteem was approval from their parents. Whereas other persons during adolescence typically develop meaningful relationships outside their families, these foreclosed women seemed incapable of trusting anyone other than family members. They judged all things in terms of dichotomies, bringing to mind the dualist position regarding knowledge: things were either all good or all bad, true or false, and proper or improper. These women, who could not tolerate ambiguity, were troubled with doubts and anxiety when uncertainty or ambivalence entered their lives.

The foreclosed women were to a person self-centered, materialistic, and unreflective. They imposed a Pollyanna interpretation on reality, and any struggles were projected on external sources that could not be trusted. They had remained children psychologically. Becoming a foreclosed identity had exacted a cost in terms of limited personal strengths and constrained relationships with others. By the end of their college years they were characterized by three prominent life developments: (a) in interpersonal relationships they attempted to recreate the closeness they treasured in their families of origin, (b) they accepted uncritically the values and norms of their parents, and (c) they typically were inhibited emotionally. Their adult sense of self was a definition forged during their childhood.

At the first follow-up with the 12 foreclosed women, it was clear they had not changed the decisions they had made in their childhoods. They had adapted well, many were clear successes in the world of work, they remained convinced of their self-worth, and none vacillated in her convictions. None had drifted back into diffusion or moved into a moratorium or achievement status. The one foreclosed woman who had grown personally had coped with the shattering of her marriage when her husband divorced her; however, this life crisis had not led her to question her fundamental beliefs or commitments.

Ten years later the foreclosed women still participating in the study had been pared to six. Josselson now called them Guardians rather than foreclosed. They were more rigid in their thinking and values than other women in her study, and they favored being in control, framed in terms of maintaining order and tradition. They retained their self-assurance of being correct, and found compromising difficult. Being married to men who eventually turned out not to have been what the women had dreamed led some of the women to rethink their choices and self-image.

However, Josselson reported that the women she called Guardians did change over time. Such development occurred later in life than it had for the women who were in Moratorium or in Achieved Identity statuses. She noted that the six Guardians still in the study had become "more insightful, more self-aware" (p. 49) than they had been in college and 10 years following college. She considered them "among the most interesting and lively of the women I have followed" (p. 49).

Moratorium Status Women.   Several complicated themes interweaved in the lives of the female college students in the moratorium status: guilt over disappointing their parents, strong identification with their fathers, idealization of a friend or peer, daydreams and fantasies of remarkable achievements, dedication to correct answers, intense devotion to interpersonal relationships, conflicts over emotional separation from parents, and acute insight into personal and social concerns. Unlike research that indicated the moratorium status is one of short duration for persons, the research with these college students found the moratorium status more long-lasting than transitory.

From their childhoods, these 12 young women had placed great importance on being correct, and this conviction stayed with them through their adolescence. They experienced a crisis when they discovered competing values and other persons with compelling arguments against what they believed. The moratorium female was faced with deciding which competing values to choose, and until she made her choice, her identity was in turmoil. Of all the college students studied, the moratoriums expressed ongoing interest in the great questions that have challenged philosophers, such as "Why is there evil in the world if there is a benevolent, powerful God?"

Their self-definitions reflected their interpersonal relationships. This need for relationships was unlike the quest of the foreclosed females to recover the security their parents had given them while growing up. For moratoriums, the need for relationships was fueled by a craving for new encounters with reality. The moratoriums alone sought feedback from the researchers and expressed particular curiosity over what topics had been mentioned in other interviews.

In some aspects the moratorium females resembled diffuse females. The moratoriums were anxious, expressed intense emotions, and struggled with self-esteem. However, they were more energetic and less sad than their diffuse peers and had much greater skill in exerting control over episodes of conflict and times of feeling blue.

At the first follow-up with the moratorium women, it was difficult to categorize these individuals regarding identity status. Six of the women had characteristics of an amalgamation of the foreclosure and the achievement statuses, and a new category was coined: foreclosure/achievement. On the surface, one could think these six women had simply reverted to accepting parental values in the vein of women in the foreclosed identity status. But the difference was that the women had made personal choices for these values after experimenting with other points of view and careful consideration of options. Three of the women who had been in the moratorium status had entered identity achievement. For the six women who were now "foreclosed/achieved" and the three who were in identity achievement, such changes in identity status occurred only because of an adult relationship with someone who cared about them. Women who were still in the moratorium status continued to struggle over options that foreclosed/achieved and achieved identity women had resolved.

Ten years later the moratorium women still participating in the study had been pared to nine. Josselson now called them Searchers rather than using Marcia's term moratorium. They were women with many questions about life and wanted to find answers that were integral to a larger picture about the meaning of life. They were self-reflective, and Josselson found the "women in this group to be enormously engaging" (p. 106).

By middle age these individuals had much less in common within their group than Josselson found in the other women she studied. For some of them their searching did not end, whereas others found a direction after college but engaged in more searching in their forties. Some needed professional assistance to deal with "powerful inner demons, old and tenacious conflicts from childhood . . . before they could move ahead" (p. 112). Others experienced life after college so difficult that they returned home to a safer harbor.

Achieved Identity Status Women. While heterogeneity marked the women who had become identity achieved in college, in all there were some common characteristics. The chief characteristic found in all the women was autonomy; they were attracted to men who promoted and responded favorably to independence in others. Unlike foreclosed females, the achieved identity women selected male partners who cared for them rather than took care of them.[3] These women had learned to be self-reliant, preferred instrumental activity rather than introspection, and tempered their fantasies with experiences linked to reality.

These achieved identity women had strong trust in their ability to accomplish things that mattered to them, called in some circles an internal locus of control and in other circles a sense of self-efficacy. They invested in achieving personal goals, and accepted that some things that they desired could be beyond their powers to effect. Who they might be was of greater importance to them than whose love they might win.

At the first follow-up with the achieved identity women, all but one of the individuals was still in the achieved status. One woman had reverted to the moratorium status because she had become unsure of the choices she had made and was struggling with other possibilities. The differences between the achieved women and the foreclosed could seem hard to identify in terms of daily functioning. The fundamental difference between these two groups was psychological: the achieved women demonstrated greater flexibility, more openness to experience, and more security from outside validations of self-worth. They placed value on intrinsic rewards, whereas foreclosed women were focused on external rewards. The achieved women tolerated ambiguity and were open to learn more about themselves.

Ten years later the achieved women still participating in the study had been pared to seven. Josselson now termed these women Pathmakers rather than achieved. They were self-confident, interested in doing things, and not inclined to introspection. They were marked by flexibility and interest in resolving problems. Josselson considered that the Pathmakers in their mid-forties were confident, capable, and engaged in the wider world; they had achieved intentionally chosen goals that mattered to them. "They made compromises along the way, but most ended up feeling that, in the end, they arrived where they had intended to go" (p. 73).

Research into Adolescent Self-Concept

Daniel Offer studied adolescent growth from early into later adolescence, and argued that both longitudinal research on American teenagers and cross-sectional research on adolescents from 10 separate countries demonstrated conclusively that adolescent development is marked by relative calm and stability rather than storm, stress, and conflict. The great majority of teenagers have been shown to be normal (that is, stable and well-adjusted) rather than at odds with society (that is, delinquent) or at odds with themselves (that is, psychiatrically disturbed).

One of Offer's approaches was to interview teenage boys over a 4-year period, and another approach used a self-report instrument called the Offer Self-Image Questionnaire for Adolescents (OSIQ). For instance, in the interview there was interest in such issues as goals, relations with family members, and coping with stress.

The OSIQ is an instrument that adolescents fill out regarding 11 areas that comprise aspects of self-concept. These 11 areas are:

1. Impulse control; that is, the extent to which the adolescent can ward off stress
2. Emotional tone; that is, the extent to which the adolescent has achieved emotional harmony
3. Body and self image; that is, attitudes of the adolescent toward his or her body and feelings of security about self
4. Morals; that is, the extent to which the person's conscience has developed
5. Family relationships; that is, measures of the parent–child relationship and of the emotional atmosphere in the home
6. Mastery of the external world; that is, a measure of how well the adolescent adapts to the external environment
7. Vocational-educational goals; that is, the extent to which the adolescent is learning and is planning for a future in the world of work
8. Psychopathology; that is, the extent to which the adolescent manifests severe and abnormal symptomatology
9. Social relationships; that is, the strength of relationships with persons outside the family
10. Sexual attitudes; that is, attitudes, feelings, and behaviors toward the opposite sex[4]
11. Superior adjustment; that is, the extent to which the adolescent copes with self, significant others, and the world at large

Norms have been produced on adolescent responses to the OSIQ based on gender and on age. Significant differences separate normal adolescents from delinquent and from psychiatrically disturbed adolescents. The great majority of adolescents are in the grouping considered normal, and their responses differ from delinquent and disturbed adolescents at a remarkably consistent and statistically significant level.

More than any other controversy about adolescents, the assertion that the adolescent years are marked by turmoil has been challenged by the OSIQ findings. However, there is such widespread belief that stress and mayhem mark adolescent development—the assertions from G. Stanley Hall and from Anna Freud—that these OSIQ findings about normality typically are dismissed as out of touch with reality.

The 4-year longitudinal study of teenage boys encouraged the researchers about the capacity of normal teenagers to profit developmentally from life crises, using these experiences as opportunities to mature.[5] Some prominent aspects of their growth toward adulthood included (a) an overall acceptance of the values espoused by their parents and (b) a capacity to remain psychologically centered when life events, such as the death of a father or permanent injury to a sibling, challenged. Regarding their overall acceptance of parental values, one could speculate that these youths were in foreclosed identity status, but there was nothing in Offer's longitudinal study that indicated either uncritical acquiescence to parental values or an aversion to experiment or explore options.

Regarding remaining psychologically centered when challenged by life crises, the basic message is that these normal teenagers were resilient and possessed successful coping skills rather than being by definition overwhelmed with emotional troubles. The boys had resources to master troubling life events. It was not that these adolescents did not experience anxiety, but even when experiencing anxiety the boys' coped by

> attending to manageable details first, concentrating on them and thereby minimizing the threat (or even repressing it altogether). They were able to keep shifting gears and to concentrate on different aspects of the same problem. . . . (They) adapted to traumatic situations such as a death of a parent, with initial overconcern over the reality of the situation. (Examples: Will Mother have enough money to support me? Should I still plan to go to the college of my choice?). . . . They would proceed a little more quickly into adulthood than their contemporaries, who had been left in a world where dependency-independency issue needed no immediate resolutions.
>
> (Offer, 1969, p. 221)

Concluding Comments

Changes in many important dimensions of life take hold during the adolescent years. It is possible to study these changes as though they are discrete phenomena, but any parent of a teenage boy or girl knows that adolescent development occurs in multiple arenas. Development during adolescence cascades. We see these effects in our adolescents' physical growth, their cognitive makeup, and their interpersonal conduct.

The meta-cognitive skills that emerge during adolescence do more than disclose changes in brain processing. They enable growing adolescents to ponder the changes occurring in their body and in their relations with other persons. They allow for decisions that require self-control and self-reflection.

A singularly important product of the changing mental processes during adolescence is trial-and-error with various selves so that by the onset of early adolescence "individuals are indeed producers of their own development" leading to "an increasingly firm sense of personal identity" (Kuhn & Franklin, 2008, p. 543). This discussion of the adolescent's growing sense of "Who I am" dovetails into the coming two chapters: a chapter on the ecological niches that influence adolescents and in which adolescents interact, and a chapter on adolescent coping.

Notes

1. Some female college undergraduates who have heard me present these findings have expressed their disagreement. In short, they will say, "I was a late-maturing girl, but it did not affect me negatively with my friends or with adults."
2. I am not claiming Perry knew all these connections, though it is clear he was familiar with the works of Polanyi.
3. At the time of the research, little thought apparently was given to females whose sexual orientation is not heterosexual. It is implausible that the four identity statuses apply only to heterosexual persons. The commitments and crises may have a different frame for homosexual and heterosexual adolescents, but there will be crises to resolve over religion, power, and interpersonal relationships.
4. The sexual attitudes scale proved problematic for several years. The apparent assumption of heterosexuality may have been part of the trouble, but that is my speculation. However, for whatever the reasons, of all the areas measured in the OSIQ, the sexual attitudes scale could not distinguish the responses of normal, delinquent, and emotionally disturbed adolescents.
5. In a follow-up with these research subjects nearly 35 years later, Offer and his colleagues (2004, p. 6) wrote, "Our subjects remained centered on mainstream values and moved in the general direction their parents had . . . they remained centered on a core of values and self-definition. There was a stability, a psychological equilibrium, among these psychologically normal teenagers that acknowledged and reacted to, but was not overwhelmed by, the events that swirled around them."

Sources

Atkinson, R. C. & Shiffrin, R. M. (1968). Human memory: A proposed system and its control processes. In K. W. Spence & J. T. Spence (Eds.), *The psychology of learning and motivation: Advances in research and theory*. Vol. 2 (pp. 89–195). New York: Academic Press.

Brooks-Gunn, J. (1987). Pubertal pressures: Their relevance for developmental research. In. R. H. Munroe, R. L. Munroe, & B. B. Whiting (Eds.), *Handbook of adolescent psychology* (pp. 111–130). New York: Pergamon Press.

Crockett, L. J., Petersen, A. C., Graber, J. A., Schulenberg, J. E., & Ebata, A. (1989). School transitions and adjustment during early adolescence. *Journal of Early Adolescence, 9*, 181–210.

Erikson, E. H. (1968). *Identity: Youth and crisis*. New York: Norton.

Giedd, J. N., Stockman, M., Weddle, C., Liverpool, M., Wallace, G. L., Lee, N. R., Lalande, F., & Lenroot, R. K. (2012). Anatomic magnetic resonance imaging of the developing child and adolescent brain. In V. F. Reyna, S. B. Chapman, M. R. Dougherty, & J. Confrey (Eds.), *The adolescent brain: Learning, reasoning, and decision making* (pp. 15–35). Washington, DC: American Psychological Association.

Josselson, R. (1987). *Finding herself: Pathways to identity development in women*. San Francisco: Jossey-Bass.

Josselson, R. (1996). *Revising herself: The story of women's identity from college to mid-life*. New York: Oxford University Press.

Kuhn, D. & Franklin, S. (2008). The second decade: What develops (and how)? In W. Damon & R. M. Lerner (Eds.), *Child and adolescent development: An advanced course* (pp. 517–550). Hoboken, NJ: John Wiley & Sons.

Marcia, J. E. (1964). *Determination and construct validity of ego identity status*. Unpublished doctoral dissertation, The Ohio State University, Columbus, OH.

Meynell, H. (1990). Newman's vindication of faith in the *Grammar of Assent*. In I. Ker & A. G. Hill (Eds.), *Newman after a hundred years* (pp. 247–261). Oxford, UK: Clarendon Press.

Mitchell, B. (1990). Newman as a philosopher. In I. Ker & A. G. Hill (Eds.), *Newman after a hundred years* (pp. 223–246). Oxford, UK: Clarendon Press.

Newman, J. H. (1985). *An essay in aid of a grammar of assent.* (I. T. Ker, Ed.). New York: Oxford University Press. [Original work published 1870]

Newman, J. H. (2006). *Fifteen sermons preached before the University of Oxford between AD 1826 and 1843.* (J. D. Earnest & G. Tracey, Eds.). New York: Oxford University Press. [Original work published 1872]

Offer, D. (1969). *The psychological world of the teenager.* New York: Basic Books.

Offer, D. (1984). *The adolescent: A psychological self-portrait.* New York: Basic Books.

Offer, D., Offer, M. K., & Ostrov, E. (2004). *Regular guys: Thirty-four years beyond adolescence.* New York: Plenum.

Offer, D., Ostrov, E., & Howard, K. I. (1977). The self-image of adolescents: A study of four cultures. *Journal of Youth and Adolescence, 6*, 265–280.

Orlofsky, J. L. (1978). Identity formation, achievement, and fear of success in college men and women. *Journal of Youth and Adolescence, 7*, 49–62.

Pascarella, E. T. & Terenzini, P. T. (1991). *How college affects students: Findings and insights from twenty years of research.* San Francisco: Jossey-Bass.

Pascarella, E. T. & Terenzini, P.T. (2005). *Liberal arts colleges and liberal arts education: New science on impacts.* San Francisco: Wiley.

Perry, W. G. (1970). *Forms of intellectual and ethical development during the college years.* New York: Holt, Rinehart & Winston.

Piaget, J. (1983). Piaget's theory. In P. H. Mussen (Ed.), *Handbook of child psychology. Vol. 1. History, theory, and methods.* New York: Wiley.

Pitt, R, B. (1983). Development of a general problem-solving schema in adolescence and early adulthood. *Journal of Experimental Psychology General, 112*, 547–584.

Polanyi, M. (1958). *Personal knowledge: Towards a postcritical philosophy.* Chicago: University of Chicago Press.

Roche, A. F. (1976). Growth after puberty. In E. Puchs (Ed.), *Youth in a changing world: Cross-cultural perspectives on adolescence* (pp. 17–53). The Hague, Netherlands: Mouton.

Savin-Williams, R. C. & Weisfeld, G. E. (1989). An ethological perspective on adolescence. In G. R. Adams, R. Montemayor, & T. P. Gullotta (Eds.), *Biology of adolescent behavior and development* (pp. 249–274). Newbury Park, CA: Sage.

Sternberg, R. J. (1988). Intellectual development. Psychometric and information processing approaches. In M. H. Bornstein & M. E. Lamb (Eds.), *Developmental psychology: An advanced textbook* (pp. 261–295). Hillsdale, NJ: Erlbaum.

Sternberg, R. J. & Downing, C. (1982). The development of higher order reasoning in adolescence. *Child Development, 53*, 209–221.

Tanner, J. M. (1962). *Growth at adolescence.* Oxford, UK: Blackwell Scientific.

Toulmin, S. E. (1972). *Human understanding: The collective use and evolution of concepts.* Princeton, NJ: Princeton University Press.

Toulmin, S. E. (1990). *Cosmopolis: The hidden agenda of modernity.* New York: Free Press.

Toulmin, S. E. (2003). *The uses of argument* (Updated edition). New York: Cambridge University Press.

Waterman, A. S. (1985). Identity in the context of adolescent psychology. *New Directions for Child Development, 30*, 5–24.

3 Ecological Niches for Adolescents
Family, Peers, School, Media, and Gangs

A Prolegomena to Chapter Three

This chapter examines various explicit as well as tacit social influences on the development of adolescents. The conflicts and issues facing adolescents take place on various stages and with varying casts. Making sense of reality and learning their way in the world present important challenges for adolescents, and the forms these challenges take occur within various ecological niches: the family, peer relationships, the school environment, and the omnipresent electronic media including radio, television, phones, movies, and, above all, the Internet. Gangs hold paramount importance in the lives of a subset of adolescents.

Culture, ethnicity, and gender present three fundamental, frequently tacit influences on socialization and assumptive worlds of adolescents. As I worked on this chapter and on others in this book, I remained aware that much of the research conducted about adolescents has come from studies with white, middle-class adolescents who live in the United States. In the field of bereavement research, to consider an example from a field of inquiry other than adolescent development, it has become increasingly apparent that norms of grieving have been derived from clinical and research experience with white females, primarily adults whose spouses have died.

Mentioning "white females" means talking about ethnicity, gender, and, perhaps without realization, culture as well. The intricacies and ambiguities of such constructs as culture, ethnicity, and gender are apparent to anyone who reflects on the matter of ecological niches and adolescent development. For instance, rules and expectations and interactions within an Orthodox Jewish family differ markedly from the rules, expectations, and interactions within such families as a working-class Roman Catholic family of first-generation Polish immigrants living in Chicago, a Navajo family living in rural New Mexico, an upper-class, "old money" Episcopalian family of Boston natives whose ancestors have been in the United States since the 17th century, and a middle-class Black AME (African Methodist Episcopal) family living in Brooklyn whose ancestors were brought to this continent as slaves. It is painfully clear that little is known about the cultural values that tacitly and explicitly impinge on the development of adolescents in families—not only the few mentioned in the previous sentence but also the legion of others throughout this world. My decision has been to acknowledge this fact, proceed with what I know about the ecological niches identified in the chapter's title, and where possible bring in vignettes and slices of life detailing adolescent experiences both within and outside white, middle-class America.

The Notion of an Ecological Niche

An ecological niche, in brief, is the environment in which an organism responds to survival demands and prospects for thriving.[1] By organism I am referring to any living being, whether a one-celled animal, a plant, a chimpanzee, or an adolescent human, to give but a few examples. The evolutionary concepts of fitness, adaptation, costs, and benefits are applied to understand the influences of an ecological niche. Obviously, some ecological niches foster optimum development and growth (consider the value of positive parenting on children, for instance), and some ecological niches threaten well-being (consider the dangers refugee camps present to displaced persons).

Adolescent development and behavior occur within a variety of intertwined and distinct ecological niches. The diversity of these niches will be contingent on culture and ethnicity. The matter of gender takes cues from culture and ethnicity and plays out in such niches as the family, peers, and school. The media have become an overarching, pervasive ecological niche in the development and behavior of adolescents. Within certain subsets of adolescents, gangs present an attractive, powerful ecological niche. "The bottom line is that the psychological 'meaning' attributed to any given social behavior is, in large part, a function of the ecological niche in which it is produced" (Rubin, Bukowski, Parker, & Bowker, 2008, p. 145).

The adolescent's efforts to develop a stable identity involve trying out a proliferation of selves that differ according to the ecological niche in which the adolescent is acting. Thus, the self an individual puts on display with close friends varies from the self on display with teachers, with a coach, with an employer, and with one's parents; there is even the prospect that an adolescent's self-projection varies when with his or her mother and when with his or her father. These diverse selves remain without synthesis until later adolescence because early adolescent and middle adolescent youth have yet to attain the critical thinking skills that allow reaching "realistic conclusions about the self" (Harter, 2008, p. 238).[2]

The Family as Ecological Niche

The Family Life Cycle

One influential theme in the study of family life is the family life cycle. The notion here is that families change over time by responding to various normative life transitions such as the birth of children, the onset of puberty for an adolescent, and the time when a youth leaves home and launches an independent life. One model of the family life cycle proposes that families develop over time in six stages that begin with unattached young adults, move into marriage and raising children at various points in development, and end with later life once children have moved on. Another model suggests eight stages that begin once a couple marries and end with the elderly married couple in retirement. These family life cycle models present normative views dominant in the 20th century that do not encompass such variations as divorced families and blended families; they do not take into account women who choose to become pregnant and raise children without a spouse, same gender spouses who raise children, and couples who choose not to have children.

The Family Systems Perspective

Researchers into family functioning have been greatly impressed by the contributions of the systems perspective in understanding and explaining human interaction and in offering a platform for effectively changing a dysfunctional family. The critical assertion of a systems perspective on family functioning is that families are sets of mutually influential, interconnected relationships. Rather than a mixture of totally discrete individuals, a family is considered to be greater than the sum of its members. In systems terms, the whole exceeds the sum of its parts.

While some family systems advocates maintain that individual family members cannot be understood apart from the family as a whole, I consider that position extreme and simplistic. Individuals come into contact with many systems other than their families. Examples of systems that influence adolescent development and behavior are schools, peers, and media. However, I concur that it is sheer ignorance to disregard the role of the family in a person's life, and I accept that family functioning is more clearly explained by applying systems theory ideas.

Consider, for example, these ideas from systems theory to explain family functioning.

- Family cohesion refers to how emotionally attached family members are to one another and how much autonomy the family encourages in its members. Effective families are considered to foster attachments that nurture individual development and promote autonomy, and such effective family functioning is termed balanced cohesion.
- Family adaptability is the capacity of a family to respond positively to stressful life circumstances. Adaptability involves both the capacity to change and the capacity to resist change. At one extreme is the family that resists all demands for change, while at the other extreme is the family that has no stability. For instance, in a family that resists all demands for change, the parents refuse to revise discipline as children mature, whereas in a family with no stability, the parents constantly change the rules and enforce them inconsistently. Family systems advocates tout the effectiveness of families with balanced adaptability; such balance comes from open communication about rules to be followed and roles to be accepted.
- Problem solving refers to a family's ability to resolve matters that affect its functioning as a family. Such matters are either instrumental problems such as finances, food, shelter, education, clothing, and transportation, or affective problems, which involve emotions. In a related field, group process and dynamics, instrumental problems are seen as task functions whereby the group accomplishes things, and affective problems are seen as maintenance functions whereby communication within the group is maintained and encouraged.
- Family roles are the repetitive behavior patterns whereby families fulfill necessary functions such as giving nurturance and support and providing shelter. Facilitating personal development is another necessary family role. Several miscellaneous functions are included under the idea of family roles: decision-making, paying bills, and maintaining discipline are examples. Dealing with instrumental and affective problems shapes family roles. Some family roles are ascribed, that is, delegated to an individual because of certain assumptions about the role, for instance, ascribing

preparation of meals to females or ascribing household maintenance such as maintaining the yard to males. Some family roles are achieved, or engaged in, because the individual has talent in the area not because of a priori assumptions.

- Communication provides the linkage between problem solving, role acceptance, and role execution in families. Families characterized by open communication engage in problem solving more consistently acceptable to members, and open communication enables family members to understand, carry out, and revise their various family roles.

- Affective responsiveness involves the ability of family members to respond with feelings that fit a situation. Responsiveness is not the expression of emotion per se, but rather is measured by whether specific emotions are congruent to the situation and whether the family allows individuals to express how they feel.

- Affective involvement refers to interpersonal attachment and empathy, and the notion designates the amount of family interest in and appreciation for the activities of individual members. Affective involvement ranges along a continuum from total lack of involvement (labeled disengagement) to extreme involvement (labeled enmeshment). Well-functioning families engage in balanced affective involvement; disengagement and enmeshment progressively incapacitate families.

Genograms[3]

Family therapists, who extensively rely on a family systems perspective, have produced an intriguing tool, called a genogram, to accentuate awareness of the history of problems in families. The genogram casts light on emotions and on interpersonal relationships over three generations in a family. Genograms can disclose how certain patterns of conduct reappear in successive generations. For instance, some families teach their children, both explicitly and indirectly, to negotiate interpersonal difficulties and to develop and express secure bonds of attachment; other families teach their children to camouflage interpersonal issues and to remain ambivalent about attachments to others.

A genogram can disclose how three generations of a family have dealt with significant developmental tasks in the lives of its children. As an example, a significant developmental task for any family is to shape the children so that by late adolescence they are ready to launch out into the world on their own. Charting how earlier generations have prepared their late adolescents to be independent adults provides clues to what is occurring in a current generation.

Genograms use symbols to identify individuals, indicate relationships, and identify quality of communication. These symbols are presented in the key of Figure 3.1. This figure presents a hypothetical family headed by George and Joanna Mitchell and their two living children, the fraternal twins Phyllis and James. In addition, other individuals include Ralph and Phyllis Mitchell, George's parents; Henry Mitchell, Ralph and Phyllis's deceased son; John Mitchell, George's brother; James and Rose Johnson, Joanna's parents; James Johnson, Jr., and Marie, Joanna's siblings; both Joanna's father and brother are deceased; and Wendell Smith, a young man interested in marrying George and Joanna's daughter.

The Mitchells live on a farm. Our interpretation of the Mitchell family genogram focuses on James, the 20-year-old son; however, there is plenty of data in the genogram to examine the other persons identified in the figure.

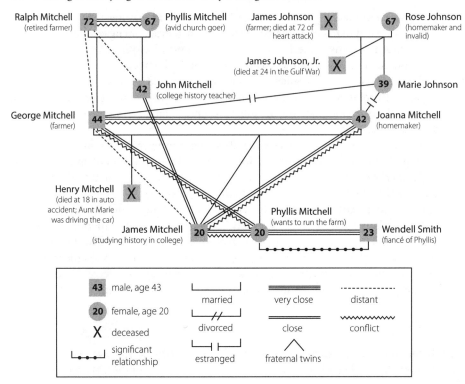

Figure 3.1 A Genogram of James Mitchell's Family

The first lesson we learn concerns intimacy. Males in the Mitchell family for the most recent three generations have close but conflictual relationships with females. Through years of interacting within his family and observing others interact, James has learned that relationships with females are risky. He has learned males and females protect themselves by mixing intimacy with conflict. Like many sons, James perceives his father as distant; James also sees that his father and paternal grandfather are emotionally distant with each other.

The Mitchell farm has been in the family for five generations. Each oldest son has inherited the farm and improved it. James is expected to take over the farm from his father. The mantle of inheritance was passed to him when his older brother, Henry, died in an automobile accident a year and a half ago.

There is conflict for James and his family over this family tradition. James, first of all, entered the state university 2 years ago with the intention to become a college history professor like his Uncle John. James has no desire to study agriculture, and he does not want to return home to run the farm. Communication between James and his uncle is open, and the two feel close to one another. They text and email one another regularly.

Second, the family farm is in serious economic crisis, and James's father might lose it before the end of the year unless arrangements can be made with creditors. The level of distress in the family over the potential loss of the farm has three generations of

Mitchells deeply upset. James feels guilty about his desire for an education in history at a time when his family is in such need. He feels pulled to change majors and accede to his parents' wishes about inheriting the farm. There is actually more pressure on James than wishes from his parents: The night after Henry's funeral, George became very autocratic and gave his younger son a lecture on family responsibility and on the need to sacrifice for what was in the best interests of the whole family. So far James is holding out against these pressures. If the farm is to remain in the family, George can see no alternative to James's managing the farm.

A third dynamic has entered the picture and might provide James and his family an outlet if they can get beyond gender stereotypes. Phyllis Mitchell, the 20-year-old twin of James, has expressed her desire to take over the farm and keep it in the family. She began to express her interests about a year after Henry's death. James and Phyllis are close, but argue a lot, particularly now over the future of the farm.

James's father is also close with Phyllis, but like other males in the Mitchell family, tempers this closeness with conflict. He is, however, beginning to say to others in the family that perhaps his daughter can help to save the family's inheritance. He respects Phyllis's fiancé, a young man who knows a great deal about farming and who last year earned a college degree in agricultural economics.

James is feeling confused about what is appropriate for men and women to do now that he knows his father's opinions about his sister's interest in taking over the farm. James is suspicious of Phyllis's fiancé, whom he thinks is an outsider more interested in getting the farm than in marrying his sister. While he wants to follow in the footsteps of his uncle, he is confused about what his duty is to his family. Were it not for Henry's death, he would not have had the role of inheritor placed on him and, without any distress, could have been given the family's blessing to become a college history teacher.

John feels very torn about what advice to give his nephew. Although he thinks James will make a very good college teacher, he feels hesitant to interfere in an issue that is so emotionally charged for his brother's family. He also is sure that many unresolved bereavement issues linger regarding Henry's death for George, Joanna, and their surviving children.

James would like to talk to his Aunt Marie about the confusion he feels. For some reason James cannot understand, he is relaxed around his aunt. However, the Mitchells have a family rule not to share family secrets with anyone the parents do not approve of. James's parents have cut off communication with Aunt Marie, and they expect their children to follow suit. They blame Marie for Henry's death. She was driving the car when Henry died. The car was hit by a sudden gust of wind, went out of control, turned over, and caused Henry to die of massive internal injuries. Marie suffered a broken arm and some cuts and bruises, but for the most part was unscathed.

James believes his parents are blaming Marie for something that was not her fault. James knows that Marie and her brother, who was killed in the Gulf War and after whom James was named, were very close. If you look at the genogram, you will see that Marie and her brother were twins, just as Phyllis and James are. In his physical appearance, James reminds everyone of his Uncle James.

Unresolved grief seems to haunt the Mitchells, preventing any closure to the death of their older son, Henry. An unspoken but well-understood rule in this family was that there would be no discussion of Henry's death after the funeral. The estrangement with

Marie over Henry's death has made unwelcome one relative James feels at ease with. One wonders how Marie and her sister Joanna dealt with the death of James Johnson, Jr., when he was killed in the Gulf War.

The genogram in Figure 3.1 helps to concisely portray these family dynamics. A key example is the presence of so many close but conflictual relationships between males and females. It is little wonder that separation from his parents is a matter of difficulty for James given the family dynamics illustrated in the genogram.

Opening up to his family now about what he wants leaves James vulnerable to conflict and being pressured by his parents at a time when he wants to be his own person. He is beginning to become emotionally isolated from his parents.

Separating from Parents and Becoming an Adult

Adolescent separation from parents involves four multidimensional aspects:

- Functional independence—managing personal and practical affairs with little assistance from parents
- Attitudinal independence—seeing oneself as unique from one's parents and possessing a personal set of beliefs, values, and ideas about adult life
- Emotional independence—being free from excessive need for parental approval, closeness, and emotional support
- Conflictual independence—being free from excessive guilt, anxiety, resentment, responsibility, and anger in relation to one's parents

In addition to these four independence issues, adolescents themselves have identified several kinds of evidence that signify having achieved separation from parents. Among items on their lists are gaining economic independence, establishing a separate residence, graduating from school, and making independent choices.

Achieving self-governance is an important aspect of separating from parents. Achieving self-governance is manifested in adolescents' responses to such queries as

- How often do you make your own decisions?
- How much do you do things for yourself?
- How much do you feel like an adult?
- How independent are you?

Adolescents who live successfully on their own and achieve self-governance have ongoing, positive relations with their families. Maintenance of such relations is a distinguishing feature of families who launch adolescents into the world. These adolescents consider achieving such separation while remaining close to family members to be an acquired competency. In fact, most adolescents downgrade the importance of emotional detachment in gaining separation from parents.

Some adolescents, however, whose relationships with parents are dysfunctional, seem to see separation from parents achievable primarily in terms of escaping problematic family interactions. For these adolescents, the key characteristic of separating is emotional detachment from parents.

The less traveled road for achieving separation, that of emotional detachment, is considered less optimal for adolescent males than for females. In choosing this path, males are believed to be less likely to achieve well-being as an adult. It seems unlikely that problems males experience in life satisfaction as an adult are caused solely by construing separation from parents in terms of emotional detachment. By the time late adolescent males define separation in these terms, several years of personal development and family interactions have shaped them.

Viewing separation in terms of emotional detachment may signify that these late adolescent males have difficulty becoming securely attached to other persons and have difficulty giving and receiving nurturance. They may find it inconceivable that separation could be anything other than a form of emotional isolation, and inconceivable that independence can be achieved when one retains ties.

If nothing else, the data on adolescents' achieving separation and becoming self-governing adults indicate that family relationships influence the adolescent transition toward achieving a separate, independent identity. A history of detachment between parents and adolescents produces particular risks for males seeking to establish autonomous identities.

Compared to males, females who associate separation with emotional detachment are marked by less loneliness, greater self-esteem, greater life satisfaction, less difficulty leaving home, and greater achievement of an identity separate from their parents. One hypothesis about why females whose separation is marked by emotional detachment are more effective than males in coping with separating from parents is that males are less competent with emotional intimacy and with relationships in general. It has been argued that females internalize richer emotional relationships with other persons than do males. Therefore, reserves of internalized personal relationships insulate late adolescent females during times of separation and make them less emotionally dependent on their parents.

A Case Study

Rachel, a 22-year-old college senior majoring in Economics, will graduate in this year's Spring Commencement. Shortly thereafter, she and Tom, her fiancé, will marry and move to a city in the Southwest where Tom has been offered a good job in an engineering firm.

Rachel comes from an intact family. Her father is a hospital administrator, and her mother is a homemaker. Both have college degrees. Rachel said, "Mom and I get along better since I have been in college and living away from home. When I was in high school, we had mother-daughter quarrels over friends, boys I was dating, that sort of stuff. Mom believed I was too nice and let my friends use me. At the time it felt like she was trying to run my life. Now, when I look back on it, I think a lot of what she said made sense."

Rachel hesitated when asked if she feels close to her Mom. After some reflection, she replied, "For our relationship, yes, I'd say we're close. I've seen worse mother-daughter relationships. I know some daughters who don't even talk to their mothers. I feel fortunate my Mom and I are as close as we are, particularly considering how we got along in the past. In the past, I had just such a troubling relationship with her that I feel fortunate we are as close as we are. Mom has said she thinks we were close in the past. I just sit there dumbfounded to hear her say that. I never really felt close to her just because I talked to her."

She paused a bit, and then Rachel said, "I was never really close with my Dad until about 2 years ago when I started working over the summer at the hospital where he works. I used to ride in with him, and we talked in the car a lot about things that matter. We talked a lot about Tom and our upcoming marriage. I really feel that now I can talk to my Dad about a lot more stuff. I've found out that Dad listens and seldom gives advice. He doesn't lecture me and tell me what I am supposed to do. He treats me like I'm an adult, and he's interested in me.

"I really hope I don't become my mother in my new family. I can see a lot of things in my Mom coming out in me. Around Tom I can be a real cold fish if we get in an argument. I can just leave and refuse to discuss it. Mom does that a lot. But she leaves because she is convinced she is right. I leave because I know I'm wrong."

Rachel talked about her upcoming separation from her parents and said, "I don't think it's really quite hit me yet that I am going to be on my own, and that I won't be calling Dad to tell him I need money. And I won't be calling Mom when I am upset about things. While I don't do that excessively, I do it even less since I've met Tom. I turn to him when things go wrong. I think I'll be able to rely on myself after Tom's company moves him to his second job in the next year. I could hardly believe my ears when Mom and Dad agreed with the decision Tom and I made to buy a car. I thought they would be finding fault, but they just treated us like we were adults and had the right to make such a decision."

Peers as Ecological Niche

As youths develop from early through late adolescence, they spend increasingly less time with their families and increasingly more time with peers and by themselves. Both gender and age influence these interpersonal and intrapersonal changes. It is widely held that peers play a significant role in adolescents' maturation regarding interpersonal relations.

Increased interpersonal competence that comes from ongoing peer interactions and relationships emerges in at least five domains. These domains involve competency in initiating relationships, managing conflict, providing emotional support, expressing disapproval of and dislike for another person's actions, and disclosing personal thoughts and feelings.

As certain relationships develop, some domains of competency increase in importance and others decline. For instance, competency in beginning a relationship and opening up about oneself are especially important early when moving from acquaintanceship to friendship, and skills at providing emotional support and managing conflict enable persons to keep and enrich a relationship with another person.

Early and middle adolescents place more importance on being members of a popular group than do later adolescents; early and middle adolescent peer groups expect greater conformity than peer groups of older (that is, later) adolescents. Conflict with and antagonism toward peers outside the group are common experiences for early and middle adolescents. Girls are particularly bothered when in conflict with members of their peer group, but the boundaries of girls' peer groups are more permeable than the boundaries of boys' groups.

On the whole interactions with peers benefit adolescent maturation. Relations with peers provide a base for developing independence from parents and learning early forms of intimacy outside of one's family. Relations with peers form a source for becoming involved in the wider world.

Friendship

Friendship is a special type of interpersonal relationship. Adolescents understand the importance of friendship and value their friends. Loyalty, keeping confidences, trust, empathic understanding, and support in emotionally difficult times distinguish friends from acquaintances. There is some skepticism from adults about these matters, however, because adolescents use the term *friend* loosely and identify as friends persons who, at most, are acquaintances. The exponentially growing number of persons who "friend" someone on Facebook offers an example of this shallow use of the idea of friendship. Is it possible—let alone plausible—to have 100,000 or more friends? Does it matter that someone I don't know has "unfriended" me because I did not respond to unsolicited Facebook contact? It is comforting that undergraduate students who use Facebook— perhaps that phrase is redundant as Facebook use seems universal among 18- to 23-year-old college students today—clearly specify different expectations of close friends, casual friends, and acquaintances about communication and deception when using Facebook.

Changes in cognitive development enable adolescents to form relationships unavailable to school-age children. Unlike school-age youths, adolescents gain increased empathic understandings and sensitivity to the perspectives of others. Increasing social skills allow adolescents who are friends to explore the emotional tensions that characterize both individual and interpersonal development.

Adolescent friends understand that their relationship poses mutual obligations. Chief among these obligations for females is being available when a friend is in need. For males, the chief obligations of friendship are remaining loyal to and protecting one another.

Many studies of the effects of college on peer relations have been faulty. The studies included relatively small samples, used cross-sectional designs, and gathered data at only one institution. Many researchers have not controlled for maturation effects (changes that occur due to development over time) that mark undergraduates. However, some large-scale research with college students has overcome these failings and examined longitudinal change and stability in social extroverts and introverts over a 4-year period. Social extroverts prefer to be with other persons, and they seek out social activities. Introverts withdraw from social gatherings and prefer to be by themselves or with one or two select persons. Over a 4-year period there was no change from the freshman to senior year in students' interests in social events and interpersonal gatherings. However, over a 4-year period both introverts and extroverts became more interested in a select group of friends and spent more time in intimate activities with a few individuals or with one person who had become a close friend.

Longitudinal research with female college students has disclosed the many fundamental benefits for intellectual and personal growth that friendship with other women brought. For one, the friendships with other women stimulated intellectual growth by offering safe milieus for discussing new ideas and listening to trusted criticism. Such explorations of new ideas can readily be seen as promoting growth into committed relativism. Further, college females' friendships with other women fostered "self-authorship" (Martinez-Aleman, 2010, p. 556), a highly-prized, value-laden outcome identifying autonomy in action and independence in thought. Overall, college students' friendships with other women promoted achieving two key developmental tasks of later adolescence: maintaining intimate relationships and achieving self-identity.

It was clear that underlying these benefits afforded by close friendships between women in college was psychological well-being. The literature on adolescent development is replete with the value of friendship for psychological well-being. One recent finding bolstering assertions about friendship and psychological well-being has come from functional magnetic resonant imaging studies showing the neural pathways that develop to buffer adolescents against peer rejection when they spend time with friends.

The influence of friendship during college has been traced to the development of such higher order thinking skills as postformal reasoning. In particular, college students who enter into "cross-category" friendships profit from the development of postformal reasoning. Definitions will help. The term *cross-category friendship* denotes friendships between persons of distinctly dissimilar social backgrounds, such as persons from different generations or different socioeconomic classes. The term *postformal reasoning* refers to the integration of subjective and objective experiences when applying logic to particular situations, such as questions asking whether there are multiple ways to define life problems. College students with cross-category friendships demonstrated greater use of postformal reasoning than did students whose friends were just like them.

Case Study on Loneliness during Adolescence

Daniel Offer and his colleagues conducted cross-cultural studies of adolescent development in three countries: Australia, Ireland, and the United States.[4] The researchers used a standardized self-report instrument focused on various aspects of self-concept (the Offer Self-Image Questionnaire for Adolescents). One item in the instrument is phrased "I am so very lonely," and the item is answered on a six-point scale ranging from "describes me very well" to "does not describe me at all."

Offer's sample included nearly 3,000 participants: 1,513 males and 1,426 females. Australians comprised 46% of the sample, Americans 43%, and Irish 11%. The responses of the great majority (88%) to the self-concept instrument indicated they were normal, psychologically healthy teenagers.

Among the findings in this cross-cultural study, Offer reported that

- Early adolescents, whether boys or girls, reported more loneliness than later adolescents.
- Contrary to predictions that girls overall would report more loneliness than boys, the findings turned up no gender differences overall in expressions of feeling lonely.
- Gender differences did appear, however, when the adolescents' nationality was brought into the analysis: American adolescent males were found to endorse feeling lonelier than their male counterparts in Australia and in Ireland, but no differences were found among girls from the three countries. The researchers were caught off guard by these results and speculated that cultural factors they did not understand may have produced the differences separating American males from Irish and Australian males; there was no explanation for the lack of differences on feelings of loneliness among the American, Irish, and Australian girls.

Loneliness strikes me as an endemic condition for some persons who are introspective and, perhaps, socially awkward. However, with the advent of social media sites, particularly Facebook, new outlets for social connections have entered the world of adolescents and young adults. Would the social isolation felt by the adolescents in Offer's multinational study be as pronounced should a comparable study be conducted in today's social media climate?

School as Ecological Niche

A prime location where adolescents interact with peers and adults is school. The impact of this niche differs for early, middle, and later adolescents.

The Middle School

Evaluation of the transitions from the elementary school to the middle school (sometimes called junior high school) and from the middle school to high has led to differing viewpoints on how well these transitions serve the prominent social and individual issues facing early and middle adolescents. For instance, early adolescents have specific developmental tasks to accomplish, such as gaining increased independence and placing more reliance on peers, and the middle school was formed to promote achievement of these tasks. Whether the middle school enables early adolescents to accomplish developmental tasks is debated. Overall evidence indicates the middle school environment serves youth whose development is occurring on time, but that early adolescents who are more developmentally mature than their peers find the middle school frustrating and stifling.

Qualitative studies have produced more positive portraits of the effects of the middle school. The typical early adolescent copes well in this new environment, and the research conclusion is that resiliency marks the response of youth to the middle school. The adolescents seek and use information to succeed in their new school setting, and they employ various communication strategies to cope. For instance, some strategies are practical and direct, such as asking someone for help in doing a math problem. Other strategies include interpersonal skills such as being open and friendly; testing limits such as deliberately violating a school rule to learn if it will be enforced; observing others to find out what is acceptable behavior; and wandering through the school to discover markers that will help one navigate the maze of corridors.

A national task force comprised of experts on education and adolescent development made eight recommendations based on essential principles for making the middle school responsive to the needs of early adolescents. Chief among these essential principles was that the middle school "should be a place where close, trusting relationships with adults and peers create a climate for personal growth and intellectual development" (Task Force, 1989, p. 37). The task force recommended that middle schools needed to be milieus where

1. A community for learning exists, and such a community would be fostered by dividing large, impersonal middle schools into smaller communities where individuals are recognized and known.

2. The curriculum centers on a common core of substantive knowledge that evokes both cognitive and affective learning such as critical thinking, problem solving, openness to ideas, and learner curiosity.
3. Success is made much more likely for all students.
4. Decision-making is in the hands of principals at the local level.
5. Middle school teachers are prepared to work specifically with early adolescents.
6. The curriculum would be integrally linked to health and fitness.
7. The school forms alliances with families of students.
8. The school and community organizations engage in collaborative partnerships.

The High School

The current assessment of the American high school is that we poorly educate students. Sources of concern involve continually declining scores on standardized achievement tests, particularly in student comprehension of mathematics and science. However, the sweeping condemnations of high schools have been tempered with the realization that there are some schools where students' achievement is exemplary. These good high schools emphasize high academic standards, promote a core curriculum, provide for some electives, and have a vision of what it means to be an educated person. The importance of a clear educational vision, sometimes called a rationale, has been found at the center of good high schools; the good schools' clear educational vision expressed commitment to four central objectives: developing critical thinking, promoting student investment in continued learning, exploring diverse career options, and building community spirit.

Bullying in Middle Schools and in High Schools

All is not happiness and joy for each student in middle school or high school. Some experience academics as drudgery and learning the school subjects as irrelevant. Another set of issues involving interpersonal conflict, however, also leads some youth to dread being in school.

All human relationships involve the prospect of conflict. The organization of the middle and high school milieus seems to exacerbate these prospects, enabling some students to single out others for harassment. We term this type of harassment "bullying."

A student may take a dislike to someone else and use the Internet to forge nasty statements online in the name of the youth picked out for bullying. The case of D.C. (a pseudonym for a student bullied online) provides an illustrative lesson. Someone forged Facebook messages that made it appear D.C. was mocking other teenagers online. Students turned away, excluding D.C. from their social circles. When confronted with accusations about his Facebook statements, D.C. protested that he did not even have a Facebook account; his protests were dismissed as obvious lies. The forged Facebook identity was fairly convincing; it had D.C.'s name and a picture of him jogging. D.C.'s mother uncovered the Facebook account. When she protested to school authorities, she was told the matter was out of their jurisdiction; none of the cyber bullying had been done on campus. This form of harassment, called "cyber bullying," is all the more insidious because it permits the attacker to stay hidden and to spread the poison for all the Internet world to see.

One form of bullying occurs when a student's sexual orientation, perhaps without any truth to what peers say, is made the subject of ridicule. Accusations of being gay or lesbian are thrown around fairly loosely by early and middle adolescents. When the accusations stick, an individual can be targeted for intensifying moments of bullying that bleed over into physical assault.

We know that only some students engage in bullying. It is not common to all early and middle adolescents; that is, not all early and middle adolescent youth target others for harassment. What triggers bullying? Is there something about an individual student that sets him or her so apart from another person or group and leads to being bullied? The issue is layered: It may be an individual's looks or clothing or social awkwardness mark a student as different. An individual's being different stands out and is not considered cool; being different and cool would encompass such talents as athletic prowess, musical talent, or high intelligence. However, social awkwardness, not fitting into the standards that the in-crowd sets, and not having a powerful subgroup of one's own, marks some students as targets. Two patterns that have been uncovered are bullying is directed (a) at peers with noticeable social withdrawal and social anxiety and (b) at peers with poor impulse control, annoying social behavior, and a propensity to provoke aggression.

Another part of the concatenation of influences encouraging bullying is a school climate that permits bullying. Social learning also plays a part and interacts within a school climate in which bullying is tolerated. In short, when an aggressive child observes that bullying behaviors are tolerated, the frequency of aggressive acts against other students increases: ridiculing, taunting, and making life miserable for an unfortunate few become normative beliefs for some adolescents. A school climate that offers no reinforcement for bullying and, in fact, enforces severe consequences for engaging in bullying, reduces the frequency of such acts. (Note: I did not state that the reduction in bullying behavior also tempered dispositions toward being a bully. Changing the bully's character is not what youth who are harassed desire. An end to being bullied is gain enough for youth who are tormented.)

The College

College as an ecological niche for adolescents has been studied from several perspectives. Longitudinal studies from the decades of the 1970s, 1980s, 1990s, and the first years of the 2000s have looked particularly at two overarching perspectives: (a) the college environment and (b) student involvement.

The most sweeping environmental effect of college on adolescent development was attributed to the influence of the student's peer group. Certain peer group characteristics exerted more influence on development than did others. Specifically, the most influential peer group influences came from the socioeconomic status, attitudes, values, and self-concept exerted by the student group. Faculty had some impact on development of late adolescent undergraduates, particularly faculty who were oriented toward the growth of students; unlike faculty whose primary orientation was research accomplishments, student-oriented faculty not only had positive effects on student satisfaction with their college experience but also with the students' cognitive achievement and affective development.

Evidence from a variety of sources indicates the significant changes that accrue for undergraduates occur because of a series of connected experiences over a period of time. Some of these experiences occur in the classroom, and others involve living in campus residences as well as living off campus; interacting with faculty outside the classroom; gaining focus through an academic major; and participating in the diverse intellectual, social, and cultural life available on a campus. An example of a positive effect of undergraduate study is exposure to cultural differences that parlays into receptivity toward and growing interest in various facets of culture.

Social Media as Ecological Niche

The exponential changes that the electronic revolution has wrought validate the prophetic vision of Marshall McLuhan who in the 1960s wrote generously, even rhapsodically, of the deep qualitative changes occurring to human development, interactions, and expectations due to the technological possibilities of electronic media. Persons in developed countries who were born since the 1980s have not known a time without the Internet, FAX machines, e-mail, instant messaging, and cell phones. We have a cultural divide between the digital natives, persons whose development takes the electronic marvels for granted, and digital immigrants, persons whose experiences occurred without immediate communication and whose social lives do not depend on involvement with Facebook or some such electronic system.

The Pew Research Center conducted a national survey in late 2012 to ascertain the demographics of social media users in the United States. The results indicate wide use of the Internet, particularly among persons younger than 50. Social networking sites are particularly popular among 18- to 29-year-olds; 83% of survey respondents in this age group use social media, and Facebook by far is the preferred social networking platform. Other sites such as Twitter, Pinterest, Tumblr, and Instagram are significantly much less used than is Facebook, and are much more likely to be used by urban rather than rural residents. Although social media are used by both genders, females significantly use these sites more than males (71% of the females as compared to 62% of the male survey respondents). There are some differences that indicate greater use among urban versus rural respondents.

Digital Natives

Adolescents today are part of the increasingly growing cohort of persons who have never known a time without the Internet. Various phrases have been tried out to depict these young persons: "the Net Generation," "the digital generation," "Millennials," and "digital natives." I like the phrase "digital natives" because it provides for a counterpart term, "digital immigrants." Persons who grew up in an era when the Internet was nonexistent are "digital immigrants."

Digital natives simply know of no social fabric without the pervasive presence of the technology of the Internet. The last thing they touch before going to bed will be a smart phone, and checking for text messages will be the first thing digital natives do upon waking. It is estimated that digital natives have spent close to a third of their lives using smart phones, playing video games, texting, downloading movies, books, and music, and engaging in various forms of social media such as Facebook. Failing to remain in touch with peers by means of social media leads to social isolation.

For digital natives, multitasking is the normal mode of operation. Digital natives send and receive instant messages, surf the Internet, and listen to music while also reading course assignments. Critics of multitasking argue that such behavior leads to superficial understanding at best; the distractions built into multitasking militate against forming the discipline and character needed to master complex, nuanced, challenging ideas. Multitaskers are characterized as having short attention spans and an impatience when results take time. Some neuroscientists are convinced that the brains of digital natives are being rewired due to their constant engagement with digital tools.

There are some skeptics to this wholesale depiction of a self-absorbed, impatient, shallow generation hooked on digital technology. Some educators as well as researchers strongly contest the sweeping and negative generalizations made about digital natives. For example, though remaining connected through social media is important and having access to the Internet is crucial to digital natives, only a small minority of this cohort is considered addicted to constant texting.

Radio and Adolescent Development: A Bygone Influence

At one point feverishly listening to the radio demarcated one of the rites of passage into early adolescence. A team of researchers at the University of Illinois at Urbana-Champaign in the late 1980s considered that adolescence began when, in conjunction with spending more time with peers and less time with families, "a young person begins to seriously invest him or herself in the popular music of the day" (Larson, Kubey, & Colletti, 1989, p. 597). These "radio days" are passé. Radio no longer holds importance for today's adolescents who have smart phones and iPads and have never known a time without the Internet. Adolescents invest themselves in the popular music of the day, but don't need to turn to the radio to do so.

Case Study: Marshall McLuhan's Point of View

The ideas of the Canadian scholar Marshall McLuhan became suddenly popular in the United States in the 1960s. Admittedly, social change involving electronic technology has moved exponentially beyond the state of affairs people knew 50 or 60 years ago. However, the gist of McLuhan's thesis strikes me as more relevant today than it was when he proposed it. In short, McLuhan asserted that the contemporary human environment is fundamentally technological, and that technological advances are extensions of the human species. He maintained that few persons were aware of how pervasively technology influences human life. Technology provides extensions of our own faculties so that, in McLuhan's words, "The book is an extension of the eye … clothing an extension of the skin … [and] electric circuitry an extension of the central nervous system" (McLuhan & Fiore, 1967, pp. 26–40). Remember: He was writing before there was an Internet. Computers were beyond the reach of the typical person, and social media such as Myspace and Facebook had yet to revolutionize how persons interact.

For McLuhan, the most revolutionary technological influence on the human species is the marriage of electronic media, primarily television, with communication satellites.

McLuhan said already in the late 1980s we lived in a global village due to the presence of communication satellites. Think how that "proscenium arch around the planet" has so dramatically made the globe a stage "on which everybody can do his thing" in the 21st century (McLuhan, 1989, p. 4).

The year before McLuhan published those words just quoted directly, my daughter at the age of 10 told her mother and me she could not imagine a quality life without radio, television, and video cassettes. "What did people do with their time before television?" was my daughter's wonder. (Actually, I told her before there was television, my family used to gather in the family room and stare at the wall.)

Now we have more than radios, TVs, and video cassettes. We have an electronic media revolution demarcating generations. As mentioned in earlier in this chapter, there are digital natives and digital immigrants. There is speculation that extensive exposure to and active involvement with electronic media is rewiring synapses. See the section "Social Media as Ecological Niche" in this chapter for that discussion.

Gangs as Ecological Niche

Subsets of adolescents gravitate to gang membership, and gangs are not a new phenomenon. Books such as *Street Corner Society* and *Do or Die* and movies such as *West Side Story, Gangs of New York,* and *The Warriors* testify to the awareness of gangs in popular and scholarly circles. As one scholar wrote in the early 1990s, "Los Angeles is a city of gangs. There are Chinese gangs and Central American gangs, Vietnamese and Cambodian gangs, Phillipino [sic], Korean, and Samoan gangs. There are white gangs. The oldest street gang in L.A., dating back to the thirties, is Mexican-American.... But the white hot glare of public interest focused sharply on gangs only a little more than two and a half years ago [1988]. And then it centered on the ghetto gangs, the Bloods and the Crips" (Bing, 1991, p. xiv).

Gang activity and gang organization have spread across the United States, from large metropolitan areas such as Los Angeles and Washington, D.C., to medium size towns, and to small towns. Problems involving gang violence often involve distribution and sale of drugs, a major income source for gangs. Drive-by shootings, gun battles between rival gang members, and killing of bystanders caught in the crossfire are forms of gang violence that mark gang presence in a community. Illegal activities lead to the arrest, conviction, and imprisonment of gang members. One of the ironies is that youth correctional facilities and prisons become fertile grounds for recruiting gang members.

Gangs are predominantly male, although there are female gangs and females who are involved with male-dominated gangs. Youths enter gangs earlier and stay longer than gang members did previously, except for females, who still enter later than males and leave earlier. Whereas the age range of gang members on average extends from 8 to 30, there are gang members who are older.

Theories to Explain Youth Gangs

Three main theories to explain youth gangs are *strain theory, cultural deviance theory,* and *dysfunctional families*. The fundamental idea of strain theory is that young people in an impoverished underclass strive to solve the problem of economic oppression. Finding no doors opening to permit economic advancement, the youths experience strain over the obstacles preventing attainment of their economic desires and ambitions. This strain leads to frustration, discontent, and anger; however, rather than becoming helpless, the youths develop (or join) their own economic development program—a gang.

Cultural deviance theory explains youth gangs as the creation of adolescents who follow behavioral norms that vary considerably from the norms of mainstream society. Norms in the youth gang subculture endorse gratuitous violence, instant gratification, rebellion against social restraints imposed by the police and the courts, and group autonomy. Loyalty to the gang and to one's fellow gang members is valued highly. Gang members understand that they engage in illegal activities, but they consider the violation of mainstream social norms irrelevant and that participating in the gang is the only course of action available to overcome the constraints whereby mainstream society keeps impoverished youth from economic success. From the viewpoint of the gang member, deviance is a word used by persons in power in mainstream society to label nonconformists and rebels. For the gang member, not participating in the gang is economically impractical; furthermore, gang members consider following mainstream rules means remaining members of an oppressed underclass and would be the epitome of submitting to a social order out of their reach.

Dysfunctional families is a theory used to explain the presence and staying power of gangs. According to this theory, adolescents turn to gang membership to achieve the nurturance, support, and protection denied them in their biological families. When applied to members of gangs in Los Angeles, data indicated invariably that these youths' families were beset by drug addiction, alcoholism, chronic illness, impoverished housing, physical and emotional abuse, and parental conflict. According to one person who studied gang members' motivation, the gang provides "affection, understanding, recognition, loyalty, and emotional and physical protection" (Morales, 1992, p. 137).

Case Study on Gang Violence

Gang violence has increased substantially since the 1930s. Relatively few gang homicides were reported in the 1950s and 1960s, but in 1980 the city of Los Angeles alone reported 351 deaths due to gang violence. By 1989 nearly two-fifths of all the murders in Los Angeles were gang killings. By the end of the first decade of the 21st century, slightly more than half of all murders in Los Angeles were gang-related (see www.streetgangs.com/homicides).

Numbers fluctuate. Whereas Wichita, Kansas, police in the 1990s had expressed growing concern over the spread of gangs and of gang violence, by 2010 this police department was reporting a noticeable decline in gang homicides. The total number of homicides in the two largest cities in Oklahoma, Tulsa and Oklahoma City, oscillated in the first decade of the 21st century, but gang-related killings increased. Police in Flint, Michigan, reported most homicides in its town were linked to drugs and gangs. And in 2010 the police in Chicago, Illinois, reported an overwhelming majority (81%) of homicides were due to gangs; the trend continued in 2011 and 2012 with high numbers of homicides, most attributed to gang members with firearms.

Police say that gang members hold human life in utter disregard, and feel no remorse for persons they kill. As a police officer who works with gangs said, "macho to these guys is you kill someone" (Tachsler, 1993, 2A). Consider this example as an illustration that vengeance holds a prominent place in the core values of gangs: Gang members went to the home of a rival gang member, knocked on the front door, and shot in the face the person who opened the door. The victim was the mother of the rival gang member. In retaliation, the woman's son took members of his gang and did the same thing to the mother of one of the members of the offending gang.

Concluding Comments

In this chapter the focus is on ecological niches that exert influence on the development and well-being of the individual adolescent. It seems reasonable to juxtapose the influence of the family with the influence of the peer group, and there are some researchers who maintain that the peer group gains such ascendancy over the adolescent that family, particularly parents, take at best a secondary role. Longitudinal research into adolescent self-concept indicates that the growth of the influence of peers does not replace the value the adolescent looks to in his or her parents when it comes to decisions that have far-reaching consequences.

Throughout the developed world adults have arranged a social structure that forces children into greater and greater interaction with peers for many hours each week. This social organization is the school. Whereas in earlier times a young person would be apprenticed to an adult to learn a trade or occupation and thereby remain within adult influence and supervision, the school leads to norms developed and enforced by youth. Of course, we have marketing campaigns from various industries (clothing, music, movies, television, for instance) that establish, cater to, and exploit youth trends.

The pervasive power of social networking sites to shape youth is one of the watershed events of our era. The digital natives simply act differently than youth from earlier generations. To remain current with one's social set, the digital natives must interact on such social media outlets as Facebook. Surely you have observed many adolescents who are obsessively texting and checking for text messages. I suspect a whole new form of carpal tunnel syndrome will emerge as adolescents' and young adults' thumbs get overused in feverishly sending text messages. But this 24/7 power to communicate also provides resources for youth dealing with serious life crises, such as a life-threatening illness or the death of someone loved; we will not lose sight of this phenomenon when turning to issues of coping with dying or grieving.

Finally, there is a subset of adolescents, raised predominantly in impoverished circumstances in urban settings, who turn to gangs for interpersonal support, income, and physical protection. The infusion of drugs and firearms makes gangs particularly deadly, as does the wanton disregard for human life that becomes a norm in the behavior of a gang.

Notes

1. Ethologists study animals in their natural environments. Jane Goodall is one well-known example of an ethologist who studied chimpanzees in jungle settings in Africa. The jungle offers one type of ecological niche for chimpanzee development and behavior. A zoo offers another setting that is also an ecological niche for chimpanzee development and behavior.

2. A speculation I think well worth testing with longitudinal studies of bereaved and nonbereaved adolescents is that having to cope in early adolescence with the death of a family member or friend leads to finer grained self-realizations that peers unaffected by such severe losses do not acquire in the early adolescent years.
3. The material about genograms originally appeared in *Helping the Bereaved College Student* (Balk, 2011, pp. 139–143).
4. See the discussion in Chapter Two of Daniel Offer's research into adolescent self-concept.

Sources

Amichal-Hamburger, Y., Kingsbury, M., & Schneider, B. H. (2013). Friendship: An old concept with a new meaning? *Computers in Human Behavior*, **29**, 33–39.

Balk, D. E. (2011). *Helping the bereaved college student.* New York: Springer.

Bing, L. (1991). *Do or die.* New York: HarperCollins.

Brown, E. R. & Saltman, K. J. (Editors). (2005). *The critical middle school reader.* New York: Routledge.

Bryant, E. M. & Marmo, J. (2012). The rules of Facebook friendship: A two-stage examination of interaction rules in close, casual, and acquaintance friendships. *Journal of Social and Personal Relationships*, **29**, 1013–1035.

Chase, J. M. & Leibold, M. A. (2003). *Ecological niches: Linking classical and contemporary approaches.* Chicago: University of Chicago Press.

Galupo, M. P., Cartwright, K. B., & Savage, L. S. (2009). Cross-category friendships and postformal thought among college students. *Journal of Adult Development*, **17**, 208–214.

Gendron, B. P., Williams, K. R., & Guerra, N. G. (2011). An analysis of bullying among students within schools: Estimating the effects of individual normative beliefs, self-esteem, and school climate. *Journal of School Violence*, **10**, 150–164.

Hagedorn, J. M. (2009). *A world of gangs: Armed young men and gangsta culture.* Minneapolis, MN: University of Minnesota Press.

Harter, S. (2008). The developing self. In W. Damon & R. M. Lerner (Eds.), *Child and adolescent development: An advanced course* (pp. 216–260). Hoboken, NJ: John Wiley & Sons.

Hoffman, J. (December 4, 2010). As bullies go digital, parents play catch up. *New York Times.* Retrieved May 12, 2012, from www.nytimes.com/2010/12/05/us/05bully.html.

Larson, R. W., Kubey, R., & Colletti, J. (1989). Changing channels: Early adolescent media choices and shifting investments in family and friends. *Journal of Youth and Adolescence*, **18**, 583–599.

McLuhan, H. M. (1964). *Understanding media: The extensions of man.* New York: McGraw-Hill.

McLuhan, H. M. (1989). A McLuhan mosaic. In G. Sanderson & F. Macdonald (Eds.), *Marshall McLuhan: The man and his message* (pp. 1–4). Golden, CO: Fulcrum.

McLuhan, H, M. & Fiore, Q. (1967). *The medium is the message.* New York: Bantam.

Manning. M. L. (2000). A brief history of the middle school. *Clearing House*, **73**, 192.

Martinez-Aleman, A. M. (2010). College women's female friendships: A longitudinal view. *The Journal of Higher Education*, **81**, 553–582.

Masten, C. L., Telzer, E. H., Fuligni, A. J., Lieberman, M. D., & Eisenberger, N. I. (2012). Time spent with friends in adolescence relates to less neural sensitivity to later peer rejection. *Social, Cognitive, and Affective Neuroscience*, **7**, 106–114.

Morales, A. T. (1992). Therapy with Latino gang members. In I. A. Vargas & J. D. Koss-Chioino (Eds.), *Working with culture: Psychotherapeutic interventions with ethnic minority children and adolescents* (pp. 129–154). San Francisco: Jossey-Bass.

Offer, D., Ostrov, E., & Howard, K. I. (1977). The self-image of adolescents: A study of four cultures. *Journal of Youth and Adolescence*, **6**, 265–280.

Olson, D. H., Russell, C. S., & Sprenkle, D. H. (1983). Circumplex model of family and marital systems. VI. Theoretical update. *Family Process, 22,* 69–83.

Pew Research Center. (2013). The demographics of social media users—2012. Retrieved May 6, 2013, from http://pewinternet.org/Reports/2013/Social-media-users.aspx.

The Prevention Researcher. (2004). Juvenile bullying. **11**(3). Special issue.

The Prevention Researcher. (2010). Social media and youth. **17**(Supplement). Special issue.

The Prevention Researcher. (2012). Adolescent bullying. **19**(3). Special issue.

Rubin, K. H., Bukowski, W. M., & Laursen, B. (Editors). (2011). *Handbook of peer interactions, relationships, and groups.* New York: Guilford.

Rubin, K. H., Bukowski, W. M., Parker, J. G., & Bowker, J. C, (2008). Peer interactions, relationships, and group. In W. Damon & R. M. Lerner (Eds.), *Child and adolescent development: An advanced course* (pp. 141–180). Hoboken, NJ: John Wiley & Sons.

Strong, B. & DeVault, C. (1989). *The marriage and family experience* (4th ed.). St. Paul, MN: West.

Tachsler, J. (1993, February 2). Mindset of gangs: No remorse. *Topeka Capital Journal,* **119**(95), 1A–2A.

Task Force on Education of Young Adolescents. (1989). *Turning points: Preparing American youth for the 21st century.* Washington, DC: Carnegie Council on Adolescent Development.

Venkatesh, S. (October 4, 2012). Understanding kids, gangs, and guns. *New York Times,* **CLXII**, A35.

4　Coping Responses of Adolescents

The two central topics of this book, dying and grieving, present life crises with few if any parallels in terms of the fundamental importance each holds for humans. Considerable attention has been paid to the topic of coping with life crises, and the results of those inquiries into coping form the basis for this chapter.

Models for understanding adolescent coping will be reviewed within the overall cognitive framework that dominates contemporary thinking about coping with life crises, and a specific coping model using this cognitive framework—the one developed by Rudolf Moos—will be presented. Attention will be paid to Alexander Leighton's seminal model that looks at community and sociocultural influences on individuals facing distressing life events. Coleman's focal theory of adolescent coping will be brought into the mix.

The Cognitive Framework for Current Thinking about Coping

A monumental shift occurred in the field of psychology in the decades of the 1960s and 1970s. For several decades in the 20th century, the reigning model for examining and explaining human responses had been behaviorism; the psychologist's focus we were told was to examine behavior and to avoid any study of the activities of the mind. A key figure extolling behaviorism as the key to psychology's advance as a science was the Harvard University psychologist B. F. Skinner.

There was not a denial that human beings think, plan, analyze, or imagine, but studying human cognition was considered beyond the capability of empiricism. Then several persons began a rebellion by looking specifically at the actions of using the mind: planning, analyzing, decision-making, and creative expression. And now the tide has greatly turned in favor of a cognitive approach to studying human psychology. This cognitive approach dominates the leading scholars who study coping.

The Coping Model Developed by Rudolf Moos

Rudolf Moos has developed an approach to understanding how individuals cope with developmental transitions and stressful life events. He proposes that coping with life crises involves several dynamically interacting aspects; background and personal factors, event-related factors, environmental factors, cognitive appraisal, adaptive tasks, coping skills, and crisis outcome. A concern I have with the Moos model is that it seems to be pointing in only one direction, namely, the box in Figure 4.1 labeled "Outcome of the Crisis." In the model, cognitive appraisal, adaptive tasks, and coping skills are the mediating factors whereby an individual can move to some form of crisis resolution. However, the impact that resolving a crisis has on adaptation to new life events remains overlooked. Outcomes of crises bode either ill or good—perhaps a combination of both—for an individual and point to the future. I suggest adding a box denoting the individual's future. I also suggest that the outcome for a crisis be seen as becoming part of the person's background and personal factors. These modifications are illustrated in Figure 4.1.

This model of coping assumes that certain structural features are common to life crises. For instance, (a) life crises threaten a person's well-being, (b) the person's normal repertoire of coping proves inadequate to resolve the situation, and (c) crises hold both the prospects for growth and gain as well as dissolution and loss. Erikson's notion of human growth over the life span is built on the notion that identity formation occurs as a response to fundamental crises (what we could call developmental transitions) that occur at identified points from infancy through old age. Along with Erikson's endorsement of the central place of crisis resolution in human growth and development, the Moos model is part of that tradition asserting that life crises present danger and opportunity.

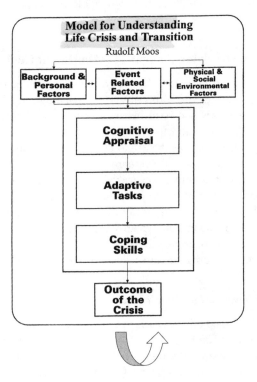

Figure 4.1 Model for Understanding Life Crisis and Transition

author?.

Background and Personal Factors. A <u>person brings</u> to a life crisis how he or she <u>has</u> dealt <u>with crises in the past</u>. The person's beliefs about ability to attain difficult goals will be part of background and personal factors. Other examples of background and personal factors are the person's gender, temperament, emotional maturity, self-concept, socio-economic status, sexual orientation, intelligence, previous experience with crises, locus of control, and religious beliefs.

Bandura?

Event-Related Factors. These are situation specific and would <u>include</u>, for instance, the extent to <u>which the crisis was anticipated</u> and the extent to which <u>the person is respon-</u> <u>sible for the crisis</u>. <u>For</u> instance, a life crisis that is anticipated is the death of a loved one from an incurable, fatal illness. Other event-related factors include who else the crisis will affect, whether the crisis could have been prevented, <u>and the overall impact of the</u> <u>crisis if handled well versus if handled poorly.</u> *Boekh?*

Environmental Factors. These factors include the quality and <u>accessibility of interper-</u> <u>sonal support</u> (both from <u>family and others</u>), the availability of counseling, and safety nets established within society to assist persons in specific types of life crises. Societal responses address some anticipated life transitions, such as the movement of early adolescents from an elementary to a middle school. Some societal responses emerge from growing awareness of problems that cannot be overlooked, such as safe havens for women and children who are victims of domestic violence. Some life crises interventions have grown up from the grass roots efforts of persons who found no plausible help for people in their situation. Examples include Alcoholics Anonymous; Compassionate Friends, a social support group founded and run by bereaved parents; and National Students of AMF, a support group for bereaved college students founded by college students.

Cognitive Appraisal. Background and personal factors, event-related factors, and environmental factors mediate the person's **cognitive appraisal** of a life crisis. With cognitive appraisal, the person sizes up the situation, assesses threat, and chooses what response to make. Cognitive appraisal triggers five adaptive tasks and three domains of coping skills.

Five Adaptive Tasks. Human beings employ **five adaptive tasks** to cope with a life crisis. In the following presentation, I use bereavement over the death of a friend as an example to illustrate each task. Note that the tasks do not occur in any definitive sequence, and they are certainly not understood to form a series of sequential steps. They do not denote stages in coping. I could present them in another order than is presented here. A person needs to engage all these tasks and will return to them over time as events demand; for example, when an adolescent faces expected developmental transitions such as graduating from high school, getting one's first job as a young adult, or becoming a parent.

1. *Establish the Meaning of the Event and Comprehend Its Personal Significance.* The person employs this task throughout crisis resolution. For instance, an adolescent faced with the death of a friend must initially accept such a loss intellectually and, at later points, integrate the loss into a coherent view of the world.
2. *Confront Reality and Respond to the Situational Requirements of the Event.* This task is dictated by the event itself. For instance, an adolescent whose friend has died will

make plans to attend the funeral, think about what to say to the friend's bereaved parents, and what to text on social media about the death and its impact.

3. *Sustain Interpersonal Relations.* A fundamental lesson we have learned is that social support greatly assists individuals to master crises. An adolescent whose friend has died needs to sustain relationships with other friends and with family members in order to ameliorate the distress and confusion presented by the death. There is little doubt that sharing one's feelings and thoughts and hearing other points of view prove beneficial to someone coping with a significant loss. A problem that adolescents report when bereaved is that few persons around them are willing to listen to their expressions of grief and begin to shy away if the grieving adolescent does not muffle saying what he or she feels or thinks about the death.

4. *Maintain Emotional Balance.* Significant, irreparable losses produce painful, unsettling emotions. The distress over the death of a friend can produce unexpected and intense emotional reactions. It is not uncommon for deaths of friends to leave adolescents overwhelmed with anger, confusion, fear, guilt, and perhaps despair. A vital aspect of this adaptive task is to maintain a sense of hope. Bereaved adolescents, particularly grieving college students, have told me they would never have anticipated their emotional reactions to a friend's death would endure so long and remain so intense. At times the grief adolescents feel is so intense and long lasting that they fear they will never find anything to look forward to and will never regain balance in their lives. In fact, when individuals are grieving acutely, the intensity of the emotions may lead to fears they are going crazy.

5. *Preserve a Satisfactory Self-Concept and Maintain a Sense of Self-Efficacy.* Momentous life events such as the death of a friend can shake a person's self-confidence and threaten his or her self-image. Research evidence suggests that positive crisis resolution is intertwined with positive self-image. Thus, it is essential for individuals coping with crises to maintain a sense of self-control and belief in their abilities to achieve outcomes they desire. The death of a friend can shake an adolescent's belief in his or her competency.

Domains of Coping. How do persons coping with life crises accomplish the five adaptive tasks? They do so by engaging three domains of coping: appraisal-focused coping, problem-focused coping, and emotion-focused coping.

1. *Appraisal-focused coping* involves the skills of logical analysis, mental preparation, cognitive redefinition, and cognitive avoidance or denial. For instance, grieving the death of a friend, an adolescent may gather information to be sure of what happened; may think how to approach peers upon returning to school; may need to reassess erroneous assumptions that bad things don't happen to good people; and may now and then take a break from thinking about the death and do something else, such as go to a movie with friends.

2. *Problem-focused coping* involves the skills of seeking information and support, taking action, and identifying alternatives to pursue. For instance, grieving the death of a friend, an adolescent may ask someone trusted what to expect in grief; may make sure that rumors about the friend's death get corrected when inaccurate stories start circulating; and may begin looking for someone else in whom to confide now that this trusted friend has died.

3. *Emotion-focused coping* involves the skills of emotional control, emotional release, and emotional acceptance. For instance, grieving the death of a friend, an adolescent may hold grief inside when at work or with a study group; may become involved in energy-demanding activities such as aerobic exercises as a means to release feelings; and—in league with the skills of cognitive redefinition and gaining information— may come to a new set of beliefs about human existence that permit emotional acceptance of the friend's death.

Alexander Leighton's Sociocultural Model of Responses to Life Crises

Over half a century ago, Alexander Leighton, the Director of the Program in Social Psychiatry at Cornell University, directed a remarkable study about the emergence of psychiatric disorders in sociocultural environments. The investigators studied communities in Nova Scotia, Canada, marked by various indicators of social disintegration: extreme poverty, high frequency of broken homes, widespread ill health, high frequency of crime and of juvenile delinquency, widespread aggression, few and weak community leaders, and few or weak associations of people. The research project found communities characterized by these indicators and other communities that, in contrast, were marked by opposite social indicators. Leighton and his associates persuasively demonstrated a significant contrast between stable and unstable communities in the development of psychiatric disorders in the population. Social disintegration was shown to be a major influence in the development of mental illness.

Implicit in Leighton's study is the notion that certain social indicators facilitate people to cope with crises. It is a small step to make connections with the Moos model of coping. The Moos model emphasizes environmental factors such as interpersonal support and societal safety nets; it also emphasizes the adaptive task of sustaining interpersonal relationships and the coping skill of seeking information and support. Disintegrating and disintegrated communities lack such factors crucial to coping with a crisis.[1]

Essential Human Strivings

In addition to the identification of important social indicators, a substantial contribution from the Leighton project is the hypothesis that certain essential strivings (sometimes called "sentiments") mark human personality and the hypothesis that these strivings change as one matures over the life span (what Leighton called "the life arc"). Leighton postulated that stable communities foster individuals to achieve these strivings in healthy ways, whereas disintegrating and disintegrated communities frustrate individuals from achieving these strivings.

While he acknowledged that there is no certain list of strivings that apply to humans in every culture, and thus the strivings vary from culture to culture and from person to person, Leighton offered a basic set for consideration. These **essential human strivings** are to

- Achieve physical security
- Obtain sexual satisfaction
- Express hostility

- Express love
- Receive love
- Secure recognition
- Express creativity
- Be oriented in terms of one's place in society and in relationship to others
- Secure and maintain membership in a definite human group
- Belong to a moral order

The relative importance of the essential human strivings varies, as indicated earlier, at different points in a person's life. Take as an example the manner and form the sentiments of expressing and receiving love take in the life of a 5-year-old toward her father. These sentiments will develop over time as both she and her father age. By the time he is elderly and infirm, he may be in the same position his daughter was in when a young child in terms of dependence on the good will and loving care of others, including his adult daughter.

The Cross-Section of the Moment

A central idea in Leighton's model is **the cross-section of the moment.** By this phrase he means what we would call a distressing life situation or a life crisis. He examined the structural properties of cross-sections of the moment and noted that *temporal thickness* is a key property. By temporal thickness he meant that all cross-sections of the moment are influenced by an individual's past, by present circumstances, and by anticipations of the future. The example of the death of a friend used to illustrate points in the Moos model will be used here to examine the concept of temporal thickness. I will use two examples, one the death of a friend in an accident and the other the death of a friend due to cancer.

- Let's imagine Harry's friend Roger died in an automobile accident. Harry and Roger had met each other in middle school where they became good friends, continued their friendship in high school, and then went to the state university where they roomed together. One night after a big basketball victory over the university's main rival, Harry and Roger partied hard with a large group of students. Then the two of them, a bit under the influence, piled into Harry's car to drive back to their apartment. Harry was driving. There had been a steady snowfall mixed with sleet much of the day. Two blocks from where they lived, Harry's car hit a patch of black ice and careened into a stone wall encircling the campus; Harry suffered a broken collar bone, a broken leg, and face lacerations, but Roger was killed. The police determined that the car went out of control because of the icy patch; Harry passed a breathalyzer test.

The accident occurred in a discrete moment in time. Yet the significance of this event (this cross-section of the moment) is deeply colored by the history of Harry and Roger's friendship. Further, Harry's acute grief over a death he feels he caused influenced his standing in school: studying became very difficult, and Harry's grades suffered, leading to eventual problems getting into graduate school. His injuries took various durations of time to heal. For over a year Harry found it difficult to look forward to anything or to plan for a meaningful future.

In addition to this look at temporal thickness, you can also apply the essential human strivings and how they changed over time for Harry following Roger's death. Harry and Roger were sources of love and recognition for each other. For several months after the accident, Harry felt hostility toward such a chance event and also toward himself for being slightly inebriated. He wondered what sort of universe we live in that allows such a good person as Roger to be killed in such a freak occurrence (that is, he questioned the moral order of things). In the coming year and a half, Harry reflected deeply on what matters in life and whether things just occur randomly, and he came to believe strongly that life is precious but fragile, that some things are very hard to explain, that he still believed God gives meaning to the world, and that it was important to let persons he loves know how he feels. It takes little imagination to consider that his life from Roger's death would have been shaped differently had Harry become a cynic who adopted a sheerly absurdist view of existence.

• In this vignette we will imagine Susan, a 14-year-old high school freshman, whose 16-year-old sister Helen died after a 2-year battle with pancreatic adenocarcinoma, a very rare form of cancer for children and adolescents that is quite resistant to chemotherapy and radiation therapy, and is very painful in its final stages.[2]

Helen and Susan were best friends. Susan stayed with Helen during the good and the bad days of her illness, and became distraught as Helen's pain became excruciating and could not be managed by the medical team. Watching her older sister, whom she loved deeply, waste away troubled Susan in ways outsiders to this cross-section of the moment did not understand.

In the last months of the illness, Susan began to realize Helen was not going to make it. Helen, her parents, and Susan talked about this reality. Following Helen's death, Susan and her parents went through some very difficult times as each one pulled into a cocoon, did not say much to one another, and walked around the house as if on egg shells. Susan feared her family was going to disintegrate. Within 4 months the family fell back on its history of close, personal communication, and Helen's death became a topic all could talk about. Susan found her parents not only offered consolation but also enforced rules that she had to follow; she was grounded once for not keeping the curfew that had been set.

Unlike the accident that took Roger's life, Helen's illness lasted over 2 years, and she became worse over time. During the illness, everyone in the family openly talked about the implications of the cancer and even admitted that Helen was going to die. There was a 14-year history of sibling bonding and rivalry between Helen and Susan that gave considerable poignancy to Helen's eventual death. The death changed her family's dynamics for a while and led Susan to fear that her whole family would never recover from Helen's death. Finally, this close family regained its pattern of shared communication. Helen had talked about becoming a physician. Four years after Helen's death, by the end of high school Susan had decided to become a medical doctor who specialized in pediatric oncology.

In addition to this look at temporal thickness, you can also apply the essential human strivings and how they changed over time for Susan following Helen's death. The suffering and death of her sister threatened Susan's sense of physical security: what had happened to Helen could just as well happen to her mother, her father, or her. She was angry over how her sister died and found difficulty letting go of the hostility she bore toward God. She lost a solid, true friend, a source of love and companionship, but found anew the love she and her parents felt toward each other. Her ultimate choice to enter the medical profession was testament to her decision to contribute to making her place in society, to express her creative vision about bringing hope and comfort to very ill children, and to being oriented as a member of the medical profession.

Coleman's Focal Model of Adolescent Coping

Facing One Issue at a Time

John Coleman has argued that the majority of adolescents deal with the many changes of adolescent development—for example, changes in physical development, school transitions, family relations, interpersonal perspective-taking, and emotional understanding—by facing one issue at a time. Adolescents spread out the process of coping with issues by concentrating their efforts on resolving one issue before focusing attention on another. By maintaining such focus, adolescents can deal with what otherwise would be turmoil. Daniel Offer reported this coping strategy in his longitudinal study of adolescent boys.

Knowledge about the changes in the developing adolescent brain provides means to explain how adolescents engage in such selective focusing on individual crises: The metacognitive components of the brain's executive functions make it possible "to temporally 'bracket' the perspectives dictated by one's own beliefs" (Kuhn & Franklin, 2008, p. 542), to organize and select from a variety of responses, and even to inhibit initial impulsive reactions.

The Sequencing of Identity Formation during Later Adolescence

It seems unlikely that an adolescent facing the threat of a severe illness or grieving the death of someone loved has the luxury of compartmentalizing issues. Perhaps what occurs is that the issue of dying or of grieving takes precedence over other issues that would be more important in different circumstances. I have not uncovered any research that has examined Coleman's focal theory applied to the lives of adolescents faced with unanticipated life crises.

One area in which the focal theory has been applied is the sequencing of identity formation during later adolescence.[3] In this domain of an anticipated life transition, focal theory was upheld: later adolescents deal with one domain of identity formation at a time and then, if necessary, move on to another.

1. *Movement from Diffusion to Foreclosure or Moratorium, or Remaining Diffuse.* Movement from diffusion to foreclosure occurs when the adolescent selects the first clear alternative found and forgoes exploration of other options. As an example, consider the dilemma of a college student who, uncertain about which major to choose, selects accounting because the student newspaper reported it is the most popular major on campus.

Movement from diffusion to moratorium occurs when social expectations are nonspecific but cover areas of personal importance to the adolescent. As an example, consider the case of another college student who grasps the importance of preparing for a career that suits her talents and works from the expectation that the decision must be solely hers. She delays making any career decision so she can explore various possibilities and because making a decision seems so formidable in the teeth of all the options possible.

In some cases, a person may not move from the diffused identity state. The lack of movement out of diffusion, for instance, with regard to choosing a major or a career, may grip the individual because views about making headway in the world of work never attain significance for the person.

2. *Movement from Foreclosure Back to Diffusion or Ahead to Moratorium, or Remaining Foreclosed.* Movement from foreclosure to diffusion can occur when an individual's commitments become obstructed, and the person decides exploring other options is not worth the effort. For example, consider a person who decided getting married and raising children was the right thing to do for personal fulfillment. An abusive husband, a divorce, and lack of opportunities led to a radical revision of her position, but she had no sense of plausible alternatives. Or consider a person who wanted since childhood to become a veterinarian. She volunteered at animal hospitals, excelled in a college curriculum pointing toward the study of veterinary medicine, but now for the third time has been denied admission to every college of veterinary medicine to which she has applied. Her dreams shattered, she decides not to explore other options lest she be hurt by further rejection.

Movement from foreclosure to moratorium occurs when an adolescent's early choices are challenged, and the adolescent begins exploring new options. An example is presented by an individual who had thought since the age of 10 to become a Catholic priest, but when he examined during his later adolescence options not open to the priesthood (intimate, romantic relationships; becoming a politician; rejecting some positions of the Catholic Church regarding homosexuality and about family planning), the young man set out on new explorations.

In some cases persons remain foreclosed, especially when an early commitment leads to immediate and continuing success. Consider the young woman who decided in childhood to become a teacher, received ongoing encouragement from her teachers and parents, excelled in learning both pedagogy and content (in her case, mathematics), landed a beginning position as a high school teacher, and has never looked back.

3. *Movement from Moratorium Ahead to Achievement or Back to Diffusion.* There is argument in some quarters that because of the unsettling elements of crisis experienced in moratorium and the desire to find resolution, individuals find it improbable to remain in moratorium indefinitely. Two choices are to move to achievement or to move to diffusion.

Movement from moratorium to achievement occurs when a person's exploration leads to synthesis of his or her potential, and social support exists for expressing these potentials. One can see in this expression of potential links to Leighton's human sentiments of belonging to a definite group and of acting creatively. An example is offered in the case of Susan who, searching for answers about the meaning of existence following the death of her sister from cancer, found resolution to her quest in the choice of becoming a medical doctor specializing in pediatric oncology.

Movement from moratorium to diffusion occurs when an adolescent relinquishes the struggle to choose and decides no meaningful options exist. Consider a college student who is majoring in philosophy and searching for the meaning of human existence; his girlfriend is stricken with acute lymphoblastic leukemia, and dies. He decides it is absurd to think human existence has ultimate meaning, but even faced with the existentialist choice offered by Camus or Sartre, for instance, to struggle despite the lack of ultimate meaning, the young man just succumbs to despair. And again, imagine another adolescent whose search for meaning to existence following the murder of his father ends with his surrender to a belief that nothing gives meaning to existence, not even human defiance in the face of absurdity.

As noted earlier, because of the elements of crisis present in moratorium and the desire to find resolution, researchers consider it highly improbable that someone may remain in moratorium indefinitely. Ruthellen Josselson's longitudinal study of females suggests, on the other hand, a lengthy duration in moratorium occurs for some individuals.

4. *Movement from Achievement Back to Moratorium or Diffusion, or Remaining Achieved.* Movement from achievement to moratorium occurs when the pursuit of important personal concerns is obstructed, and the person is forced to review alternatives. As an example, consider a young woman who chose veterinary medicine for her career, but after half a dozen years as a practicing veterinarian and growing disillusionment over how many owners needlessly call upon her to euthanize their pets, finds her career unrewarding and leaves veterinary practice to search other options. Consider as well the situation of a young man who chose law as a career after exploring numerous options; upon entering the practice of law he has found to his dismay that it is unrewarding and leaves him acting duplicitously in order to win cases at all costs. While his colleagues consider his qualms juvenile and naïve, he begins reassessing his life path and what he can do that does not leave him feeling, as he puts it, "slimy."

Movement from achievement to diffusion occurs when a person's ideals are deeply shattered, and the individual begins to question fundamental beliefs. While for some persons such an identity crisis precipitates reentering the moratorium phase, others abandon their sense of commitment to and interest in exploring alternatives. Crises in religious faith present a prototypical example. Severe, unshakeable doubts about the truth of one's religion can lead to loss of confidence and even of hope. The person has no commitment to explore alternatives because of a feeling of having been betrayed. Another example is presented by persons committed to a cause who become disillusioned after heroic efforts prove futile on behalf of that cause. Imagine for instance a person who entered social work to protect children from domestic violence and sexual abuse, worked herself to exhaustion while providing the best possible care, eventually lost hope because of relentless encounters with grisly instances of parental abuse of children, and began to blame the children for her own feelings of inadequacy.

An application of focal theory linked to identity sequencing that seems a fruitful area for inquiry is the trajectory of changes in identity formation for adolescents facing life-threatening illness or bereavement. One hypothesis worth testing is: Coping with the death of a loved one will move adolescents out of moratorium and into achievement status. Another topic worth testing is: Unresolved challenges to a grieving adolescent's assumptive worlds will move adolescents out of foreclosure and into either diffusion or moratorium.

I have not found any research that has examined identity status and coping with bereavement. Given the central position of identity formation in the development of adolescents and also the influence of coping with life crises on persons' assumptive worlds, it would seem a logical area for study. Of course, making any solid inroads would require longitudinal research over several years in order to map changes over time in areas as fundamental as identity status.

Concluding Comments

This chapter looks at models constructed to describe and to explain human coping with distressing life events. We looked at three models: the model developed by Rudolf Moos, the model developed by Alexander Leighton, and the model developed by John Coleman. A refrain I have heard from some persons when they are presented with the Moos model or the Leighton model is that no one in a crisis would turn to these models to instruct them how to act. I speculate the same dismissive attitude would be applied as well to Coleman's focal theory. This criticism strikes me as a shallow understanding of what these models denote.

I think it nonsense to hand someone in crisis a copy of the Moos model of coping: "Here's what you need to do, Shakera, to cope with your loss. Good luck." The model has value for counselors working with persons coping with a crisis. The same evaluation applies to the use of the Leighton model and of Coleman's focal theory. These models provide guidance to counselors. The models are based on extensive study of how persons in crises respond naturally. Successful coping leads people to master certain adaptive tasks, to employ specific domains of coping skills, to find healthy outlets for attaining essential human sentiments, and to sequester issues one at a time. The extent to which a person is avoiding an adaptive task (for instance, establishing the meaning of the event and comprehending its personal significance) offers concern for maladaptive coping and suggestions for focusing interventions to help the person employ that task.

My personal and professional tack is to meld the theoretical with the practical, and I consider coping to be at the heart of discussions of dying and grieving during adolescence. It is not that, for instance, I automatically dismiss research findings about adolescence and bereavement, that, although fascinating in themselves, have no immediate application for managing grief. However, I do come awfully close to that position because I think asking researchers the question "So what?" applies quite readily when working in the arena of adolescent dying and grieving.

Our next task in this book is to examine issues about mortality during the adolescent years.

Notes

1. The ecological niches of disintegrating and disintegrated family and community do not provide the nurturance and support that adolescents need. Disintegrating and disintegrated families would propel some youth to become runaways. Perhaps the presence of pervasive social disintegration provides a means to understand the attraction of some youth to join gangs, akin to the attraction that self-help groups such as Alcoholics Anonymous have for individuals in specific distress and not finding any official help in the society in which they live.
2. "Pancreatic adenocarcinoma, the most common type of pancreatic cancer, is notoriously resistant to chemotherapy and radiation therapy, leading to an overall 5-year relative survival rate of less than 5 percent." Retrieved May 12, 2012, from www.cancer.gov/ncicancerbulletin/032012/page3
3. This information builds on the concept of identity status set forth in the research of James Marcia and of Ruthellen Josselson. See the discussion of identity formation and identity sequences presented in Chapter Two.

Sources

Balk, D. E. (1983). Adolescents' grief reactions and self-concept perceptions following sibling death: A case study of 33 teenagers. *Journal of Youth and Adolescence, 12*, 137–161.

Balk, D. E. (1996). Models for understanding adolescent coping with bereavement. *Death Studies, 20*, 367–387.

Balk, D. E. (2011). *Helping the bereaved college student.* New York: Springer.

Coleman, J. C. (1978). Current contradictions in adolescent theory. *Journal of Youth and Adolescence, 7*, 1–11.

Garbarino, J., Wilson, J., & Garbarino, A. C. (1986). The adolescent runaway. In J. Garbarino, C. J. Schellenbach, & J. M. Sebes (Eds.), *Troubled youth, troubled families: Understanding families at risk for adolescent maltreatment* (pp. 41–54). New York: Aldine.

Kerr, S. R. (1995). *Attrition from the veterinary profession: Twelve case studies.* Unpublished doctoral dissertation, Manhattan, KS, Kansas State University.

Kuhn, D. & Franklin, S. (2008). The second decade: What develops (and how)? In W. Damon & R. M. Lerner (Eds.), *Child and adolescent development: An advanced course* (pp. 517–550). Hoboken, NJ: John Wiley & Sons.

Leighton, A. H. (1959). *My name is Legion: Foundations for a theory of man in relation to culture.* New York: Basic Books.

Moos, R. H. & Schaefer, J. A. (1986). Life transitions and crises: A conceptual overview. In R. H. Moos (Ed.), *Coping with life crises: An integrated approach* (pp. 1–28). New York: Plenum.

Osofsky, J. D. (Editor). (1997). *Children in a violent society.* New York: Guilford Press.

The Prevention Researcher. (2008). *Teen coping.* 15(4). Special issue.

Saldinger, A., Porterfield, K., & Cain, A. C. (2004). Meeting the needs of parentally bereaved children: A framework for child-centered parenting. *Psychiatry: Interpersonal and Biological Processes, 67*, 331–352.

Shorter, N. A., Glick, R. D., Klimstra, D. S., Brennan, M. F., & Laguaglia, M. P. (2002). Malignant pancreatic tumors in childhood and adolescence: The Memorial Sloan-Kettering experience, 1967 to present. *Journal of Pediatric Surgery, 37*, 887–892.

Waterman, A. S. (1985). Identity in the context of adolescent psychology. *New Directions for Child Development, 30*, 5–24.

5   Principal Causes of Death during Adolescence

Accidents, Murder, Suicide

This chapter focuses on some grim statistics, namely, the principal causes of death during the adolescent years. The three primary reasons adolescents die—accidents, homicide, and suicide—are due to human involvement, and all three entail preventable violence. Mortality statistics not only from the United States but from various developed and developing countries show that this pattern of violent death is true across the globe.

On a happier note, the adolescent years are among the healthiest in the human life span. Deaths are much less likely for persons in this age group than in others. Such was not the case but a century ago when the majority of deaths in the United States and around the world were to persons 14 years of age and under. Advances in medical science, in public health, in food production, and in the standard of living have all but eliminated in developed countries the risk of infectious diseases.

World Health Organization Data

The World Health Organization (WHO) places issues of life and death for older children and adolescents into clear perspective in a 2003 document.[1] In the document the WHO expressed grave concern over several threats to health that place older children and adolescents around the world at risk for severe injury and death. For example, the WHO noted, "The transition from childhood to adulthood will be marked for many in the coming years by such potentially deadly 'rites of passage' as violence, delinquency, drugs, alcohol, motor accidents and sexual hazards such as HIV and other sexually transmitted diseases." Socioeconomic conditions will play a significant influence in marking who is most at risk for these dangers from deadly rites of passage: according to the WHO, impoverished urban youth will be at greater risk than youth in other living conditions. In fact, data indicate the alarming statistic that, even in the United States, with its legion of health care practices, the adolescent population alone of all age groups in this country has had a decline in life expectancy since the 1980s.

The WHO paints a gloomy picture for child and adolescent health around the world in the first quarter of the 21st century. "One of the biggest 21st century hazards to children will be the continuing spread of HIV/AIDS. In 1997, 590,000 children age under 15 became infected with HIV. The disease could reverse some of the major gains in child health in the last 50 years."

Adolescents in developing countries were considered to be particularly vulnerable to sexually transmitted diseases, and "more than 40% of all new HIV infections in 2000" occurred in persons between 15 and 24 years of age. Complications from pregnancy and childbirth accounted for the major causes of death for females aged 15 to 19.

The main causes of death for adolescents around the world are some form of violence: accidents, homicide, suicide. See Table 5.1 for a breakdown of mortality statistics of 15- to 24-year-olds from several developed and developing countries.

As you can tell in most cases frequencies of various causes of death for 15- to 24-year-olds differ according to developed versus developing county. For instance, even though a very small portion of 15- to 24-year-olds in these countries die, in developing countries they are two or more times more likely to die than are their same-aged peers in developed countries. Second, deaths due to homicide are prevalent in developing countries, but only the United States of all developed countries has homicide rates that mimic the rates in developing countries. Third, in all countries males are more at risk of dying in the 15- to 24-year-old age group than are females. Fourth, accidents, homicides, and suicides form the three major causes of death for 15- to 24-year-olds around the world. It is unfortunate that the WHO data do not include countries on the African continent other than South Africa. It would be instructive to learn the incidence and prevalence of HIV-related deaths that are considered to be of growing concern for African nations.

Deaths Due to Violence

As stated earlier, around the world, whether in developed or developing countries, adolescents (and young adults) typically die from some form of violence: accidents, homicides, or suicides.[2] Violent deaths account for a majority of all deaths of 15- to 24-year-olds, regardless of country of residence. For example, accidents in the United States account yearly for approximately 45% of deaths to 15- to 24-year-olds, homicides for 16%, and suicides for 12%. No other cause of death—for instance, diseases of the heart, malignant neoplasms, leukemia, or circulatory system diseases—accounts for even 6% of the deaths of 15- to 24-year-olds in this country. In Australia, accidents account yearly for around 46% of deaths to 15- to 24-year-olds and suicides 20%, whereas deaths due to malignant neoplasms account for nearly 8%; in Mexico, accidents annually account for around 35% of deaths in this age group, suicide 6%, homicide 15%, and malignant neoplasms 7% to 8%.

Accidents

Accidents form the major cause of death, and vehicular accidents by far outdistance other accidental causes of death for 15- to 24-year-olds in nearly all developed and developing countries. In the United States the leading causes of adolescent death due to injuries are motor vehicle accidents and gunshot wounds; there is practically no difference in the number of adolescent deaths per 100,000 population for these two causes of death in the United States. No other developed country came even close to the prevalence of firearm-related deaths for 15- to 24-year-olds. Take for instance France and Norway: in France, motor vehicle accidents account for approximately 28 deaths per 100,000 population, and firearms approximately 5 per 100,000; in Norway, motor vehicle accidents accounted for approximately 14 deaths per 100,000 population, and firearms approximately 7 per 100,000 (see Table 5.2).

Table 5.1 Some Causes of Death for 15- to 24-Year-Olds in Selected Developing and Developed Countries

Developing Countries	Sex	Total Pop 15–24 yr old	All Deaths	% of deaths per pop	HIV	Malignant Neoplasms	Leukemia	Diabetes	Circulatory System	Heart Disease	Preg & Birth	All Accidents	Vehicular Accidents	Drowning	Suicide	Homicide
Belarus	M	772000	1573	0.2	NR	63	11	3	66	51		780	235	215	288	106
	F	741000	492	0.1	NR	47	9	8	19	12	9	89	62	46	48	33
Brazil	M	no report	32832		NR	864	244	88	1081	744		9927	5444	1735	1084	11649
	F	no report	10016		NR	621	184	141	898	598	558	2193	1423	246	347	947
Cuba	M	769000	680	0.1	7	49	15	3	37	32		251	117	45	104	71
	F	736000	360	0.05	2	46	9	6	23	13	15	79	56	5	51	27
El Salvador	M	no report	1613		32	35	12	2	43	27		360	246	91	115	748
	F	no report	465		6	32	13	1	34	34	0	60	41	15	94	50
Kazakhstan	M	1349000	3291	0.2	NR	115	22	7	220	170		1031	150	162	609	276
	F	1359000	1221	0.09	NR	82	15	11	119	92	25	282	46	43	124	73
Mexico	M	10006000	12494	0.1	296	786	271	90	440	295		5123	1735	592	870	2240
	F	9949000	4888	0.05	86	512	215	113	336	197	426	949	339	65	231	287
Russia	M	10025000	39996	0.4	39	1048	245	99	1999	1633		NR	5438	1785	6578	3602
	F	9648000	10876	0.1	10	800	158	178	666	429	296	NR	1771	374	1015	1162
South Africa	M	no report	12055		165	176	51	40	302	205		NR	NR	NR	NR	NR
	F	no report	6561		589	149	35	63	416	317	187	NR	NR	NR	NR	NR
Australia	M	1374000	1354	0.09	1	91	34	4	41	30		647	350	23	303	28
	F	1312000	474	0.04	0	48	12	1	25	20	1	187	115	4	70	16
Canada	M	2091000	1740	0.08	2	103	26	6	42	29		763	476	49	457	62
	F	1993000	620	0.03	2	60	11	5	29	16	2	238	181	6	105	25
France	M	3886000	3572	0.09	8	222	62	3	124	79		1964	1579	36	477	26
	F	3768000	1243	0.03	2	141	35	1	64	30	2	562	466	5	127	11
Germany	M	4669000	3752	0.08	7	256	65	12	152	113		1751	1323	32	594	57
	F	4448000	1337	0.03	2	155	34	8	91	59	4	538	425	8	138	35

(Continued)

Table 5.1 (Continued)

Developing Countries	Sex	Total Pop 15–24 yr old	All Deaths	% of deaths per pop	HIV	Malignant Neoplasms	Leukemia	Diabetes	Circulatory System	Heart Disease	Preg & Birth	All Accidents	Vehicular Accidents	Drowning	Suicide	Homicide
Japan	M	8383000	4960	0.06	1	383	144	11	360	280		2064	1562	158	1385	34
	F	7974000	2017	0.03	0	266	86	10	146	101	5	535	396	26	581	26
Norway	M	279000	255	0.09	0	14	4	2	9	8		104	65	7	79	5
	F	268000	85	0.03	1	8	0	0	3	0	0	21	12	1	24	2
United Kingdom	M	3694000	2638	0.07	3	207	60	10	90	57		908	584	32	393	66
	F	3505000	1026	0.03	3	132	35	7	90	56	3	243	174	6	88	14
United States	M	19334000	22414	0.1	95	1023	291	80	812	672		10061	6949	592	3325	4177
	F	18439000	8242	0.04	103	701	191	75	533	390	84	3631	2962	55	575	806

Source: Data calculated from WHO Mortality Database: http://www.who.int/healthinfo/statistics/mortality/en/index.html; NR = No Report

Table 5.2 Deaths Due to Certain Types of Accidents per 100,000 Population of 15- to 24-Year-Olds in Six Developed Countries, Late 1990s

Country	Motor Vehicle	Firearm	Poisoning	Drowning
Australia	21.2	3.7	6.6	1.9
Canada	19.7	5.0	4.0	2.1
France	27.6	4.8	2.0	1.9
New Zealand	48.7	4.4	7.3	4.4
Norway	14.1	6.6	3.1	3.0
United States	29.1	27.2	3.2	2.4

The Accidental Deaths of Three Adolescents

Jimmy was a high school junior in a rural school district in the Midwest. His father was an accountant for a farming cooperative and his mother was an elementary school teacher whose specialization was math education. His sister Sarah was a college junior at the land grant university about three hours away.

Jimmy was a fairly typical teenager. He looked up to his parents and his sister, had occasional emotional outbursts when rules chafed, and was gradually carving out for himself a sense of who he was. He had friends, and there were some kids he didn't get along with, but on the whole he was liked by his peers and because of his athletic ability was part of the high school's elite group.

Jimmy was a B student and hoped to get a college scholarship to play basketball, preferably at the university his sister attended. He was a starting forward on his high school team. The team was very good this year. They had so far gone undefeated, and on this night in question had just beaten their arch rival in double overtime. Jimmy had played nearly the whole game and scored key baskets to keep his team in the game. In the last 10 seconds of the game he led a fast break that resulted in his team's winning points.

Jimmy and his friends were ecstatic. Following the game they went to a party where they ate pizza and drank beer while celebrating the victory. After the party Jimmy and two of his friends piled into a car to drive home. All were drunk. They were traveling over 80 miles an hour down a state highway when the young man driving the car lost control. The vehicle left the road, traveled 100 feet across a field, and plowed into a tree. Jimmy was killed instantly, and the two other boys in the car died within the next hour.

Homicides

The homicide rate among adolescents and young adults in this country is alarming. When compared to youth in other developed countries of the world, 15- to 24-year-olds in the United States are 44 times more likely to be murdered than are 15- to 24-year-olds in Japan, 22 times more likely than are persons in this age group in Denmark, nearly 16 times more likely than in France and in Switzerland, and nearly 10 times more likely than in Sweden. After vehicular accidents, homicides are the leading cause of death in the United States among 15- to 24-year-olds. However, these statistics have even more alarming aspects because the incidence and prevalence of adolescent and young adult homicides are gender-related and race-related.

Homicide is the leading cause of death for African American males between the ages of 15 and 24. Nearly 48% of all deaths to 15- to 24-year-old African American males are due to homicide, whereas homicide accounts for 16% of the deaths of 15- to 24-year-old African American females. For White males and females in this age range, homicide accounts for 10% and 7% of the deaths, respectively, whereas unintentional injuries, not murders, accounted for nearly half of all the deaths of 15- to 24-year-old White males and females in the United States. In the mid-1990s, it was predicted that in the United States murder would become the cause of death for 1 out of every 27 African American adolescent males, for 1 out of every 117 African American adolescent females, for 1 out of every 205 White adolescent males, and for 1 out of every 496 White adolescent females. Among 15- to 24-year-old Native American males homicide accounts for slightly over 11% of deaths to this group, and 9% of the deaths among Native American females in this age group.

One could accurately say that African American males are particularly vulnerable to being murdered; at the turn of the century, 15- to 24-year-old African American males were 28 times more likely to murder someone and 17 times more likely to be murdered than anyone else in the United States. Between the early 1980s into the middle 1990s, the homicide rate and HIV rate among African American males led to a decrease in life expectancy among African American males between the ages of 15 and 24 and a decrease in life expectancy overall among African Americans, a phenomenon not seen in any other racial or ethnic group. Early in the 21st century, however, the National Center for Health Statistics indicated this decrease in life expectancy for African American males had been stemmed. This change is attributed to a decline in homicide and HIV rates within African American males. While there is still a gap in the life expectancy of White males and African American males, the gap narrowed to less than 5 years' difference whereas it had increased to a gap of over 7 years between 1983 and 1994. The life expectancy of 15- to 24-year-old White males born in 1985 is now approximately 76.5 years whereas the life expectancy of same-aged African American males is around 72.

The Murder of One Adolescent

Terrance was a 17-year-old African American male living in Chicago; he was 9 days from turning 18. He attended a private high school that contracted with the City's public school system to educate older students with troubled high school records. The students at Terrance's former school either had dropped out of high school or were at risk of dropping out. In Terrance's case, he had transferred to his new school to escape persistent bullying. Some relatives said Terrance had adjusted well to his new school because he found peers who accepted him; other relatives said bullying had not stopped and was at the heart of what led to the fatal attack on the boy.

A couple of weeks before Halloween, Terrance was walking home from school. Five teenagers surrounded him around 3:40 PM and demanded money. Terrance refused to hand over any money, and one of the robbers, a 14-year-old boy with a gun, began going through Terrance's pockets. Terrance pushed the boy away, and the 14-year-old shot Terrance in the chest. Then the five would-be robbers scattered.

Terrance was rushed to an emergency room. The attending physician pronounced him dead at 4:31 PM. Upon performing an autopsy, a medical examiner concluded that Terrance died because of the gunshot wound to his chest. The death was ruled a homicide.

Nine days after the incident, the 14-year-old gunman was arrested. His mother called the police to report his complicity in the crime. A second youth, a 16-year-old boy, was arrested 2 days later. Both boys were charged with murder and attempted robbery. The 16-year-old was charged with murder in the first-degree, and the State Attorney decided to try him as an adult. The 14-year-old would be tried in Juvenile Court. (See Sobol, October 29, 2012; October 30, 2012).

Suicides

The World Health Organization indicates that adolescent suicides have increased worldwide to such an extent that in a third of all nations adolescents are considered the group most at risk for self-destructive acts (www.befrienders.org/suicide/statistics.htm). As of 2012 suicide was the eleventh leading cause of death for all Americans, and formed the third leading cause of death for American adolescents. In this country, of 15- to 24-year-olds, on average, nearly 11 take their own lives daily, for an annual total of 3,971. This annual figure is lower than the number of suicides reported for 15- to 24-year-olds in the middle 1990s (approximately 6,000), but then that statistic only makes sense given that since 1997 the rate of suicides among 15- to 24-year-olds has declined each year. Because there is widespread suspicion that many suicides are reported as accidental deaths in order to spare the bereaved survivors even more distress, could it be that the steady decline in reported suicides actually masks the reality of self-destructive acts in this country?

It is estimated that for every individual who takes his or her own life, at least six persons are left to deal with the aftermath following such a death.[3] Thus, of 15- to 24-year-olds, if 3,971 committed suicide, there were an estimated 23,826 intimately affected and left to deal with the wake of those self-destructive acts. In other words, in the United States in 2001 there were 66 new additions daily to the group coping with the aftermath of a loved one's suicide.

A Sociological View of Suicide.   Emile Durkheim presented a sociological model that categorized suicide into four types: (1) altruistic, (2) anomic, (3) egoistic, and (4) fatalistic. There is some correspondence between altruistic suicide, in which a person's regard for community values overrides any other issues, and what is presented later in this chapter as cultural suicide. Features of anomic and fatalistic suicides, in which a person feels extremely isolated or oppressed, have features akin to referred suicide. Egoistic suicide, in which persons exhibit (a) little if any acceptance of their culture's values, (b) react powerfully to societal undercurrents of despair, and (c) remain isolated in their own worlds, seems more a type unlike any of the four categories presented next in this book.

Four Categories of Suicidal Acts. Some researchers have placed suicidal acts into four categories: surcease suicide, psychotic suicide, cultural suicide, and referred suicide. We look at each in turn.

- Surcease suicide is the intentional act to end one's own life, prompted by the desire to be released from pain. The word "surcease" means to bring something to an end. The chief example is the decision of a terminally ill person who is in unremitting, excruciating pain to be released from that pain. Another example is the decision of a person with progressively worsening Alzheimer's disease to end her life before she becomes incapable of rational thought and action. The emphasis is on a clear, rational decision in which one's reasoning is not impaired by emotional disturbance such as clinical depression.
- Psychotic suicide is the ending of one's life prompted by delusions or hallucinations. For instance, schizophrenic persons may hear voices urging or compelling them to kill themselves. In these cases, the person is incapable of using normal reasoning skills. There seems a valid question whether the person's suicidal act is voluntary.
- Cultural suicide emerges from self-concepts grounded in strong cultural values about honor and obedience to tradition. Examples are the ritual suicide of *seppuku* among Samurai in feudal Japan and the kamikaze pilots in World War II; the act of Roman nobles found guilty of treason who were offered the option of ending their lives and thereby preserving the lives of their family; *suttee*, the practice of Hindu wives to be burned alive on the funeral pyre of their dead husband; political protests such as the death through self-immolation of Buddhist monks protesting the Vietnam War and, possibly, the acts of terrorists who blow themselves up in the act of killing others.
- Referred suicide denotes the acts of persons who are in troubling life situations. They are extremely despondent, perhaps feel deep shame, and see themselves as trapped. There is a sense of personal failure. The person sees death as the only escape from an intolerable situation; however, unlike surcease suicide, in referred suicide the person's confusion and emotional turmoil is paramount; unlike psychotic suicide, the person is not under control of delusions or hallucinations.

A catchy phrase to describe referred suicides is "a permanent solution to a temporary problem." That assertion seems to me debatable; some problems seem more than transient or momentary; an example that comes to mind is permanent paralysis. However, the phrase implies that suicide is a maladaptive response to stress and that other responses are possible, such as seen in the activity of persons afflicted with amyotrophic lateral sclerosis (Lou Gehrig's disease) to remain alive and engaged in the world while they live.

Interacting Influences to Consider. Several interacting influences have been identified as risks associated with adolescent suicide. Some of these influences are feelings of depression, low self-image, excessive parental expectations, drug and alcohol use, communication breakdowns with parents or friends, a history of suicide attempts, and a major confrontation with an important figure in the adolescent's life. Motives that have been attributed to adolescents who kill themselves include a craving to get help, to escape a difficult situation, to punish people who have hurt the adolescent, to join someone who has died, and to assert a sense of independence in defiance of authorities the adolescent sees as repressive.

Other risks for adolescent suicide include psychiatric problems, psychosocial issues, cognitive problems, and biological concerns. For instance, the psychiatric problems include major depression, schizophrenia, anorexia, and alcohol abuse. Psychosocial issues include poor family relationships, romantic breakups, feelings of hopelessness, and domestic violence. Cognitive problems include perseverating self-defeating thoughts, low appraisal of ability to resolve problems, and constricted thinking (sometimes called "tunnel vision"). Biological concerns include difficulties regulating mood and problems handling distress.

Actually, psychiatric problems, psychosocial issues, cognitive problems, and biological concerns interact within the increasingly complex, differentiated journey from childhood into adolescence. An example illustrating the interactive influences on development is Chris, an adolescent who since childhood has learned he is of little value, does not quite fit in with peers, sees no prospects of worth in his future, has problems controlling feelings of anger, and lashes out impulsively at others when frustrated. A counter example is offered by Samantha, an adolescent who since childhood has developed a positive self-image, feels loved and lovable, sees goals worth striving for, anticipates consequences to actions, and can step back from distressing situations to consider how to respond.

Earlier discussions about coping and about brain development come into play when thinking about risks for adolescent suicide. The coping models emphasize cognitive processes such as planning, organizing, inhibiting impulses, and regulating emotions. Neuroscientific findings have disclosed (a) the significant role of the prefrontal cortex in these cognitive processes, particularly self-regulatory practices, and (b) the notable development of the prefrontal cortex during adolescence.

From early through later adolescence, an adolescent is developing conscious, intentional self-regulation of emotion and behavior. Early and middle adolescents' brains are much less mature than brains of later adolescents "in terms of the capacity for effortful, cognitive self-regulation," and such findings "may go a long way toward explaining why early to midadolescence is associated with a jump in the rates of risky behaviors, including suicidal behaviors" (Wagner & Zimmerman, 2006, p. 293).

1. *Hopelessness and adolescent suicide.* There are links between depression and suicidal behavior, illustrated by suicidal youth with low perceptions of self-worth, negative attitudes toward the world, and gloomy expectations about relations with other persons.[4] Hopelessness, a key feature associated with depression, has been found in suicidal adolescents, and the more hopeless an adolescent feels, the risk of suicide attempts increases.

The term "hopelessness" may be too academic and abstract to convey the anxiety and dread the person feels; he or she senses no way out of an emotionally wrenching dilemma. The person feels trapped, with no control over events overtaking him or her. The hopelessness may be colored by feelings of blame and of failure. Rumination sets in; that is, the person continually has negative thoughts about self and his or her predicament.

2. *Deficient coping and adolescent suicide.* While intentionally ending one's own life is a commonly accepted, general definition of suicide, the coping literature focuses on suicide as failed or maladaptive coping in the face of crushing stress. Research discloses that completed and attempted suicides during adolescence are often triggered by some undesired life situation for which the youth feels hopeless to resolve; this hopelessness manifests in such deficient coping as restricted problem-solving, an overreliance on avoidant coping, and difficulty regulating emotions.

    • Restricted problem-solving is seen in the adolescent's lack of confidence in dealing with the situation. Suicidal youth commonly have internalized parental expectations that the youth find impossible to meet. The adolescent's restricted problem-solving emerges in the youth's unyielding concentration on why no solution will help. This rigidity in problem-solving manifests itself as well in inflexible responses to interpersonal relationships. You may recall that one of the adaptive tasks for coping with a life crisis is to maintain interpersonal relationships. Inflexibility in interpersonal matters leaves persons isolated, thereby restricting their problem-solving skills even more.

    • Overreliance on avoidant coping is found in persons who attempt or complete suicide.[5] The operative word here is "overreliance." There are times when it is healthy for a person to back off from confronting distress; however, data indicate the suicidal tend to rely on withdrawing from others, steering clear of confronting difficulties, and engaging in fantasies (that is, wishful thinking). This avoidant style goes hand-in-glove with beliefs that problem resolution is beyond one's control.

    • Difficulty regulating emotions refers to the troubles some persons face when they experience keen levels of emotion (for instance, anger, fear, sadness, confusion, or anxiety). The emotions may incapacitate the person; the emotions may elicit impulsive behavior. Suicidal adolescents often have difficulty exerting control when keen emotions, particularly sadness and anger, engulf them. There is a reasonable hypothesis that suicide presents itself as "a strategy for dealing with negative emotion … a means of escape from emotional pain" (Wagner & Zimmerman, 2006, p. 299). This hypothesis is focused on the referred suicide category.

3. *Cyberbullying.* Cyberbullying is a pervasive matter of concern. Some adolescents use social media to harass peers, sometimes to the extent that a distraught youth completes suicide. Suicides stemming from cyberbullying have led to a new term, *cyberbullicide.* Noted cases include the completed suicides of Jamey Rodemeyer, who hanged himself after over a year of online harassment, Tyler Clementi, the Rutgers University student who jumped to his death after online assaults regarding his sexual relations with another male, and Phoebe Prince, a new student from Ireland

who took her own life after nine peers nicknamed "the mean girls" hounded her relentlessly both physically and online.

Cyberbullicide discloses a malevolent power available via social media. One colleague, Anne M. Smith, a co-author with Corinne Cavuoti of Chapter Eleven, mentioned in conversation how vulnerable adolescents are when posting information about something that happened—for instance, an illness in the family—or about how one feels: bullies use that open disclosure as ammunition to target the teen. And the harassment that ensues can be so unendurable that the only recourse looks to be suicide. My anger and disgust with bullies runs so deep that I have had to restrain myself from pontificating in this part of the chapter. I'll simply say it appalls me to find out not only how socially vicious are some preteens and adolescents but also to marvel that they feel no remorse over deaths they cause through cyberbullying. When they talk of being sorry when put on trial, they are just sorry they got caught and are being punished.

4.   *Race and gender.* There are some racial and gender aspects associated with suicide in the United States: males are four times more likely than females to take their own lives, whereas females are three times more likely than males to make suicide attempts. Suicide is predominately a male problem, and in particular a White male problem. White males in the United States are twice as likely as Black males to take their own lives, four times as likely as White females, and more than 11 times as likely as Black females. The disparities between male completed suicides and female attempted suicides are attributed to the lethality of the means chosen: males are more likely than females to use firearms or hanging, whereas females are more likely than males to use drug overdoses. Note, however, that epidemiological data gathered for the past several decades indicate that since 1960 the rates of suicide for females and members of ethnic and racial minority groups in the United States "have risen more sharply than those of white males" (Peck, 2003, p. 324).

Myths about Suicide.   Nonsuicidal adults and adolescents view the motives for suicide quite differently than do adolescents who are considering killing themselves. While suicidal youth frequently see suicide as a means to escape an intolerable situation, others typically consider suicidal acts come from weak individuals acting out of self-pity, perhaps as clumsy efforts to get attention and manipulate others. These perceptions about suicide from nonsuicidal individuals have led to various myths, among them:

1st myth. People who talk about suicide don't carry out the act. In fact, data indicate about 75% of suicides were forecast in some way by the person who took his or her own life.

2nd myth. Suicidal individuals want to end their lives. In fact, data indicate most persons are ambivalent about ending their lives, and a growing belief in the counseling field is that many suicide attempts are gestures for help.

3rd myth. Sudden improvement in a suicidal individual's emotional state signals the risk has passed. In fact, data indicate severely depressed, suicidal individuals are likely at greatest risk when their moods unexpectedly improve; improvement can actually signal that the person feels better because of having made a plan to end his or her troubles.

4th myth. People who commit suicide leave a note. In fact, some persons do, but others don't. Failure to leave a note does not rule out that the person intentionally ended his or her life.

Developmental Sequences as Keys for Examining Suicidal Acts. Seven developmental sequences or narrative plot lines have been identified in constructing coherent life stories of persons. The seven basic developmental sequences that have been identified include:

- A stable plot line in which the person's story shows no change over time. This plot line can incorporate either a basically negative or positive life story. There is no significant change in either direction up to and including the person's act of suicide.
- A progressive plot line in which the person's story shows slow, positive changes over time.
- A regressive plot line in which the person's story shows an intensification of negative changes.
- A tragic plot line in which the person's story initially is characterized by positive developments followed by drastic, negative changes.
- A tragic-comic plot line in which the person's story begins with negative developments followed by dramatic positive changes.
- A happy-ever-after plot line in which the person's story is one continuing sequence of positive occurrences.
- A romantic plot line in which the person's story oscillates continually between positive and negative developments.

Investigators into completed suicides have used developmental sequences or narrative plot lines to gain insight into the last weeks in the lives of persons who took their lives. Researchers used a procedure called a psychological autopsy to reconstruct the psychological makeup of persons who took their lives.[6] The researchers then examined the data in light of the basic developmental sequences listed earlier to analyze the motives and circumstances of 67 late adolescent Israeli soldiers who committed suicide, in nearly all cases by self-inflicted gunshot wounds. We will look at four narrative plot lines that comprised all of the 67 suicides examined.

1. *The regressive plot line.* The story of a soldier we will name Samuel illustrates the regressive plot line, which was found in 47% of the 67 cases studied. A main feature of this plot line is an accumulation of negative life events and steady, gradual deterioration in self-esteem, coping, and overall functioning. Samuel's military service began with superior performance. He won distinction in his unit. He requested and was granted a transfer to a combat unit, where he ran into several difficulties, including poor relations with his peers. His superiors described him as aloof, confused, and depressed. Samuel was granted a transfer to another unit where the same problems emerged again for him. He was transferred without requesting such a change to a clerical unit. He became a disciplinary problem, and was punished for his behavior. Peers reported he openly talked of feeling inferior and of disliking his new unit. Samuel asked to be transferred to his original unit where he had performed successfully. However, his violations of rules continued, leading eventually to his being placed under military arrest. Around this time Samuel learned he had little chance to return to his original unit. He took his own life a short while later.
2. *The stable plot line.* The story of a soldier we will name Adam illustrates the stable plot line, which was found in 21% of the 67 cases studied. Fellow soldiers in the

Israeli Defense Forces described Adam as quiet and friendly but without a wide social network. His superiors said his work met expectations. Nothing unusual or unexpected occurred in Adam's military service except for a failed effort to start a relationship with a female soldier. Adam took his life about midway through his military service, but he had given no indications of distress prior to his act and he did not leave a note.

3. *The tragic plot line.* The story of a solider we will name Miriam illustrates the tragic plot line, which was found in 21% of the 67 cases studied. Miriam's trajectory shows initial experiences of satisfaction and well-being as an Israeli soldier. Her expectations were high, and her performance led to fulfillment of her expectations. Following her superior achievements in basic training, Miriam was picked for officer training. She did well there. Acquaintances noted she was socially active, liked by subordinates and peers, and seemed destined for continued success. Then she was given an assignment to train recruits she had difficulty disciplining; her problems with this assignment led to severe depression. Shortly into the new assignment, she took her life.

4. *The romantic plot line.* The story of a soldier we will name Benjamin illustrates the romantic plot line, which was found in 11% of the cases studied. This plot line exhibits wide fluctuations, a roller coaster of emotions, and extreme ups and downs in behavior and thoughts. Benjamin entered military service with considerable dread, and his performance record during basic training noted he overcame his evident anxiety and distress and completed basic training satisfactorily. Things started looking up for him when he was assigned to paramedical training; he excelled as a paramedic and was promoted to being an instructor. He did well as an instructor, was appreciated by fellow soldiers, and expressed both confidence and competence. However, when his girlfriend broke up with him, he became depressed, temporarily performed poorly, then righted himself. He entered into a relationship with a new girlfriend, but they broke up after a short time. His depression returned, along with negative self-evaluations, and then he took his life.

5. *Analysis of the 67 cases.* Nearly 80% of the soldiers expressed some intent to kill themselves, in some cases directly (for example, "I'll shoot myself in the head") and in other cases indirectly (for example, "There's no reason to fear death"). However, when asked about their intentions, all denied they were thinking of suicide.

Depression was found in 43% of the soldiers who took their lives. Note that in nearly 20% of the cases, evidence indicated the predominant mood was positive, not one of agitation, anxiety, or depression. Such a sudden shift to a positive mood has been found in other suicides: the person has identified a way out of his or her troubles.

The triggering event could be identified in most but not all cases. Typically, the triggering event was an external stressor, such as being transferred to an undesired unit; interpersonal conflict, such as breaking up with a girlfriend; or failure, such as doing poorly in some aspect of military duties. The plurality of triggering events came from external stressors. Of considerable interest is that no triggering event could be identified in nearly one third of the cases. Also of considerable interest is that in almost every case, the soldiers who took their lives had no trust that professionals could help them.

The Completed Suicide of One Adolescent

Mary Beth was a high school junior. She played in the school's marching band and was a pretty good student. She was also the target of various forms of bullying that ranged from graffiti spray painted on her locker to physical assaults from other students, including members of the band. Once these band members had surrounded Mary Beth on the practice field and beat her up. The students singled her out for these assaults because they were offended at Mary Beth's sexual orientation. More than once her locker got spray painted with various slurs such as "Dyke" and "Lesbo."

Mary Beth's parents were deeply upset that their daughter was attracted to other women. Confirmed Christians with deeply fundamentalist views, her parents had taken Mary Beth to their pastor for counseling; they wanted to get her straightened out, and they were concerned she would go to hell if she did not give up homosexuality.

In his conversation with her, the pastor focused on the depravity of homosexuality and emphasized how it was a sin that offended God. The pastor said that Scripture expressly forbids homosexual relations, and insured Mary Beth that homosexuals were destined to suffer hell fire for eternity. Choosing homosexuality put her immortal soul in deadly peril, he told her, and she must renounce any homosexual feelings and actions.

Mary Beth was not swayed by the pastor. She had already told her Mom and Dad and attempted to tell the pastor that she had known since she was about 11 that she did not feel attracted to boys the ways other girls her age did. On the contrary, she found she was attracted to girls. It wasn't something she had chosen, but was something that defined very much who and what she was. She said to the pastor, "With all the trouble and problems my being attracted to girls causes me, don't you think I'd choose differently if I could?"

When Mary Beth's parents heard the pastor's report that the girl was "hard-hearted and unrepentant," they physically beat her, called her vile names, and told her she was confined to her room for the coming month. She could only go to school when she left the house, and then had to come immediately home. Each evening she would be questioned whether she had changed her mind about how she felt toward girls, and each night when she said she had not, her father beat her with a belt. This state of affairs went on for 4 days. On the fifth day, Mary Beth's mother found the girl in a coma in bed; she had taken an overdose of sleeping pills.

The mother phoned 911, and the emergency medical technicians arrived in time to revive Mary Beth and rush her to the emergency room of the local hospital. Once discharged from the emergency room, she was admitted to the inpatient psychiatric unit where she stayed for 2 weeks.

Upon being discharged from the psychiatric unit, Mary Beth returned home where she found a frightened, fragile mother and an angry father. The bullies at school taunted her for "not being smart enough even to know how to 'off yourself'" as one girl put it. The abuse at school intensified. When told of the bullying by one of Mary Beth's friends, school officials said the security guards would remain vigilant to prevent problems; that very day a group of students surrounded Mary Beth again and beat her up.

When she got home after having been beaten up once again, she told her parents she couldn't take it anymore. She wanted them to get her out of the school so she would no longer be hurt. She'd earn a GED, she said.

Her father asked whether she still was a "damned lesbian." If she would just become normal, the kids would leave her alone, he told her. She said her feelings had not changed. Enraged, her father told her to get out of the house. Appeals to her mother did not help.

Before leaving the house Mary Beth took her father's pistol and some bullets from her parents' bedroom closet. Her body was found the next morning on a hill overlooking the city. She had shot herself in the head.

Concluding Comments

The story line in this chapter is about sudden, preventable violence that takes the lives of adolescents. All the violent acts occur because of human behavior. It is a sobering fact that the age group most vulnerable to die used to be youth 14 years of age and younger; the principal cause of death was infectious disease. Now because of advances in medical care and public health, death is an unlikely occurrence to youth. But when it does occur, death will almost assuredly come from violence due to human neglect or human intent.

Deaths due to motor vehicle accidents take more adolescent lives around the planet than any other cause. Another sobering fact to consider is that nearly the same proportion of adolescent deaths in this country occurs because of homicides, primarily perpetrated by persons with firearms. The number of firearm-related homicides in Chicago and in Detroit is staggering. The great majority of these homicides are linked to gang activity, though the person who is killed may not be a gang member but rather an innocent in the wrong place at the wrong time.

Suicidal acts have increased exponentially since 1950, and in many countries suicide vies with unintentional injuries as the principal cause of adolescent mortality. The overwhelming proportion of adolescent suicides (attempted and completed) are placed in the referred suicide category. These suicidal acts are seen to be influenced by transitory emotions and impulsive acts, often associated with reduced inhibitions brought on by alcohol or drugs. Narrative plot lines offer a means to construct plausible scenarios to understand the suicide of an adolescent; the large plurality of these plot lines involve an accumulation of negative life events and steady, gradual deterioration in self-esteem, coping, and overall functioning. The vignette presenting Mary Beth's suicide shows this regressive plot line.

Notes

1. www.who.int/whr/1998/media_centre/50facts/en/
2. Often mortality statistics are calculated per every 100,000 persons in the age group. For instance, for every 100,000 persons 15 to 24 years of age in the United States between the years

1999–2001, 37 died due to accidents, 13 were murdered, and 10 committed suicide (see Arias, Anderson, Hsiang-Ching, Murphy, & Kochanek, September 18, 2003).
3. It is unclear what the source is, and how trustworthy this claim is about suicide's impact on six persons.
4. Not all suicidal persons acting out what are considered "referred suicides" manifest depressive symptoms, a research and clinical finding that some persons may find counterintuitive.
5. Note that the research refers to persons who were emotionally distressed (a "referred suicide"), not to persons whose act of suicide can be categorized as surcease or cultural.
6. Conducting a psychological autopsy uses interviews with acquaintances of the person who died and analysis of documents and other records such as diaries, letters, and performance evaluations from supervisors.

Sources

Arias, W., Anderson, R. N., Hsiang-Ching, K., Murphy, S. L., & Kochanek, M. A. (September 18, 2003). Deaths: Final data for 2001. *National Vital Statistics Reports, 52*(3).

Balk, D. E. (1995). *Adolescent development: Early through late adolescence.* Pacific Grove, CA: Brooks/Cole.

Bryant, C. D. & Peck, D. L. (Editors). (2009). *Encyclopedia of death and the human experience.* Los Angeles: Sage.

Conger, J. J. (1990). *Adolescence and youth: Psychological development in a changing world.* New York: HarperCollins.

Corr, C. A. & Corr, D. M. (2013). *Death & dying, life & living* (7th ed.). Belmont, CA: Wadsworth, Cenage Learning.

Curran, D. K. (1987). *Adolescent suicidal behavior.* Washington, DC: Hemisphere.

Fingerhut, L. A., Cox, C. S., & Warner, M. (1998). *International comparative analysis of injury mortality.* Center for Disease Control and Prevention, National Center for Health Statistics.

Ho, J. (2012). Bullied to death: Cyberbullying and student online speech rights. *Florida Law Review, 64,* 789.

Kastenbaum, R. J. (2001). *Death, society, and human experience* (7th ed.). Boston: Allyn & Bacon.

King, K. A. & Vidourke, R. A. (2012). Teen depression and suicide: Effective prevention and intervention strategies. *The Prevention Researcher, 19*(4), 15–17.

Luxton, D. L., June, J. D., & Fairall, J. M. (2012). Social media and suicide: A public health perspective. *American Journal of Public Health, 102*(S2), S195–S200.

National Center for Injury Prevention and Control. (2003). *Fatal injuries: Leading causes of death reports.* Washington, DC: Centers for Disease Control and Prevention.

Norman, J. O. & Connolly, J. (2011). Mimetic theory and scapegoating in the age of cyberbullying: The case of Phoebe Prince. *Pastoral Care in Education: An International Journal of Personal, Social and Emotional Development, 29*(4), 287–300.

Orbach, I., Gilboa-Schechtman, E., Ofek, H., Lubin, G., Mark, M., Bodner, E., Cohen. D., & King, R. (2007). A chronological perspective on suicide—the last days of life. *Death Studies, 31,* 909–932.

Pirkis, J. Blood, R. W., Beautrais, A. Burgess, P., & Skehan, J. (2006). Media guidelines on the reporting of suicide. *Crisis, 27,* 82–87.

Range, L. M. (2009). Suicide and adolescents. In D. E. Balk, & C. A. Corr (Editors), *Adolescent encounters with death, bereavement, and coping* (pp. 81–97). New York: Springer.

Sobol, R. R. (October 29, 2012). "Authorities: Boy, 14, charged with Far South Side murder." *Chicago Tribune.* Retrieved January 27, 2013, from http://articles.chicagotribune.com/2012–10–29/news/

Sobol, R. R. (October 30, 2012). "2nd teen charged in murder of teen outside South Side high school." *Chicago Tribune*. Retrieved January 27, 2013, from http://articles.chicagotribune.com/2012–10–30/news/

Wagner, B. M. & Zimmerman, J. H. (2006). Developmental influences on suicidality among adolescents : Cognitive, emotional, and neuroscience aspects. In T. E. Ellis (Ed.), *Cognition and suicide: Theory, research, and therapy* (pp. 287–308). Washington, DC: American Psychological Association.

World Health Organization. (1998). *50 facts: Global health situation and trends 1955–2025*. Retrieved July 3, 2013, from www.who.int/whr/1998/media_centre/50facts/en/

6 Chronic, Life-Threatening Disease and Terminal Illness during Adolescence

Mortality statistics establish clearly that adolescents' deaths due to illness are uncommon. The rarity of such problems is irrelevant to an adolescent and his or her family when a life-threatening disease invades the adolescent's body. What matters is dealing with this crisis and finding experts who know what to do and who do it well.

As stated in Chapter Five, youth practices add to the increasing exposure of children and adolescents to mortality. The World Health Organization (WHO) expressed grave concern for several threats to health that place older children and adolescents around the world at risk for severe injury and death due to rites of passage involving violence, unprotected sex, delinquent behavior, vehicular accidents, and substance abuse. Socioeconomic conditions, particularly those conditions impoverished urban youth face, play a significant influence in marking who is most at risk for these dangers from deadly rites of passage.

Issues an Ill Adolescent Faces

In this chapter we look at life-threatening diseases that affect some adolescents: diabetes, HIV/AIDS, human papillomavirus (HPV), and three forms of cancer. We begin with a look at diabetes and adolescence.

Diabetes during Adolescence

The term *diabetes mellitus* denotes a chronic disease for which no cure has yet been devised. Diabetes mellitus has two forms: (a) insulin-dependent diabetes mellitus, usually referred to as Type 1 diabetes and sometimes as juvenile-onset diabetes; (b) non-insulin-dependent diabetes mellitus, sometimes termed adult-onset diabetes or Type 2 diabetes. Type 1 diabetes emerges usually during childhood or adolescence, hence the term *juvenile-onset diabetes,* and Type 2 does not usually emerge before middle adulthood. However, Type 2 diabetes has been seen increasingly in children between the ages of 10 and 14 in the United States; these children are typically obese and come from a family with a history of diabetes. Overall life expectancy in the United States, despite its legion of health care practices, is in danger of being shortened due to the epidemic of obesity in childhood and adolescence. There is growing talk that obesity will increase numerous risks for mortality in the US population. Obesity has been identified to make children vulnerable to developing childhood cancers as well as diabetes. In this section we will focus on Type 1 diabetes.

Type 1 diabetes results from the autoimmune system's progressive destruction of beta cells in the pancreas, with the subsequent result that the body cannot produce insulin. Insulin, a hormone that enables muscle and adipose tissue[1] to use glucose in the blood, also enables the body to activate glucose stored in the liver. Without insulin, the body develops high glucose levels in the blood (called hyperglycemia), a condition with symptoms of thirst, weight loss, extreme urination, and fatigue. Lacking insulin, the body responds by breaking down adipose tissue, which leads to weight loss; if unchecked, hyperglycemia leads to a worse condition called ketoacidosis,[2] and the person eventually falls into a coma and may die.

Deaths due to diabetes among 15- to 24-year-olds are relatively rare. As examples, diabetes accounts for approximately one half of 1 percent of all deaths among middle and late adolescents in such countries as Australia, Brazil, France, Japan, Mexico, Russia, and the United States. Yet Type 1 diabetes is one of the most prevalent chronic conditions that adolescents face worldwide: only asthma and cerebral palsy are more common chronic conditions affecting youth. Recent evidence indicates an increasing incidence of Type 1 diabetes in the urban areas of developed countries; for instance, from 1980 through 1999 the number of new cases doubled in the United Kingdom, going from 7 to 13.5 per 100,000. Why there should be any discussion of diabetes among adolescents in a book examining issues of death, dying, and bereavement is that (a) the number of deaths to this chronic condition increase as people age and (b) risk of dying is influenced by how diabetic adolescents view their condition and the proper way to manage it.

Diabetes produces both acute and chronic complications. Acute complications are time-limited and present moments of grave concern for the well-being of the diabetic adolescent. Chronic complications are effects with longer lasting results that take time to develop.

Acute Complications of Type 1 Diabetes

The two types of acute complications of Type 1 diabetes are low levels of blood glucose (hypoglycemia) and ketoacidosis. Low levels of blood glucose make persons sweat and tremble and can progress, if not checked, to coordination difficulties and cognitive confusion and, eventually, to loss of consciousness and death. Ketoacidosis emerges when hyperglycemia (high levels of blood glucose) goes unchecked, and it typically is noted when the diabetic youth is first diagnosed to have Type 1 diabetes; medical responses to ketoacidosis include hospitalizing the person "to correct fluid loss, institute insulin therapy, and prevent complications" (Hampson et al., 2001, p. 2). The onset of ketoacidosis is attributed to three common causes: an acute illness, excessive alcohol consumption (seen particularly in Type 1 diabetic adolescent males), and improper insulin administration.

Chronic Complications of Type 1 Diabetes

Chronic complications of Type 1 diabetes group into three categories: (a) microvascular complications, (b) neuropathic complications, and (c) macrovascular complications. Microvascular complications typically are noted in impaired vision (retinopathy) and in kidney dysfunction (nephropathy). The prognosis for retinopathy is grim, and although prevalence rates vary, "long-term follow-up studies show that retinopathy is virtually inevitable in conventionally managed Type 1 diabetes" (Hampson et al., 2001, p. 2). Blindness eventually results for up to 9% of persons affected by Type 1 diabetes.

Kidney problems are a major contributor to death in Type 1 diabetes. Up to half of all persons diagnosed with Type 1 diabetes after 40 years or so develop diabetic nephropathy, a condition that can lead to kidney failure, a situation 17 times more common among persons with Type 1 diabetes than among persons without the disease. Kidney failure, commonly called renal failure, is estimated to cause 15% of all deaths to persons under 50 years of age with Type 1 diabetes.

Neuropathy refers to motor nerve dysfunction, is considered common in nearly three-fourths of persons as soon as they develop Type 1 diabetes, and primarily affects loss of sensation, particularly in the feet. Additionally, autonomic nerve dysfunction can occur; for instance, erectile dysfunction is found in around 6% of 20- to 24-year-old males with Type 1 diabetes and as high as 75% of Type 1 diabetic male adults in their late fifties; rates of erectile dysfunction in same-aged persons without Type 1 diabetes range from 0% to 18%.

Macrovascular complications involve circulatory system problems that lead to increased risks of heart disease, stroke, and deterioration of intellectual functions. It is estimated that Type 1 diabetics run a two- to five-fold greater risk of coronary heart disease that do their unaffected same-age peers.

Implications of Diabetes for Adolescents

The rapid physical, cognitive, and interpersonal changes during adolescence make this period of life especially crucial for persons with diabetes. Of concern for medical researchers and health care providers is the fact that during adolescence individuals develop inadequate habits about taking care of themselves and managing their diabetes. Beliefs about diabetes and its care and management, which are integrated during the adolescent years, have an ongoing impact on well-being into the adult years. For example, physiological changes that mark puberty make it increasingly difficult to keep glucose levels under control and require these levels be monitored more carefully than in childhood. Such changes create more intrusive demands in an adolescent's life, and youth may fear maintaining safe insulin regimens will interfere with making and keeping friends and prevent the adolescent from having fun. In short, adolescents with Type 1 diabetes may place themselves in harm's way in order to be accepted by their unaffected peers. An example would be the diabetic early adolescent girl who eats junk food with her friends in order not to appear abnormal and who in the process triggers high levels of glucose that lead to ketoacidosis.

In summary, the physiological changes during adolescence place persons with Type 1 diabetes at greater risk of damage than experienced by children without Type 1 diabetes. These dangers can have long-term effects because they speed up the development of microvascular, neuropathic, and macrovascular complications, shorten the individual's lifespan, and create acute situations in which the individual is in danger of dying.

HIV/AIDS and Adolescents

Medical researchers have expressed concern at the growth of HIV infection among adolescents and young adults in both the developed and developing world. Researchers have noted with alarm the spread of HIV infection among youth in Latin America, Africa,

Asia, and the United States. Changing demographic conditions, government inaction, and deepening economic crises have made for high HIV infection rates among adolescents in Mexico, Ecuador, and Brazil; HIV infection was found in nearly 40% of 15- to 19-year-old females in urban areas of four African countries: Benin, Cameroon, Kenya, and Zambia; at least 10% of the estimated 300,000 HIV infected individuals in China were teenagers, who contracted the virus primarily through contaminated drug syringes; researchers within the Philippines reported the growing worldwide economic crisis of the late 1990s led to an increase in HIV infections among Asian adolescents as more and more young females resorted to prostitution to support their families; finally, a quarter of all new cases of HIV infections in the United States occur in the 13- to 21-year-old age group.

According to the World Health Organization (WHO), "15 to 24 year olds accounted for an estimated 40% of all new HIV infections among adults worldwide in 2009. Every day, 2400 more young people get infected and globally there are more than 5 million young people living with HIV/AIDS" (www.who.int/mediacentre/factsheets/fs345/en/index.html retrieved December 12, 2012). The WHO noted that if unchecked the ongoing spread of HIV/AIDS in children and adolescents could undo the significant gains made in child health in the latter half of the 20th century.

Human Papillomavirus (HPV) and Adolescents

Human papillomavirus (HPV) is the most prevalent form of sexually transmitted infection in the United States. The World Health Organization estimates that about 630 million persons across the globe have contracted the virus. Consequences of HPV infection include skin warts, genital warts, cervical cancer, and cancer of the throat, anus, penis, vulva, and vagina.

Over 100 types of HPV have been identified, and about one-third infect genital mucosa. Epidemiological data indicate about 67% of persons who have sexual contact with someone infected with HPV will themselves show signs of HPV infection within 3 months. The great majority of these infections dissipate; however, a minority of women who become infected with HPV develop cervical cancer within 10 years of HPV infection. Cervical cancer is the most common form of cancer to be linked to HPV infection and is considered the second leading cause of women's death from cancer worldwide. According to the American Cancer Society, annually over 11,000 women in the United States are diagnosed with cervical cancer. The mortality rate is 35%.

The link between HPV infection and the onset of cervical cancer has been solidly established. HPV DNA has been found in nearly 100% of cases of cervical cancer. Four types of HPV (named #16, 18, 31, and 45) are particularly active in the development of cervical cancer. HPV types 16 and 18 account for nearly 70% of cervical cancers[3] identified worldwide; however, more than infection with one of these four types of HPV is deemed necessary for cervical cancer to develop. Risky, carcinogenic behaviors such as smoking and exposure to stressors that lead to a compromised immune system also have been identified in HPV-infected women who develop cervical cancer. Increasingly, clinical researchers are uncovering evidence that disorders in the immune system play a key role in the link between HPV infection and cervical cancer. Such disorders can originate from such stressors as strep throat, the common cold, and severe anxiety. It is well-documented that one of the consequences of bereavement is a compromised immune system, particularly in the first few months following a death.

Studies of new cases of HPV-infected women have uncovered that infection typically occurs soon after the females become sexually active, and an overwhelming percentage of new cases involve middle and later adolescents, both males and females. Public health researchers estimate that currently (a) over 20 million persons in the United States are infected with HPV, (b) over 6 million new cases occur each year, and (c) over 80% of sexually active women will contract HPV by the age of 50.

HPV vaccines have been developed, and they have proven effective in the prevention of HPV infection and in the prevention of cervical cancer. The data for these efficacy studies came from research with middle adolescent to young adult women. There is no evidence that the vaccines are effective if the person was infected with HPV prior to being vaccinated. Further, how long the vaccine protects someone has not been determined, although none of the vaccinated women followed for over 5 years after receiving the vaccine showed any symptoms of HPV infection.

As of 2013, many states have adopted public health policies urging that early adolescent females receive the HPV vaccine. Some of the states mention males as well should receive the vaccine. These states include Hawaii, Iowa, Kentucky, New York, Ohio, and South Carolina. Efforts in Texas to require HPV vaccination of early adolescent females led to a fierce debate; among issues expressed have been concerns over serious side effects yet to be uncovered (as in the case of thalidomide) and accusations over unwarranted and dangerous government intrusion into people's lives.

Cancers and Adolescents

The types of cancer are legion in numbers. Some cancers are more common in different portions of the human life span. For instance, cervical, breast, and colorectal cancer are more prominent in persons ages 25 to 39. Statistics kept on middle and later adolescents indicate that the cancers most common to that age group are acute lymphoblastic leukemia (ALL, pronounced with each letter identified, not as the word "all"), malignant melanoma, thyroid cancer, non-Hodgkin's lymphoma, central nervous system (CNS) tumors, germ cell tumors, and Hodgkin's lymphoma. Aging seems to be one of the greatest risk factors associated with contracting cancer. The elderly are much more likely than other persons to develop cancers in the rectum, lungs, bladder, stomach, colon, pancreas, and prostate. We will look at three of the cancers found in adolescence: Hodgkin's lymphoma, malignant melanoma, and ALL.

Hodgkin's Lymphoma

While quite rare in younger ages, Hodgkin's lymphoma is the most common form of cancer found in middle and later adolescents; it appears in 12% of all cancers reported in the adolescent years. This form of cancer appears more frequently in 15- to 19-year-old female than male adolescents; however, over the full human life span, more males contract Hodgkin's lymphoma than do females. White, non-Hispanic youth have a greater incidence of Hodgkin's lymphoma than do other groups.

It is a cancer that originates in white blood cells, called lymphocytes, attacks lymph nodes, and spreads from one lymph node group to others. One of the suspected risk factors in the development of Hodgkin's lymphoma is an earlier case of mononucleosis. By the year 2004 epidemiology data indicated that Hodgkin's lymphoma, like other cancers of childhood and adolescence, was increasing, and it was found in nearly 23 of every 1 million adolescents.

Signs of Hodgkin's lymphoma are many and, as in the case of several diseases, mimic other illnesses. The symptoms include irritated, itchy skin, night sweats, fever, back pain, weight loss, shortness of breath, and exhaustion. The most common symptom of Hodgkin's lymphoma involves swollen lymph nodes, particularly in the neck, shoulders, and chest.

When detected early, Hodgkin's lymphoma responds well to radiation therapy and to chemotherapy. The survival rate for adolescents with Hodgkin's lymphoma has reached 90%. As in all cases of survival from cancer, there are concerns over long-term negative effects from therapy. These concerns are addressed later in this chapter.

Malignant Melanoma

Malignant melanoma, cancer of the skin, is increasing more rapidly across the planet than any other cancer. It comprises 11% of the various cancers that affect 10- to 19-year-olds. Excessive exposure to the sun is a leading cause of malignant melanoma and, while lighter skinned individuals are at greater risk of contracting this disease, darker skinned persons are not necessarily immune. There is also the puzzle that melanoma occurs in some persons' skin areas seldom exposed to sunlight, suggesting that risk for some persons involves factors other than exposure to excessive sunlight.

It is conjectured that artificial tanning (sometimes called the bikini effect) is producing increased numbers of cases with melanoma. Females are at greater risk of contracting malignant melanoma than are males; however, that statement does not mean males cannot contract this cancer. In fact, males with melanoma on their head or neck have a poor survival rate as compared to females with melanoma confined to the torso.

Deaths from malignant melanoma have steadily decreased since the last quarter of the 20th century. It is considered a curable disease when detected in time. Treatment involves such methods as surgical removal of normal tissue surrounding affected skin, removal of lymph glands, and efforts to stimulate immune system responsiveness. Protecting the skin from sun radiation by applying sunscreen is a preventive technique.

Acute Lymphoblastic Leukemia

This cancer affects two different age groups the most: children between the ages of 2 and 6 and adults over 40. ALL comprises 6% of cancers affecting adolescents, and except for infants below the age of 1, adolescents and young adults have the lowest rate of ALL among the different age cohorts in the United States. It occurs more frequently among males than females, regardless of age, and more often among Caucasians (particularly European Americans) than other ethnic groups.

As indicated by the term "leukemia," ALL is a cancer of the white blood cells. The term "lymphoblastic" refers to immature blood cells that originate in bone marrow; following normal development, lymphoblasts become mature white blood cells (called lymphocytes) that act as a key part of the body's immune system; the serious problem denoted by the phrase "acute lymphoblastic lymphoma" is that the lymphoblasts multiply out of control, do not become mature cells, and migrate in large numbers to the blood. If unchecked, this explosion of lymphoblasts proves fatal. Symptoms that may indicate the presence of ALL include enlarged lymph nodes, fatigue, anemia, unusual bruising, pain in the joints or in the bones, and marked weight loss. Obviously, a definitive diagnosis of ALL involves analysis of lymphoblasts in the person's blood.

Various approaches to treatment are available in the battle against ALL. The data indicate that success in treatment increases greatly the earlier that ALL is diagnosed. The major forms of treatment include chemotherapy regimens, radiation therapy, bone marrow transplants, and steroid injections. Chemotherapy is the preferred treatment in the initial efforts to combat the cancer. The typical case involves multimodal treatment, not just one of the treatment forms mentioned earlier.

Survival following the diagnosis of ALL improved dramatically in the last quarter of the 20th century and first decades of the 21st century. In the 1960s few persons survived ALL, and today survival has reached 60% to 75%, particularly for younger patients, persons in whom the cancer has not metastasized to the central nervous system, and persons whose response to the initial treatment was positive. Let's look at a brief case study of an adolescent boy who contracted ALL. All the children with leukemia in Bluebond-Langner's classic study died; given the advances in medical research and treatment since that study, it is almost a certainty that none of the children would die today.

Dying at a Young Age

James Samuelson was almost 11 when he became very ill, more ill than his parents, his sister, or James realized. His prolonged descent into death began innocently enough as a high temperature and overall "achy" feelings; James thought it resembled the time he had a really bad case of the flu. All of these complications started in early 1980.

When his temperature rose to 102, his mother rushed James to an emergency room where the staff stabilized his condition and contacted Dr. Hunt, the Samuelson's family physician, who ordered blood work be done. Upon reviewing the blood analysis, Dr. Hunt took a deep breath, picked up his phone, and called the Samuelsons with the news that James had leukemia.

Mr. and Mrs. Samuelson were stunned. They asked what Dr. Hunt could do for James. Dr. Hunt said the best course was to get James admitted to the cancer treatment program for children at the University Hospital across town. Trembling and unsure what to say or do, Mrs. Samuelson agreed to let Dr. Hunt phone the children's cancer program to see if they would admit her son and treat him. It seemed clear that if James did not get into the program, it would not be possible to save his life. The admitting nurse asked Dr. Hunt several questions about James's condition, and finally said it sounded as though he were a good candidate for their program and asked would his parents bring James in the next day for an initial screening.

In the waiting room at the cancer program, Mrs. Samuelson sat with other parents while a team of physicians examined her son. She realized the other parents were "veterans," that is, they were used to the procedures and talked fairly easily with one another about their children's conditions. She, however, couldn't even bring herself to say the word "leukemia."

James was admitted to the program and given an aggressive course of chemotherapy. The drugs made him very sick and he lost all of his hair. But his leukemia went into remission, and James returned home. Because he was now completely bald, he usually wore a wig unless the people around him were persons he trusted. He regained all of his energy, returned to school, teased his sister, and was pretty much his old self, except for feeling isolated from many his age and at times feeling angry with students who made fun of his illness. The remission lasted 2 years.

James's relapse occurred one weekend when he and his father were getting ready to go fishing. He began to feel weak, and his temperature shot up. The cancer program's staff had told Mr. and Mrs. Samuelson the signs that would indicate James's cancer had returned, so they immediately phoned the program and were told to bring James in at once. An examination confirmed their fears: the leukemia was back.

For the next 2 years James went in and out of remission as he was given new drugs to combat his disease. The emotional and physical ordeal on everyone was dreadful as James's health vacillated; fortunately, medical insurance enabled the Samuelsons to avoid financial ruin. Everyone in the family knew that James would eventually die from this illness, and they did not hide their knowledge from one another. They also did not talk about his condition incessantly.

Finally, one cold, wet Spring morning James became very ill. He was now 15 years old. This time there was nothing the specialists could do for him. He died surrounded by medical personnel at the cancer clinic. His family was in the room with James, and his mother noted he fought to remain alive until the end. When he finally succumbed, she murmured, "Good," because now his suffering was over.

Demands on Coping with a Life-Threatening Illness

What demands on coping does an adolescent with a life-threatening illness face? Beliefs about the multidimensionality of the human person apply to any effort to understand adolescent responses when coping with a life-threatening illness. In short, the illness will require responses to physical issues, interpersonal issues, cognitive issues, emotional issues, behavioral issues, and spiritual issues.

Responding to Physical Issues

The adolescent will be faced with changes in energy, very likely with changes in appearance (for instance, notable weight reductions and hair loss, perhaps amputations), with invasive treatments, pain, nausea, and constipation, and with the ultimate possibility of dying. For instance, to quote one adolescent with cancer (Rich, 2002, p. 571), "When I was first diagnosed, I thought I was going to die. There was no way I could be cured." The various changes to body image that adolescents with cancer face come at a point in the life span when appearance matters very much. Outsiders may not realize how upsetting these changes in appearance are to an adolescent "because many patients put on a brave front, but the pain of the experience is often felt for many years" (Stevens & Dunsmore, 1996, p. 110).

Responding to Interpersonal Issues

The adolescent will be faced with challenges from peers, even friends, who do not understand the constraints imposed by the illness—and from some whose anxiety and fear lead them to shun the adolescent with a life-threatening illness. Longitudinal findings indicate that adolescents with cancer remain more socially isolated than healthy peers; however, the adolescents do not differ from their peers on a variety of measures of social acceptance and seem well-adjusted psychosocially. Dying adolescents may narrow their interpersonal focus to a small set of individuals. There is no universal formula to be applied, however, regarding how a specific adolescent will respond.

Responding to Cognitive Issues

Adolescents will want to learn as much as possible about their illness and may over time become quite knowledgeable about symptoms, treatments, and prognosis. Another cognitive issue for adolescents with a life-threatening illness will involve appraising the significance of their illness. Some researchers in Finland have reported cognitive impairments in late adolescent and young adult cancer survivors who contracted cancer before age five; these cognitive impairments particularly involved short-term memory difficulties and were attributed to effects of cranial radiation.

Responding to Emotional Issues

The adolescent will face a panoply of emotions. There may well be anger and frustration over loss of independence. Marc Rich noted that fear was a primary theme around which to understand responses about death and dying of adolescents at a cancer camp. However, he questioned the opinion that a constant fear of death characterized adolescents with cancer. Fears of death were prominent at diagnosis for the various adolescents he knew over a 5-year period at a cancer camp, but over time such fear dissipated for most of the youth: "The campers I have interviewed have been surprisingly open and comfortable discussing issues related to death and dying. It appears that having childhood cancer may actually make some of the campers at (the camp) more comfortable with a topic that is taboo in Western culture" (Rich, 2002, p. 573). A portion of the campers actually had no fear of death, a result Rich attributed to having faced the real possibility of dying.

Responding to Behavioral Issues

In addition to expected behavioral issues that emerge from fatigue due to the illness and to treatments, a salient behavioral issue for adolescents involves becoming dependent on others. This concern gains greatest prominence with behaviors healthy individuals take for granted they will do on their own. As examples, consider such common tasks as dressing, eating, washing, making one's bed, and going to the toilet. Medical staff can add to the frustration adolescents feel over loss of behavioral control by treating adolescents as though they are children.

Responding to Spiritual Issues

Life-threatening illnesses prove to be catalysts for questions about threats to meaning, loss of connections that lend coherence to a person's life, and to transcending the limits of human existence. Obvious questions asked include "What is the point of continuing to suffer?", "How does my one life matter in the midst of this enormous universe?", and "Where is a benevolent God in the death of so many innocent persons?"

Finding hope provides a means to accept these questions, even when answers prove elusive. "Hope becomes an essential ingredient for living successfully for these young people. Their hopes may not necessarily be for a cure or magical recovery, but more often for joy and for success with the challenges of living" (Stevens & Dunsmore, 1996, p. 113). On her bedroom wall, one adolescent with cancer wrote, "Be realistic. Plan for a miracle." (Stevens & Dunsmore, 1996, p. 113).

Pamela Hinds and her colleagues conducted a longitudinal study to determine the extent of hopefulness and what was hoped for among 78 adolescents (12–21 years of age) in the first 6 months of their treatment for cancer. The adolescents were more hopeful than what has been found in other samples of adolescents with cancer; they hoped for many and varied things, such as, to regain health and to return to normalcy. Females were the only research participants to hope for increased family closeness and economic independence. Males were the only research participants to hope for public acclaim and success in athletics.

Responding to a Variety of Losses

Adolescents fundamentally mourn the loss of their health and the impact of not being able to live as they did when they were stronger, more energetic, and considered normal by their peers. Stevens and Dunsmore (1996, p. 109) quote an adolescent who said, "People don't treat me like the person I used to be."

Think about the avalanche of losses, primary and secondary, that the adolescent with a life-threatening illness can face. Among these losses are

- The person prior to cancer's onslaught (the "prediagnosis person" in the words of Stevens & Dunsmore, 1996, p. 109)
- Body image
- The family prior to the diagnosis
- Independence
- Relationships with parents, siblings, and peers
- Certainty about one's future
- Education
- Hope

None of these losses occurs without interaction with other losses. For instance, mourning the loss of the "prediagnosis person" includes pining away after lost relationships with one's peers and mourning loss of body image. Mourning the loss of one's body image involves relationships with peers due to fears of being rejected and of actually being ostracized by peers in some cases; concomitantly, loss of body image affects the adolescent's sense of independence and self-worth. "The insult to body image is internal and cannot be restored properly by an external prosthesis" (Stevens & Dunsmore, 1996, p. 110). One can readily infer the valued role of sensitive counselors, child life specialists, and psychologists to help adolescents adjust following physically altering effects of cancer.

Significant differences have been found for adolescents' self-reports comparing how they engaged in exercise now that they have completed treatment for cancer with memories of these activities prior to the onset of cancer and during treatment. While these findings are subject to some skepticism due to the documented difficulties with the reliability of retrospective findings, it is notable that adolescents who maintained an active exercise regimen had lower depression scores and higher self-concept scores than did adolescents who (1) previously had been active but no longer were, (2) temporarily curtailed their activities due to treatment and then became active again, or (3) had never been active in exercise or sports. Keep in mind that the researchers had no reliable data on the adolescents' self-concepts and depression scores prior to their contracting cancer.

Experiences and Reactions of Adolescents with Cancer

The experiences and reactions of adolescents with cancer can be organized according to the stage of cancer that the adolescent is experiencing. We will look at reactions in four separate stages: diagnosis, treatment, relapse, and beyond treatment.[4]

Diagnosis Stage

At diagnosis the most common reaction is denial, followed quickly by expectations that the worst would happen. The reactions reported seemed to be what Kubler-Ross indicated seeing in adults dying of a terminal illness; however, experts who work with adolescents coping with a life-threatening illness do not consider the adolescents enter a progression of "stages of dying" when they discover they have cancer.

A key goal at diagnosis is to help adolescents and their parents appraise the situation realistically, linked to the adolescent's actual prospects. The quality and accuracy of communication at diagnosis sets the stage for what develops in the struggle to overcome the disease, and has been shown to be instrumental in enabling terminally ill adolescents to accept palliative care if that form of care becomes the necessary option.

Communicating with the adolescent is a key factor. Adolescents want medical staff to talk with them about their illness, and resent being talked about when in the same room as their parents and the medical staff. An extensive literature search conducted by researchers at the University of California at Berkeley indicated that very few efforts have been made to provide systematic information to adolescents about their cancer or to assess the effectiveness of these efforts.

Treatment Stage

During and following treatment adolescents with cancer manifest what others consider remarkable resilience. For instance, because of having to deal with the adversity of their terminal illness, adolescents with cancer consider themselves more able to cope with difficult times and more mature than their unaffected peers. In this regard, these adolescents seem to have grown from their harsh conditions much as other researchers have reported is the case for bereaved adolescents: they are more sensitive to others' hardships, unafraid to be in the presence of people experiencing emotionally painful times, and more grown up than their unaffected peers.

Growing research evidence indicates developmental factors are involved in resilience of youth battling cancer and coping with other traumatic experiences. The basic conclusion is that resilience in at-risk youth occurs when a set of basic human protective systems, including a supportive family, are present and active. Clearly such empirical findings pose opportunities for a host of professionals who work with adolescents coping with cancer.

Terminal Stage

Adolescents in the later stages of cancer respond with various reactions to dying. These variations in response are attributed to personality differences, disparities in the history of each adolescent's illness, different expectations about what caregiving the adolescent will accept, and what is needed to provide adequate palliative care. The different responses include such contrasts as denial that death is imminent versus resigned acceptance of death, desire for peace and quiet versus preference for noise and bustle, wishing to be alone versus wishing to be surrounded by family and friends, and wanting to be alert to the end versus choosing to be heavily sedated.

There is a remarkable parallel between the needs expressed by older adults with a terminal illness and the needs expressed by adolescents in the later stages of cancer: the need to maintain a sense of identity, to remain active in decisions that affect them, to feel worthwhile and valued, and to receive fitting, satisfactory care. Rather than fearing being dead, adolescents dread the loss of control they associate with the process of dying. Some adolescents when first diagnosed with cancer progress from an overwhelming fear of death to a weakened fear to a lack of fear. While not true of all adolescents with cancer, some adolescents' views about death are captured well in such comments as "Having cancer has changed my views about death. I realize that death is not something horrible but just another chapter in one's life" (Rich, 2002, p. 573).

It is important to remember that not all adolescents reach such equanimity: some remain in denial and others are afraid at the end. It would be an injustice to impose on any adolescent with cancer the expectation that becoming poised and composed about death is the norm. Equanimity in the face of dying is one possibility seen in some adolescents.

Life after Treatment Succeeds

Cancer survival has steadily increased in the last quarter of the 20th century and first decades of the 21st century. Survival is commonly measured as being cancer-free for

5 years. For example, among adolescents with malignant melanoma the survival rate was over 90%; with Hodgkin's lymphoma, 90% of adolescents attain the 5-year survival rate; for adolescents with ALL the 5-year survival rate is around 60%.

Elation, even euphoria, are common reactions when first learning that treatment has succeeded and no signs of the cancer remain. The reality that the cancer could return is not lost on the adolescent, however, and uncertainty about the future can lead to concern, even dread, not only for oneself but also for peers with the same cancer. This state of anxious uncertainty over the return of the cancer was christened in the early 1980s the "Damocles syndrome," referring to a tyrant in the ancient world who placed dinner guests beneath a sword suspended by a light cord over their heads; just as at any moment the sword might fall and kill the person, the adolescent realized the cancer could return in virulence. Given the increasing success since the early 1980s in treating cancers during adolescence and the growing numbers of individuals living cancer-free well beyond 5 years, it would be a worthwhile public health endeavor to determine whether survivors of adolescent cancer show signs of the Damocles syndrome.

Clinical teams report that psychological reactions to relapse contain more distress than reactions when the cancer was diagnosed initially. Reasons for the distress include the realization that prognosis is poor. The wind goes out of the ill adolescent's sails, as it were, and hopelessness becomes a danger. The adolescent picks up on the nonverbal cues of family members and medical professionals whose fear and disappointment are often palpable. One 16-year-old in relapse said, "I sailed through treatment the first time. I always believed I would make it. This time it's more difficult. I see the pain and fear in the faces of my family. I see the pity in the eyes of my nurses and doctors" (Stevens, Dunsmore, Bennett, & Young, 2009, p. 132).

Concluding Comments

The focus of this chapter is on life-threatening illnesses, primarily threats to adolescent mortality from diabetes, HIV/AIDS, and cancer. Emphasis was on issues faced when coping with Type I diabetes and with the epidemic of obesity in the United States leading to an increase in the incidence and prevalence of diabetes. Further, developmental changes during the adolescent years can increase the danger of long-term effects and risk of dying when adolescents contract Type I diabetes.

The primary concern worldwide about HIV/AIDS is the virulent spread of the virus in some African, South American, and Asian countries. The somber reality is that 15- to 24-year-olds account for 40% or more of all new cases of HIV infection. Crushing economic needs lead in many cases to female adolescents becoming infected as they engage in prostitution to provide money for their families. A variety of prevention measures were introduced in this country by the Centers for Disease Control; a significant proportion of new cases of HIV infection is found in the early through later adolescent years, often among members of ethnic minority groups, particularly African Americans.

Breakthroughs in curing many forms of cancer continue to occur. However, cancer remains one of the leading causes of death for adults around the world, and some adolescents contract cancer and die. We looked at three forms of cancer that may prove fatal to adolescents: Hodgkin's lymphoma, malignant melanoma, and acute lymphoblastic leukemia.

The holistic framework provides a means to comprehend the demands on coping that an adolescent faces when struck by a life-threatening illness. The youth faces physical demands, cognitive demands, behavioral demands, interpersonal demands, emotional demands, and spiritual demands. In addition, life-threatening illnesses lead to grief over an assortment of finite, nontangible losses, and all can be seen tied back into the holistic framework. For instance, losses concerning body image involve at the very least cognitive and emotional aspects to an adolescent's makeup. Uncertainty about the future and diminished hope involve by definition issues of spirituality.

Notes

1. Adipose tissue lies under the skin and around body organs and is made up of fat-storing cells.
2. Ketoacidosis is a condition produced by high ketone levels. Ketones are molecules formed in the liver when carbohydrates, proteins, and fats are not being properly metabolized.
3. HPV infection has been linked to 90% of anal cancers, 40% of penile, vaginal, and vulvar cancers, and 12% of throat cancers.
4. There is also a prediagnostic stage during which the symptoms of the illness emerge but are not always seen for what they are. Rather than seek out expert advice, the person may dismiss the symptoms or discount their severity. Life prior to diagnosis provides all the memories for what becomes known as the prediagnostic person.

Sources

American Society of Clinical Oncology. Cancer in older adults. Retrieved July 28, 2012, from www.cancer.net/

Bassett, L. (September 13, 2011). Rick Perry's HPV vaccine law sparks political fight that ignores health issues. *The Huffington Post*. Retrieved March 27, 2013, from www.huffingtonpost.com

Bendel, A., Beaty, O., Bottom, K., Bunin, G., & Wrensch, M. (2007). Central nervous system cancer. In *Cancer epidemiology in older adolescents and young adults 15–29 years of age. Including SEER incidence and survival: 1975–2000* (pp. 65–80). Washington, DC: National Cancer Institute.

Betts, P. R. Jefferson, I. G., & Swift, F. (2002). Diabetes care in childhood and adolescence. *Diabetic Medicine, 19*, 61–65.

Bluebond-Langner, M. (1978). *The private worlds of dying children*. Princeton, NJ: Princeton University Press.

Centers for Disease Control. (2001). *Young people at risk: HIV/AIDS among America's youth.* Retrieved December 12, 2012, from www.thebody.com/content/art17256.html

Centers for Disease Control. (2012). Human papillomavirus: Epidemiology and prevention of vaccine-preventable diseases. *The Pink Book* (12th ed.). Retrieved March 26, 2013, from www.cdc.gov/vaccines/pubs/pinkbook/hpv.html#epi

Chabon, B. & Futterman, D. (1999). Adolescents and HIV. *AIDS in Clinical Care, 11*, 9–11, 15–16.

Corr, C. A. (1992). A task-based approach to coping with dying. *Omega, 24*, 81–94.

Doka, K. J. (2013). Historical and contemporary perspectives on dying. In D. K. Meagher & D. E. Balk (Eds.), *Handbook of thanatology: The essential body of knowledge for the study of death, dying, and bereavement* (pp. 17–23). New York: Routledge.

Diabetes. (2012). Washington, DC: National Diabetes Information Clearinghouse. Retrieved December 12, 2012, from www.niddk.nih.gov/

Foltz, L. M., Song, K. W., & Connors, J. M. (2006). Hodgkin's lymphoma in adolescents. *Journal of Clinical Oncology, 24*(16), 2520–2526.

Freyer, D. R. (2004). Care of the dying adolescent. *Pediatrics, 113*, 381–388.

Gottschalk, S. M. & McClain, K. L (2009). Overview of Hodgkin lymphoma in children and adolescents. Retrieved July 28, 2012, from www.uptodate.com

Gurney, J. G., Linel, M., Tamra, T., Young, J. L., & Bunin, G. (Editors). (1999). *Cancer incidence and survival among children and adolescents: United States SEER program 1975–1995*. NIH Publication No. 99-4649. Bethesda, MD: National Cancer Institute, SEER Program.

Hampson, S. E., Skinner, T. C., Hart, J., Storey, L., Gage, H., Foxcraft, D., Kimber, A., Shaw, K., & Walker, J. (2001). Effects of educational and psychosocial interventions for adolescents with diabetes mellitus: A systematic review. *Health Technology Assessment, 5*(10).

Herzog, C., Pappo, A., Bondy, M., Bleyer, A., & Kirkwood, J. (2007). Malignant melanoma. In *Cancer epidemiology in older adolescents and young adults 15–29 years of age. Including SEER incidence and survival: 1975–2000* (pp. 54–63). Washington, DC: National Cancer Institute.

Hinds, P. S., Quargnenti, A., Faairclough, D., Bush, A. J., Betcher, D., Rissmiller, G. Pratt, C. B., & Gilchrist, G. S. (1999). Hopefulness and its characteristics in adolescents with cancer. *Western Journal of Nursing Research, 21,* 600–620.

Jeha, S. (2003). Who should be treating adolescents and young adults with acute lymphoblastic leukemia? *European Journal of Cancer, 39,* 2579–2583.

Keats, M. R., Courneya, K. S., Danielsen, S., & Whitsett, S. F. (1999). Leisure-time physical activity and psychosocial well-being in adolescents after cancer diagnosis. *Journal of Pediatric Oncology Nursing, 16,* 180–188.

Mattano, L., Nachman, J., Ross, J., & Stock. W. (2007). Leukemias. In *Cancer epidemiology in older adolescents and young adults 15–29 years of age. Including SEER incidence and survival: 1975–2000* (pp. 39–50). Washington, DC: National Cancer Institute.

More and more young people get HIV/AIDS. (1999). *ReproWatch, 5,* 1–2.

Mukherjee, S. (2010). *The emperor of all maladies: A biography of cancer.* New York: Scribner.

National Cancer Institute. Adolescents and young adults with cancer. Retrieved July 28, 2012, from www.cancer.gov/cancertopics/aya

Noll, R. B., Bukowski, W. M., Davies, W. H., & Koontz, K. et al. (1993). Adjustment in the peer system of adolescents with cancer: A two-year study. *Journal of Pediatric Psychology, 18,* 351–364.

O'Leary, M., Sheaffer, J., Keller, F., Shu, X-O, & Cheson, B. (2007). Lymphomas and reticuloendothelial neoplasms. In *Cancer epidemiology in older adolescents and young adults 15–29 years of age. Including SEER incidence and survival: 1975–2000* (pp. 25–38). Washington, DC: National Cancer Institute.

Olshansky, S. J., Passaro, D. J., Hershaw, R. C., Layden, J., Carnes, B. A., Brody, J., Hayflick, L., Butler, R. N., Allison, D. B., & Ludwig, D. S.(2005). A potential decline in life expectancy in the United States in the 21st century. *The New England Journal of Medicine, 352,* 1138–1145.

Pagliusi, S. (July 18, 2011). Vaccines against human papillomavirus. Retrieved March 26, 2013, from www.who.int/vaccines

Ribera, J-M. & Oriol, A. (2009). Acute lymphoblastic leukemia in adolescents and young adults. *Hematology Oncology Clinics of North America, 23*(5), 1033–1042.

Rich, M. D. (2002). Memory Circles: The Implications of (not) grieving at cancer camp. *Journal of Contemporary Ethnography, 31,* 548–581.

Schwimmer, J. B., Burwinkle, T. M., & Varni, J. W. (2003). Health-related quality of life of severely obese children and adolescents. *JAMA, 289*(14), 1813–1819.

Scott, J. T., Harmsen, M., Prictor, M. J., Sowden, A. J., & Watt, I. (2008). Ways of improving communication with children and adolescents about their cancer. Retrieved December 10, 2012, from www.ncbi.nlm.nih.gov/pubmedhealth/PMH0011718/

Skinner, T. C., Hampson, S. E., & Fife-Schaw, C. (2002). Personality. Personal belief models, and self-care in adolescents and young adults with Type 1 diabetes. *Health Psychology, 21,* 61–70.

Snoek, F. J. & Skinner, T. C. (Editors). (2005). *Psychology in diabetes care.* Chichester, West Sussex: UK: Wiley.

Stevens, M. M. & Dunsmore, J. C. (1996). Adolescents who are living with a life-threatening illness. In C. A. Corr & D. E. Balk (Editors), *Handbook of adolescent death and bereavement* (pp. 107–155). New York: Springer.

Stevens, M. M., Dunsmore, J. C., Bennett, D. L., & Young, A. J. (2009). Adolescents living with life-threatening illness. In D. E. Balk & C. A. Corr (Eds.), *Adolescent encounters with death, bereavement, and coping* (pp. 115–140). New York: Springer.

UNICEF. (2011). Adolescence: An age of opportunity. Retrieved December 12, 2012, from www.uis.unesco.org/Library/Documents/state-world-children-adolescence-age-opportunity-education-2011-en.pdf

Vance, Y. H. & Eiser, C. (2002). The school experience of the child with cancer. *Child Care, Health and Development, 28,* 5–19.

Zha, B. (1998). AIDS in China. *China Population Research Newsletter,* June(1), 4–5.

7 Trauma

One Saturday morning when I was a late adolescent, I cut my hand while working in the yard. My father, who was a physician, looked at the cut and called it a trauma. The medical notion of trauma is an injury to living tissue caused by an external agent. Thinking of the psychological notions of trauma, I said it seemed a bit dramatic to call my cut a trauma. Dad just smiled and put a bandage on the cut. The medical notion is one prominent sense of trauma, but not one I suspect that comes to mind when many persons hear the word.

In this chapter we are talking about the psychological sense of trauma, not the medical. We are talking about horrific events, such as one's daughter being run over by a car, being sexually assaulted, finding the body of a friend who has completed suicide, being held hostage by criminals in a bank robbery gone bad, having a loved one killed in a terrorist bombing, seeing a family member waste away and die in pain from a terminal illness, or coming under constant bombardment in a firefight during a war. These kinds of awful events present grave, imminent threats to one's own life or to the lives of persons we care about. Persons who have not experienced the terror of such events typically dismiss the intensity and the duration of suffering the event induces. The aftermath of such horrific events can be devastating and lead to Acute Stress Disorder (ASD) or to Post-Traumatic Stress Disorder (PTSD). I am not claiming the only reactions to such horrific events are ASD or PTSD, but I don't want to overlook the ramifications being traumatized can have on the person in the aftermath of the event.

Information about Post-Traumatic Stress Disorder

Many people with PTSD repeatedly reexperience the ordeal in the form of flashback episodes, memories, nightmares, or frightening thoughts, especially when they are exposed to events or objects reminiscent of the trauma. Anniversaries of the event can also trigger symptoms. People with PTSD also experience emotional numbness and sleep disturbances, depression, anxiety, irritability, persistent negative emotional states, and sudden outbursts of anger. Feelings of intense guilt are also common. Most people with PTSD try to avoid any reminders or thoughts of the ordeal. PTSD is diagnosed when symptoms last more than 1 month. Three categories of response to trauma are intrusive thoughts and images, avoidance of remainders of the event, and hypervigilance (sometimes called hyperarousal). The new *Diagnostic and Statistical Manual* (*DSM-5*) allows diagnoses of PTSD for children age 6 or younger as long as certain developmental criteria are present.

PTSD can develop at any age, including childhood and adolescence, and symptoms often begin within 3 months following a traumatic event; there are occasions that PTSD symptoms remain dormant for years. The severity and duration of PTSD symptoms differ from case to case: whereas some PTSD victims recover within 6 months, others suffer much longer.

Are some persons more vulnerable to PTSD than are others? Evidence indicates that individuals abused physically and/or sexually as children, individuals who have experienced other types of traumatic experiences, and individuals with psychiatric disorders are at increased risk of developing PTSD. Researchers continue to identify other influences that contribute to developing PTSD. At one time researchers and clinicians believed that emotional neutrality or numbness following a traumatic experience demonstrated a healthy response to the trauma, but there is growing suspicion that such emotional detachment discloses vulnerability to having been traumatized.

Acute Stress Disorder

Acute Stress Disorder (ASD) is a diagnostic category in the *DSM-5*.[1] Similarities with PTSD will immediately become apparent in this review of ASD. ASD is a severe reaction to a horrifying event. However, the recently published *DSM-5* has removed the requirement that the person must have reacted with horror or terror or helplessness. It is also no longer required in *DSM-5* for the person with ASD to exhibit dissociative symptoms. Examples of dissociative symptoms include depersonalization and inability to recall chief characteristics of the event. To be diagnosed with ASD a person must manifest at least 9 of 14 symptoms in the categories of intrusion, negative mood, dissociation, avoidance, and arousal.

The interest in identifying ASD as a diagnostic category in the early 1990s was partly—perhaps prominently—to obtain a means to identify persons at risk for developing PTSD. However, a wide range of persons with PTSD—from 29% to 72%—never manifested ASD symptoms. It has become evident that using only ASD symptoms as a screening device to identify persons at risk for PTSD would lead to both false positives and false negatives.

Long-Term Consequences of Trauma

An analogy used by scholars to explain the effects and sequelae of trauma, particularly experienced during childhood and adolescence, is to liken trauma to rheumatic fever. Rheumatic fever is a serious disease of childhood that can lead to damage that proves lethal in adulthood. Some of the consequences of rheumatic fever can include obsessive-compulsive behavior, tic disorders, and subsequent damage to body tissues because the person is vulnerable to reoccurrences of the disease.

The sense is that childhood trauma can operate analogously to rheumatic fever's serious debilitating consequences for an individual. Childhood traumas have been linked to such serious problems in adulthood as anxiety disorders, psychotic thinking, eating disorders, suicidal ideation, drug abuse, self-mutilation, and disastrous interpersonal relationships. Causal comparative research with adults who were raised by alcoholic parents has identified the presence of several of these serious problems, and one plausible inference is that the ongoing insecure and unpredictable parenting from alcoholics had traumatic outcomes in adulthood for the children.

Two Overarching Categories of Trauma

There are two categories into which traumas are grouped: Type I Traumas and Type II Traumas. The categories are quite distinct, and symptoms differ considerably depending on the type of trauma experienced.

Type I Traumas are sudden, discrete experiences such as being kidnapped, being sexually assaulted, and being shot at by a sniper. *Type II Traumas* are longstanding in nature and come from repeated exposure to horrific ordeals. Examples include long-term physical or sexual abuse. The consequences for children raised by alcoholic parents suggest a Type II trauma.

Individuals who experience Type I traumatic experiences exhibit symptoms quite different from the symptoms that follow exposure to Type II experiences. Table 7.1 provides the symptoms in parallel columns, and a discussion follows the table.

More Detail about Type I Symptoms

1. *Etched in memories* refers to nearly complete, precise verbal recounts of what the person endured. These memories are seemingly indelibly carved into the psyche. No matter how the person tries to suppress these memories, the memories stubbornly persist. One thinks of what the Impact of Event Scale denotes as intrusive thoughts and images. In short, individuals who experience Type I traumas can remember almost every second and minute of the contents of the event that traumatized them. However, they seem incapable of remembering how they felt or how they acted during the ordeal.
2. *Continual rumination about the event* refers to the person's thinking over and over about the event. This symptom too—like "etched in memories"—has intrusive aspects to it. Perhaps the continual rumination and the etched in memories interplay and reinforce each other.
3. *Cognitive impairments* refers to certain maladaptations in coping. Persons who experience Type I traumas are at risk of developing a pattern of forgetting and trouble concentrating. They develop problems with "narrative coherence," which is the

Table 7.1 Symptoms of Type I and Type II Trauma

Type I Symptoms	Type II Symptoms
Fully detailed, etched in memories	Massive denial of the traumatic events
Continual rumination about the event	Psychic numbing
Cognitive impairments	Indifference to pain
Emotional displacement	Lack of empathy
Reenactment of the traumatic event	Anger
Transpositions	Avoidance of intimacy with others
Sense of foreshortened future	Aggression
Interpersonal attachment difficulties	Refusal to acknowledge their emotions

ability to organize material into a recognizable beginning, middle, and end. Lack of narrative coherence has direct implications for reading, writing, and other forms of communication, and for understanding the history of one's life.

4. *Emotional displacement* refers to shifting or displacing emotions about the trauma to a related time, to an associated idea, or to another person. For instance, in the case of a child seeing a psychiatrist following a kidnapping, the child became convinced the psychiatrist was placing in her school locker damaging notes about her ordeal.

5. *Reenactment of the event* refers to behaviors apparently performed with the intent to determine a reason for the event or to assign blame or responsibility. For children, such reenactment literally takes the form of play. For adolescents the form reenactment takes can be rebellious or delinquent behavior such as truancy, sexual activity, theft, or drug abuse. The adolescent may be engaging in such behavior because the trauma has convinced the youth he or she is really no good and only a bad person would be doing such bad things.

6. *Transpositions* is a technical term that denotes such phenomena as visual hallucinations, time misperceptions, and superstitious attributions. For instance, the person may consider the event is an omen of disastrous things yet to come, or the child may have problems sorting out what happened before and after the trauma. Distortions of time seem to become part of the personality of the person who develops PTSD following a Type I trauma. PTSD experts see these time distortions as coping efforts to take control of events in the person's life, even if that effort means having to accept blame for events over which the person had no control. An example is found in the response of a boy who was supposed to come home from school immediately after class was dismissed, who dallied on the playground with friends, and then attributed his having been kidnapped and assaulted by a pedophile to his not having obeyed his parents.

7. *Sense of a foreshortened future* manifests itself in recurring nightmares with themes of death and destruction. Children who have these nightmares say their frightening dreams are highly predictive of the future, a reaction linked to the sense that the event was an omen of disaster to come.

8. *Attachment difficulties* can emerge in what is called "anxious attachment" in which the person suffers severe separation anxiety when loved ones are absent. These attachment difficulties may lead children to regress socially, which produces rejection and teasing from peers. Imagine the problems an 8-year-old child has with peers if the 8-year-old regresses to behavior of a 5-year-old. Attachment difficulties may manifest themselves in the person's appraisal that caregivers (for instance, the parents) are unable to help when needs are the greatest; after all, the caregivers provided no help during the traumatic ordeal. The result may involve emotional separation from the parents or other caregivers.

More Detail about Type II Symptoms

Persons who have experienced continual physical and sexual abuse exhibit these symptoms. Refugees from war-torn countries are another group prone to exhibit Type II symptoms. The typical features of Type II traumas are *massive denial* and *psychic numbing*. These traumatized individuals avoid talking about themselves or the traumas they experienced. They try to look as normal as they can. If they do tell someone their stories, later they may deny they did so, or deny the story was the truth. Note the difference with Type I children who tell the story over and over. For Type II children the coping mechanism of denial may become so pervasive that the children forget whole spans of their lives.

Persons who experience Type II trauma are indifferent to pain (both their pain and others' pain) and lack empathy. They absolutely avoid psychological intimacy and will not recognize or acknowledge their emotions. The main character in the emotionally riveting movie *The Pawnbroker* portrays someone whose Holocaust experience in concentration camps has produced a cipher of a person who takes great care to never let anyone get close.

It would be a serious mistake to conclude that individuals from Type II traumatic ordeals do not have emotions. In particular, the emotion they feel and act on is rage. They have an inwardly turned anger against themselves for having been powerless to stop the trauma and an externally focused rage directed at others. The outcomes of this rage can be self-mutilations, suicide, or murders.

Type I trauma victims reenact in some form the event that happened. What Type II victims reenact is the anger they feel at what was done to them. They become angry so often that is not uncommon for Type II trauma victims to form habitual patterns of turning to aggression in response to what they feel or in response to how others behave.

Crossover from Type I to Type II Trauma

At times a single event, for instance, a traumatic accident, can evolve into ongoing trauma. As an example, consider a young teenager who emerges from a car accident with permanent physical disfigurement or long-term pain or abandonment due to the deaths of significant others in the accident. In this case of loss produced by the trauma, there is increased attention being paid to the problems that can ensue when traumatic shock interferes with the normal course of bereavement, leading to major depression as grief becomes more and more complicated. We will take up in Chapter Eight the complex issues that ensue when trauma and bereavement intersect.

Secondary Stressors Resulting from Maladaptive Coping

Maladaptive coping with trauma can lead to secondary stressors in a person's life. For example, consider the adolescent who copes with a traumatic event by sexual promiscuity and develops in the process a communicable, perhaps deadly, disease. An individual who takes control by blaming himself for having caused a traumatic event ("If I had only gone home like Mom told me, this wouldn't have happened") can become overwhelmed with undeserved feelings of guilt and shame.

Thus, in addition to the initial trauma, negative coping patterns can produce additional stressors and present further psychological burdens.

An Episode Providing Information to Explore the Effects of a Type I Trauma

I will present information about a sniper's multihour attack on an elementary school in Los Angeles and the immediate reactions as well as the reactions over time of the children to this very distressing event. The older children were in early adolescence, but most of the children were younger. See if the information meshes with or diverges from the information about PTSD just given.

Here is some background information:

1. The school had about 1,100 students enrolled.
2. The school operated on a year-round schedule, so that at any one time during the school year 25% of the students were on vacation and thus not at the school.
3. Children on vacation were called "off track" students. All the other students were called "on track."
4. On the day of the sniper attack, the majority of the "on track" students had either already gone home before the shooting started or had hurried home when the shooting began.
5. For children still at school during the sniper attack, there were two groups:
   a. Those students on the playground during the attack.
   b. Those students in the school building during the attack.

Information about the Sniper Attack

The sniper was a 28-year-old male named Tyrone Mitchell. Mitchell lived in a house directly across from the school, and he had an upstairs window with a clear view of the playground. He had a reputation in the neighborhood as a habitual user of the drug PCP. Relatives told police after the shooting that Mitchell had been under the influence of drugs on the day of the attack. Mitchell had been a member of the People's Temple in Guyana whose leader, the Rev. Jim Jones, had convinced his followers to commit mass suicide in November 1978. Mitchell had not been part of the mass suicide because on the day it happened Mitchell had been in the capital city of Guyana; Mitchell's parents and two other close relatives died in the mass suicide.

The attack on the school children started at approximately 2:30 PM on February 24, 1984. Witnesses estimated about 100 children were on the playground when the shooting started. Mitchell killed a 10-year-old girl, and an adult pedestrian walking by Mitchell's house; he wounded 11 children and 2 adults. Except for the adult walking by Mitchell's house, all the persons shot were on the playground.

Mitchell fired repeatedly at figures on the playground. The child fatally wounded did not die immediately but lay bleeding and crying for help. The 11 children and adults who were wounded also lay on the playground. Three of the injured children suffered severe wounds. One of the adults was a playground attendant who had been shot while rushing to help the injured child who eventually died.

Bullets shattered school windows, pierced metal doors, and put holes in playground equipment. Children on the playground hid behind trees or trash cans, or lay motionless on the ground if they could not get to cover.

Several students were still in the school building when the shooting started. Some teachers put groups of children in closets or directed them to hide under classroom furniture. Some teachers covered with paper the windows to their classroom doors so that any potential intruders would not be able to see inside the room.

The SWAT team evacuated persons from adjoining homes and surrounded Mitchell's house. Mitchell could not be talked into surrendering. Four hours after Mitchell began shooting, the police flooded his house with tear gas and entered the place. They found Mitchell had killed himself. The police found several weapons, including a high-powered rifle, and considerable ammunition in the house. No one else was in the house during Mitchell's assault on the school.

First Research Study

Robert Pynoos, a psychiatrist who specializes in the effects of traumatic stress on human beings, and his colleagues gained access to the school shortly after the attack, and they followed the children for the next 14 months. The researchers began gathering data within 1.5 to 3 months after the attack. They focused on two broad categories of information: (a) the children's memory of the attack and (b) the children's stress response reactions.

Pynoos and his colleagues interviewed 10% of the student body. The children interviewed fell into one of four groups: (a) children on the playground during the attack, (b) children in the school building, (c) children in their classrooms, and (d) children not at school during the attack. Each child was taken through the same interview process, and the researchers asked each child to do some or all of the following:

- Review the event as if was occurring in slow motion.
- Make a drawing of the attack.
- Walk through the actual sequence at the school yard.
- Talk about "the worst moment."

Findings

The researchers discovered that proximity to the violence had a recognizable influence on what the children recalled about the event in the first several weeks after the attack. Further, the researchers reported that certain aspects of the event influenced recall.

Proximity to the violence. Remember there were groups of children whose proximity to the violence differed considerably: children on the playground, children in the school building, children in their classrooms, and children not at school. Here is information on how proximity to the violence influenced recall of the event.

1. *Children on the playground.* This group of children could actually be subdivided into three separate groups. There were those children who remained trapped on the playground in clear line of fire throughout the ordeal; there were children who remained on the playground but managed to get to protective covering; there were children who were able to get off the playground and back into the school building. For children on the playground when the attack began, their first memories of the event minimized the threat to their lives. Children who had not been injured remembered being in safer locations than they actually had been. For instance, children who could not escape from the line of fire to safer locations but who had not been shot placed the injured children and the sniper's house farther away from where the children were pinned down. As an example, one girl had been only a few feet away from the girl who was fatally wounded; she recalled being much further away from both the injured girl and the sniper.

Many of the children who were on the playground when the shooting began escaped to safer locations during a pause in the firing. When these children initially talked about the attack, they left out the parts of the event that were most life-threatening. For instance, one boy on the playground who made it back into the school building remembered he had been on the playground, remembered seeing the girl who was killed when she was shot, and remembered there was gunfire as he ran inside the building. What he had forgotten was that he had been pinned down for some time on the open playground and that bullets struck on either side of him.

Another girl was near the teachers' cafeteria when the shooting began. She saw the girl who died get shot and saw the playground attendant get shot while trying to reach the wounded child. The girl ran to an exit from the playground and got away safely. In her first recall of the event, she placed herself at the exit, not at the teachers' cafeteria.

Other children on the playground made it to protective cover. They hid behind trash cans or behind trees. These children did not make it back inside the building, but were outside the sniper's line of fire.

In all cases children on the playground who were not shot recalled what they had done to protect themselves. For instance, some children remembered hiding behind a large garbage dumpster. Once they knew they were safe behind their protective cover, they said they wondered how they could get to a safer location. Only after describing their actions to protect themselves did these children begin to remember the people on the playground who had been shot.

Children on the playground who were shot also exhibited the same kind of psychological defenses of minimizing the risk to their lives. They did not mention their wounds and only recalled knowing that shooting was occurring and remembering getting to safety. In actual fact, these children who were wounded remained pinned down during the whole sniper attack and did not make it to a safer location.

2. *Children in the school building.* Some children were just about to leave the school building and go on the playground as the shooting began. Other children were still in their classrooms waiting for their teachers to dismiss them.

    The children who were about to enter the playground when the shooting started remembered they stayed in the building and were never on the playground during the attack. They remembered being safe. However, they did not minimize the danger to staying alive as did the children on the playground when the shooting began. On the contrary, children who had almost entered the playground emphasized the danger they had avoided. One child who had stayed in the school building recalled seeing the dying girl and seeing the sniper standing over the girl. In reality, this student could not possibly have seen the dying girl from her vantage point in the school building and the sniper never left his house during the attack.

3. *Children in the classrooms.* All these children and their teachers heard the gunfire, but some thought it was just firecrackers. Others seemed to recognize the sounds as gunfire. Some classroom windows faced the sniper's house, whereas other windows faced away.

    Children in the classrooms relied on their teachers' actions to assess what was happening. They also remembered discrepancies between what their teachers said and how their teachers acted. For instance, some teachers assured the children everything was going to be okay, but were seen to be in tears or shaking. In one case, a teacher dismissed his class, assuring his students that nothing was the matter and the noise was only firecrackers. Other teachers heard the children in the hallways and sent them back to their classroom; these other teachers knew the sounds were from gunfire. Children in this man's classroom remembered their teacher's mistake and indicated being upset with him for sending them into danger.

The children in the classroom recalled fearing there were intruders in the building who were going to harm them. They said seeing teachers placing paper on classroom windows increased their fears for their safety. Some students said they saw police officers crawling along corridors in the school building, and seeing the police increased their alarm about intruders harming them. For children in the classroom during the attack, fear of intruders remained for a time following the attack.

4. *Children not at school.* These children tended to remember being closer to the violence than they actually had been. They remembered being closer in time and closer in location. They did not describe themselves as being in the line of fire, but they tended to place themselves nearer the attack than they had been. As an example, one girl was already walking home and was nearly a block away from the school when the shooting began. She initially remembered both being much closer to the school and actually near the sniper's house. A boy who was "off track" recalled being on his way to the school and seeing someone lying shot on the playground. In reality, the police had quickly cordoned off the area, and no one could get within a block of the school. Many children not at school during the attack came to school the next day, and in their initial recall placed this visit as occurring on the day of the shooting.

Anchor points for memory of the event. In addition to the children's memories being influenced by proximity to the event, other aspects of the sniper attack influenced what they remembered. There were four aspects: (a) cues of distress, (b) sight of blood or sight of persons wounded, (c) worry about a sibling, and (d) previous moments of trauma.

1. *Cues of distress.* Some children on the playground could hear the girl who eventually died calling for help. Each child with this memory changed the experience so that they could increase their prospects of helping the dying child. For instance, one girl reported she went over to the girl and told her, "I love you." Later she acknowledged she had not been able to approach the girl but had wanted to let her know how much she wanted to help.

2. *Sight of blood or sight of persons wounded.* Blood remained an exceedingly vivid image for the children. Children who saw the shooting of the girl who died described over and over the horror of seeing "all that blood coming out." Other children remembered seeing the shooting of a girl who was playing on the monkey bars. They recalled the girl falling from the monkey bars and "lying in blood." When asked to draw what they had seen, some children specifically requested red crayons to represent blood; however, other children seemed reluctant to include any reference to blood in their drawings.

3. *Worry about a sibling.* The interviewers asked the children if they were concerned about anyone during the attack. Often the children expressed concern for their brother or sister. These concerns for siblings did not emerge until the children felt

they had minimized the immediate danger to their own lives. One boy, for instance, told in detail how, after escaping to the protective cover of the teachers' cafeteria, he began scanning the playground for his sister, placing himself in danger to do so.

Seeing a brother or sister lying motionless was often misinterpreted as the sibling had been shot. Siblings who were together on the playground during the attack did not express the same worries as children who did not know whether their sibling had been shot. Older siblings usually expressed feeling responsibility for getting the younger one to safety.

Children in the school building or in classrooms worried about their own safety and feared their siblings were in grave danger. This fear remained tangible even after the sibling's safety was verified.

Children not at school heard about the shooting from news coverage or from students who had gotten away from the school just before the shooting started. If these children had siblings at school, they imagined the worse.

4. *Reminders of previous trauma.* Previous life experiences that had been traumatic influenced how children remembered the sniper's attack. For example, one girl who was trapped on the playground had 2 years earlier lost a sister who drowned in a swimming pool. The sister had been pulled from the pool while still alive, but paramedic efforts to revive her had failed. The girl on the playground wondered if the paramedics would have saved her sister had they been able to get to her sister more quickly. In her memory of the sniper's attack, the girl whose sister had drowned emphasized how quickly help had arrived for the girl bleeding to death on the playground. Her initial memory actually shortened the period of time for the paramedics to reach the wounded girl. But then she corrected herself and talked about how it was already too late because by the time the paramedics got there, the girl had lost too much blood.

Follow-Up Study 14 Months Later

Fourteen months after the sniper's attack, Pynoos and his colleagues interviewed the same students they had interviewed in the weeks following the attack. They were interested now to see what stress reactions had endured or even emerged since the first interview; they were clearly interested to see if the children were exhibiting symptoms of PTSD.

Actually, their longitudinal study had three time frames to it:

1. Phase One: Reactions to stress in the immediate aftermath of the event.
2. Phase Two: Stress reactions 6 months after the event.
3. Phase Three: Stress reactions 14 months after the event.

Two aspects of the data gathering are worth mentioning. One, whereas 159 children were interviewed at phase one, only 100 children participated in the follow-up. Some had moved and could not be located and some would not participate further in the study. Two, data for the 6- and 14-month follow-up were gathered at the same time: at the 14-month follow-up session.

Let's talk about the method of gathering data at the follow-up. The method was to gather data at one point in time about distress symptoms currently experienced

14 months after the event and symptoms experienced 6 months after the event. How could children's recall of what they felt like 8 months prior to the interview be trusted? How, in other words, could the researchers frame the interview questions so that school-age children would be able to give an accurate account of their reactions 8 months ago? Here is what the researchers did to frame the experience in memorable chronology.

1.   The sniper attack occurred in February, 1984.
2.   The Olympics were held in Los Angeles July through August, 1984.
3.   The children were asked to remember how they felt about the attack during the time when the Olympics were being held.
4.   The children reported their current reactions to the sniper attack.

The Follow-Up Sample

Of the 159 children originally interviewed, 100 took part in the follow-up interview (~63%). There were four groups of children interviewed:

1. Children on the playground	19
2. Children inside the school building	21
3. Children on track but not at school	28
4. Children off track	32
Total	100

Children in the follow-up study included every grade, including children who in the intervening year had moved from the elementary school and gone to the nearby junior high school. What data did the researchers gather from the children?

Symptoms of distress. The researchers gathered data on 17 symptoms of distress following a traumatic event. Examples of these symptoms are emotional detachment, intrusive thoughts, difficulty concentrating, intrusive images, guilt, and feeling isolated in one's distress.

How the symptoms are scored. The researcher adds the number of symptoms that are reported. A PTSD score is determined based on the number of symptoms reported.

•   0–6 symptoms—No PTSD
•   7–9 symptoms—Mild PTSD
•   10–12 symptoms—Moderate PTSD
•   13–17 symptoms—Severe PTSD

Differentiations over time in symptoms. In the first few weeks and months following the attack, all the children who were studied reported mild to moderate PTSD. Age, gender, and ethnic background were not significantly linked to symptoms of distress. What really mattered was the proximity of the child to the attack. That is, the greater the child's expo-sure to the life-threatening attack, the more the number of symptoms of distress the child reported. In particular, four symptoms were endorsed by children with greater proximity to the event: fear the event would occur again, emotional detachment, jumpiness, and trouble sleeping. All the children, regardless of proximity to the attack, identified the sniper attack as an extreme stressor in the first few weeks and months after the event.

Six months after the event the number of symptoms declined for all groups of children except for the children on the playground during the attack. Children on the playground reported about 10 symptoms (moderate PTSD). Children in the school building reported seven symptoms (mild PTSD). Children not at school and children off track reported four symptoms (no PTSD).

At the 14-month follow-up session, the number of symptoms barely declined for children who had been on the playground. They now reported on average nearly 10 symptoms (moderate PTSD). Children in the school building reported at most six symptoms (no PTSD). Children not at school and children off track reported around four symptoms (no PTSD).

An Overview of Results 14 Months after the Attack

Children with the most exposure to the event continued to report the greatest number of symptoms. Over the 14 months span of time, the PTSD reactions declined for everyone except for children on the playground. There were significant differences in the PTSD symptoms reported after 14 months by children on the playground and all the other children. See Table 7.2, which reports the information in terms of the percentage in each group with PTSD symptoms.

After 14 months a very high number of PTSD symptoms were reported by children on the playground, but not by any of the other groups of children. This information is presented in Table 7.3.

Discussion of the Findings at 14 Months

The two primary predictors of on-going PTSD reactions were proximity to the violence and the degree of threat to one's life. For children with less exposure to the violence and the threat to life, stress responses rapidly diminished. Fear of reoccurrence of the traumatic event faded for all but the most directly exposed children. Even for children in safe areas on the playground, no "reality-based appraisal" minimized their fear of a reoccurrence. By "reality-based appraisal" I mean the child acknowledged that the sniper could not have shot him or her because the child was in a safe area of the playground. This logic made no impact on how the child feared a reoccurrence.

Table 7.2 Percentage of Children Grouped by Proximity Reporting PTSD Symptoms 14 Months after the Sniper Attack

	Report of PTSD Symptoms	
Proximity to Sniper	*Reported PTSD Symptoms*	*Did Not Report Symptoms*
On playground	74%	26%
All other locations	19%	81%

Table 7.3 Symptoms Significantly Reported by Children on the Playground but Not by Other Children 14 Months after the Sniper Attack

1.	Attack still considered distressing
2.	Fearful when thinking about the attack
3.	Intrusive images of the attack
4.	Intrusive thoughts of the attack
5.	Nightmares
6.	Fearful the event will happen again
7.	Wish to avoid feelings
8.	Feeling jumpy or nervous
9.	Trouble sleeping
10.	Avoid reminders of the event
11.	Upset by thoughts of the event
12.	Feel alone in their distress

For children in the school building or away from the school, the sniper attack no longer was a distressing event for them. Over the intervening months they had been able to assess the event and realize it had not posed a threat to them. Children on the playground continued to be troubled by such intrusive imagery as images of the dying girl, images of bleeding classmates, images and sounds of bullets striking around them, and images of children crying for help. As time progressed, children with enduring symptoms of distress suffered their thoughts and feelings alone, silently. They stayed alone with their distress and did not experience anyone else as supportive. There are expectations by persons unaffected by a traumatic episode that recovery will occur fairly quickly. People who have experienced the traumatic episode may place these unrealistic expectations on themselves. Many of the children with the most exposure to the violence and threat to their lives expressed their expectation that they should already be over how the sniper attack had affected them. They thought there was something very wrong with them, and that belief caused them further distress.

Treatments Following Trauma

Some persons demonstrate resilience both during and in the aftermath of a trauma. Various factors have been identified to influence resiliency in the face of trauma. Among these factors are maintaining and acting on interpersonal support, positive self-assertions about one's actions when coping with danger, using a successful means of coping with the trauma and reflecting on applying that method to other parts of life, and acting effectively despite being afraid. George Bonanno, a clinical psychologist who has been studying bereavement extensively, has asserted that the typical human response to trauma—natural and manmade disasters, horrendous experiences, and deaths of loved ones—is resilience.

Interventions found useful when persons are coping with PTSD include psychological and pharmaceutical approaches. For adolescents and adults, the psychological treatment of choice in the face of PTSD is cognitive behavioral therapy. Cognitive behavioral therapy includes such techniques as relaxation procedures, anger management, desensitization to feared stimuli, and stress management. Cognitive behavioral therapy is also recommended for use with traumatized children. Cognitive behavioral therapy is intended to give a child a feeling of efficacy, empowerment, and self-control.

The National Institute of Mental Health (NIMH) noted that the severity of PTSD calls for expertly trained mental health professionals to deliver treatment. To place the severity of these problems in context, NIMH mentioned that a person coping with PTSD may also be dealing with other significant problems, including suicidal ideation, panic disorders, or major depression. All these concerns point clearly to the need for well-trained psychotherapists.

A variety of psychotherapy approaches have been found effective, but it may take some trial-and-error to find which approach (or combination of approaches) work best with an individual. Regardless which treatment(s) are used, NIMH emphasizes the invaluable part that support from friends and family members play in helping someone recover from PTSD.

For many instances of PTSD, cognitive behavioral therapy (CBT) has proven successful. One form of CBT is called exposure therapy; this treatment provides the person gradual exposure to their fears, and uses a variety of techniques such as mental imagery and writing about the trauma. Another CBT approach is cognitive restructuring in which the therapist engages the person in reframing the trauma and dealing with guilt and shame. A third form of CBT is stress inoculation training; this approach focuses on reducing anxiety and facing memories without becoming overwhelmed with fear and dread.

Pharmaceutical approaches to treat PTSD primarily involve administration of antidepressant medications. Two antidepressant medications have FDA approval for treating adults with PTSD: sertaline also known as Zoloft; paroxetine also known as Paxil. These medications may alleviate such PTSD symptoms as anger, numbness, and worry and thereby prove an asset when a person is in psychotherapy.

There are cautions about possible side effects attributed to these two antidepressant medications. Among the most commonly recorded side effects are headaches (typically of short duration, perhaps 1 or 2 days), nausea (also typically of 1 or 2 days' duration), insomnia or drowsiness (typically of one or two weeks in duration), restlessness, and loss of interest in sex as well as lack of pleasure from sex.

The authors of the NIMH document highlighted a caution from the Food and Drug Administration (FDA) about dangerous side effects of antidepressant medications. While noting that the great majority of young persons benefited from these drugs, NIMH drew attention to risks pertaining to suicide in a small portion of adolescents and young adults. About 4% of youth taking these antidepressants engaged in suicidal ideation as compared to 2% who were taking placebos. Concerns over these serious life hazards attributed to the drugs led to explicit warnings about the need to monitor carefully any youth on these medications. Physicians and family members were warned to be aware of any indications of trouble such as insomnia, restless agitation, and suicidal thinking.

Concluding Comments

Trauma has become increasingly discussed when bereavement is the main topic of concern. Horrific events all too frequently these days not only traumatize persons but leave them grieving the deaths of loved ones. The example of the sniper attack on school children in Los Angeles, once an anomaly, has become a common occurrence. Witness the killings at Dunblane Primary School in Scotland, at Columbine High School in Littleton, Colorado, at a holiday island in Denmark, at Virginia Tech University, at the movie theater in Aurora, Colorado, at the elementary school in Newtown, Connecticut, at the School of Nursing at the University of Arizona, and at the Sikh temple in Oak Creek, Wisconsin. The list could be extended much longer, and it would include acts of mass terrorism such as the bombing of the Alfred P. Murrah Federal Building in Oklahoma City, the destruction of the Twin Towers in New York City, and the attack on the Pentagon.

The linkage between trauma and bereavement will be explored more in the next chapter on bereavement, grief, and mourning. Two issues to keep in mind are that (a) a traumatic event may be what has caused one's bereavement, as in the horrific death taking the life of a friend or family member and (b) the bereavement itself may be traumatic. We will examine the implications of each issue.

Note

1. ASD is the acronym for Autism Spectrum Disorder in the recently published *DSM-5*.

Sources

American Psychiatric Association. (2013). *Highlights of changes from DSM-IV-TR to DSM-5.* Washington, DC: Author.

Blackham, G. J. & Silbernan, A. (1975). *Modification of child and adolescent behavior* (2nd ed.). Belmont, CA: Wadsworth.

Bonanno, G. A. (2009). *The other side of sadness: What the new science of bereavement tells us about life after loss.* New York: Basic Books.

Bryant, R. A., Friedman, M. J., Spiegel, D., Ursano, R., & Strain, J. (2011). A review of Acute Stress Disorder in DSM-5. *Depression and Anxiety, 28,* 802–817.

Deblinger, E. & Reflin, A. H. (1996). *Cognitive behavioral interventions for treating sexually abused children.* Thousand Oaks, CA: Sage.

Friedman, M. J., Foa, E. B., & Charney, D. S. (2003). Toward evidence-based early intervention for acutely traumatized adults and children. *Biological Psychiatry, 53,* 765–768.

Horowitz, M. J. (1976). *Stress response syndromes.* Northvale, NJ: Aronson.

Horowitz, M. J., Wilner, N., & Alvarez, W. (1979). Impact of events scale: A measure of subjective stress. *Psychosomatic Medicine, 41,* 208–218.

International Society for Traumatic Stress Disorders. (1997). *Practice guidelines for the treatment of posttraumatic stress disorder.* www.istss.org/quick/tg.doc.html

Landreth, G. L. (1987). Play therapy: Facilitative use of child's play in elementary school counseling. *Elementary School Guidance and Counseling, 21*(4), 253–261.

Landreth, G. L. & Bratton, S. (1999). *Play therapy.* Eric microfonn ED 430172.

Lindsey, R. (February 25, 1984). Sniper kills girl in Los Angeles; Suspect is dead. *New York Times,* 16.

Lindsey, R. (February 26, 1984). Schoolyard killer: Cult and drugs seen as clues. *New York Times,* 126.

Molina, M. H. (2000). *Interpersonal relationships of adult children of alcoholic: Evaluating intimacy and attachment.* Unpublished doctoral dissertation, California School of Professional Psychology, Los Angeles, CA.

Morgenthau, T. & Pedersen, D. (March 5, 1984). A sniper in the schoolyard. *Newsweek, 33.*

Mowbray, C. T. (1988). Post-traumatic therapy for children who are victims of violence. In F. M. Ochberg (Ed.), *Post-traumatic therapy and victims of violence* (pp. 196–212). New York: Brunner/Mazel.

Nader, K. O. (1997). Assessing traumatic experiences in children. In I. P. Wilson & T. M. Keane (Eds.), *Assessing psychological trauma and PTSD* (pp. 291–348). New York: Guilford.

Nader, K. O., Pynoos, R., Fairbanks, L., & Frederick, C. (1990). Children's PTSD reactions one year after a sniper attack at their school. *American Journal of Psychiatry, 147,* 1526–1530.

National Institute of Mental Health. (n.d.). Post-traumatic stress disorder (PTSD). Retrieved July 7, 2013, from www.nimh.nih.gov/health/publications/post-traumatic-stress-disorder-ptsd/nimh_ptsd_booklet.pdf.

Pynoos, R. & Nader, K. O. (1989). Children's memory and proximity to violence. *Journal of the American Academy of Child and Adolescent Psychiatry, 28,* 236–241.

Pynoos, R. S. & Nader, K. O. (1998). Psychological first aid and treatment approach to children exposed to community violence: Research implications. *Journal of Traumatic Stress, 1,* 445–473.

Pynoos, R. S., Steinberg, A. M., & Goenjian, A. (1996). Traumatic stress in childhood and adolescence: Recent developments and current controversies. In B. A. van der Kolk, A. C. McFarlane, & L. Weisaeth (Eds.), *Traumatic stress* (pp. 331–358). New York: Guilford Press.

Weiss, D. (2007). The impact of event scale: Revised. In J. P. Wilson & C. S. Tang (Eds.), *Cross-cultural assessment of psychological trauma and PTSD* (pp. 219–238). New York: Springer.

8   Bereavement

Our knowledge of bereavement (and its corollaries grief and mourning) has undergone a major swing, akin to what Thomas Kuhn called a paradigm shift. Major figures predominantly responsible for this shift in thinking about bereavement include George Bonanno, Margaret Stroebe, Dennis Klass, and Robert Neimeyer. They have moved us from adherence to the long-standing model of human responses to bereavement initiated by Sigmund Freud, modified and expanded by Erich Lindemann, and challenged to a degree by John Bowlby. The approach in this chapter is to examine the material historically, starting with Freud's seminal ideas. Other topics to be reviewed are (a) the symptoms endemic to bereavement and (b) bereavement complicated by trauma. We begin with reflections on the effects of bereavement to obstruct an individual from achieving essential human sentiments needed for psychological fulfillment and mental health.

Leighton's Framework for Reflecting on the Impact of Bereavement

Alexander Leighton's sociocultural model was introduced in Chapter Four. Examples used to illustrate the model involved persons responding to bereavement. I now return to his sociocultural model as a means of examining the dynamism inherent in human grief and mourning. Leighton did not intend his model as an explanation of bereavement, but rather as an overarching framework for understanding the human personality's continual efforts to maintain healthy interaction with the environment and the issues that influence the development of psychiatric disorders. However, the sociocultural model is rich and nuanced in its review of the roles the individual and the community play in assisting or impeding a person from achieving psychological health, and one event Leighton used to illustrate the struggle for such health is bereavement.

The key concepts in Leighton's sociocultural model are laid out in Chapter Four. These concepts are the cross-section of the moment, temporal thickness, essential human strivings, the life arc, and community integration versus disintegration. A concept not presented in Chapter Four is a notion influenced by Leighton's acceptance of psychodynamic views of human personality. This concept is what Leighton termed "the essential psychical condition."

By this term Leighton meant a dynamic, ongoing human process to achieve the healthiest psychological functioning and that striving for such a condition focuses on attaining what Leighton termed "essential striving sentiments." None of us strives after abstract, general sentiments but rather after particular objects that embody one or more of the essential striving sentiments. Thus, a father may work hard to provide for the needs of his wife and children, enjoy a mature bond with his wife, offer his children both nurturance and discipline, and understand that by being a good husband and father he is part of a meaningful social order. Surely among the essential striving sentiments involved in this man's case are achieving physical security, obtaining sexual satisfaction, expressing and receiving love, and being oriented in terms of his place in society and in relationship to others.

Because of the dynamism that characterizes our being in the world, humans are constantly in the process of gaining, losing, and regaining essential striving sentiments. A singular reason such striving can be obstructed is when a cross-section of the moment—in the case of the father mentioned earlier, the death of the man's son—presents obstacles to achieving the sentiments that matter most to an individual. Working through the obstacles, in this case coping with bereavement, is a matter both of individual style and community presence. Insecure, doubting individuals in marginal relationships struggle to take initiative, whereas persons with self-belief and secure attachments to others—particularly, a coherent community such as constructed in a loving family—are empowered to grapple with the loss they have experienced. How we grapple with loss is the subject of the next section in this chapter, namely, the various models that have been devised to explain human responses to bereavement. At the end of this chapter, I intend to return to Leighton's model as a fertile set of ideas for assessing both the impact of bereavement over time and the transformations that grieving can produce.

Three Traditional Models of Bereavement

The Contribution of Sigmund Freud

Two names recognized by any educated person in the West are Sigmund Freud and Albert Einstein. While the intricacies and formidable challenges inherent in the scholarship of each man typically elude many persons, these men have become cultural icons of genius whose ideas remain influential, both inside their respective areas of work and within the wider culture.

Freud understood grief and mourning are normal human responses to an irreparable loss, particularly to the death of someone with whom one had deep emotional investment. He thought bereavement and its sequelae to be a prototype of the misfortunes that beset human beings, and he considered persons have the wherewithal to manage the distress and turmoil that bereavement causes. He believed recovery from bereavement is not only possible but normal; however, the steps for such recovery occur only with considerable difficulty. The steps he identified for achieving recovery from bereavement have come down to us as "the grief work theory."

What Freud Said Successful Coping with Bereavement Entails. The death of someone loved creates a rupture between what the grieving person wants to be true and what the person knows is true. In short, Freud used his notion of two of the mental processes that comprise human personality and activity, namely, the id and the ego, to explain why coping with bereavement is so difficult. The id received pleasure from relating with the person, has a deep emotional investment in retaining that relationship, and vigorously struggles against any notion that the relationship has ended. In Freud's technical vocabulary, the id found in the relationship an outlet for libidinal energy (primarily sex and love) and strongly connected with (that is, "cathected to") that relationship. Freud called the energy "the libido" and intrapsychic connections between the id and the other person he called "cathexis." Even though the relationship has been irrevocably ended, Freud wrote the id keeps attempting to keep the connection intact. The task for the ego during bereavement is to shape the id's acceptance that (a) the death has occurred, (b) the death removes from possibility the satisfactions gained when the person was alive, and thus (c) the id needs to withdraw its libidinal connections from that outlet. The hard work of grieving is how the ego accomplishes such acceptance on the part of the id.

Freud

This grief work requires three emotionally challenging tasks. One task is for the griever to experience the distress that the death causes. The grieving individual is expected to consciously and deliberately expose him- or herself to all reminders that stir up grief over the death. A person looks at pictures of the dead person, listens to music that elicits memories, goes to places special to the relationship, and opens him- or herself to the emotionally wrenching realization that the person is gone forever. Contemporary psychologists would consider such perseverating activity rumination. For Freud, the purpose is to remove gradually the intrapsychic emotional hold that all these reminders have on the griever.

A second task in Freud's work of grieving is to detach emotionally from the person who died. Freud placed a technical meaning on what he calls detachment; in short, he was arguing that the issue of grieving occurs intrapsychically, and thus the challenge is for the id to let go its tenacious hold on a relationship that no longer had any prospect of reciprocity. Popular understanding of this step in Freud's model of grief ignores the notion of the id's severing its libidinal connections as a necessary condition for recovery. Popular notions consider that the call is to let go of any love or caring for the person who died. I am convinced Freud did not have such a popular notion in mind; in letters Freud wrote and some technical papers he published after his first discussion of bereavement, Freud acknowledged that he held warm, strong feelings for persons who had been taken forever from his life (his daughter Sophie for instance). Freud called for reshaping the attachment one had to the person, not obliterating that attachment.

And thus a third task in Freud's idea of grief work is to form a mental representation of the person who died. This memory store allows a person to think about the person without the pangs of grief intruding. It is not that the mental representation is emotionally neutral so much as the memory is free of the id's incessant clamor for the person still to be alive. This mental representation is the reshaping of the id's libidinal connection to an ego-constructed memory.

Accomplishing these three tasks takes place only over time, and in Freud's estimation occurs as a natural process. People who are bereaved engage in this process as the normal means the human mind has evolved to deal with bereavement. A person beset by bereavement does not need professional help, and according to Freud referring someone who is grieving for such help is contraindicated. In Freud's assessment, grief becomes resolved with the passage of time. Efforts to intervene he considered futile or even posed hazards. He did recognize that some persons' responses are outside this normal pattern of recovery, and for these persons whose grief is enduring and resisting amelioration, Freud did understand the value of professional intervention.

Further, Freud was intrigued by the resemblance between grief and clinical depression. However, he considered this resemblance misleading, and he cautioned that at its core grief was nothing like depression. To paraphrase Freud, the bereaved individual finds nothing worthwhile or enjoyable in the world whereas the depressed individual finds nothing worthwhile or enjoyable in himself. While the intensity and duration of grief would naturally lead an observer to conclude that the reactions are disturbingly abnormal, Freud countered that his experience with bereavement had taught him that such intense, long-lasting reactions are the normal response to an irreparable loss.

Erich Lindemann's Contribution to the Grief Work Theory

Erich Lindemann was a psychiatrist who taught at Harvard University and practiced at Massachusetts General Hospital. His major contributions were made from the 1940s into the 1960s. Along with Alexander Leighton and Gerald Caplan, Lindemann was a key figure in the ideas that led to the community health movement. His work with grieving individuals led to a paper with remarkable influence on our understanding of bereavement (Lindemann, 1944), particularly our knowledge of grief responses in the first weeks and months after a death.

Lindemann and his clinical team of psychiatrists, clinical psychologists, nurses, and social workers were tasked with working with persons grieving the deaths of family members and friends who had died in the conflagration that engulfed Boston's Cocoanut Grove Restaurant on November 28, 1942. Nearly 500 persons died in this fire, and until the burning of the Twin Towers in 2001, the fire remained the worst such disaster in the United States, easily outdistancing the 146 deaths that occurred in the Triangle Shirt Factory fire of 1911.

Wondering how to approach this task of assisting the persons affected by the Cocoanut Grove fire, Lindemann turned for direction to Freud's writings on bereavement. Lindemann laid out the steps Freud asserted account for recovery when bereaved, is credited with naming this process "the grief work theory," chose to intervene in an arena Freud said did not call for intervention, and made a lasting contribution with his identification of an acute grief syndrome. Lindemann also identified the work being done with these grieving individuals was but a precursor of demands that would be made in American society due to the numerous deaths sure to accrue as the United States fought World War II.

The Acute Grief Syndrome. Reflecting on the 101 persons treated by his clinical team, Lindemann noted that there were some remarkable consistencies in the thoughts, behavior, and emotions of these grieving patients in the first several months of their bereavement. Culling through the massive amount of data recorded about interactions with these persons, Lindemann noted patterns that he termed "an acute grief syndrome."[1] This synthesis of information produced a map of what to look for when entering the terrain of someone recently bereaved. The syndrome identified responses endemic to grief, and thus provided clinicians a useful conceptual framework (a) for understanding what are normal grief reactions and (b) for assessing changes over time in terms of amelioration of these reactions. The duration of a person's acute grief was seen to hover around 2 to 3 months, thus giving a yardstick for identifying if someone is stuck in grief (what we now term respectively "a prolonged grief disorder" or "an enduring grief trajectory").

The four main points Lindemann makes in his paper are:

1. Acute grief is a definite syndrome with psychological and somatic symptoms.
2. The syndrome of acute grief may appear in one of three manners:
   a. immediately after a crisis
   b. after the passage of time
   c. in an exaggerated fashion

   If acute grief is completely absent, there would also be concerns for complicated grief.

3. Whereas acute grief has a typical set of symptoms, in some cases unusual responses representing an individual aspect of the syndrome appear.
4. Appropriate clinical techniques can transform these distorted pictures into a normal grief reaction with resolution.

The elements of the acute grief syndrome include specified thoughts, behaviors, and emotions. Table 8.1 provides a listing of these elements.

The Course and Duration of Acute Grief. How long the acute grief syndrome lasts depends on "the success with which a person does the *grief work,* namely, emancipation from the bondage to the deceased, readjustment to the environment in which the deceased is missing, and the formation of new relationships" (Lindemann, 1944, p. 143) (italics in Lindemann's article).

Table 8.1 The Acute Grief Syndrome

---

1. Sensations of somatic distress that occurred in waves lasting from 20 to 60 minutes, receding, and then returning—for instance, tightness in the throat, choking and shortness of breath, continual sighing, empty feelings in one's stomach, intense headaches, constant exhaustion and fatigue.
2. A sense of unreality—something had to be wrong since everything in the world seemed normal even though an irreparable loss had occurred.
3. Increased emotional distance from other persons.
4. Intense preoccupation with images of the person who had died.
5. Feelings of guilt—for instance, searching for something prior to the death that indicated personal negligence caused the death.
6. Irritability, anger, lack of warmth toward others, even outbursts of hostility that both surprised the bereaved person and led to questions of losing sanity.
7. Loss of patterns of conduct, manifested in several ways:
   a. Agitated restlessness
   b. Aimlessness
   c. Inability to remain focused
   d. Difficulty making decisions
   e. Lack of initiative
   f. Going through the motions, with no zest for living

According to Lindemann, it is absolutely essential for bereaved persons to feel the intense distress bereavement produces and to openly express the feelings that grief stimulates. You will recall that Freud said resolution of bereavement required a person to encounter all reminders of the deceased person until emotional attachment had been withdrawn fully from the person. Lindemann added the requirement that persons need to give vocal expression to their grief, and he noted that men particularly resisted open expression of grief and that many patients, both men and women, prefer to avoid the "intense distress connected with the grief experience" (p. 143).

You may have noted something else that Lindemann added, something that Freud said was not needed unless you were facing bereavement that had turned pathological. Freud had said that "Although mourning involves grave departures from the normal attitude to life, it never occurs to us to regard it as a pathological condition and to refer it to medical treatment" (Freud, 1957/1917, pp. 243–244). Lindemann placed all these persons with acute grief in treatment. That change to provide professional intervention in cases of bereavement is a legacy Lindemann gave to the mental health profession. Later in this book when discussing interventions and the debate over the efficacy of grief counseling, we will return to Freud's admonition that such interventions were not only of no benefit but could prove harmful.

Lindemann said the chief task for the bereaved is to engage in grief work, which means "extricating oneself from bondage to the deceased and finding new patterns of rewarding interaction" (1944, p. 147). People need more than comfort and more than the passage of time to recover from bereavement. Lindemann said recovering from bereavement requires eight separate tasks, all tied to grief work:

1. Accept the distressing pain of bereavement.
2. Review one's relationship with the person who died.
3. Work through the fears of going insane triggered by surprising, intense responses (such as unexpected outbursts of hostility).
4. Understand changes in emotional responses since the death.
5. Give expression to one's sorrow.
6. Construct an acceptable relationship to the person who died (perhaps Lindemann is referring to Freud's mental representation of the deceased).
7. Express feelings of guilt.
8. Find others who will stimulate acquiring new patterns of behavior.

How long did the bereaved person need to engage in grief work in order for the acute grief syndrome to diminish? Lindemann said acute grief resolved in 4 to 6 weeks when the psychiatrist and the patient met 8 to 10 times and the bereaved person confronted the distress bereavement caused and openly expressed feelings. One question I have goes to the heart of Lindemann's evaluation of the effectiveness of his intervention: Because acute grief typically diminishes within 2 to 3 months of a death and the long duration of normal grief then sets in, isn't it likely that what Lindemann reported would have happened in a few more weeks without any influence from his efforts? There is also the issue whether the persons grieving the deaths caused in the Cocoanut Grove Restaurant fire were also dealing with an overlay of trauma. Later in this chapter we look at the issues raised when bereaved individuals are also traumatized.

John Bowlby's Appeal to Attachment Theory

While Erich Lindemann was working out his ideas on bereavement, grief, and mourning, a British psychiatrist named John Bowlby was studying the effects of separation from parents that had occurred in England during World War II when the government removed children from urban areas to prevent them from being killed during the Nazi bombing campaign. This detailed research provided the ground work for his comprehensive thinking about human responses to loss. Instead of using psychoanalysis's appeal to intrapsychic struggles between the id and ego as the basis for human grief responses,[2] Bowlby appealed to ethology, which demonstrated that the survival of mammals depends on close bonds established between infants and caregivers. Caregivers and their young, vulnerable dependents become attached to each other.

Such attachment bonds become prominent in higher order mammals, and there is a mutuality to the bond: it is not just that the child is attached to the parent or the parent to the child, but their relationship is defined by a mutuality of attachment bonds. These attachment bonds are biologically wired, so to speak, into the human species (as well as other mammalian species), and they form a survival function: the attachment bonds enable the vulnerable young to be protected, to learn, and to grow to adulthood. The types of attachment bonds a youngster has with caregivers greatly influence the kinds of attachments that the youngster will form with others over his or her life span; in Bowlby's terms, an infant's experience of attachment produces cognitive schemas of what to expect from others and how to interact with others.[3]

Psychologists interested in child development have grabbed up the ideas that attachment theory suggests, and have used the theory as a means to explore and to explain human development in childhood. One of the most influential of these researchers was Mary Ainsworth, a colleague Bowlby acknowledged with respect, who constructed some strict protocols for measuring the impact on 12- to 18-month-old children when their mothers are present or absent and a stranger is in the room. She called her research design "the Strange Situation," in which young children and their mothers enter a room where there are toys. "There is a series of separations and reunions where the mother and child are first alone in the room and then the researcher enters, and after a few minutes, the mother leaves. A few minutes later, the mother returns and the researcher observes the child's reaction to this return" (Retrieved March 25, 2013, from www.webster .edu/~woolflm/ainsworth.html).

From her work emerged the notion of various types of attachment bonds: a secure bond, an anxious/avoidant bond, and an anxious/resistant bond. "Secure infants either seek proximity or contact or else greet the parent at a distance with a smile or wave. Avoidant infants avoid the parent. Resistant/ambivalent infants either passively or actively show hostility toward the parent." (Retrieved March 25, 2013 from www .personalityresearch.org/attachment.html)

Perhaps you have seen the direction that Bowlby's thinking was taking him to explain bereavement and its consequences. Bowlby explained bereavement, grief, and mourning as the responses that naturally occur when bonds of attachment are sundered. Whereas Freud explained bereavement as the natural consequence of refusal to accept that an object of libidinal investment was lost forever, Bowlby said bereavement occurred due to the irreparable rupture of attachment bonds. In Freud's thinking, without intrapsychic libidinal cathexis, there would be no bereavement; in Bowlby's thinking, without attachment bonds to someone in the external world, there would be no bereavement.

The empirical data demonstrating various types of attachment bonds have come to influence greatly current thinking about responses to bereavement. Secure attachments have been found to influence normal bereavement responses; insecure attachments complicate resolution of bereavement.

Types of attachment in league with different styles of coping with distress are seen to produce different responses to bereavement. Bereaved persons whose bond to the deceased had been a secure attachment are flexible in response to their loss; persons with insecure attachments (either of an avoidant or a resistant/ambivalent type) exhibit constrained thinking and action. In particular, insecure attachments are seen to produce bereavement complications. One such complication is difficulty constructing the meaning of the loss. Meaning reconstruction in the face of bereavement is at the heart of the thinking of several influential scholars (Stroebe, Schut, Neimeyer, Attig, and Kauffman are prime examples). More on meaning making and bereavement is coming up later in the chapter.

Phases of Mourning. Bowlby—along with Colin Murray Parkes—described the process of recovery from bereavement as a series of phases that involve protests and shock over sundered attachment bonds, yearning for reunion with the person who was missing, loss of hope when it becomes clear that such a reunion is out of the question, and finally reengaging in the world and with other persons. Lillian Range (2007, p. 270) eloquently summarized these phases: ". . . death of a loved one requires reorganization of attachments, a process that progresses through four phases: experiencing and expressing outside of oneself the reality of the death, tolerating the emotional suffering inherent in the grief while physically and emotionally nurturing oneself, converting the relationship with the deceased to a memory, and developing a sense of identity based on a life without the deceased."

Here in a bit more detail are descriptions of these phases.

1. *Numbing.* In this first phase, the bereaved person seems incapable of comprehending the loss. A person will say such things as, "I can't believe this has happened" or "It can't be true."
2. *Yearning or searching.* In the second phase, the bereaved person seems preoccupied with thoughts and feelings about the deceased. There is what Bowlby considered a "desire to recover the person who is now gone" (Cook & Oltjenbruns, 1989, p. 48). Sounds in the house will prompt thoughts that the person has returned. Someone who resembles the dead person may lead the bereaved individual to think they are seeing the one they miss. The phone will ring, and the person will initially think the call is from the person they miss.
3. *Disorganization and despair.* This third phase emerges as the bereaved person realizes the dead person cannot be recovered. Apathy may set in as the person struggles to find ways to cope with an irreparable loss. The challenge is to discard patterns of thinking, feeling, and acting. The person feels helpless and can become very vulnerable to bad advice or to unscrupulous individuals who prey on the bereaved. In the 2 weeks following my father's death, my mother received numerous phone calls

from realtors, all couched in words expressing a desire to help her in her time of trouble.

4. *Reorganization.* The fourth phase of Bowlby's model denotes a time when a person begins redefining his or her identity and place in the world. Not uncommonly such reorganization requires learning new roles, as when a middle-aged widow returns to the work force after a 20-year absence or a widower learns how to cook and do laundry. Reorganization can be ascribed to the actions of bereaved adolescents when they emotionally reinvest in life goals, make a career choice and pursue it, or simply accept that their dead brother or sister would want them to make the most of the life ahead of them.

Recent Thinking Extending, Modifying, or Challenging the Traditional Models of Bereavement

Worden's Tasks of Mourning

The American clinical psychologist J. William Worden made at least two enduring contributions to our knowledge of bereavement, grief, and mourning. One of his contributions is the action framework he devised as the tasks that naturally and necessarily people engage as they cope with bereavement; he has revised the model as he reflected on research data and clinical experience. The other contribution he accomplished when collaborating with Phyllis R. Silverman: they completed a respected longitudinal study of childhood and adolescent bereavement following the death of a parent. Worden's task-based model is a focus of this chapter; the results of the longitudinal work are presented principally in Chapter Nine.

The first presentations of Worden's task model involve straightforward actions that put into operation Lindemann's understanding of how grieving persons manage bereavement. In short, Worden's tasks present the steps whereby Lindemann operationalized the grief work theory. Worden's connections with Lindemann encompass conceptual frameworks (namely, the grief work model), academic environments, and practice settings. As had Lindemann when completing his work about bereavement, Worden was a member of the faculty at Harvard and on the staff of Massachusetts General Hospital when he devised his task-based model. However, in personal conversation, Worden told me his work on the tasks of mourning was much more influenced by contact with Colin Murray Parkes, who was in Boston completing a longitudinal study of widows and bereavement in the 1960s.

Worden revised some aspects of his tasks as new evidence presented itself, and now the model seems an amalgam of the grief work theory and continuing bonds. Here is the first construction he gave to tasks to be accomplished to manage bereavement.

In his first edition of his book (Worden, 1982), Worden's four tasks were to

1. Accept the reality of the loss.
2. Work through to the pain of grief.
3. Adjust to an environment in which the deceased is missing.
4. Withdraw emotional energy and reinvest it in another relationship.

Enduring relationship in absence

Because of fairly persuasive empirical and conceptual challenges from Dennis Klass, a researcher who has studied bereaved parents for over 25 years, and from his research colleague, Phyllis Silverman, Worden revised the fourth task in the second edition of his book. Klass showed that for many if not all of the parents he had come to know, they did accomplish tasks 1 through 3 but remained emotionally attached to the child who had died. On the same score, a woman I know whose husband died in a car accident said she absolutely refused to accept the initial version of task 4: "If that is what recovery from bereavement means, then the hell with it" was her statement when she read task 4 in Worden's 1982 task-based model.

The revised task four in Worden's 2002 model reads, "To emotionally relocate the deceased and move on with life" (p. 35). The rephrasing actually adheres strongly to Freud's overall idea of letting go and forming a mental representation. More recently, Worden radically altered the phrasing of task 4. The wording now is "To find an enduring connection with the deceased in the midst of embarking on a new life" (Worden, 2009, p. 60). This new phrasing represents a bow in the direction of what is called "continuing bonds" and incorporates Bowlby's fourth phase of bereavement recovery, namely, reorganization in which a person gets a renewed interest in being alive. In short, Worden now presents coping with bereavement as a combination of the grief work theory, continuing bonds, and Bowlby.[4]

Commentators see Worden's task-based model provides a significant advance over the phases of mourning described by Bowlby. One aspect that critics like about Worden's approach over their criticism of the phase models of grieving is that tasks to accomplish make grieving a proactive process. The phases describe a passive process requiring only endurance and sufficient time. In short, the critics say the phase models liken grieving to a car wash in which a dirty vehicle is linked to a line that pulls the car through, requiring no effort on the part of the vehicle's owner except to sit patiently in the car.[5] Working on the tasks provides a renewed sense of control, a sense of autonomy. Coping with grief in terms of tasks to accomplish probably explains in part the appeal of this model to Americans who appreciate a pragmatic focus on things to do.

The Argument for Continuing Bonds

The construct "continuing bonds" leaped onto the stage of bereavement scholarship and clinical practice and received an enthusiastic welcome. Dennis Klass was a primary figure in bringing the idea of continuing bonds to the forefront of thanatology. Other prominent figures were Phyllis Silverman and Nancy Hogan.

The basic idea is that maintaining ties to the deceased is a common, even normal, human response to being bereaved. The idea of maintaining bonds to the deceased challenges the long-standing notion from the grief work theory that grievers must sever emotional ties in order to recover from bereavement. Initially, continuing bonds was presented as a needed corrective to the sweeping generalization that persons would recover from bereavement only if they relinquished their emotional investment in the person who had died. Ongoing attachments in mainstream clinical practice were considered signs of pathology. The advocates of continuing bonds argued that some persons coped well and yet maintained an ongoing attachment to the dead person. However, rather shortly, the mantra stated that failure to maintain a continuing bond was a sign of pathology.

A small core of thanatology scholars remained skeptical of the uncritical bandwagon endorsement of continuing bonds. Eventually, some rigorous research began examining bereavement outcomes tied to type of attachment bonds the griever had formed with the deceased before the death. Type of attachment has emerged as a salient matter for coping with bereavement. Secure attachments formed before the death are closely associated with healthy bereavement resolution marked by continuing bonds. However, anxious, ambivalent, and hostile attachments formed prior to the death make ongoing, continuing bonds problematic for grief recovery; insecure attachments, in short, are better for the griever if relinquished.

The Dual Process Model of Coping with Loss

Margaret Stroebe and her research colleagues at the University of Utrecht have consistently made noteworthy contributions to thanatology. One of the more important contributions has been the notion that the natural process of coping with bereavement involves moving back and forth between (a) confronting the distress that bereavement produces and (b) engaging in living. The dual process model is a modification of the idea that coping with bereavement requires constant, conscious, and effortful focus on the pain bereavement causes. In short, the dual process model is a refinement to the grief work theory.

Eager acceptance from clinicians and researchers greeted the dual process model. It was as though the obvious had been hidden and was now disclosed. A similar reaction occurred with the publication and discussion of the continuing bonds model.

Work with bereaved persons indicates two distinct processes, not merely a confrontation with distress, enable bereaved persons to adapt to their loss. Stroebe and Schut acknowledge that the grief work hypothesis is correct as far as it goes, namely, it is important at times to focus on the distress of one's loss. However, it is also important to attend to other aspects of life. Stroebe and Schut proposed that part of bereavement requires us to have a loss orientation (the grief work notion) and also to have a restoration orientation (life goes on). Bereaved persons oscillate between these orientations as they deal with their bereavement. See Figure 8.1 for an illustration of the oscillation process the dual process model presents. This oscillation is normal; it is what people do naturally. A bereavement care program that emphasized only the grief work hypothesis would be incomplete.

The Two-Track Model of Grieving

Simon Shimshon Rubin, an American clinical psychologist now living in Israel, introduced in 1981 a model of coping with bereavement called the Two-Track Model of Grieving. This model emphasizes the multidimensionality of bereavement, and one can find in it aspects of the holistic framework, of the fundamental relationships highlighted in existential phenomenology, and of the grief work theory. I am sure that there are aspects as well of narrative therapy, of the dual process model, and of continuing bonds.

Track 1 of the Two-Track Model centers on biopsychosocial functioning, such as feelings of anxiety, somatic issues, interpersonal relationships, self-concept, and work. This track clearly incorporates the features of Lindemann's acute grief syndrome; for

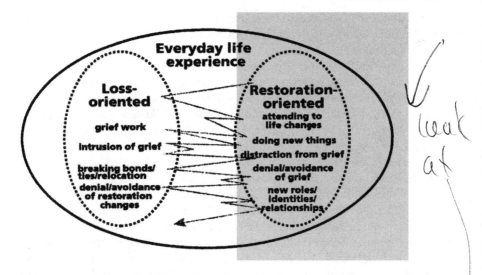

Figure 8.1 The Dual Process Model

instance, it includes Lindemann's focus on somatic distress, emotional distance, feelings of guilt, and loss of patterns of conduct. The track emphasizes the importance of a meaning structure, and thus incorporates narrative therapy, especially as more recently elaborated in Neimeyer's notion of meaning making, and the emphasis in existential phenomenology on relearning fundamental relationships to others and the world. The outcome desired from successful coping in Track 1 is healthy functioning in the world.

Track 2 of the Two-Track Model centers on the development of a healthy relationship to the deceased. What seems most at stake in this track is giving full play to the ideas Freud put forth in his writings about coping with bereavement. There is considerable emphasis on use of imagery and building accessible memories of the deceased; the griever must come to terms with negative feelings linked to the person who died, and deal with the distress that the loss stirs in one's mind and body. The outcomes expected from successful coping in Track 2 include an ongoing bond to the deceased, a coherent account of the death story, and a new life narrative. One can find in Track 2 elements faithful to existential phenomenology's notion of relearning one's relationship to oneself.

Successfully dealing with the demands of each track requires an adaptive process that takes time and is emotionally wrenching. It is possible for a griever to cope very well in one of the tracks but struggle to cope in the other. Difficulties resolving either of the tracks hold forth keys to intervention, and the goals and strategies of interventions can be established by a comprehensive assessment of the aspects in either track that the griever is not attending to.

Trajectories of Bereavement

George Bonanno is a stress researcher at Columbia University who has challenged assumptions about bereavement that were held for most of the 20th century. One of his major contributions has been identifying three separate bereavement trajectories. The three paths are (a) a resiliency trajectory, (b) a recovery trajectory, and (c) an enduring grief trajectory. I will discuss each in turn. First, we will look at what has been uncovered about the resiliency trajectory.

Of great surprise to many scholars, the plurality of grieving persons whose bereavement trajectories have been studied follow a path that shows initial difficulty with intense sadness but fairly quick resiliency and low symptoms of grief; by quick it is meant a return to normal functioning within a couple of weeks following the death. In some studies, the persons in this trajectory form a majority of bereaved individuals. The proportions of bereaved persons in this trajectory range from slightly under 50% in some studies to nearly 60% in others. These persons find happiness and solace when thinking about or talking about the person who died. For them the grief process produces comfort. This path following bereavement has been named the *resilient* trajectory.

Consider the case of Joanne, a 22-year-old college senior I knew at Oklahoma State University, whose father died suddenly of a heart attack. Her father's death bothered her, but it presented no challenge to her assumptive world. She believed firmly in her Mormon faith. She continued with her classes, did well in her courses, graduated on time, and found a job related to her college major. She had a very secure bond with her mother, whom she saw often and to whom she had introduced me at a college function several months before her father's death. A few weeks into her bereavement, Joanne approached me on behalf of her mother, who wondered if there were any books I could recommend for her to read. I suggested Attig's *How We Grieve,* and a few months later Joanne told me that her mother had found the book very helpful. When she graduated, Joanne came to my office and gave to me a treasure that she said had proven enormously helpful to her, *The Book of Mormon.*

Another bereavement trajectory that many scholars have long assumed was that the more typical path is found in 40 to 44% of grieving persons. This trajectory involves sadness, anxiety, guilt, confusion, and other intense symptoms that last for several months, even beyond a year following the death, eventually leveling off to a noticeably improved situation. This path was for years assumed to be the expected course of grief. It has been called the *recovery* trajectory.

Roberto was a 19-year-old college sophomore I met at Brooklyn College, and he provides an example of someone in the recovery trajectory. His family had moved to New York City from Puerto Rico when he was a baby. Roberto was a devout Roman Catholic who was grieving the death of his grandfather due to an illness. The death had occurred not quite 9 months ago. Several aspects of his bereavement indicated that it either distressed him moderately or in some cases quite a bit. For example, Roberto said he was having some troubles staying asleep, he felt irritable and got angry quite a bit since the death, and he frequently had intrusive thoughts about his grandfather's death. He experienced troubles concentrating and acknowledged he had yet to deal with a lot of feelings about the death. He was managing his course work, though problems concentrating got in the way, and he had a 30-hour-a-week job to boot. On top of his grandfather's death, in the past year Roberto had experienced the end of a close friendship and the death of his dog.

A third bereavement trajectory, one of unremitting distress, accounts for the experience of approximately 15% of grieving persons. For these persons their acute grief never lessens. They may well experience clinical depression in response to the death, and their grief symptoms remain intense. Only professional intervention seems able to assist persons in this trajectory. This complicated bereavement path has been called the *enduring grief* trajectory.

Marie, a 20-year-old who had been majoring in biology with the intent to enter veterinary school, offers a glimpse into the emotionally wrenching experience of someone caught in the enduring grief trajectory. Her mother died following a 2-year battle with breast cancer. Not quite 9 months later, Marie still found her mother's death impossible to accept. It was as though an essential part of her had also died. She felt bitter and angry about the suffering her mother had experienced and the inability of the medical profession to find a cure. She no longer had any zest for living and walked around seemingly dazed and emotionally numb. She daily longed for her mother's presence and consciously avoided any reminder of the death. She had dropped out of school, stopped seeing her friends, and found it difficult to trust other people. There seemed no point in making plans for a better tomorrow such as getting good grades so that she would gain admittance to a veterinary college.

Existential Phenomenology Applied to Bereavement

In the late 1950s, Rollo May and his colleagues introduced Americans to the use of existential phenomenology in psychiatry and psychology. Existential phenomenology asserts human existence at its core involves the lived experiences of relationships with the external world, with other persons, and with oneself.

Tom Attig, a gifted philosopher who founded the graduate program in practical philosophy at Bowling Green State University, has used the lens of existential phenomenology to unravel what grieving entails. See his book *How We Grieve*. In my estimation *How We Grieve* is the best single volume to give a bereaved person who is looking for a book to read about bereavement, grief, and mourning.

Attig maintains that grieving involves relearning our relationships to the world, other persons, and ourselves. The features of the acute grief syndrome provide examples that illustrate the disruptions bereavement wreaks on these three fundamental relationships. Bereavement can seriously disrupt a person's normal functioning in everyday affairs (consider the loss of patterns of conduct), interactions with other persons (consider the emotional distance from other people), and self-perceptions (consider the sense of unreality).

Attig makes fundamental distinctions between bereavement and grieving. Bereavement is something that happens to you. A loss is inflicted on you. Grieving can also remain passive, but Attig argues it can and should become an active choice. Whereas humans are thrust into bereavement, we are then left with choosing how to respond.

Active grieving involves relearning our relationships to the world, other persons, and oneself. Grievers don't simply learn information. What occurs in active grieving is making sense of our human existence by

- Relearning our place in the wider world and how we may shape this world into which we are thrown, grievers must come to terms with places and objects that bring to mind their loss. They must come to terms with what Worden calls an environment in which the deceased is missing. They must reengage in the wider world and in making a living. Part of relearning our relationship with the world is expressed well in the restoration orientation of the dual process model.

- Relearning our social surroundings, not only who we are in relation to the person who died but also who we are in relation to the people in our lives. Part of this relearning our relations with other people encompasses assessing the relationship we had with the person who died. Part of this relearning means forming new relationships.
- Relearning our selves by examining what we care for, our core set of beliefs, and by framing our own biography now that a person we cared for has died. Bereavement can shatter a person's assumptions about existence and undermine confidence in accomplishing things that matter.

Disenfranchised Grief

To be disenfranchised means to be deprived of a right. In politics, to be disenfranchised means to be deprived of the right to vote. A substantial goal in the civil rights struggle in the United States has been to remove rules and practices that take away people's right to vote.

The term *disenfranchised* has been applied to certain circumstances involving bereavement, grief, and mourning. The term is being applied to certain losses considered outside the bounds for grieving. Social pressure is applied against feeling grief, expressing mourning, or being bereaved over the loss of some relationships deemed marginal, illicit, or illegitimate. Examples include the death of a pet, a miscarriage, and an abortion. The death of a mistress, of an ex-spouse, or of a criminal executed for heinous crimes are other examples. In some milieus protecting oneself from any show of vulnerability militates against expressing grief over a loss; an example is the experience of incarcerated females who keep tight reins on reactions to the loss of a family member on the outside.

Disenfranchisement may lead to social isolation and exacerbate feelings of guilt, depression, and anger. Lacking acceptable outlets for expressing, communicating, and receiving support places grievers in the place Shakespeare depicted in *Macbeth (IV.iii.245– 246):* "The grief that does not speak whispers the o'er-fraught heart, and bids it break."

Disenfranchised grief spills over to sanctions even against recognized or accepted losses. Consider the anxiety and discomfort that persons unaffected by a loss manifest when in the presence of someone who is bereaved over the death of a family member. Adolescents and young adults learn that peers become impatient and intolerant of ongoing grief. The grieving middle school student, high school student, and college student learns to camouflage grief in order to maintain a social circle.

Instrumental and Intuitive Approaches to Grieving

The grief work theory maintains that effortful, conscious, planned confrontations with the distress that bereavement causes is essential for a person to recover from irreparable loss. We have already seen that the dual process model has introduced a modification to the grief work model, namely, with the assertion that the normal process of grieving involves oscillating back and forth from confronting the distress and avoiding the distress.

Ken Doka and his colleague Terry Martin have introduced another notion that requires modification of the grief work theory. They have examined two distinct approaches to grieving: one they term "instrumental grieving," an approach that primarily involves inner reflection and external action, not focusing on the emotional distress or sharing how one feels; the other approach is termed "intuitive grieving," and it does involve primarily focusing on one's affect and talking about one's grief. While neither approach is the exclusive property of males or females, evidence indicates that males are more likely to engage grief instrumentally and females to engage grief intuitively.

There is the paradox that some bereaved persons who tend toward disclosure of feelings "adopt stoicism and curb their feelings" and some grievers who tend toward inner reflection and problem-solving "become disorganized and display their emotions (for instance, by crying)" (Balk, 2011, p. 48). Further, Doka and Martin noted that there are clear cases of approaches to grieving that involve a merging of intuitive and instrumental. Table 8.2 provides a side-by-side comparison/contrast of intuitive and instrumental approaches to grieving.[6]

One can see in this depiction of the intuitive approach to grieving the earlier work of a Yale psychologist, Susan Nolen-Hoeksema, who died much too early at the age of 53. She studied the propensity of females to ruminate about distressing experiences rather than engage in problem-solving action; Nolen-Hoeksema said men were much less likely to fall victim to rumination and much more likely to engage in action to resolve distressing problems. By ruminating on distressing situations, women were inclined to become depressed, to engage in constant negative attributions about self, and overthink matters troubling them. It is impossible to ignore the distinct challenge that Nolen-Hoeksema's analysis presents not only to the grief work theory but also to the idea that intuitive grieving is a fortunate state of affairs; Freud and Lindemann asserted that recovery from bereavement demands openly focusing on what was distressing. Nolen-Hoeksema's research as well as the evidence of an instrumental approach to grieving can also be seen as a direct challenge to Lindemann's assertion that recovery from bereavement requires persons to talk about their feelings.

Table 8.2 Intuitive and Instrumental Grieving Compared

Intuitive	Instrumental
Bereavement experienced affectively	Bereavement experienced cognitively
Outwardly express grief	Focus on mastering one's situation
Share with others one's feelings	General reluctance to discuss feelings
Primary strategy: experience the distress bereavement produces	Primary strategy is to problem solve and conceptualize
Secondary strategy: care for others and fulfill responsibilities	Secondary strategy allows for expressing feelings in private
Prolonged periods of Lindemann's acute grief syndrome	Intermittent, brief periods of cognitive confusion

Source: Taken directly from Balk, 2011, p. 49. Reproduced with the permission of Springer Publishing Company, LLC.

Bereavement Recovery as Restoration of Meaning

Considerable attention has been directed to the place of meaning making in the act of grieving. The chief architect of this attention to meaning-making when bereaved is Robert Neimeyer, a clinical psychologist at the University of Memphis.

Focusing on meaning-making is an emphasis in cognitive models of coping with life crises. Meaning-making is at the heart of George Kelly's theory of personality development called "personal construct theory." There are linkages to attribution theory as well as self-efficacy theory, both outgrowths of the cognitive revolution that has overtaken psychology and clearly surpassed the influence of behaviorism upon the work and training of psychologists.

Neimeyer refers to meaning-making as "meaning reconstruction." By this cognitive work, he means the conscious pursuit of three activities that enable the griever to restore equilibrium and possibly to find growth and transformation in the midst of coping with irreparable loss. These three activities are (a) sense making, (b) benefit finding, and (c) identity change. It has struck me that persons whose grief is part of the recovery trajectory or the enduring grief trajectory would want to engage in meaning reconstruction. A person in the resiliency trajectory would seem to have no impetus for such meaning-making as the loss has not challenged the person's basic assumptions about existence. I remain open to changing this opinion should there be evidence indicating persons in the resiliency trajectory engage also in meaning reconstruction.

The following discussion of the three activities Neimeyer identifies as involved in meaning reconstruction occurred originally in the book *Helping the Bereaved College Student* on pp. 52–54. To repeat, the activities in meaning reconstruction are named sense making, benefit finding, and identity change.

Sense Making.   Neimeyer notes that difficult life experiences that fail to make sense are the ones that most challenge personal equanimity. They plant seeds of self-doubt and stir up mental and emotional turmoil. To regain a sense of predictability and control, the natural step is to find a reason for what happened.

In cases of bereavement, people look for information about how the death happened, and look for answers to why it happened, for answers how the death is going to impact life from now on, and perhaps for answers why this burden came to them. Thus sense making is a three-fold process for Neimeyer:

1.   The grieving person questions her bereavement.
2.   The grieving person looks for meaning in her loss.
3.   The grieving person makes sense of her bereavement.

In the third step, if making sense of the bereavement leads the griever to determine that the meaning corresponds to assumptions about reality, then she fits the experience into her overall constructs about existence. If, however, her assumptions about existence fly in the face of the experience she has had, then making sense requires her to construct a new sense of reality. Persons who search for meaning but find none are the most distressed grievers.

Some persons have asked, "Why can't some grieving persons find meaning?" I will identify some of the cases of persons left bereft of meaning when they search for it following a death, and perhaps inferring the difficulties involved will be apparent. Think of the parents of a child who is kidnapped, tortured, and killed by a serial killer. Think of parents whose apparently perfectly healthy infant dies in his sleep. Think of the college student whose best friend is killed in a drive-by shooting. In each case is it difficult to imagine the assault on beliefs in a moral order and a just world? What purpose could such a wanton death serve?

Benefit Finding. Coping theorists talk about "reframing" or "positive reappraisal." One form such benefit finding takes is becoming more attuned to letting other persons know they are loved. The notion that benefit finding comes quickly is dispelled by Neimeyer, who notes that some benefits emerge only over time as the person matures, gains experiences, reflects on her life, becomes more educated, and interacts with others.

A coping skill noted among persons dealing with life crises is pursuing alternative rewards. Such an example of benefit finding can be seen in the investment that some persons make in assisting individuals to manage similar events, for instance, the persons who start support groups for bereaved college students.

Identity Change. Reconstructing meaning in the face of bereavement, the prototypical life crisis, in effect, means constructing oneself anew. Responding to loss in adaptive ways can result in transformation or personal growth. Such growth does not mean anguish is eliminated. The person matures, gains a deeper perspective on the tragedy embedded in human existence, and becomes attuned to the suffering of others.

In constructivist theories of meaning making, it is the distress inherent in the bereavement that impels the person to attempt to make sense of a significant loss. The hypothesis proposed is that without distress there would be no need to make sense out of the loss. There is the prospect, however, that too much distress immobilizes efforts or depletes energy to search for what will make sense of the situation. There is also the possibility that some persons by temperament simply are not reflective and do not engage in sense making. Perhaps these persons are more likely to be, for instance, kinesthetic rather than self-reflective, and to become physically active when dealing with an event challenging their coping skills and presenting a threat to their well-being.

Making sense of a crisis seems to be more helpful when accomplished early in the process of coping. In fact, Neimeyer has concluded that benefit finding fortifies adjustment as the person's coping continues over time. However, decreases in distress are not the earmarks of personal growth or identity change for bereaved persons. They learn how better to deal with the tragic side of life, but such growth does not eradicate the distress inherent to bereavement.

Empirical studies have uncovered the unexpected finding that some bereaved persons who do not engage in a process of meaning making perform well on all measures of functioning (for instance, school work, job performance, personal relationships, spirituality). The concern that these persons are at risk for delayed grief reactions has been dispelled by Bonanno, whose extensive longitudinal research has uncovered no evidence that delayed grief occurs.

I noted earlier that there are some persons plagued because they cannot find any meaning in their loss, and this failure to make meaning out of the event has left them worse off than bereaved individuals for whom loss does not inspire them to search for meaning. The fact that some persons apparently would have been better off had they not needed to find meaning but looked for it and it eluded them underscores the constructivist ideas. The very fact of such painful outcomes to bereavement highlights that meaning making is central for these persons: they cannot find meaning and desperately want to, and if they could they would be able to deal with their loss.

However, the fact that meaning making is not central to the experience of some bereaved persons could be seen (but I think mistakenly) to challenge the constructivists' assertion. A plausible explanation leads us back to the ideas of George Kelly about personal constructs about reality. The reason some persons experience no need to reconstruct meaning out of a loss or even to look for meaning is that the experience of this loss is in accord with their constructs about reality. What happened does not challenge their assumptions about the world. Consider the case of a student whose brother dies in a high-speed car crash; she grieves his death, but she doesn't find the death out of synch with her expectations about this world: Physics indicates persons in vehicles that crash at high rates of speed are likely going to be hurt, even killed.

The Symptoms Endemic to Bereavement

Within the latter part of the 20th century and the early part of the 21st century, it dawned on some bereavement scholars that many studies of loss, grief, and mourning were confounding psychiatric symptoms of distress with what constitutes bereavement. Measures of psychiatric symptoms examine responses not specific to bereavement; these psychiatric symptoms are shared across a variety of groups experiencing distress. Nonspecific psychiatric symptom scales "systematically preclude assessments of psychosocial responses that are unique to loss, such as attachment difficulties signaled by missing the deceased" (Neimeyer & Hogan, 2001, p. 91). Numerous measures of psychological distress—such as measures of clinical depression and of anxiety—were being used to identify core bereavement phenomena and track the course of bereavement. For instance, although it is possible for some bereaved individuals to be depressed, the realization grew that (a) depression was not at the core of bereavement and (b) more careful analysis was needed to uncover the core phenomena.

Lindemann's acute grief syndrome provides an excellent start for what is at the core of bereavement: somatic distress, a sense of unreality, emotional distance, loss of patterns of conduct, impulsive irritability, preoccupation with thoughts about the deceased, and feelings of guilt. Some of the acute grief symptoms are also part of other psychological reactions; for example, somatic distress is also associated with clinical depression and somatoform disorders. Guilt is associated with PTSD and also with obsessive-compulsive behavior. It is the overall constellation of the symptoms, not individual manifestations, that sets apart the acute grief syndrome as a breakthrough in identifying grief.[7]

Identification of Core Bereavement Items

There is, however, still the nagging sense that the core of bereavement may be hidden within the symptoms of the acute grief syndrome. Researchers led by Beverly Raphael, the Australian psychiatrist, engaged in extensive work to uncover the symptoms at the core of bereavement. The longitudinal work included bereaved spouses, children, and parents: members of each group were given a self-report instrument whose items had been identified from reflections on clinical experience and review of relevant literature. Factor analytic tests identified 17 items grouped into three specific aspects: frequent thoughts and images of the deceased; a sense of acute separation; and distress related to reminders (termed "grief"). The 17 items are given in Table 8.3.

The response options for the items varied somewhat. For items 1, 2, 4, and 6 the choices were scaled on this four-point rating scale: Continuously, Quite a bit of the time, A little bit of the time, and Never. For items 3, 5, and 7 the four-point scale began with Always and then used the other three options of Quite a bit of the time, A little bit of the time, and Never. For items 8 through 17 the choices were A lot of the time, Quite a bit of the time, A little bit of the time, and Never.

Expert assessment of the Core Bereavement Items (CBI) has been positive. While accepting the caution expressed by the authors of the CBI that more work is needed to validate the instrument, these experts note that the attention on core aspects of bereavement is a strength due to the credibility the items have for the majority of grievers; there

Table 8.3 Core Bereavement Items

Images and Thoughts

1. Do you experience images of the events surrounding *x*'s death?
2. Do thoughts of *x* come into your mind whether you wish it or not?
3. Do thoughts of *x* make you feel distressed?
4. Do you think about *x*?
5. Do images of *x* make you feel distressed?
6. Do you find yourself preoccupied with images or memories of *x*?
7. Do you find yourself thinking of a reunion with *x*?

Acute Separation

8. Do you find yourself missing *x*?
9. Are you reminded by familiar objects (photos, possessions, rooms, etc.) of *x*?
10. Do you find yourself pining for/yearning for *x*?
11. Do you find yourself looking for *x* in familiar places?
12. Do you feel distress/pain if for any reason you are confronted with the reality that *x* is not present/not coming back?

Grief

13. Do reminders of *x* such as photos, situations, music, places, and such cause you to feel longing for *x*?
14. Do reminders of *x* such as photos, situations, music, places, and such cause you to feel loneliness?
15. Do reminders of *x* such as photos, situations, music, places, and such cause you to cry about *x*?
16. Do reminders of *x* such as photos, situations, music, places, and such cause you to feel sadness?
17. Do reminders of *x* such as photos, situations, music, places, and such cause you to feel loss of enjoyment?

Source: Taken directly from Burnett, Middleton, Raphael, & Martinek, 1997, p. 56. Reproduced with permission of Cambridge University Press.

is concern that exclusion of less centrally important items such as feelings of unreality and anger is a limitation of the CBI. Overall, these experts concluded this inventory "is probably best suited to the study of 'normal' grief responses" (Neimeyer & Hogan, 2001, p. 98).

Other scholars have winnowed the essence of bereavement to yearning after the person who died, feeling intense pain over the loss, struggling to keep connected to the deceased, and attachment difficulties indicated by missing the person who died. You can find this sense of the core to bereavement in the work of clinical researchers working to identify what distinguishes complicated bereavement from normal.

The Hogan Grief Reaction Checklist

Another effort to measure responses endemic to bereavement is found in the Hogan Grief Reaction Checklist (HGRC). This self-report inventory contains 61 items and captures information on six distinct factors relevant to bereavement: despair, panic behavior, personal growth, blame and anger, detachment, and disorganization. Respondents are asked to look at a list of thoughts and feelings they may have had in the past 2 weeks and to select from five ratings that range from "does not describe me at all" to "describes me very well." Some of the items from the inventory include "I don't believe I will ever be happy again," " I am a more forgiving person," and "I have hope for the future." The HGRC has high internal consistency, and comparisons with other standardized instruments have demonstrated its validity.

A Holistic Approach

The holistic philosophy of caring for the terminally ill emphasizes the whole person, and identifies six dimensions of human existence that comingle; the interrelation of these six dimensions comprise fundamental aspects of being in the world. The six dimensions are behavioral, emotional, cognitive, physical, interpersonal, and spiritual. The philosophical framework that emphasizes these six interrelated dimensions of human existence is called holism, and it has clear, richly evocative applications to understand the complexities and nuances of bereavement on an individual.

Behavioral Impacts of Bereavement. Lindemann reported that acute grief produces a "loss of patterns of conduct" (1944, p. 44). Routines are shot. Agitated restlessness is common; that is, the person just can't keep still for even a short period of time. Crying is common. Some persons take up dangerous behaviors such as drinking excessively, smoking, or promiscuously engaging in sex. Scanning crowds to find the person who has died is common in the first few months following a death. Turning to religious practices such as praying or reading Scriptures offers comfort to some. For grievers whose faith the death has undermined, religious practices repel them.

Emotional Impacts of Bereavement. Emotional impacts are common. Emotions often reported by the bereaved include confusion, fear, sadness, loneliness, guilt, anxiety, and anger. Some grievers report self-doubt; that is, an undermining of trust they can accomplish things that matter. Guilt may emanate from being alive, from feeling complicit in the death, from concerns they are not grieving enough, or from beginning to enjoy life once again. Deaths from suicide typically elicit both anger and guilt. A parent's death may leave a teenager anxious over his or her future, such as being worried about affording college. Confusion may dominate when questions remain unanswered about how the death happened. An enduring sadness seems present from then on, not always in the foreground but part of one's whole back story as time goes on. While the term "depression" is often used in every day conversations about bereavement, the fact of the matter is that few grieving persons feel utterly worthless. For the small percentage whose bereavement is complicated (around 10–14%), clinical depression will be a factor in their lives.

Cognitive Impacts of Bereavement. Having one's consciousness flooded with thoughts and images of the deceased is common in the first few weeks and months following a death. Grievers report they have trouble concentrating and difficulties remembering things. For most adolescents, particularly adolescents in school, problems concentrating and remembering adversely affects their academic work. Bereaved college students commonly mention their grades plummet during the first semester of grieving a death, and independent research at such campuses as Purdue University, Oral Roberts University, and the University of Wisconsin at Green Bay supports students' anecdotal remarks about negative impacts on grades. More than one college student has told me how they misjudged what coping with a loss would require in the first few months following a death, how grieving interfered with their studies, and how they wish they had taken a leave of absence for at least a semester.

A minority of grieving adolescents have told me of auditory and visual hallucinations or of sensing the presence of the dead person. For some, such "paranormal" experiences prove uncanny and a bit scary, and for others they offer comfort. Many adolescents who have not had such hallucinations have expressed the wish such experiences would happen. Of course, terming these experiences "hallucinations" begs the question for some persons: these experiences are true encounters with the spirit of the person who died.

Physical Impacts of Bereavement. These include exhaustion, chills, nausea, diarrhea, and trouble sleeping. People may get headaches. Waves of somatic distress lasting from 20 to 60 minutes, tapering off, and then returning once again were reported by Lindemann as common in all the persons he treated. The distress bereavement wreaks upon the body can compromise the immune system, leaving persons prey for opportunistic infections they would otherwise have overcome. Anhedonia—inability to find pleasure in experiences typically enjoyable—may envelop a griever.

Interpersonal Impacts of Bereavement. Persons unaffected by a death have little patience for expressions of grief. I have been struck by how filled with dread and anxiety people who have not coped with bereavement feel when in the presence of someone who is grieving. Grievers learn to camouflage their grief in order to maintain contact with others. There is also the reality that bereaved persons may prefer to stay to themselves; being with others is both awkward and unsettling, particularly when other adolescents are having a good time and the griever is hurting.

Spiritual Impacts of Bereavement. Transcending oneself is a major mark of human spirituality. Such transcending of self occurs in multiple fashions: we strive to understand the world around us, we give ourselves in love and friendship to others, and we accept offers of love and friendship. We search for meaning and purpose. Many seek communion with a divine presence. Many strive to construct meaning, value, and purpose in a world they consider devoid of divine presence.

Bereavement can shatter our transcendence of self. Our assumptions about reality may no longer seem plausible. Reasons to hope may have evaporated. And yet a spiritual impact of bereavement can emerge in a renewed, even transformed sense of purpose, connections with others, and deeper insight into others, the world, and ourselves.

It is not a difficult leap in judgment to see the spiritual outcomes of coping with bereavement connect to the developmental transitions that mark adolescence. One would expect spiritual transformations to permeate one's fundamental relationships: with self, others, and the world. Further, the adolescent transition toward forming an autonomous identity, making career decisions, and entering into faithful, intimate relationships will also be impacted in the spiritual growth that bereavement elicits.

Concern over Assigning Depression to the Core of Bereavement

There has been a fierce struggle within the psychiatric and psychological fields to differentiate bereavement and depression. Freud noted that the intensity and duration of bereavement tempts observers to think grief reactions are matters for clinical intervention, and he particularly took exception to diagnostic conclusions that found depression in normal reactions to loss.

The American Psychiatric Association (APA) has resisted efforts to include bereavement as a distinct diagnostic category and for several years expressly cautioned against seeing depression as part of a person's acute grief. This distinction, known as the exclusion criterion, stated that if after 2 months from the onset of bereavement a griever is manifesting symptoms of depression, the exclusion criterion is withdrawn and psychiatric treatment for depression is considered appropriate. The APA recognized that in the first 2 months of bereavement a person may be clinically depressed over matters not related to the death; if it can be determined that the depression is related to matters other than the death, for instance, to a person's feelings of utter worthlessness or to guilt over something other than the death, then a diagnosis of clinical depression was considered warranted. The caution, in other words, is to take seriously that bereavement mimics depression and to refrain from treating a person for depression when the person is not depressed over the death but rather is grieving. Proponents for doing away with the exclusion criterion won the day with the latest edition of the *Diagnostic and Statistical Manual of Mental Disorders;* treatment for depression related to the death is now allowed within the first 2 weeks of the onset of grief.

Trauma on Top of Bereavement

The basic notion of trauma is a terrifying event that poses a mortal danger to oneself and/or to persons one loves. The experience of trauma can undermine one's basic assumptions about the world, expectations about one's ongoing safety can be seriously undermined, and belief in one's ability to achieve desired outcomes can be seriously damaged. The insidious effects of trauma are to disrupt a sense of coherency (that is, trauma dislocates a person's sense of temporal continuity). Such temporal disjunction confounds reflecting on oneself and relating to other people. Jeffrey Kauffman (2013, p. 276) wrote that persons in the grip of trauma live "on the thin ice of the vulnerability of the traumatized self to disintegrate."

By obvious inference, trauma's assault on a person's basic assumptions attacks the five core issues at the heart of adolescent development: predictability of events, mastery/control, belonging, fairness/justice, and self-image. Trauma attacks the core relationships that define human existence: relationships to the external world, to other persons, and to oneself. Part of coming to terms with trauma requires reframing one's assumptions about reality and relearning the fundamental relationships that frame human existence. Inability to construct a new, meaningful set of assumptions and relationships leave the traumatized person at risk for prolonged grief disorder.

It is crucial to recognize that human resiliency is a common response to terrifying events. Bonanno stresses that resiliency rather than dysfunction is the more common response of many survivors of disasters such as the atomic bombings of Hiroshima and Nagasaki; mass murders by lone gunmen in such places as Newtown, Connecticut, and Virginia Tech University; terrorist attacks on the Murrah Federal Building in Oklahoma City, the World Trade Center, and in the city of Mumbai; and devastation from severe storms such as Hurricane Katrina and Hurricane Sandy and F-4 and F-5 tornadoes that have struck places such as Joplin, Missouri, and Moore, Oklahoma. Not all persons, however, cope resiliently in the wake of trauma.

We have become aware that post-traumatic stress disorder (PTSD) is one of the possible consequences of being exposed to a traumatic event. PTSD has a set of disturbing reactions that overwhelm the traumatized individual both when conscious and asleep. Thus, when conscious a person will persistently be flooded with intrusive thoughts and images about the event. When asleep, dreams come unbidden and force the person to relive the trauma rather than sleep peacefully. Persons who have not been in the grip of such disturbing thoughts and images underestimate the fear these assaults on consciousness induce.

Bereavement caused by horrendous deaths may present problems with trauma for the griever. In some literature these sorts of deaths are called disastrous losses, and typically what is being referred to is death due to murder, drug overdose, or suicide. You can add to that list of devastating losses deaths that stem from natural and manmade disasters. The excellent research of Amy Saldinger has brought to our attention as well the devastating loss that can characterize observing the wasting away of a loved one due to terminal illness. Clinical lore—backed by some evidence-based practice—strongly indicates that attending to trauma must precede any efforts expended on grief counseling or grief therapy. For instance, "children who were both traumatized and bereaved by witnessing their parents violently murdered had acute posttraumatic stress reactions, which interfered with their ability to grieve" (Neria & Litz, 2004, p. 80). Kathleen Nader (1997, p. 17) concluded, "Normal grief resolution may be impeded without first attending to the traumatic nature of the death(s)."

Bereavement Itself as Traumatic: Prolonged Grief Disorder

Another scenario presents itself: The loss itself traumatizes the griever. This phenomenon is what is known colloquially as "being stuck in one's grief," identified more technically as the realities of an enduring grief trajectory. Increased attention has been paid in the past several years to the difficulties accompanying the phenomenon of enduring grief. Various terms have been proposed for this phenomenon: "traumatic grief," "pathological grief," "complicated grief," and "complicated mourning" are some of the more common terms. The term "prolonged grief disorder" was introduced a few years ago, and now authors of the *DSM-5* have coined the term "persistent complex bereavement-related disorder." In this book I use the terms "prolonged grief disorder" and "complicated grief" interchangeably. Estimates of the percentage of grieving individuals at risk of complicated grief vary from 4% to as high as 37%. Bonanno's research identifying an enduring grief trajectory narrowed the percentage to 10% to 14%.

Bill Worden has noted there are four types of complicated grief. These four types of abnormal reactions to loss are:

1. Chronic grief reactions, in which acute grief endures and the person does not return to being a functioning member of society.
2. Delayed grief reactions, in which the person's reaction to a loss is somehow stifled but emerges later in an extreme reaction to some triggering event, perhaps another loss.
3. Exaggerated grief reactions, in which the bereaved individual's grief is both excessive and disabling. Worden cautions that such complicated grief can lead to phobias, physical symptoms, and exceedingly deviant behavior.
4. Masked grief reactions, in which the person experiences difficulty in living but does not realize their difficulties are due to unresolved reactions to loss.

There is debate over the reality of delayed grief reactions. George Bonanno declared there were no indications of delayed grief in the many widows and widowers who were part of the research he conducted. However, researchers working with families bereaved by parental death noted that bereaved mothers consciously put on hold their grief because they had children to care for following the deaths of the children's fathers.

Bereavement researchers have focused attention (a) on identifying criteria that differentiate complicated grief from major depression and (b) on developing an empirical screening device to assess complicated grief as a distinct psychiatric disorder. Holly Prigerson and her colleagues[8] have constructed what they call an Inventory of Traumatic Grief, and this instrument has proven to possess reliability, validity, and practicality of use.

There is a significant correlation between complicated bereavement, depression, and anxiety. Physiological indicators distinguish bereaved individuals who are coping with depression and/or anxiety from bereaved individuals whose bereavement is considered normal. Consensus has built that psychological indicators of complicated grief include the severity and duration of intrusive thoughts and images, spasms of acute emotions, excessive loneliness and isolation, extreme avoidance of reminders of the deceased, and enduring sleep disturbances.

It is mistaken to consider a horrific event the core, defining characteristic of complicated grief disorder. Extensive research has convinced Prigerson and her colleagues that the trauma involved in complicated grief "appears to be a result of separation, which causes separation distress, rather than a result of exposure to a particularly horrific or gruesome experience" (Prigerson & Jacobs, 2001, p. 618). In short, the source of this trauma is not death from a horrendous event but rather the existential crux of the matter, namely, the person is gone forever.

The symptoms endemic to complicated grief disorder are "yearning or searching for the deceased or loneliness resulting from the loss of the loved one" (p. 618). Such yearning is akin to what traumatized individuals experience when in the grip of intrusive but unwelcome thoughts and images. However, the griever constantly longs to be reunited with the person who died, and in fact such ongoing effort to be in the presence of the deceased "tends to be a source of comfort" (p. 618).

There are some corollaries in complicated grief disorder to the hypervigilance, sometimes called hyperarousal, that is characteristic of trauma from a horrendous event. For the person "stuck in her grief," hypervigilance involves scrutinizing the milieu in efforts to locate the deceased; in other words, the person is constantly on the lookout for reminders of the person who died. This hypervigilance does not involve concern that a horrific event will reoccur.

Avoidance is a common indicator of trauma. However, studies of complicated grief disorder suggest avoidance may not be relevant for identifying persons with the disorder. While not yet definitive, these findings about avoidance and prolonged grief disorder led Prigerson and her colleagues to assert that avoidance alone does not provide salient information to identify a true case of this disorder. However, they don't completely dismiss the prospect that avoidance still is worth examining in regard to prolonged grief disorder. They include items in their self-report instrument to measure avoidance, and they call for more studies to verify whether avoidance should be included in measures of this disorder.

A central conclusion is that prolonged grief disorder may mimic PTSD, but of fundamental importance is that separation trauma marks this form of bereavement and it does not mark PTSD. As Prigerson and Jacobs (2001) summarize the matter, the intrusion, avoidance, and hypervigilance of prolonged grief disorder refer to very different experiences than found in persons suffering from PTSD:

> . . . reexperiencing refers to thoughts of the person rather than the event; avoidant thoughts and behaviors appear to be less central than the numbness and dissociative features of the disorder; hyperarousal relates to searching for the missing loved one rather than being rooted in the threat posed by a dangerous event.
>
> (p. 619)

Further, studies of bereaved persons who do meet the criteria for PTSD did not meet the diagnostic criteria for prolonged grief disorder. In short, these grievers' trauma stemmed not from the separation but from the horrific event itself.

As has been found in studies of persons whose bereavement forms an enduring grief trajectory, persons identified with prolonged grief disorder have grim long-term prospects. Unless they receive professional intervention, the intensity and duration of their complicated grief will continue unabated. This conclusion, paired with the evidence that prolonged grief disorder is a distinct psychological reality, raises the obvious question of whether there are valid, reliable means to diagnose the presence of the problem.

Two Standardized Measures to Identify Complicated Grief

Prigerson and her colleagues have developed, administered, and verified the psychometric properties of an instrument to identify grievers with complicated grief disorder. The instrument is titled the Inventory of Traumatic Grief (ITG). Validity and reliability studies have established high internal consistency (Cronbach's alpha = 0.95) for the ITG and have identified criterion-related validity by establishing strong associations with the Medical Outcomes Survey.

ITG Criteria to Rule in Complicated Grief Disorder

The first criterion to be met is someone significant to the griever must have died. The cause of death (accident, homicide, suicide, illness) is not specified. Other criteria involve the frequency and intensity of (a) separation distress, (b) traumatic distress, (c) duration of the feelings, and (d) serious disruption to functioning in the world. The five items measuring separation distress include distressing memories, constant yearning, and continual loneliness. The 12 items measuring traumatic distress include difficulties accepting the death, constant anger over the death, feeling dazed due to the death, lack of empathy, avoidance of reminders, guilt, bitterness, and aimlessness. The person needs to endorse 3 of the 5 separation distress items, and 6 of the 12 traumatic distress items. The person must have experienced the symptoms for no less than 2 months and must indicate that problems engaging in the world are severe or extreme.

A Shorter Version

A shortened version of the Inventory for Traumatic Grief is available in a 13-item questionnaire titled Prolonged Grief Disorder—PG-13. The 13-item self-report instrument measures prolonged grief disorder using the following criteria: bereavement over a death, separation distress, certain cognitive, emotional, and behavioral symptoms with a duration of at least 6 months, and functional impairment. Specifically, to qualify as someone who is experiencing prolonged grief disorder the following conditions must be met:

- The loss must be due to the death of someone important to the person who is grieving. The cause of death (accident, homicide, suicide, illness) is not specified.
- Symptoms of separation distress involving such indicators as emotional pain and yearning must be experienced at least daily and have persisted for at least 6 months.
- At least five of nine markers of traumatic distress must be experienced either daily or quite a bit over the preceding 6 months. These symptoms include avoiding reminders of the person who died, feeling dazed or astounded by the death, aimlessness about oneself, difficulties trusting others, problems admitting the death happened,

bitterness over the death, problems engaging in the world, emotional deadness, and feeling empty overall about life.

- The person must have significant impairment in important areas of functioning, such as on the job or with one's family.

This easily administered, psychometrically sound instrument provides a useful tool for both diagnosis and treatment. The indicators of prolonged grief disorder line up in clear juxtaposition opposite what Prigerson and Jacobs term normal grief. To end this discussion of trauma and grief, I will quote at length what they wrote to distinguish traumatic grief from normal grief.

> . . . individuals who are able to acknowledge the death (who do not feel disbelief); who do not feel extremely lonely or empty after the loss; who are able to feel emotionally connected to others; who feel that life still holds meaning and purpose; whose sense of self, personal efficacy, and trust in others has not been shaken by the loss; and who are not extremely angered over the loss, would appear to be adapting to life in the absence of the deceased. These survivors would be expected to feel sad about the loss and miss the deceased, particularly in the first few months following the loss, but would experience a gradual return over the first few years after the loss of the capacity for reinvestment in new interests, activities, and relationships. They would also experience an attenuation of their distress (i.e., not have marked and persistent levels of TG {traumatic grief] symptoms and generally appear capable of adjusting to their new circumstances without undue difficultly).
>
> (Prigerson & Jacobs, 2001, p. 633)

Concluding Comments

The models and concepts developed to describe and, in some cases, to explain human responses to bereavement point toward human resolution of irreparable loss. Either tacitly or explicitly the models endorse that humans do resolve bereavement, but how such resolution occurs is not settled ground. Efforts at synthesizing the main tenets of these models and concepts discloses the shift in thinking as new approaches have been applied to examine what at one time were considered settled viewpoints. In some cases, the thinking about grief is clearly value-laden, as in the discussion of disenfranchised grief with the implications that marginalizing grief over some loss experiences is a matter of social oppression, even of injustice.

The thrust of my review about models to explain bereavement, grief, and mourning is on the reaction to the loss of a family member or friend. I do not discount other losses, such as the death of a pet or the loss of one's ideals; however, I have centered my writing on grief over deaths of loved ones. Embedded in this discussion is the expectation that resolution is not only possible, but expected. I contend that massive research evidence supports the assertion that grievers typically recover.

However, embedded also in any discussion of models of bereavement must be a focus on how people cope as well as attention on interventions to promote coping. Portions of this chapter have looked at various viewpoints about coping with bereavement. For instance, Leighton's sociocultural framework with its essential striving sentiments and Attig's ideas about relearning fundamental human relations to self, others, and the world offer promising leads on markers of the whole person responding to living after bereavement.

> In short, we can define relationships with self, the world, and others as indicated by the presence of striving after specific human sentiments. As an example, relearning our relationship to others will contain sentiments of giving and receiving love. Striving after the essential human sentiments provides a mechanism to examine the multidimensionality of bereavement. How the person understands belonging to a moral order provides a link to spiritual aspects of seeking meaning and having hope in the face of loss. Thus, we would systematically examine bereavement resolution by seeing the extent to which the essential human sentiments are being achieved; and striving after the sentiments would indicate the work toward relearning the relationships that Attig has written comprises the essence of how we resolve grief. Such examinations of bereavement resolution would inspect the various types and levels of recovery, assume that recovery is not an all-or-nothing phenomenon but rather an ongoing process of integration and reintegration, and expect there to be both qualitative and quantitative opportunities to understand recovery following bereavement.
>
> (Balk, 2004, pp. 371–372)

Further, there are Freud's and Lindemann's ideas in what is called grief work, the Moos model for coping with life crises, the dual process model of coping with loss, Neimeyer on meaning making, the notion of intuitive and instrumental approaches to grieving, and Rubin's Two-Track Model. There is the deeply hope-filling work of George Bonanno on both resiliency and recovery trajectories, and the sensitive work of researchers to examine the phenomena of what lay people term "being stuck in one's grief" and what bereavement scholars and practitioners variously term complicated grief, traumatic grief, and now prolonged grief disorder or the newest phrase, persistent-complex bereavement-related disorder. While the intensity and duration of a clearly specified set of symptoms form boundaries between normal and traumatic grief, we also know from these many models of human grief that recovery is more than the absence of symptoms but also involves active reinvestment in the world.

Our next step is to look at bereavement, grief, and mourning during adolescence. The focus will be on adolescent grief over the deaths of parents, the deaths of siblings, and the deaths of friends. We begin that discussion in Chapter Nine.

Notes

1. A syndrome refers to a set of symptoms that are endemic to a specific condition.
2. Anna Freud bitterly disputed Bowlby's writings about bereavement; she recognized he was offering a powerful challenge to her father's thinking that grieving is fundamentally an intra-psychic matter.
3. Harry Harlow, the influential psychologist, studied the effects on development of infant rhesus monkeys when contact with a biological mother was substituted for contact with a doll made from wire and cloth. His experiments showed that infant rhesus monkeys preferred affection over food, even if the affection was from a wire and cloth doll. The results of being deprived

of the course of attachment to a natural caregiver were devastating for the infant monkeys, particularly in terms of their interactions with peers as they grew older.

4. In the 2009 edition of his book, Worden slightly adjusted task 2 to read, "To process the pain of grief" (p. 43).

5. Two other arguments raised against phases of mourning are (a) the models have been invalidly generalized to all persons. In short, there is no evidence supporting the assertion that these phases mark the grieving in all populations. (b) Inadequate research methods produced the data that led to assertions that people experience these phases when grieving.

6. This table appeared originally in *Helping the Bereaved College Student*, p. 49.

7. The fact that nearly all of Lindemann's patients were possibly also suffering from trauma needs to be taken into account as a factor that may actually differentiate those persons from individuals whose grief can be termed normal.

8. A main figure in the study of complicated grief disorder, Holly Prigerson, on the faculty at Harvard University and Director of the Center for Psychooncology and Palliative Care Research at the Dana Farber Institute in Boston, is a key player in efforts to have complicated grief admitted as an accepted diagnosis of psychiatric disorder. Prigerson and her colleagues noted that young adults whose grief is complicated are at risk for suicide.

Sources

Attig, T. (1995). *How we grieve: Relearning the world.* New York: Oxford University Press.

Balk, D. E. (1996). Attachment and the reactions of bereaved college students: A longitudinal study. In D. Klass, P. R. Silverman, & S. Nickman. (Eds.), *Continuing Bonds: New Understandings of Grief* (pp. 311–328). Washington, DC: Taylor & Francis.

Balk, D. E. (2004). Recovery following bereavement: An examination of the concept. *Death Studies, 28,* 361–374 (special issue in honor of Herman Feifel).

Balk, D. E., Noppe, I., Sandler, I., & Werth, J. Bereavement and depression: Possible changes to the *Diagnostic and Statistical Manual of Mental Disorders:* A report from the Scientific Advisory Committee of the Association for Death Education and Counseling. *Omega, 63*(3), 199–220.

Bonanno, G. A. (2009). *The other side of sadness: What the new science of bereavement tells us about life after loss.* New York: Basic Books.

Bonanno, G. A., Boerner, K., & Wortman, C. B. (2008). Trajectories of grieving. In M. S. Stroebe, R. O. Hansson, H. Schut, & W. Stroebe (Eds.), *Handbook of bereavement research and practice: Advances in theory and intervention* (pp. 287–307). Washington, DC: American Psychological Association.

Bowlby, J. (1961). Processes of mourning. *The International Journal of Psychoanalysis, 42,* 317–340.

Bowlby, J. (1969–1980). *Attachment and loss.* Vol. 1, *Attachment;* Vol. 2, *Separation: Anxiety and anger;* Vol. 3, *Loss: Sadness and depression.* New York: Basic Books.

Burke, L. A., Neimeyer, R. A., McDevitt-Murphy, M. E., Ippolito, M. R., & Roberts, J. M. (2011). Faith in the wake of homicide: Religious coping and bereavement distress in an African American sample. *The International Journal for the Psychology of Religion, 21,* 289–397.

Burnett, P., Middleton, W., Raphael, B., & Martinek, N. (1997). Measuring core bereavement phenomena. *Psychological Medicine, 27,* 49–57.

Calhoun, L. G. & Tedeschi, R. G. (2013). *Posttraumatic growth in clinical practice.* New York: Routledge.

Carey, B. (2013). Susan Nolen-Hoeksema, psychologist who studied depression in women, dies at 53. *New York Times,* January 13.

Christ, G. (2011). *Bereavement of widows of firefighters who died on 9/11/01.* A presentation at the Annual Conference of the Association for Death Education and Counseling, Miami, FL, June 23.

Doka, K. J. (Editor). (2002). *Disenfranchised grief: New directions, challenges, and strategies for practice.* Champaign, IL: Research Press.

Doka, K. J. & Martin, T. L. (2010). *Grieving beyond gender: Understanding the ways men and women mourn.* New York: Routledge.

Elison, J. & McGonigle, C. (2003). *Liberating losses: When death brings relief.* Cambridge, MA: Perseus.

Feigelman, W., Jordan, J. R., McIntosh, J. L., & Feigelman, B. (2012). *Devastating losses: How parents cope with the death of a child to suicide or drugs.* New York: Springer.

Folkman, S. F. (2001). Revised coping theory and the process of bereavement. In M. S. Stroebe, R. O. Hansson, W. Stroebe, & H. Schut (Eds.), *Handbook of bereavement research: Consequences, coping, and care* (pp. 563–584). Washington, DC: American Psychological Association.

Frankl, V. E. (1959). *Man's search for meaning.* New York: Pocket Books.

Freud, S. (1957). Mourning and melancholia. In J. Strachey (Ed. & Trans.), *The standard edition of the complete psychological works of Sigmund Freud* (Vol. 14, pp. 243–258). London: Hogarth Press. (Original work published 1917.)

Gillies, J. & Neimeyer, R. A. (2006). Loss, grief, and the search for significance: Toward a model of meaning reconstruction in bereavement. *Journal of Constructivist Psychology, 19*, 31–65.

Hogan, N. & DeSantis, L. (1992). Adolescent sibling bereavement: An ongoing attachment. *Qualitative Health Research, 2*(2), 159–177.

Horowitz, M. J., Siegel, B., Holen, A., Bonanno, G. A., Milbrath, C., & Stinson, C. H. (1997). Diagnostic criteria for complicated grief disorder. *American Journal of Psychiatry, 154*, 904–910.

Jacobs, S. (1993). *Pathologic grief: Maladaptation to loss.* Washington, DC: American Psychiatric Press.

Kauffman, J. (2013). Culture, socialization, and traumatic death. In D. K. Meagher & D. E. Balk (Eds.), *Handbook of thanatology: The essential body of knowledge for the study of death, dying, and bereavement* (2nd ed.) (pp. 276–284). New York: Routledge.

Kelly, G. A. (1955). *The psychology of personal constructs.* Vol. 1. New York: Norton.

Klass, D. (1997). The deceased child in the psychic and social worlds of bereaved parents during the resolution of grief. *Death Studies, 21*(2), 147–175.

Klass, D., Silverman, P. R., & Nickman, S. L. (1996). (Editor). *Continuing bonds: New understandings of grief.* Philadelphia: Taylor & Francis.

Lehman, D. R., Wortman, C. B., & Williams, A. F. (1987). Long-term effects of losing a spouse or child in a motor vehicle crash. *Journal of Personality and Social Psychology 52*, 218–231.

Leighton, A. H. (1959). *My name is Legion: Foundations for a theory of man in relation to culture.* New York: Basic Books.

Lindemann, E. (1944). The symptomatology and management of acute grief. *American Journal of Psychiatry, 101*, 141–148.

May, R., Angel, E., & Ellenberger, H. F. (Editors). (1959). *Existence: A new dimension in psychiatry and psychology.* New York: Basic Books.

Moos, R. H. & Schaefer, J. A. (1986). Life transitions and crises: A conceptual overview. *Coping with life crises: An integrated approach* (pp. 3–28). New York: Plenum.

Mulholland, K. A. (2001). *Experiencing and working with incongruence: Adaptation after parent death in adolescence.* Unpublished doctoral dissertation, University of Wisconsin at Madison.

Nader, K. O. (1997). Childhood traumatic loss: The interaction of trauma and grief. In C. R. Figley, B. E. Bride, & N. Mazza (Eds.), *Death and trauma: The traumatology of grieving* (pp. 17–41). Washington, DC: Taylor & Francis.

Nader, K., Pynoos, R., Fairbanks, L., & Frederick, C. (1990). Children's PTSD reactions one year after a sniper attack at their school. *American Journal of Psychiatry, 147*, 1526–1530.

Neimeyer, R. A. (Editor). (2001). *Meaning reconstruction and the experience of loss.* Washington, DC: American Psychological Association.

Neimeyer, R. A. & Hogan, N. S. (2001). Quantitative or qualitative? Measurement issues in the study of grief. In M. S. Stroebe, R. O. Hansson, W. Stroebe, & H. Schut (Eds.), *Handbook of bereavement research: Consequences, coping, and care* (pp. 89–118). Washington, DC: American Psychological Association Press.

Neria, Y. & Litz, B. T. (2004). Bereavement by traumatic means: The complex synergy of trauma and grief. *Journal of Loss and Trauma, 9,* 73–87.

Nickman, S. L. (1996). Retroactive loss in adopted persons. In D. Klass, P. R. Silverman, & S. L. Nickman (Eds.), *Continuing bonds: New understandings of grief* (pp. 257–272). Philadelphia: Taylor & Francis.

Nolen-Hoeksema, S. (1998). The other end of the continuum: The costs of rumination. *Psychological Inquiry, 9,* 216–219.

Nolen-Hoeksema, S. & Larson, J. (1999). *Coping with loss.* Mahwah, NJ: Lawrence Erlbaum.

Oltjenbruns, K. A. (2001). Developmental context of childhood: Grief and regrief phenomena. In M. S. Stroebe, R. O. Hansson, H. Schut, & W. Stroebe (Eds.), *Handbook of bereavement research: Consequences, coping, and care* (pp. 169–197). Washington, DC: American Psychological Association.

Prigerson, H. G. & Jacobs, S. C. (2001). Traumatic grief as a distinct disorder: A rationale, consensus criteria, and a preliminary empirical test. In M. S. Stroebe, R. O. Hansson, W. Stroebe, & H. Schut (Eds.), *Handbook of bereavement research: Consequences, coping, and care* (pp. 613–645). Washington, DC: American Psychological Association.

Prigerson, H. G., Maciejewski, P. K., Newsom, J., Reynolds, C. F., Frank, E., Bierhals, E. J., Miller, M., Fasiczka, A., Doman, J., & Houck, P. R. (1995). The Inventory of Complicated Grief: A scale to measure maladaptive symptoms of loss. *Psychiatry Research, 59,* 65–79.

Prigerson, H. G., Vanderwerker, L.C., & Maciejewski, P. K. (2008). A case for inclusion of Prolonged Grief Disorder in DSM-V. In M. S. Stroebe, R. O. Hansson, W. Stroebe, & H. Schut (Eds.), *Handbook of bereavement research and practice: Advances in theory and intervention.* (pp. 165–186). Washington, DC: American Psychological Association.

Pynoos, R. S., Nader, K., Frederick, C., Gonda, L., & Stuber, M. (1987). Grief reactions in school age children following a sniper attack at school. *Israel Journal of Psychiatry and Related Science, 24,* 53–63.

Range, L. (2007). Historical and contemporary perspectives on traumatic death. In D. E. Balk, C. Wogrin, G. Thornton, & D. Meagher (Eds.), *Handbook of thanatology: The essential body of knowledge for the study of dying, death, and bereavement* (pp. 269–275). New York: Routledge.

Rindt, S. E. M. (2002). *Sudden sibling loss: Reflections of women on their experience during adolescence.* Unpublished doctoral dissertation, Alliant International University.

Rosenblatt, P. C. (1983). *Bitter, bitter tears: Nineteenth-century diarists and twentieth- century grief theories.* Minneapolis: University of Minnesota Press.

Rubin, S. S. (1981). A two-track model of bereavement: Theory and application in research. *American Journal of Orthopsychiatry, 51,* 101–109.

Rubin S.S. (1999). The Two-Track Model of Bereavement: Overview, retrospect and prospect. *Death Studies, 23*(8), 681–714.

Rubin, S.S. (2012). Tracking through bereavement: A framework for intervention. In R. Neimeyer et al. (Eds.) *Techniques of grief therapy.* New York: Routledge.

Rubin, S.S., Bar Nadav, O., Malkinson, R., Koren, D., Gofer-Shnarch, M., & Michaeli, E. (2009). The Two-Track Model of Bereavement Questionnaire (TTBQ): Development and findings of a relational measure. *Death Studies, 33,* 1–29.

Rubin, S.S., Malkinson, R., & Witztum, E. (2003). Trauma and bereavement: Conceptual and clinical issues revolving around relationships. *Death Studies, 27,* 667–690.

Rubin, S.S., Malkinson, R., & Witztum, E. (2008). Clinical aspects of a DSM Complicated Grief Diagnosis: Challenges, dilemmas, and opportunities. In M. S. Stroebe, R. O. Hansson, H. Schut &

W. Stroebe (Eds.), *Handbook of Bereavement Research and Practice: Advances in Theory and Intervention* (pp. 187–206). Washington, DC: American Psychological Association Press.

Rubin, S. S., Malkinson, R., & Witztum, E. (2012). *Working with the bereaved: Multiple lenses on loss and mourning.* New York: Routledge.

Rubin, S. S., Malkinson, R., & Witzum, E. (2013). On bereavement interventions: Controversy and consensus. In D. K. Meagher & D. E. Balk (Eds.), *Handbook of thanatology: The essential body of knowledge for the study of death, dying, and bereavement* (2nd ed.) (pp. 263–272). New York: Routledge.

Rubin, S. S. & Schechter, N. (1997). Exploring the social construction of bereavement: Perceptions of adjustment and recovery for bereaved men. *American Journal of Orthopsychiatry, 67,* 279–289.

Salazar, M. J. (1992). *Retirement adjustment of professional athletes.* Unpublished doctoral dissertation, Widener University, Institute for Clinical Graduate Study.

Servaty-Seib, H. L. & Taub, D. J. (2008, Spring). *Assisting bereaved college students. New Directions for Student Services,* Number 121.

Silver, R. C. & Wortman, C. B. (1980). Coping with undesirable life events. In J. Gardner & M. E. P. Seligman (Eds.), *Human helplessness: Theory and applications* (pp. 279–340). New York: Academic Press.

Silverman, P. R. (1987). The impact of parental death on college-age women. *Psychiatric Clinics of North America, 10,* 387–404.

Silverman, P. R., Nickman, S. L., & Worden, J. W. (1992). Detachment revisited: The child's reconstruction of a dead parent. *American Journal of Orthopsychiatry, 62*(4), 494–503.

Stroebe, M. & Schut, H. (1999). The dual process model of coping with bereavement: Rationale and description. *Death Studies, 23,* 197–224.

Stroebe, M., Schut, H., & Boerner, K. (2010). Continuing bonds in adaptation to bereavement: Toward theoretical integration. *Clinical Psychology Review, 30,* 259–268.

Stroebe, M., Schut, H., & van den Bout, J. (2013). *Complicated grief: Scientific foundations for health professionals.* New York: Routledge.

Stroebe, M. S. & Stroebe, W. (1989). Who participates in bereavement research? A review and empirical study. *Omega, 20,* 1–29.

Stroebe, W. & Stroebe, M. S. (1987). *Bereavement and health: The psychological and physical consequences of partner loss.* New York: Cambridge University Press.

Tedeschi, R. G. & Calhoun, L. G. (1995). *Trauma and transformation: Growing in the aftermath of suffering.* Thousand Oaks, CA: Sage.

Tyson-Rawson, K. J. (1993). *College women and bereavement: Late adolescence and father death.* Unpublished doctoral dissertation, Kansas State University, Manhattan, KS.

Walker, A. C. (2008). Grieving in the Muscogee Creek Tribe. *Death Studies, 32,* 123–141.

Winegardner, D., Simonetti, J. L., & Nykodym, N. (1984). Unemployment: The living death? *Journal of Employment Counseling, 21*(4), 149–155.

Worden, J. W. (1982). *Grief counseling and grief therapy: A handbook for the mental health practitioner.* New York: Springer.

Worden, J. W. (1992). *Grief counseling and grief therapy: A handbook for the mental health practitioner* (2nd ed.). New York: Springer.

Worden, J. W. (2002). *Grief counseling and grief therapy: A handbook for the mental health practitioner* (3rd ed.). New York: Springer.

Worden, J. W. (2009). *Grief counseling and grief therapy: A handbook for the mental health practitioner* (4th ed.). New York: Springer.

Wortman, C. B. & Silver, R. C. (1989). The myths of coping with loss. *Journal of Consulting and Clinical Psychology, 57,* 349–357.

9 Bereavement, Grief, and Mourning during Adolescence

The focus of this chapter is on three sources of bereavement, grief, and mourning during the adolescent years. Specifically, the topics are bereavement and its sequelae when a parent dies, a sibling dies, and a friend dies. Topics not reviewed in this chapter but for which a case can be made are bereavement over the death of a grandparent and the death of a pet; frequently a grandparent's death introduces an adolescent to irreparable loss, grief, and mourning; further, the importance of pets in the lives of humans is receiving increased attention, and several teenagers and young adults have told me how wrenching it was for them when their companion animal—typically a cat or dog, but in some cases a horse or other animal—died. Very little attention has been paid to bereavement following the death of an adolescent's spouse, son, or daughter, and I anticipate a push into these areas will be made once some researchers recognize the fertile ground offered.

Parental Death during Adolescence

Researchers have developed a keen interest in the quality of separation from parents occurring during adolescence, the association between parenting styles and separation, and the relation between identity status and separation. These topics were touched on earlier in the book. The anguish of parental death is complicated by tensions over the developmental crisis of dependency versus autonomy that marks adolescent–parent relations.

A parent's death presents a severe threat on many levels. It can create financial and emotional strains that overwhelm some families. The death of a parent during adolescence can destabilize such core developmental issues as (a) trusting others and the world, (b) gaining a sense of belonging, and (c) gaining a sense of mastery. We will look at the impact of parental death on core developmental issues and examine the implications for adolescent development that emerge when a parent dies.

Bereavement over the death of a parent has proved the most scrutinized form of adolescent grief and mourning. This research focus has plausible reasons. First, there is common agreement that the death of a parent has few if any comparable losses for an adolescent; thus researchers and clinicians accept that a parent's death reverberates with cascading effects in an adolescent's life. Second, the higher prevalence of adult deaths makes parental death during adolescence more likely than the deaths of siblings or peers. The fact that bereavement over parental death is the most examined cause of adolescent grief has led some to argue that focusing on such deaths is more useful than examining other types of adolescent bereavement: specifically, there is more literature to draw on for analysis and comparison and suggestions.[1]

Core Developmental Issues and Parental Death

Recall the earlier discussion in Chapter One of five core developmental issues to be mastered during adolescence. In brief, these issues involve the gradual move into mature adulthood as the individual responds to the demands that he or she gain emotional separation from parents, develop personal autonomy, self-efficacy, and individual control, and attain skills at maintaining interpersonal intimacy and commitment. The five issues are predictability of events, self-image, a sense of belonging, mastery/control, and fairness/justice.

Bill Worden reported on four of the core issues when writing his book on the longitudinal research he and Phyllis Silverman completed regarding children's and adolescents' grief following parental death. Specifically,

- There was increased anxiety, depression, and worries up to 2 years following a parent's death, effects Worden inferred demonstrated concern that significant life events were not able to be predicted. These reactions were not found in a matched group of nonbereaved adolescents.
- In terms of self-image, the death of a parent and subsequent grief reactions left adolescents feeling different than nonbereaved peers. They considered their school work and overall conduct inferior to what other adolescents accomplished. Males particularly had been explicitly urged by adults "to act more grown up" (Worden, 1966, p. 89) in order to help others and themselves cope with the loss; typically, adolescents who got this message believed they were not reaching what adults expected of them. However, perhaps paradoxically, the bereaved adolescents thought of themselves as more mature than other persons their age, and Daniel Offer reported dealing with significant family adversity such as a parent's death thrusting teenagers more quickly into adulthood.
- Problems with interpersonal relations, such as withdrawal from acquaintances and feeling different than peers, marked these adolescents' perceptions of not belonging. A link to Leighton's sentiment of the need to feel part of a human group suggests itself as an obvious link worth pursuing.
- During the second year of bereavement, the adolescents' sense of being less in control of their lives was most prominent. This finding about the core issue of mastery and control could be examined further by researchers interested in locus of control variables and in attribution theory.

Internalizing and Externalizing Symptoms

Researchers into stress and coping during adolescence often look into what are called internalizing and externalizing symptoms. Internalizing symptoms such as personal thoughts and feelings as well as clinical issues such as anxiety are hidden from others, whereas externalizing symptoms such as expressions of hostility or delinquent behavior—both status offenses and criminal offenses[2]—by definition are open to observation by others.

When compared to a matched group of adolescents who were not grieving, bereaved adolescents showed no differences in delinquency, expressions of anger, or frequency of accidents. However, for girls whose mothers had died, acting out behavior became prominent. Bereaved girls reported more anxiety than bereaved boys, as well as greater sensitivity over family tensions.

Irwin Sandler and his colleagues in the Family Bereavement Project have reported on gender differences involving externalizing and internalizing symptoms following the death of a parent. For instance, over time bereaved males' anxiety and depression lessen, whereas without intervention the anxiety and depression of girls increase; acting out behavior decreased for bereaved boys over time, but decreased for girls only who were part of an intervention program. Other research with bereaved adolescents has reported that bereaved female youth exhibit externalizing and internalizing symptoms more than do boys, but—unlike what Worden's research uncovered—bereaved adolescents engaged in externalizing behavior more than nonbereaved controls.

Research with college students who experienced parental death indicated adolescents who report fewer grief responses to their parents' deaths also report greater feelings of loneliness and lower self-esteem. Parentally bereaved high school students disclosed higher scores on the Beck Depression Inventory than a comparable set of control subjects; further, school work typically plummeted in the first months and more following a parent's death for bereaved high school students. Similar findings have been reported by sibling bereaved high school students and by bereaved college students grieving the deaths of family friends or friends. Somatic complaints and alterations in sleeping and eating habits have also been noticed in parentally bereaved adolescents.

Career Decisions and Bereaved Adolescents

A key developmental task for adolescents is to identify a career goal that provides an answer to the question, "What do you want to do when you grow up?" Convincing evidence has shown that self-concept and career decision-making are tightly linked. Bereaved adolescents manifest self-concepts that either mirror how most adolescents think about themselves or, in a noticeable proportion of cases, develop self-perceptions more mature than most nonbereaved adolescents.

Career counseling is at the core of counseling psychology and has been throughout the history of the profession. A link between career decision-making and bereavement may give the acceptable framework for counseling psychologists to devise graduate curricula that include more than marginal interest in issues of loss and grief. Alexandra Dueck appreciates the prospects for such a shift in counseling psychology when she notes on the very first page of her thesis that "little is known about loss . . . and its impact on career development" (Dueck, 2011, p. 1).

Dueck's exploratory study into career decisions and adolescent bereavement offers a beginning look at this critical aspect of growth into young adulthood while coping with grief.[3] Most of the persons in her study acknowledged that the person who died had been a role model with ongoing influence in their lives. The adolescents wanted to be like that person, and "their selection of a career was based on carrying on the legacy of the family member or friend who had died" (Dueck, 2011, p. 91). Constructing a core set of beliefs about the meaning of life was bound up with making sense of the death of the person they loved and transforming that meaning-making into a personally satisfying career choice.

Donald Super's model of career decision-making, tied to self-concept, bears significance for interpreting the impact of bereavement on career decisions. Examining the interplay between career decisions, self-concept, and bereavement offers an explanatory tool for understanding certain sequelae of grief in the development of adolescents.

A college student I interviewed put into her own words the ongoing influence of her dead father on the impetus she felt toward making a career. The interview question she answered was not "How did the death influence your career decision-making?" but rather was "How has bereavement impacted you behaviorally?" Tara, a 20-year-old physics major whose father's death from prostate cancer had occurred 18 months ago, told me,

> As a result of my father's passing I have been trying really hard to succeed in life like he did. I have been more aggressive when it comes to gaining experiences and opportunities that will help to advance my career. I got into research because I wanted to try and make a difference when it comes to fighting the disease my father died from. I recently got a major science scholarship which I don't think I would have pursued if my father was still around.
>
> (Balk, 2011, p. 124)

Factors Promoting Resiliency in the Face of Parental Death

The construct *resiliency* has captured the imagination of many psychologists. We see this conceptual shift in the writings of Seligman on positive psychology, a counterbalance to his seminal work on learned helplessness. During the latter half of the 20th century, great interest was expressed about uncovering intrapersonal and environmental factors that promote resiliency in children and adolescents, particularly when they lived in impoverished conditions that usually left persons cynical and feeling helpless. This focus on promoting resiliency in children from impoverished backgrounds became a mission within NIH, the William T. Grant Foundation, and among community psychologists.

Scholars in Great Britain have examined the various psychological variables and social factors that promote resiliency when an adolescent is coping with the death of a parent. Table 9.1 provides a list of 12 factors the scholars have identified. Among these factors are a positive temperament, a sense of competency, attachment to an adult, and a repertoire of effective problem-solving skills.

Here is the case of an adolescent following the death of her mother from a heart attack. The case illustrates resiliency in the face of some challenging odds, such as (a) personal assumptions that one has to relinquish personal plans and dreams and (b) the difficulties of reengaging in academic studies at a university. The young woman—Roberta—is fortunate to have a father and siblings who support her. Resiliency seems to be not only an individual trait but also a characteristic fostered by family interactions and interpersonal dynamics.

Table 9.1 Factors Promoting Adolescent Resiliency Following Parental Death

Hope and trust in the future
Realistic, balanced appraisal of personal strengths and limitations
Goals that can be attained
Internal locus of control
Peer relationship skills
Problem-solving skills
Emotional regulation
Valued by others
Outgoing, responsive temperament
Self-esteem and self-efficacy
Continuing bond with the parent who died
Able to accept surviving parent's entering into new relationships

Source: Adapted from Stokes, Reid, & Cook, 2009.

Roberta

Roberta Branson was a 20-year-old college student living in a dorm at the state university about an hour from her home town. She was a history major with minors in psychology and in the classics. She was a good student, on track to graduate in four more semesters. Upon graduation she planned to earn a doctorate in American Studies and then teach at the university level and write books on issues in American society.

Roberta was the youngest child in her family. Her older sister, Margaret, lived in another state with her husband and infant son. Michael, her 22-year-old brother, was a soldier stationed at Ft. Riley in Kansas. Her father James and her mother Helen were in their early 50s, adjusting to life without any children living at home. If asked, the Branson children and parents would correctly depict their family as strongly cohesive: persons shared personal matters and trusted one another. James and Helen had raised their children by combining support and encouragement with clear limits; they enforced rules. Roberta was close to both of her parents, and felt particularly able to talk with her mother; she often phoned just to say hi.

Helen died suddenly one morning in October of 2011 while preparing breakfast for her and her husband. An autopsy revealed she had suffered a massive heart attack. Learning about the death, Roberta rushed home with the clear intent to stay there and take over care of the house. She was especially worried her father would not do well living on his own.

James was an insurance agent with an office in town. He had many friends and was an active member of the Methodist church and of the Rotary Club. He was active in politics behind the scenes, such as working on campaigns for candidates he believed in. He was a Republican both by conviction and by tradition; his parents had been Republicans, and their political views had stayed with him.

James felt blindsided by Helen's death. He plunged into work as a means to deal with his loss. Talking about his grief was foreign to him; he preferred to be doing something and figuring out how to master the problems facing him and his children now that Helen was gone. He was glad all the children had quickly found their way home for the funeral.

The presence of his three children comforted James in the days surrounding the funeral. They all shared so many memories of Helen, and all of them found solace in talking about these memories. Frequently they found themselves laughing about some of the practical jokes Helen had pulled on people. Once she had hid in Margaret's closet behind the clothes, and when Margaret reached for a dress on a hanger, Helen had grabbed Margaret's hand, leading Margaret to let out a shriek heard throughout the house. Another time at Halloween Helen had disguised herself as an old man with bushy hair and a beard, and traveled all the way to Roberta's dorm to knock on her door and say "Trick or Treat." Roberta at first said, "Oh, just a second." And then she took a close look and said, "Mom?"

After the funeral, Roberta disclosed her intention to stay home and take care of things around the house. James was not only dumbfounded at this offer, he also was adamant that Roberta return to the university "unless," as he put it, " studying would be too hard on top of your grief. I don't want you to jeopardize your education." James went on, "Your mom and I are so proud of you, of the scholarship you earned, of your grades and your plans, and you can't give that up. You have to go back to school and finish. Wait out a semester if that's what you need, but don't give up your future." Margaret and Michael joined in, telling Roberta their dad was right—and that he would be able to care for himself.

Roberta reluctantly at first returned to school. The first few weeks were difficult as she worried about her dad and found concentrating on school work a chore. Few persons at the university appreciated her situation, but she found a chapter of National Students of AMF on her campus. Roberta began going to meetings, and helped organize a 10 K walk on behalf of heart research.

Roberta and her siblings are members of the digital generation. They arranged for long-distance visits with one another and with their dad on Skype. Her dad let them know he appreciated these visits. He even did the unthinkable only a year ago; he started using Facebook.

Roberta is now in her senior year and is on track to graduate. The semester of her mother's death had proven a challenge, but she pulled through. She applied to several doctoral programs in American Studies, and has been accepted by three programs. Now she is debating which offer to accept. Talking things over with her father and siblings via Skype has been a great help.

Anticipated Death Due to Terminal Illness

An assumption that seems to make common sense is that anticipated deaths prove easier for the bereaved than do sudden. Being aware both my father and mother were terminally ill helped me to prepare for the inevitable, irrevocable losses that were looming in the wings. However, are people always better off when a death can be anticipated?

Empirical research has produced equivocal if not outright counterintuitive results comparing grief following anticipated and sudden deaths. While many research findings indicate sudden deaths elicit more adverse grief reactions than do anticipated, there are studies indicating bereavement following anticipated deaths proves as or even more difficult in some cases. Some longitudinal research following sudden versus anticipated bereavement indicates that initially grievers of sudden deaths do worse but that over time grief reactions ameliorate for both groups and it is not possible to determine from grief scores at 2-year follow-ups who belongs in which group.

Using the theory of locus of control, some researchers have concluded higher levels of internal control buffer grievers from the adverse effects of bereavement, whereas higher levels of external control increase vulnerability to the distress of bereavement, regardless whether the death was sudden or anticipated. Similar findings have shown significant inverse associations between self-concept and grief in adolescents following sibling death: higher self-concept was linked to less distress whereas lower self-concept was linked to greater distress, regardless whether the death was sudden or anticipated.

Watching a loved one waste away from the ravages of cancer or some other terminal illness can traumatize people. Observing a loved one dying in agony, physically wasting away, cognitively slipping into dementia can prove devastating. In addition to holistic pressures such as emotional, cognitive, interpersonal, and spiritual, there can be heavy financial burdens added to the mix. Such overwhelming cases make one wonder if a sudden death—rather than a lingering, drawn out affair—would not have been a blessing to all concerned.

Many years ago when I was doing my dissertation, a 17-year-old adolescent whom I will call Charlene told me of the death of her brother. The story has stayed with me since. Charlene's brother was undergoing an experimental procedure to bring his cancer into remission. What happened was that his body had an extremely adverse reaction to the procedure, the treatment attacked his skin tissue, and he died in excruciating pain. Charlene looked so distraught as, her eyes filled with tears, she said she was relieved he had died because now he would no longer suffer. The death had created rifts in the family, there were financial burdens that would take years to overcome, and anger and confusion governed her family's reaction to the death "of this beautiful young guy" as Charlene described him.

In a sense you could say her brother's death was sudden. Charlene made it clear that everyone, including her brother, thought the experimental procedure was the last hope. They hated seeing him grow weaker, and had no idea that the procedure to save him would be what killed him.

A linear notion of grief is one reason some people propose there are favorable outcomes over time for grief from anticipated deaths. The notion is that there is a finite amount of grief, and anticipating a death starts the grieving process and reduces the amount of grief to be coped with when the death actually happens. Some scholars find this idea mistaken. I am one of the individuals who do not think we reduce our grief by anticipating a loved one's death, and I think anticipating a death triggers anxiety but not grief. We don't begin treating the dying person as if he or she is already dead. In the last months of my father's life and of my mother's life I felt very close to them, knew our time together was precious, and enjoyed being in their presence. But not once do I find any reactions that tell me I was in grief over a state of anticipated, irreparable loss.

Here now is a reflection on the experience of Rhonda, a late adolescent female college student whose father died following a multiyear struggle with colon cancer. Rhonda's experiences with her father's illness encompassed some of her early adolescence and all of her middle adolescent years. Consider the situation Rhonda faced with the developmental expectation of emotionally separating from her father. Given her deep bond for him and witnessing—at times in a controlled panic—her father on more than one occasion being near death, it is obvious that how Rhonda managed that developmental transition is different than how most adolescents face such a transition. The reflection about Rhonda is titled "When an Adolescent's Parent Has a Terminal Illness."

When an Adolescent's Parent Has a Terminal Illness

A parent's death from a terminal illness presents a crisis situation that contains the prospect of preparing for the worst and not being ambushed by a sudden death. As just mentioned, folk wisdom and common sense assert that coping with a death is facilitated when the death can be anticipated. On one hand, such a notion sounds reasonable; however, there are cases of exhaustion, dread, and even trauma for survivors as they attend to and witness the withering decline of someone with a terminal illness. Some lasting features of such cases are images, sounds, and smells that invade one's mind; these features get triggered by environmental stimuli and return unbidden to flood one's consciousness.

One such case is offered by Rhonda, a 19-year-old college student whose father contracted colon cancer when she was in middle school and died late in the first semester of her undergraduate studies. She wrote in her journal 3 days following his death,

Dear Dad,

Today was not so difficult as I expected it to be. I know now that you are just fine. I did not cry until I came back to school, and I'm not sure why it came out then. I guess I am lonely. I really miss you, Dad, the talks, the encouragement you always gave me. I'm going to really have to dig deep some days to find that strength you taught me all about. . . . I miss you so bad, but I have for some time now. I feel stronger and for a while (quite a while) even happy. Happy that I did not have to see you hurt inside and outside. This step in life is one of the hardest I have ever had to do. You mean the world to me and losing you is not easy. I am afraid to love another too deeply or open up too much, afraid they will leave me also. . . . I am afraid of the future somewhat. But I can't be I know. Oh how I wish I could talk to you. Dad, I'm going to keep fighting.

Love, Rhonda

(see Balk & Vesta, 1998, p. 24)

Her family owned and worked a farm, and Rhonda had moments in the 4 years following her father's death when smells, sounds, and images triggered vivid memories. One morning, for instance, when she was leaving a building on the university campus, a tractor-trailer rig was making its way on a street a short distance away; the smell of the fuel brought instant images of her father driving his tractor in the field. An example known to many grieving students is the smell of perfume or cologne bringing to mind the presence of a dead mother or father.

Consider other smells, sounds, and images integrally linked to the dying parent who was wasting away before the adolescent's eyes.

- A physically vibrant father was reduced to a frail, weak person wracked with pain.
- An active, proud man was reduced to a bed-ridden, emaciated person who had to be fed, dressed, and bathed.
- Soiled body parts and bed linens became the order of the day.

Many students in the National Students of AMF,[4] an organization whose mission is to assist college students grieving the deaths of family members and friends, mention they wish more attention was given to the issues students face when a loved one, particularly a parent, is dying from a terminal illness. Here are the words of one student:

> The most difficult thing for me has been watching those I love die slowly and painfully. And then afterward a lot of people in my life have moved on when I have not. We don't really talk about it because I feel if I talk to them I will make them uncomfortable since they never bring our loved ones up. Another difficult part was going to work when I could not get off to go to the funerals or to grieve.

Sibling Death during Adolescence

In the United States, sibling death presents an adolescent with an off-time, out-of-sequence, atypical life situation. It is off-time and out-of-sequence because siblings are supposed to live into old age and outlive their parents; coping with a sibling's death is hardly a normal developmental transition for an American adolescent, or indeed for adolescents living in the developed countries of the world.

The atypical aspect of sibling death during adolescence may account for the phenomenon that, when a family is grieving the death of a child, adolescents become forgotten mourners. This observation is not to say that adolescents are more forgotten than younger children during a family's time of grief; it is seemingly the case, however, that society accords the extraordinary pain of parental grief more credence and compassion than the pain of sibling grief. Perhaps some people believe mourning is beyond the realm of possibility when the individual is not an adult. Complications of disenfranchised grief become intertwined here when adolescents' needs are ignored or dismissed.

Initial research forays into adolescent bereavement began with studies of early and middle adolescents whose siblings had died. These studies took place in the 1980s, with some further research in the 1990s. While adolescent responses to sibling death are still of import, since the late 1990s sibling bereavement has been studied less than parental bereavement.

The principal areas of focus regarding sibling bereavement and adolescents have been self-concept, emotional responses, grades and school work, religion, and family dynamics and relationships. Here is a synthesis of research into each of these areas of interest.

Self-Concept and Adolescent Sibling Bereavement

Other than on measures of morality (i.e., the development of conscience), adolescents bereaved over a sibling's death resemble their nonbereaved peers on various aspects of self-concept; on this matter of conscience, sibling bereaved adolescents score significantly higher than do nonbereaved. In some research, during the first 12 months following a sibling's death, bereaved adolescents' self-concepts are more mature than the self-concepts of nonbereaved peers; while these differences typically did not hold over time, the bereaved adolescents' scores did not drop below the scores of nonbereaved adolescents.

Bereaved adolescents' scores on the Offer Self Image Questionnaire for Adolescents (OSIQ), a standardized self-report instrument normed particularly for adolescent populations, differentiated three groups of bereaved adolescents: (a) 25%–30% with self-concept scorers considerably higher (that is, more mature) than most adolescents' scores on the OSIQ; (b) greater than 50% with self-concept scores matching how most adolescents respond to the instrument (in effect, average self-concept); and (c) 15%–20% whose scores on the OSIQ were significantly lower than most adolescents' responses (in effect, low self-concept). In contrast to clinical and theoretical assertions that severe life crises would negatively impact adolescents from developing a stable, integrated identity, these OSIQ results support Daniel Offer's longitudinal findings that teenagers typically cope well when family tragedies strike. In related research, Hogan and Greenfield reported that low self-concepts for bereaved adolescents were particularly associated with long-term vulnerability to problems in psychological development.

Clinical lore and assumptions of persons in general assert that mothers will have a reliable, accurate understanding of how their teenage children are responding to the death of a sibling; fathers' understanding is assumed to be faulty and thus less to be trusted. Research that examined this assumption about mothers' and fathers' comprehension of their bereaved adolescents' self-concept and grief reactions uncovered unexpected findings, however.

In this research, mothers, fathers, and teenagers were given Hogan's standardized measure of adolescent sibling bereavement; the parents were asked to complete the instrument as they believed their adolescent would. Mothers' views of their bereaved teenagers' self-concepts and grief reactions significantly differed with the views of the teenagers and with the views of the fathers. The fathers' views of their teenagers' self-concepts and grief reactions fundamentally agreed with what the teenagers reported about themselves. In particular, the mothers said they thought their adolescent's self-concept was above average and their grief of considerable intensity, whereas the fathers and the teenagers reported (a) normal or average estimations of self-concept and (b) grief reactions of less intensity than expected by the mothers. How the fathers and the teenagers responded corresponds with other studies using Offer's Self Image Questionnaire for Adolescents; one can speculate that the majority of the adolescents were in what Bonanno has termed a resiliency trajectory, and that the fathers recognized their teenage son or daughter were functioning well despite being distressed over the death of their sibling. Bereaved mothers who have heard the results of this research have expressed relief that it allows them not to be the ultimate source of information about their family, and they suggest what explains the discrepancy in the mothers' and teenagers' reports is the mothers' investment in the well-being of the surviving teenager (thus, a desire for an above-average self-concept) and belief that the close attachment bonds of the children would affect the surviving teenager (thus, an expectation of considerably intense grief).

These findings are controversial. Other research has reported a greater congruence between the reports of mothers and their adolescents and less congruence between the reports of fathers and their adolescents. Unlike fathers, mothers are expected to understand their children because adolescents and mothers are seen to engage in more self-disclosure than are fathers and adolescents.

Emotional Responses and Adolescent Sibling Bereavement

Bereaved adolescents said these terms described them in the months immediately following a sibling's death: shock, guilt, confusion, depression, fear, loneliness, and anger. As time passed and the adolescents coped with their bereavement, fewer adolescents chose those terms to depict how they still felt about the death. However, and this matter has drawn the attention of scholars and clinical practitioners, a sizable minority ranging from 28% to 45% reported ongoing feelings of guilt, confusion, depression, anger, and loneliness. Through careful analysis examining family coherency and adolescents' emotional responses, we have learned that family attachment and personal communication differentially mediate immediate and ongoing emotional responses to a sibling's death; see the later section titled "Family Dynamics and Relationships."

Two internalizing problems—depression and anxiety—have been the focus of much research into adolescent sibling bereavement. For instance, Leslie Balmer, a Canadian psychologist and researcher, used standardized measures of depression and compared the responses of sibling bereaved adolescents and a matched group of nonbereaved adolescents; she reported the bereaved adolescents were more likely than the nonbereaved to endorse items indicative of depression.

Grades and School Work

Grades and study habits are noticeably affected following a sibling's death, with a decrease in both reported by a significant proportion of bereaved adolescents. Adolescents bereaved following a sibling's death report trouble concentrating on school work. As one high school student said,

> I didn't put as much importance on my studying. I wouldn't say like it really affected me like I didn't want to study or anything, but I think I probably was not as motivated. I studied less. I just had so much on my mind. I was busy thinking about myself and thinking about everything I was going through. I didn't feel like I had to study. I guess I kind of thought I had an excuse.
>
> (Balk, 1981, p. 294)[5]

Over time, grades and study habits return to normal for most teenagers following a sibling's death, but not for all. The return to normal patterns of studying seems most attributable to the teenagers' acceptance that personal goals and achievements are expected and acceptable. In the words of one teenager, "I'm starting to study more again. I don't study as much as I used to. But I want to get into college" (Balk, 1981, p. 295).

It is not clear why academic interests and skills remain below previous standards for a minority of sibling bereaved teenagers. One possibility is that this group of bereaved teenagers are stuck in complicated grief (Bonanno's enduring grief trajectory); another possibility is that striving for personal goals and achievements no longer seems reasonable or compelling when life has proven to be deeply unpredictable.

Leslie Balmer included school performance in her study of sibling bereaved adolescents. While subjects in her study reported problems concentrating, their academic performance did not differ from the grades of a matched set of nonbereaved adolescents. Because of obstacles to secure dependable data about school performance, Balmer expressed misgivings that self-reports of grades offer a useful measure of adjustment following sibling death.

Religion

Religion takes on increasing importance for many adolescents bereaved over a sibling's death. However, this turn to religion primarily occurs only after considerable questioning and anger vented at God. For instance, one bereaved teenager said, "At times (following my brother's death) religion didn't help me at all. It does at times now. You know, the way they explain about heaven and that. It sounds like a nice place for him" (Balk, 1981, p. 298).

In a survey of college students in the state of New York that focused on coping with separation and loss, a foundation of religious belief emerged as a primary means for building acceptance of irreparable losses. Further, adolescents grieving parental death had very different depression scores vis-à-vis religious beliefs: higher depression scores significantly were associated with lack of religious beliefs, whereas lower depression scores were associated with presence of religious beliefs.

The evidence indicates that religious beliefs interact in some manner with the processes of adolescent mourning. It would be imprudent to infer that adolescent bereavement resolution favors the religious believer. The current evidence indicates that specific grief reactions differentiate religious and nonreligious teenagers. For instance, in the first few months after a sibling's death, religious teenagers report more confusion, whereas nonreligious teenagers report more feelings of depression and fear. Religious belief does not necessarily make coping with a sibling's death any easier. Assumptions about human existence and a just, benevolent God may crumble for religious believers in the face of a sibling's death.

Family Dynamics and Relationships

A commonly reported observation from parents following the death of a child is that their surviving children seem less affected or troubled by the death than the parents would have expected. Inferences drawn are either something along the lines of "Thank God that my child is coping well and needs no special attention" or "It troubles me that my son (or daughter) does not care more." Discussions with bereaved adolescent siblings, however, have disclosed a different reality than what the parents infer. The sur-viving child typically camouflages his or her grief in order to rescue the family from the emotional chaos and devastation now engulfing the family and threatening its ongoing survival.

The avalanche of emotions in the immediate aftermath of a sibling's death and changes in these emotions over time are directly associated with (a) how close the bereaved adolescent was to family members prior to the death and (b) how frequently self-disclosure marked communication between the adolescent and family members. Adolescents who report greater family coherency (i.e., close attachments to family members and frequent communication about important, private matters) fare dif-ferently over time than bereaved adolescents whose families are marked by less fam-ily coherency (i.e., emotional distance and infrequent to nonexistent self-disclosing conversations).

In the immediate aftermath of a sibling's death, adolescents in families marked by greater coherency report feeling shocked, numb, lonely, and afraid their distress will never subside; over time, the adolescents share their feelings with other family members and report an enduring sense of sadness over the loss, but no longer report feeling afraid, shocked, lonely, or numb. Confusion and guilt about the deaths are practically nonexis-tent for these teenagers as they resolve their grief. The family's supportive environment served as a buffer for these adolescents.

In families marked by less coherency, bereaved adolescents report they initially feel guilty and angry, but few report feeling shocked, numb, afraid, or lonely. Over time, the dominant emotional reaction they report is confusion about their siblings' deaths; they also report a sense of relief that the ordeal of coping with the death is behind them.

What can account for these significant differences in emotional responses to a sibling's death tied to family communication and extent of emotional closeness? A reasonable explanation takes into account how valuable are family relationships and dynamics for the teenagers. In teenagers used to close emotional bonds and self-disclosing commu-nication, the death of a sibling is not only emotionally wrenching for everyone involved but poses a devastating threat for the existence of the family itself. Prior to the death, the family had been a constant source of security, support, and nurturance. The sibling's death has led to emotional and personal isolation, with emotional nerves frayed and per-sons working hard to keep others from expressing their distress. Never before have the teenagers seen their father cry, and never before have they seen their mother so willing to shut herself off from everyone else. Over time the very love and trust people have devel-oped for one another surfaces, and persons engage again in signs of affection and caring, and they begin to talk about things that matter, including the sibling's death. Confusion about what led to the death is removed, and the teenagers know again that their parents care enough about them to set limits as well as express affection.

In teenagers raised in emotionally distant families in which personal conversations are rare if not wholly nonexistent, the death of a sibling is distressing but the threat it poses for the family does not shake the teenager. The family has not been a source of support, and persons go their own ways. There is no one in the family with whom one feels comfortable to share guilt about being alive or to share feelings of anger that the sibling died. The passage of time does not lead to discussions about the death or about one's reactions to the death. Rather, over time relationships remain distant, and lack of open sharing about the death results in growing confusion to questions left unanswered.

Here are two case studies of adolescents' responses to sibling death. Each case is about a late adolescent female college student. The contrast in bereavement outcomes for these two young women is fairly sharp, and one can appeal to attribution theory to discuss these discrepant responses to a brother's death in an accident. In short, for one individual (Doris) her brother's death challenged her basic assumptions about reality and God's benevolence toward persons of good will. For the other individual (Sarah), her brother's death presented no challenges to what she assumed is true about a universe following laws of physics nor what she accepted as true about the relationship between God's presence and human existence.

Doris

Doris was a 19-year-old sophomore majoring in mathematics at a large, private university, about 2,000 miles from her home town. She was a very good student, and with a 4.0 GPA had made the Dean's list for both the fall and spring semesters of her freshman year. The new semester was going well, and then 2 weeks after the start of her sophomore year she learned her brother had died when out with friends on the lake. He had been sitting on the front of the power boat, lost his balance and fell into the water, and was severely lacerated by the boat's propellers. He died within minutes of the accident.

Doris found herself walking around in a daze. She stopped studying, and found it nearly impossible to concentrate on what was presented in her classes. Writing coherent papers became a chore, and one she only half-heartedly threw herself into. Her grades fell precipitously. She found herself thinking about her brother and how he died, even when she did not want to, and these thoughts distressed her. She cried when she did not want to, at times sobbing uncontrollably, wondering why she could not stop. She was not sure what she was feeling; she had never before had such a devastating thing happen to her, and it left her uncertain how to name her feelings. Besides feeling very sad, she felt confused. She lacked energy, and found climbing the stairs to her second-floor apartment wore her out. She closed in on herself and isolated herself from her roommates. She had been raised a devout Catholic, and now found prayers and church services grated on her nerves. Whereas before she had trusted in God's benevolence, there seemed ample room to doubt now.

(Balk, 2011, p. 120)

Sarah

Sarah went to the land grant university in her state. The school was about 3 hours from where she had grown up. She was a senior studying psychology, and she had plans to become either a counseling or a clinical psychologist and work with children and adolescents. She was a better than average student, with a 3.4 GPA.

Her brother Jimmy died toward the end of the first semester of her junior year. He was out riding with friends after a high school basketball game. His death occurred 2 weeks before Sarah's final exams. Sarah returned for Jimmy's funeral, and then came back to school and dug into her studies. She aced her finals. Her roommates were worried she would be so devastated by Jimmy's death that she would function poorly. She actually surprised them and perhaps herself. As she told me, "I love Jimmy and miss him. I wish he had not died. What a waste. He had so much promise. And we were close. But he would not want me to give up my life, and the only way I will be able to get my dream is to keep working hard here in school. Other people are counting on me, and I have obligations to myself . . . and obligations to Jimmy, actually."

It was not as though Sarah was untouched by Jimmy's death. For a couple of weeks she found it difficult to sleep, but those problems passed. Some persons thought she was suppressing her grief, but she did not believe them. She scoffed at the suggestion she see a counselor. Rather than isolating herself from friends, she remained involved. She was a member of the student government, and carried out her responsibilities. She finished her class assignments on time, and continued to tutor middle school children in an outreach program between her university and a local public school. Her grades remained mostly A's with some B's. She did not question how God could let her brother die; she did not think God controlled each and every event that occurs in this world. She did believe that when a car is going 85 miles an hour and hits a tree, people are more than likely going to be hurt, probably killed. She found it easy and comforting to think about and talk about her brother, to laugh when remembering some of the crazy things they had done together, but found few people felt comfortable talking about her brother when they learned he had died.

(Balk, 2011, pp. 120–121)

Various findings about recovery from bereavement emerge in these case portraits of Doris and Sarah. Doris experienced the sorts of problems Lindemann reported are true during acute grief: somatic difficulties were present for her and Sarah, but remained far longer for Doris; Doris had problems concentrating, keeping to a regular schedule, and maintaining contact with other persons, whereas Sarah quickly returned to her previous social commitments, investment in school, and engagement in extracurricular activities; Doris felt sad and confused, and while Sarah missed her brother, she was not overwhelmed with emotional spasms or uncontrollable bouts of crying; Doris was flooded with intrusive thoughts and images of her brother's death that distressed her, but Sarah's thoughts of her brother were comforting and left her feeling happy; fundamental questions about the meaning of existence and what she had been taught in her religion began plaguing Doris, but "Sarah did not find what had happened altered in the least what she believed about God and how this world works" (Balk, 2011, p. 122). Doris illustrates a person in what Bonanno has called a recovery trajectory following bereavement, and Sarah someone in a resiliency trajectory.

The Death of a Friend during Adolescence

Being accepted by peers, caring for someone else, entering into and maintaining friendship all form part of the normal maturation process; in addition, support from friends bolsters humans in times of need. Leighton noted the fundamental value of giving and receiving love and of belonging to a definite group as key aspects of human striving that separate well-adjusted individuals from persons whose coping with reality is troubled.

The Term "Friend"

Earlier in the book I dismissed the casual use of the term "friend," for instance, the absurd notion foisted by Facebook adherents that they have hundreds or even thousands of friends. Friendship is rare and valuable, not common and cheap. A friend keeps your trust and cares about you and "has your back" when times are hard. A friend is someone who shares with you private thoughts and feelings and keeps in confidence what you share. A friend listens to you attentively. A friend is proud and happy for you when you succeed and commiserates when things don't go well. Chaim Potok insightfully depicts the friendship of two adolescent boys in his novels *The Chosen* and *The Promise;* in the first book the father of one of the boys notes that it is not easy to be a friend. Being a friend is inestimably important, and persons with friends appreciate their fortune to have a friend in their life.

Paucity of Research into Friend Bereavement during Adolescence

It is puzzling that so little attention has been paid to adolescent grief over the death of a friend. Developmental psychologists acknowledge the increasing importance of peers in the growth of adolescents, and there is consensus that friendship is linked to healthy adjustment. Certain developmental aspects of friendship have become clear.

- With increasing age and experience, youths change their expectations about friendship. As an example, emphasis on playing together diminishes, while accent on reciprocity increases.
- Intimacy and physical support are two attributes of friendship that noticeably emerge during adolescence.

- Mutuality takes on increasingly complex content due to the cognitive changes and interpersonal contact that promote self-disclosure and perspective taking.
- Over the course of their undergraduate years, college students become more interested in a select group of friends, and may spend most of their time with one close friend.

The death of a friend violates basic assumptions adolescents make about fairness and justice. The death of a friend bears some analogous connections to the death of a child: it occurs off time and out of sequence. An adolescent is supposed to live to old age, just as a child is supposed to outlive her parents. Thus, the death of a friend can also challenge assumptions about the predictability of events.

The paucity of research into bereavement over friend deaths is doubly perplexing considering the incidence of violent deaths from accidents, murders, and completed suicides that accompany adolescent risk taking. Many adolescents will know a peer who dies, will be deeply affected by the death, and yet will be less likely to be seen as bereaved because bereavement over deaths of family members is more readily recognized. "Hidden population" and "forgotten grievers" are two terms used to depict this ignoring or undervaluing of the grief of adolescents when friends die. At least three identifiable subgroups make up the hidden population of bereaved friends: (a) the elderly, (b) same sex adult dyads, and (c) adolescents and young adults.

Responses to open-ended interviews with college students and from essays written by members of support groups indicate that dealing with the death of a friend closely parallels the grief experienced over the death of a family member. The death of a friend evokes shock, disbelief, and anger. The death of a friend can also stimulate existential concerns about one's own mortality. Grief reactions to the death of a parent, sibling, or friend frequently stir up difficulties concentrating and concomitant problems with school performance.

Attachment and Friend Grief

Attachment issues play a significant role in how an individual responds to another's death. It is important when assessing reactions to the death of someone identified as a friend to determine the extent of attachment the bereaved person ascribes to the relationship. For instance, bereaved high school and college students when asked will differentiate whether the person who died was a close friend, an acquaintance, or someone barely known.

Researchers have found that intensity of adolescent grief reactions over friend death is directly associated with closeness to the person who died. For instance, Joan McNeil and her colleagues noted high school students' reactions to the death of a peer depended on how close they were to the person who died. Synthesizing that research, Heather Servaty-Seib reported, adolescents

closest to a high school classmate who died from leukemia were more likely to report having trouble talking about the death and paying attention in class than less close peers. The closer peers were also more likely to express a belief that this death changed them in some way, including heightening their awareness of their own mortality and increasing both their thoughts about life after death and their concern about the people they loved.

(Servaty-Seib, 2009, p. 223)

Close attachments become intensified in cohesive groups such as sports teams or combat units in which individuals depend on one another and share experiences that matter to all. Such a phenomenon is manifestly true of combat troops, many who are 18 to 23 years old and whom I suspect are impelled into a maturity beyond that of their same-aged peers who are not soldiers. The intensity of grief over the death of one's buddy in combat may be complicated by sheer terror experienced when under attack and by the trauma experienced at seeing, hearing, and smelling persons being ripped to pieces by high-powered weapons.

Some researchers have reported that the grief of US combat soldiers returning from deployment in Iraq and Afghanistan is saturated with physical health issues. Links to Lindemann's identified symptomatology are obvious. The soldiers who had difficulty coping with grief reported problems sleeping, poor general health, fatigue, and difficulties carrying out normal training expectations. I suspect we are talking here about grief overlaid with trauma and about the need to design informed interventions that prove useful to persons at high risk of complicated bereavement. This type of friend death deserves considerable attention.

Here is the case study of a late adolescent male college student whose best friend died in an accident for which he holds himself at fault. Elements of trauma are present. The sequelae of Daniel's reactions following the death of his girlfriend are indicative of what we would consider an enduring grief reaction or, in the words of some clinicians I know, a portrait of someone stuck in grief.

Daniel

Daniel had been a 20-year-old college junior at a large land grant university a few hundred miles from his home. He had liked school, and the persons he had met there. He was in a pre-med program, and felt confident about his desire to become a physician. Already he had arranged for a summer placement in a rural medical clinic. He knew once he became a physician that he would make a difference in people's lives. He had met Jenna at the university, and they liked each other a lot and had been dating seriously for several months. Actually, Daniel loved Jenna, and looked to the day they would be married.

In short, Daniel had been doing well in school and felt good about being alive. Then everything changed 10 months ago when on a rainy night he lost control of the car he was driving and hit a bridge abutment. He was hardly scratched, but Jenna was severely injured, and eventually died. The police report said it looked to them that the car had hydroplaned and that what happened could not possibly be Daniel's fault.

Daniel took no comfort in what the police concluded. He had been responsible for keeping Jenna safe. He felt desolate, and had recurring panic attacks. He had trouble sleeping, found he constantly thought about Jenna and the accident, could not concentrate on school work or remember things, and was very restless. Several persons at the university knew about the accident, but only one person, Jenna's roommate, made any effort to offer condolences. When he approached his organic chemistry teacher to see about getting an extension on course assignments, the teacher told him there would be no exceptions made about when assignments were due, and he would have to take the mid-term with everyone else. It was clear to Daniel that other students became uncomfortable when Daniel was in the same room.

He made some efforts to study, but his course work seemed without meaning, and 5 weeks following the accident he simply packed up his things and came home. He had not considered contacting the Dean of Students or finding out if it was possible to take a leave of absence. Following the rules of the university for taking an official leave of absence was not a priority; getting away from school seemed a good idea. Getting away from all reminders of the accident seemed a good idea. The idea was to get away.

Daniel told himself over and over he was guilty and deserved to be punished. When his parents heard these comments, they became very concerned and arranged for Daniel to see a mental health counselor. The counselor had little understanding of bereavement and grief. He was concerned about suicidal risks and did ascertain that Daniel had no plan to take his life. After listening to Daniel's story, he explained to Daniel about Kubler-Ross's stages of grief and told Daniel it seemed clear he was in the anger stage. Daniel stopped seeing the counselor after the third session, thinking he did not deserve to get better.

Months passed. Daniel's grief remained relentless. To stop feeling bad about Jenna's death seemed to Daniel an utter betrayal of her. It would be like he didn't care. He constantly thought about Jenna and missed her intensely. Images of her bloody body came to him when asleep and when awake. He no longer had any plans for what do with his life, and did not take part in the internship with the rural clinic. It all seemed meaningless.

He had thought he could make a difference in people's lives. But now he realized life was a series of random events with no meaning. He had invested deeply, unreservedly in his school work and in Jenna. It had been a mistake. But there was one thing he was sure of: he was guilty of having killed her. And no one, not even his parents, seemed to appreciate the extent to which he had loved Jenna and how her death shattered him. He mostly stayed in his room at his parents' house, staring into space and now and then crying uncontrollably.

(Balk, 2011, pp. 223–225)

Daniel's case illustrates a bereaved person whose acute grief never lessens. Somatic distress overwhelms continually. He has shut himself off from others emotionally. His consciousness is flooded with distressing thoughts and images of his girlfriend. Most of all, he feels guilt for causing her death. Not only has he gone from a person with a purpose to being aimless and easily distracted, he now lacks initiative, has no zest for living, and has lost hope. Without expert professional intervention, it is doubtful that Daniel will ever recover from his grief over Jenna's death.

Concluding Comments

Three major sources of bereavement for adolescents are the deaths of parents, siblings, and friends. While distinctions will separate grief over these deaths—distinctions linked to the core developmental tasks adolescents are expected to master—many similarities abound. For instance, achieving an autonomous identity and emotional separation from parents provides salient if often ineffable influences on an adolescent grieving a parent's death; the phenomenology of grief reactions, however, seems true across the board, as evidenced in acute grief symptoms and challenges to make sense of the situation. Not all deaths provide challenges to meaning-making, and thus there are bereaved adolescents whose reactions fall more typically into a resiliency trajectory; however, distress can prove longer lasting and problematic, as evidenced in adolescents whose grief falls into a recovery trajectory; and then there are some whose acute grief never lessens, whose anxiety and guilt continue unabated, and so you find some adolescents whose pattern is the enduring grief trajectory. We saw examples of these three trajectories in the stories of Sarah, Doris, and Daniel. What is being reported about soldiers returning from war indicates that a notable portion have ongoing struggles with grief overlaid with trauma in some cases.

A sustaining theme concerning adolescence is the journey for self-understanding. This theme suffuses research findings about bereavement during adolescence. It is implausible that coping with the death of a parent, sibling, or friend has no influence on the psychological development of an adolescent. We see some of the outcomes in career decisions. Altruism comes to the fore in the lives of some adolescents who have coped with bereavement. Courage in the face of others' distress has been a hallmark of every bereaved adolescent I have met: whereas other persons flee figuratively or literally from individuals in emotional difficulties, adolescents who have been bereaved find the strength to remain present. Coping with bereavement has offered them opportunities for growth.

Don't misunderstand. I am not saying having to struggle with bereavement is desirable, and I am not suggesting all things turn out swell for a person who has grieved an irreparable loss. Every bereaved adolescent I know has acknowledged having been through bereavement matured them and brought them some benefits, such as not taking others for granted; however, each one said they would gladly, instantly give up these gains to have their father, mother, sister, brother, or friend back. Some note that problems concentrating in the immediate aftermath of a death led to severe setbacks in school from which they never recovered.

A supportive family plays an important part in the recovery from bereavement. Such information folds easily into the theoretical writings about human responses to life crises (think of Leighton), the explanations about coping with life crises (think of Moos & Schaefer), and the studies of interventions with bereaved adolescents (think of Sandler and his research team). Such support can be extended by designing and implementing a variety of interventions aimed at the tri-partite model of primary, secondary, and tertiary intervention. We turn next in this book to discussing the structure and place of interventions with bereaved adolescents.

Notes

1. However, in a review of depression during childhood and adolescence, Poznanski (1979, p. 57) had argued that scholars would be smart to examine sibling death rather than parental for three reasons: "In reality, sibling loss frequently brings three complicating emotional issues for the child: (1) a preceding state of parent deprivation if the sibling loss was preceded by a chronic illness; (2) sibling rivalry—which is an issue for adults as well but is much more acute for the child; (3) the parental state of grief again affecting the ability of the parents to relate to the remaining children during the period of their own bereavement."
2. A status offense is behavior prohibited to a juvenile but not illegal when done by an adult. Examples are disobeying parents and smoking cigarettes. Criminal offenses committed by a juvenile are against the law for adults also. Examples include shoplifting and assaulting someone.
3. It is important to note that Dueck's fine qualitative work included only 10 participants, and thus provides important positive suggestions but not definitive conclusions.
4. Go to www.studentsofamf.org to access the organization's Internet site.
5. Worden reported problems concentrating in school for many of the children whose parents had died, and the great majority of bereaved college students report a significant negative impact on grades in the first semester following the death of a family member or friend.

Sources

Balk, D. E. (1981). *Sibling death during adolescence: Self-concept and bereavement reactions.* Unpublished doctoral dissertation, University of Illinois, Champaign, IL.

Balk, D. E. (1983). Adolescents' grief reactions and self-concept perceptions following sibling death: A case study of 33 teenagers. *Journal of Youth and Adolescence, 12,* 137–161.

Balk, D. E. (1990). The self-concepts of bereaved adolescents: Sibling death and its aftermath. *Journal of Adolescent Research, 5,* 112–132.

Balk, D. E. (1991). Sibling death, adolescent bereavement, and religion. *Death Studies, 15,* 1–20.

Balk, D. E. (2009). Sibling death during adolescence. In D. E. Balk & C. A. Corr (Eds.), *Adolescent encounters with death and bereavement* (pp. 199–216). New York: Springer.

Balk, D. E. (2011). *Helping the bereaved college student.* New York: Springer.

Balk, D. E. & Hogan, N. S. (1995). Religion and bereaved adolescents. In D. W. Adams & E. Deveau (Eds.), *Loss, threat to life, and bereavement: The child's perspective* (pp. 61–88). Amityville, NY: Baywood.

Balk, D. E. & Vesta, L. C. (1998). Psychological development during four years of bereavement: A case study. *Death Studies, 22,* 23–41.

Balmer, L. E. (1992). *Adolescent sibling bereavement: Mediating effects of family environment and personality.* Unpublished doctoral dissertation, York University, Toronto, Ontario.

Brent, D. A., Melhem, N. M., Masten, A. S., Porta, G., & Payne, M. W. (2012). Longitudinal effects of parental bereavement on adolescent developmental competence. *Journal of Clinical Child & Adolescent Psychology, 41,* 778–791.

Clark, D. C., Pynoos, R. S., & Goebel, A. E. (1996). Mechanisms and processes of adolescent bereavement. In R. J. Haggerty & L. R. Sherrod (Eds.), *Stress, risk, and resilience in children and adolescents: Processes, mechanisms, and interventions* (pp. 100–146). New York: Cambridge University Press.

Cohen, J., Goodman, R. F., Brown, E. J., & Mannarino, A. (2004). Treatment of childhood traumatic grief: Contributing to a newly emerging condition in the wake of community trauma. *Harvard Review of Psychiatry, 12,* 213–216.

Demmer, C. & Rothschild, N. (2011). Bereavement among South African adolescents following a sibling's death from AIDS. *African Journal of AIDS Research, 10,* 15–24.

Dueck, A. G. (2011). *Bereaved university students making vocational commitments: The impact of losing a loved one on career decisions.* Unpublished Master's thesis, Trinity Western University, Langley, British Columbia.

Fleming, S. J. & Adolph, R. (1986). Helping bereaved adolescents: Needs and responses. In C. A. Corr & J. N. McNeil (Eds.), *Adolescence and death* (pp. 97–118). New York: Springer.

Fulton, R. (2003). Anticipatory mourning: A critique of the concept. *Mortality, 8,* 341–351.

Gilliland, G. & Fleming, S. J. (1998). A comparison of spousal anticipatory grief and conventional grief. *Death Studies, 22,* 541–569.

Goodman, R. A. (1986). *Adolescent grief characteristics when a parent dies.* Unpublished doctoral dissertation, Boulder, CO, University of Colorado.

Gray, R. A. (1987). Adolescent response to the death of a parent. *Journal of Youth and Adolescence,16,* 511–525.

Guerriero-Austrom, A. M. & Fleming, S. J. (1990). *Effects of sibling death on adolescents' physical and emotional well-being.* Paper presented at the Annual Convention of the American Psychological Association, Boston.

Hagan, M, J., Roubinov, D. S., Gress-Smith, J., Luecken, L. J., Sandler, I. N., & Wolchik, S. (2011). Positive parenting during childhood moderates the impact of recent negative events on cortisol activity in parentally bereaved youth. *Psychopharmacology, 214,* 231–238.

Haggerty, R. J., Sherrod, L. R., Garmezy, N., & Rutter, M. (Editors). (1996). *Stress, risk, and resilience in children and adolescents: Processes, mechanisms, and interventions.* New York: Cambridge University Press.

Hogan, N. S. (1987). *An investigation of the adolescent bereavement process and adaptation.* Unpublished doctoral dissertation, Loyola University, Chicago.

Hogan, N. S. (1988). The effects of time on the adolescent sibling bereavement process. *Pediatric Nursing, 14,* 333–335.

Hogan, N. S. (1990). Hogan Sibling Inventory of Bereavement. In J. Touliatos, B. Perlmutter, & M. Straus (Eds.), *Handbook of family measurement techniques* (p. 254). Newbury Park, CA: Sage.

Hogan, N. S. & Balk, D. E. (1990). Adolescents' reactions to sibling death: Perceptions of mothers, fathers, and teenagers. *Nursing Research, 39,* 103–106.

Hogan, N. S. & DeSantis, L. (1992). Adolescent sibling bereavement: An ongoing attachment. *Qualitative Health Research, 2,* 150–177.

Hogan, N. S. & DeSantis, L. (1994). Things that help and hinder adolescent sibling bereavement. *Western Journal of Nursing Research, 16,* 132–153.

Hogan, N. S. & Greenfield, D. B. (1991). Adolescent bereavement symptomatology in a large community sample. *Journal of Adolescent Research, 6,* 97–112.

Hogan, N. S., Greenfield, D. B., & Schmidt, L. A. (2001). Development and validation of the Hogan Grief Reaction Checklist. *Death Studies, 25,* 1–32.

LaGrand, L. E. (1986). *Coping with separation and loss as a young adult: Theoretical and practical realities.* Springfield, IL: Charles C. Thomas.

Lenhardt, A. C. & McCourt, B. (2000). Adolescent unresolved grief in response to the death of a mother. *Professional School Counseling, 3,* 189–196.

McNeil, J. N., Silliman, B., & Swihart, J. J. (1991). Helping adolescents cope with the death of a peer: A high school case study. *Journal of Adolescent Research, 6,* 132–143.

Murphy, P. A. (1986–1987). Parental death in childhood and loneliness in young adults. *Omega, 17,* 219–238.

Oltjenbruns, K. A. (2013). Life span issues and loss, grief, and mourning: Childhood and adolescence. In D. K. Meagher & D. E. Balk (Eds.), *Handbook of thanatology: The essential body of knowledge for the study of death, dying, and bereavement* (pp. 149–156). Deerfield, IL: ADEC and New York: Routledge.

Paris, M. M., Carter, B. L., Day, S. X., & Armsworth, M. W. (2009). Grief and trauma in children after the death of a sibling. *Journal of Child & Adolescent Trauma, 2,* 71–80.

Potok, C. (1967). *The chosen.* New York: Simon and Schuster.

Potok, C. (1969). *The promise.* New York: Knopf.

Poznanski, E. O. (1979). Childhood depression: A psychodynamic approach to the etiology and treatment of depression in children. In A. French & I. Berlin (Eds.), *Depression in children and adolescents* (pp. 46–68). New York: Human Sciences Press.

Rando, T. A. (2000). *Clinical dimensions of anticipatory mourning: Theory and practice in working with the dying, their loved ones, and their caregivers.* Champaign, IL: Research Press.

Rappaport, J. (1977). *Community psychology: Values, research, and action.* New York: Holt, Rinehart and Winston.

Ribbens McCarthy, J. (2006). Resilience and bereaved children: Developing complex approaches. *Grief Matters, 9,* 58–61.

Ribbens McCarthy, J. (2006). *Young people's experiences of loss and bereavement: Toward an interdisciplinary approach.* Buckingham, UK: Open University.

Saldinger, A. L. (2001). *Anticipating parental death in families with school-aged children.* Unpublished doctoral dissertation, University of Michigan, Ann Arbor, MI.

Schmiege, S. J., Khoo, S. T., Sandler, I. N., Ayers, T. S., & Wolchik, S. A. (2006). Symptoms of internalizing and externalizing problems: Modeling recovery curves after the death of a parent. *American Journal of Preventive Medicine, 31,* S152–S160.

Seligman, M. E. P. (2002). *Authentic happiness: Using the new positive psychology to realize your potential for lasting fulfillment.* New York: Free Press.

Servaty-Seib, H. L. (2009). Death of a friend during adolescence. In D. E. Balk & C. A. Corr (Eds.), *Adolescent encounters with death, bereavement, and coping* (pp. 217–235). New York: Springer.

Servaty-Seib, H. L. & Pistole, M. C. (2006). Adolescent grief: Relationship category and emotional closeness. *Omega, 54,* 147–167.

Sklar, F. & Hartley, S. F. (1990). Close friends as survivors: Bereavement patterns in a "hidden" population. *Omega, 21,* 103–112.

Stokes, J., Reid, C., & Cook, V. (2009). Life as an adolescent when a parent has died. In D. E. Balk & C. A. Corr (Eds.), *Adolescent encounters with death, bereavement, and coping* (pp. 177–197). New York: Springer.

Super, D. E. (1957). *The psychology of careers.* New York: Harper & Row.

Super, D. E. (1990). A life-span, life-space, approach to career development. *Journal of Vocational Development, 16,* 282–298.

Thompson, M. P., Kaslow, N. J., King, M., Bryant, L., & Rey, M. (1998). Psychological symptomatology following parental death in a predominantly minority sample of children and adolescents. *Journal of Clinical Child Psychology, 27,* 434–441.

Thupayagale-Tshweneagae, G. & Benedict, S. (2011). The burden of secrecy among South African adolescents orphaned by HIV and AIDS. *Issues in Mental Health Nursing, 32,* 355–358.

Toblin, R. L., Riviere, L. A., Thomas, J. L., Adler, A. B., Kok, B.C., & Hoge, C. W. (2013). Grief and physical health outcomes in U.S. soldiers returning from combat. *Journal of Affective Disorders,* **136,** 469–475.

Wolchik, S. A., Tein, J-Y., Sandler, I. N., Ayers, T. S. (2006). Stressors, quality of the child-caregiver relationship, and children's mental health problems after parental death: The mediating role of self-system beliefs. *Journal of Abnormal Child Psychology,* **34,** 221–238.

Worden, J. W. (1996). *Children and grief: When a parent dies.* New York: The Guilford Press.

10 Interventions

Prolegomena to a Chapter on Interventions

A gap continues to separate thanatology practitioners and researchers, but some progress in spanning this gap has occurred over the past 10 to 15 years. The progress has come from imaginative concepts that scholars have disclosed, such as continuing bonds or trajectories of grief; research evidence grounds these concepts. Other shared understandings have occurred via interventions, primarily psychological, to assist life-threatened or grieving persons.

Interventions are planned efforts to produce desired outcomes, and they provide fruitful meeting grounds for thanatology researchers and practitioners to examine assumptions and identify opportunities for collaboration. This chapter looks at interventions aimed at producing desired outcomes with life-threatened adolescents and with bereaved adolescents. I begin with a look at how researchers and practitioners could proceed in spanning the gap.

A Process to Consider as an Inroad for Spanning the Research–Practice Gap

Before getting into extended discussion of specific interventions, I decided to take a few moments writing about a process whereby researchers and practitioners can collaborate on the design, delivery, and evaluation of interventions meaningful to life-threatened or bereaved adolescents. I contend this process of designing, delivering, and evaluating interventions will productively span the gap. This process involves at least two phenomena:

- Clear investment of both parties in theory (a) as salient in their thinking about what they do and (b) as grounding for intelligent, respectful discussions that cross party lines
- Engagement of both parties in attentive listening to what matters to the other, openness to discuss differences, and willingness to learn from each other

Let's look at this process by identifying assumptions I make about helpful, that is, effective, counselors. Effective thanatological counselors have developed a conceptual framework that informs them how to proceed in their work with clients and enables them to explain outcomes and identify matters that don't quite go according to expectations. These components—a clear theoretical point of view, wisdom, and practical experience—provide the means for dialogue to occur between practitioners and researchers. In short, I am asserting that effective, intelligently informed thanatological counselors are planful and do not simply wing it as they move from session to session with clients. The effective, intelligently informed practitioner works with conceptual scaffolding that helps him or her to identify a client's needs and to plan interventions that will address those needs. A practitioner's conceptual scaffolding is the set of ideas that help explain human responses (such as reactions to the death of a loved one) and help predict how things will turn out should specific steps be taken. This conceptual scaffolding by any other name is a theory that informs the practitioner. Examples of some theories informing thanatological counselors are the grief work theory, social learning theory, attachment theory, family systems theory, constructivism, resiliency theory, psychoanalysis, and symbolic interactionism.

Effective, intelligently informed researchers also work from an overarching theoretical position. They derive hypotheses worth testing from deductive reflection framed by the theory that informs them. When they know of no theory to explain what they are observing, they turn to qualitative methods such as grounded theory and ethnography in order to arrive at a theoretical explanation. Consider a researcher who is examining longitudinally the impact of bereavement in the lives of parentally bereaved adolescents. He or she designs the research with the tenets of resiliency theory as the study's guiding set of principles, and from this theory identifies (a) outcomes that are predicted to occur and (b) what the research will test to see if they do occur. Or consider a researcher who is studying the outcomes of a psychosocial intervention aimed at adolescents diagnosed with early stage cancer; he or she uses the holistic framework as the theory to guide the study, designs the intervention to address each component in the holistic framework, and assesses outcomes according to changes observed in each component. Myra Bluebond-Langner used in-depth, longitudinal qualitative methods to produce a convincing explanation for the manner whereby terminally ill children come to understand and to communicate (as well as conceal their knowledge) they are dying; she closely followed the theory of childhood socialization, intermingled with symbolic-interactionism and ethnomethodology, and deliberately rejected two theoretical approaches in socialization (structural-functionalism and psychological functionalism) because those frameworks ignore the child's active role in interpreting the world, others, and self.

Practitioners and researchers intelligently informed by theory have the basis for critical discussions about what needs to be done to help persons dealing with troubling life situations; I am not just saying theory in general will fill the bill, but rather I am asserting there must be one or more theories that the practitioner finds persuasive, and one or more the researcher finds persuasive. Then the practitioner and the researcher have the intellectual grounds to discuss how they understand responses to the various issues that emerge in the lives of the bereaved and in the lives of the life-threatened. The researcher may espouse a different theory than the one guiding the practitioner, but the espousal of a theory provides a starting point for discussions aimed at producing interventions that are based in solid research evidence and are acceptable to a practitioner.

Interventions based on collaborative discussion and planning could possibly reach the gold standard of evidence-based practice. Evidence-based practices must meet certain standards, among them:

1.   The intervention has been tested on a clearly specified target population in randomized clinical trials.

2. Multiple replications at numerous sites have been run.
3. The intervention has a solid, coherent theory at its foundation.
4. The intervention produces clear benefits—or desired outcomes—in the persons who receive the intervention and such benefits do not occur in persons who did not receive the intervention.
5. Persons receiving the intervention do not suffer harm.

Theory holds paramount value in designing, administering, and assessing the outcomes of an intervention. Thus I come to this belief about the place of theory for spanning the research-practice gap: Collaborative discussions between practitioners and researchers grounded in theory offer a very promising inroad for designing research studies that (a) matter to both practitioners and researchers, (b) allow researchers to address intelligently the question "So what?" rightly raised by practitioners, and (c) allow practitioners to address intelligently the question "How do you know that what you do works?" rightly raised by everyone.

Not all interventions reach the gold standard of evidence-based practice, and practitioners cannot be expected to wait until a set of procedures is definitively examined before acting on the behalf of clients. At the same time practitioners should expect some criteria to be applied so that various interventions can be rated. One approach is the taxonomy identified in collaborative work of interdisciplinary teams interested in interventions aimed at children who are victims of physical or sexual abuse. Here in descending order is a rating system offered by this taxonomy.

1. Evidence-based: The intervention has a solid theoretical foundation and has been examined in randomized control designs. Different approaches have been compared, results have been replicated, a clear manual identifies how to carry out the intervention, and the research has been assessed via blind peer review.
2. Evidence-supported: The intervention has a solid theoretical foundation but has been examined in nonrandomized designs. All the other criteria applicable to evidence-based apply.
3. Evidence-informed: Evidence comes from case studies or the intervention was tested on a target group other than the specific population of interest to the practitioner. There have not been any replications of results. There is a manual. The possibility of harm has not been discounted.
4. Belief-based: The intervention being followed has no published research to support it, and no solid theory as its foundation; the intervention is based on ideology rather than empirically tested theory. There are no published research results assessed in blind peer review. There may be a manual to guide practitioners.
5. Harmful: Interventions with documented harmful effects are proscribed.

The five categories in the taxonomy offer guidance to a practitioner. When possible, practitioners are expected to use an intervention that rightfully belongs in the top rating, namely, evidence-based. However, when no such option is available, alternatives in other categories beckon. The rule-of-thumb is (a) to prefer an intervention higher on the rating scale than one lower on the scale, (b) to implement an intervention that fits the persons one wants to serve, and (c) to do no harm.

An Overarching Framework for Classifying Interventions:
The Tripartite Model of Primary, Secondary, and Tertiary Interventions

Community mental health was a powerful vision for providing quality mental health services to persons in the United States, particularly to persons in underserved, impoverished communities. How services were delivered was seen to be fundamentally aimed at the needs endemic to the community a particular agency served. There was an overarching framework for services borrowed from Public Health. This framework classifies interventions into one of three major categories: primary, secondary, and tertiary.

- Primary interventions are aimed at strengthening persons and/or at averting harm. A medical example would be vaccinating persons against small pox; a community mental health example would be educating adults about positive parenting with their children.
- Secondary interventions are aimed at enabling persons to adapt positively to life situations that may worsen without such involvement. A medical example would be providing physical therapy for an individual following knee replacement surgery; a community mental health example would be offering support groups for parents grieving the death of a child.
- Tertiary interventions are aimed at assisting persons to manage difficult issues that have already affected their lives. A medical example would be using dialysis with persons whose kidneys do not function properly; a community mental health example would be using cognitive behavioral therapy with persons whose bereavement is in an enduring grief trajectory.[1]

The Organization of This Chapter

The focus of this chapter is on interventions with life-threatened adolescents and interventions with bereaved adolescents. When possible, evidence-based practices will be highlighted, but I recognize that not all strategies to promote desired outcomes meet the standards for practices that are evidence-based. I have looked at interventions in terms of whether they belong in the primary, secondary, or tertiary category.

Primary Interventions

Primary interventions in thanatology encompass formal educational efforts, hospice efforts that avert the development of complicated grief, college programs promoting spiritual development, growth and transformation via exploration of life values, information campaigns, and public policy efforts. I have looked first at formal educational efforts, primarily on college campuses.[2]

Formal Education

Formal education possesses long-standing, tested means to assess outcomes. I am referring to identifying the educational objectives that formal education is designed to achieve. There is extensive scholarly work on educational objectives whereby programs, courses, and student learning can be evaluated.

Within thanatology coursework in high school and in college, the principal interests are to achieve both cognitive and affective objectives. The cognitive objectives involve the development of intellectual skills. Objectives in the cognitive domain comprise a hierarchy of ever-increasing difficulty and complexity ranging from knowledge of facts to evaluating the merit and worth of the subject matter under consideration. Here in brief is the hierarchical arrangement of the cognitive domain of educational objectives.

1. Knowledge of facts: This cognitive objective, lowest on the hierarchy, forms the basis for attaining other intellectual skills. Persons who master knowledge do so through recall of information. The person either knows the answer or doesn't. Persons who do well on *Jeopardy* have stored a lot of facts they can recall when needed. Two examples testing knowledge of facts are (a) Name the two United States senators from New York and (b) Name a statistical test for comparing the mean scores of three or more groups.
2. Comprehension of information (sometimes called understanding): This cognitive objective involves intellectual skill in stating knowledge in one's own words, and it obviously requires mastery of knowledge. Two examples testing comprehension of information are (a) State in your own words the qualifications mentioned in the US Constitution to be a United States senator and (b) Explain what analysis of variance does.
3. Application of information (sometimes called using information): This cognitive objective involves making use of what was learned in one situation when in a different situation. Predominantly, when college students are asked how they will know they are learning and whether a course is worthwhile, they say "When I find I am using the information outside of class." Two examples testing application of information are (a) Use the framework in the US Constitution about qualifications to be a senator to determine if you are eligible and (b) Determine what statistical test will best analyze your research data.
4. Analysis of information: This cognitive skill involves separating complex material into component parts. Analysis involves skill in distinguishing facts from inferences. Two examples to test analysis of information are (a) Compare and contrast the presidential campaigns of Mitt Romney and Barack Obama and (b) From research reported by the World Health Organization, what inferences can you draw about the role of vaccines in the onset of autism in children?
5. Synthesis of information: This cognitive skill involves building a coherent whole from disparate, perhaps seemingly incongruent parts. Two items to test synthesis of information are (a) Write a 5,000 word essay explaining the major issues facing the world should Iran gain nuclear weapons and (b) Write a Master's thesis on objections to death education in the elementary schools.
6. Evaluation of information (sometimes called judging): This cognitive skill involves assessing the merit or worth of something. Two items to test evaluation of information are (a) Judge the legislative accomplishments of Senator Charles Schumer and (b) Evaluate the efficacy of an intervention to reduce obesity in children.

The affective domain of educational objectives encompasses the manner in which we emotionally respond to educational material. There are five major affective categories, arranged hierarchically from lowest to highest.

1. Receiving information (sometimes called openness to information): This affective objective deals with sensitivity to or awareness of certain phenomena. Here are some examples to illustrate this first of the affective objectives: (a) The student

develops awareness of different types of jazz; (b) The student listens to viewpoints other than his or her own.

2. Responding: This affective objective deals with actively attending to phenomena, not merely perceiving or observing them. Two examples to illustrate responding are (a) The student voluntarily reads the newspaper and (b) The student seeks out research articles in his or her field of study.

3. Valuing: This affective objective involves demonstrating a commitment to something. The behavior builds on receiving and responding. It mirrors the cognitive objective of evaluating, and involves acting on what one sees is worthwhile. Two examples are (a) The student manages his or her schedule and completes assignments when due and (b) The person insures that his or her research study meets ethical standards required by the university.

4. Organization: This affective objective, closely tied to the cognitive objective of evaluation, involves placing priorities into a coherent system whereby the person can contrast and compare different values. Two examples to illustrate this affective objective are (a) The student formulates criteria for determining the credibility of a research study and (b) The individual accepts the ethical standards of behavior in his or her profession.

5. Internalizing (sometimes called character development): This last and most complex affective behavior refers to having an internalized set of core beliefs that guides actions. Here are two examples: (a) In light of new evidence, the researcher revises his or her judgments about the value of a psychoanalytic understanding of trauma and (b) The person values people for what their behavior discloses rather than what they claim or how they look.

College courses focused on death, dying, and bereavement are popular. The best organized and delivered courses have clearly stated educational objectives, and as effective interventions (at least so I strongly believe) such courses promote student attainment of cognitive and affective outcomes. Specifying the educational objectives offers a powerful starting point to promote student investment in learning and critical thinking. Specification of objectives can be (I think should be) paired with teaching methods that engage students to become actively involved in the subject matter, to connect ideas from various sources, and to gain insight by comparing and contrasting their own experiences with the course material.

An undergraduate course. I have presented information about an undergraduate college course on death, dying, and bereavement. Table 10.1 provides the educational objectives—both cognitive and affective—for this course. An abbreviated version of the syllabi for the course is found in Appendix A. The course is arranged in three parts: (a) an examination of the impact of the biomedical model on contemporary views of life, death, and dying; (b) a review of human responses to bereavement; and (c) a look at special topics, particularly responses in Europe, Australia, and the United States to physician-assisted suicide.

The course requires students to read and write; I tell students that writing is an extension of thinking, and note that reading and writing well are skills college graduates use all the time. On three occasions students are placed in small discussion groups to read

Table 10.1 Educational Objectives in an Undergraduate Course Titled Human Encounters with Death and Bereavement

The students will:

1. Identify the factors that influence personal attitudes toward death and dying.
2. Describe and analyze the various programs of care for the terminally ill.
3. Describe the process of bereavement and examine various models offered about bereavement.
4. Learn how adolescents and the elderly deal with death, dying, and bereavement.
5. Review and analyze three personal accounts about death, dying, and bereavement.
6. Engage in critical discussion of the personal accounts with a small group of students enrolled in the course.
7. Identify ways in which one may help a grieving family member or friend.
8. Critique the various arguments presented by proponents and opponents of the activities labeled as euthanasia.
9. Summarize and reflect on the feedback given to your written work.
10. Meet the due dates for assignments in the course.
11. Demonstrate willingness to listen to and understand points of view different than one's own.
12. Provide constructive critiques of others' written work, and accept constructive critiques from others about your own written work.
13. Complete a course project chosen from a variety of options listed in the syllabus.

aloud and comment on critical essays written about personal accounts: (a) reflections from a man with amyotrophic lateral sclerosis, (b) descriptions of the bereavement experiences of three college students, and (c) analysis of a medical doctor on caring for elderly persons with intractable, debilitating, chronic conditions. In each assignment the students are given questions to address that permit students to become actively involved in the subject matter, to connect ideas from various sources, and to gain insight by comparing and contrasting their own experiences with the course material. For instance, the assignment on the three bereaved college students instructs students to address the items presented in Table 10.2.

Table 10.2 Group Discussion Items

Answer 1, 2, 3, and 4.

1. Apply ideas from Lindemann's or Bowlby's understandings of grief to one of the stories.
2. Which bereavement trajectory fits Doris's story, which fits Sarah's, and which fits Daniel's? Give reasons. Don't just name the trajectory.
3. What examples of disenfranchised grief are there in any of the stories?
4. Present evidence in each story that depicts the approach to grieving—instrumental or intuitive or a combination of both—used by Doris, by Sarah, and by Daniel?

Answer either 5 or 6.

5. What evidence in one of the stories depicts the dual process model of coping with loss?
6. What evidence in one of the stories depicts the Moos model of coping with a life crisis?

Table 10.3 Worksheet for Use in Discussion of Personal Accounts

For each personal account that is discussed, review these questions and provide written responses documenting your group's discussion:

1. What are the strengths in **each person's summary** and what are some ways **each student** can improve his/her summary to provide a clear and reliable presentation of the personal account? (**Give particulars** about each group member's summary, not just a statement about the summaries in general.)
2. What were the strengths in **each person's** answers to the questions and what are some ways **each student** can improve his/her answers to the questions? (**Give particulars** about each **group member's answers,** not just a statement about the answers in general.)
3. What personal experiences and observations of group members were mentioned as experiences and observations that confirm or call into question material in the personal account? (Give particulars about each group member's experiences and observations, not just a statement about comments in general.)
4. What are areas on which people reach consensus? (**Give particulars.**)
5. What are areas on which people disagree? (**Give particulars.**)
6. How could the personal account be strengthened as an introduction to one or more topics about this course? (**Give particulars.**)

Synthesize the group's answers to the 6 items and turn in the worksheet with accompanying pages with summaries of the discussion. The summary is due at the end of the class in which the personal account is being discussed.

Take turns at each group meeting writing summaries of the items. Make sure each person in the group summarizes discussion about at least one item at the meeting. Be sure to give examples that illustrate what was discussed. Don't for instance simply say, "We agreed about everything." Give examples that verify or illustrate this agreement.

Title of personal account:_____

Date of meeting: _____

Signatures of group members present:

During the group discussion of the essays on the personal accounts, each group is instructed to address specific topics and to keep clear and specific notes on what is said. The point is to get discussions focused on the work students have written, to place students in situations where they give feedback to each group member, and to give students opportunities to listen to feedback about their work. Questions guiding the discussion groups are given in Table 10.3.

Students are to complete a semester-long project. A list of the seven possible projects is found in the syllabus reproduced in Appendix A. An example of one project is given in Table 10.4.

Continuing education. Continuing education offers a well-established primary prevention approach to reach professionals who provide services to dying and grieving adolescents. A model adopted by many professional associations is to offer continuing education via the Internet in modules called "webinars." Other terms for these education offerings are "online workshops" and "Web conferences." Webinars allow continuing education to be shipped via the Internet to multiple remote locations. Costs go

Table 10.4 A Possible Project for the Undergraduate Course

Analyze how four movies handle topics of death, dying, and bereavement. Inform me by February 13 if you have selected this project. Your analysis should examine themes pertinent to this course that you find expressed in each movie. It is not necessary that the same theme(s) be expressed in each movie although such similarity could give your project clear focus. Your analysis needs to do more than summarize each film and the theme(s) the film presents. You need to explain the themes by examining what literature (the course materials and at least two other written sources) has to say about the themes, and you need to examine and assess how well (if at all) the movies present these themes.

The format of the analysis should be:

1. **A brief synopsis** of the movies (3–4 pages)
2. **Critical analysis** of thanatology themes the films express and how the films express those themes (5–7 pages)
3. **Assessment of the value of the these movies** as vehicles to present ideas important to thanatology (1–2 pages; give reasons to support your assessment)

dramatically down for an individual to attend this kind of continuing education because there is no need to travel to a distant conference city, with the attendant expenses such as food and lodging that accrue. In the field of thanatology, the Association for Death Education and Counseling (ADEC) provides webinars, typically one a month; some topics covered in ADEC webinars have included "A Practitioner's Guide to Care of the Dying," "Working with Multiple Losses," "The Grieving College Student," "Spiritual Care at End-of-Life with Pediatric Patients and Their Families," and "Myths and Facts about Advance Care Planning: Dispelling the 'Death Panel' Claim." Information about ADEC webinars can be found at www.adec.org.

Webinars for grief counselors. Laura Breen's in-depth interviews with thanatology professionals in Australia disclosed four areas that webinars can address for these grief counselors and, presumably, address needs of grief counselors elsewhere in the world.

- Education covering the history of thinking about responses to bereavement, with comparison and contrast with more current models
- Information about assessment and treatment of Prolonged Grief Disorder
- Education about the local resources to assist in referring clients, connecting with other professionals, and improving coordinated services for the bereaved
- Education of grief counselors in research and program evaluation

Breen sees making strides in continuing education will contribute to bridging the gap separating researchers and practitioners. By increasing practitioner knowledge of the latest information in thanatology, the ground will be prepared for collaboration between practitioners and researchers on research studies. Part of this effort will be nurtured by the very fact that scholars who present webinars will be introduced to practitioners.

Webinars offer a solid way of educating graduate students in counseling and clinical psychology about coping with loss. It amazes me that the graduate curriculum in counseling and clinical psychology programs ignores issues of loss. Loss is the back story if not the presenting problem that many clients bring to sessions. That reality alone offers sufficient reasons for informed curriculum on bereavement, grief, and mourning. Given that crisis intervention started with Lindemann's work with persons grieving deaths in the Cocoanut Grove fire, it is puzzling that the graduate training of counseling and clinical psychologists carves out no room in the curriculum for such information. Perhaps once prolonged grief disorder gets added to the *Diagnostic and Statistical Manual of Mental Disorders,* there will be recognition of the need to include issues of loss in the preparation of these graduate students.

Webinars on communicating with life-threatened adolescents. Webinars can offer information to cancer and palliative care teams about communicating with adolescents who have cancer. Communicating effectively with ill adolescents is a very important skill for caregivers. Communication involves content (that is, what is communicated), style (how the message is expressed), and receptivity (listening to and observing the other person). Caregivers need to correctly decode the symbolic language adolescents use to express what they feel, what they need, and what concerns them. A webinar on communicating with dying adolescents can look at the various ways they express themselves verbally, nonverbally, and symbolically.

Adolescents coping with a life-threatening illness want to know about their illness, and they look to medical professionals for this knowledge. The webinar can stress that life-threatened adolescents have the right to know about changes in their condition and to be given the choice whether to be told they are dying. For ill adolescents to have hope, they need to feel confident in the persons providing their medical care; part of that confidence comes from having their questions about their condition clearly answered.

Another aspect of communication involves support from caregivers. Medical staff are not whom ill adolescents typically turn to for such support. They turn to family members, friends, and peers with cancer. Perhaps the difference between who is preferred for information and who is preferred for support is summed up in a young lady's comments: "I don't need my doctor to be all touchy-feely; I want her to know what she is doing. I can get support from my family and friends" (Personal communication, anonymous source).

Adolescents with life-threatening illnesses have identified a set of factors that create communication barriers and a set of factors that facilitate communication between them and caregivers. The adolescents gave examples for each set of impediments and facilitators of communication. Here are strategies that caregivers can employ to improve communication.

The four impediments to communication are (a) behaving in an impersonal, detached manner, (b) using an authoritarian style, (c) being hasty or abrupt in dealings with adolescents, and (d) letting differences in generations influence interactions. For instance, "being stuffy" was an example life-threatened adolescents gave of behaving in an impersonal, detached manner. One strategy recommended is for caregivers to accept the use of nicknames. Other strategies suggested for overcoming the impediments to communication are "avoid 'hiding' behind the patient's chart . . . talk to the adolescent, not about the adolescent . . . provide opportunity for questions. . . encourage adolescents to write down their questions . . . (and) be honest about issues of sex, fertility, relationships" (Stevens & Dunsmore, 1996, p. 334).

Education for Adolescents about HPV and Cancer

Primary prevention efforts aimed at educating adolescents about the human papilloma-virus (HPV) and about cancer include the approaches presented now. First we look at education aimed at raising awareness about HPV. Then the discussion turns to cancer and adolescents.

HPV education and adolescents. A team of medical and public health specialists designed, administered, and evaluated a program aimed at increasing adolescents' knowledge of HPV. A booklet presenting HPV information was developed for use with adolescents; a Teen Advisory Board assessed the content and overall approach used in the booklet. A companion booklet allowed an educator to provide commentary regarding the various topics in the booklet read by the adolescents.

The research design used the participants as their own controls, had 121 sexually active adolescent females answer 11 True–False questions about HPV before they took part in the educational protocol, and then assessed gains in and retention of knowledge about HPV. The assessment of knowledge gain and retention occurred immediately after the teenage completed the educational protocol and then 2 weeks later. The protocol was then revised based on feedback from the participants and administered to (a) 116 sexu-ally active adolescent females and (b) 48 peer educators in a classroom setting.

Gains in overall knowledge about HPV and retention of that knowledge went from 63% to 87%. Understanding increased for the teenagers in the first administration of the educational protocol on nearly every bit of information presented regarding HPV, spe-cifically: (a) the extent to which condoms protect against HPV infection, (b) abnormal menstrual periods for HPV-infected women, (c) sexual intercourse as the typical mode of transmitting HPV, (d) problems HPV infection creates for becoming pregnant, (e) impotency of antibiotics against HPV, and (f) the links between cigarette smoking and development of cervical cancer in HPV-infected females.

The second round of teenagers, including the 48 peer educators, also showed statisti-cally significant gains in knowledge overall. Their increase in knowledge was particularly seen regarding the five aspects of HPV just listed.

Vaccinating adolescents, particularly early adolescent females, against HPV infection has roused strong advocacy within the medical establishment and intense opposition from some quarters. Proponents argue the vaccine is safe, effective, reliable, and should be mandated; they also assert that fears about the vaccine are irrational and unfounded. Opponents express suspicion about yet-to-be uncovered side effects, government intru-sion into the lives of families, violation of religious beliefs, and sweetheart deals between pharmaceutical companies producing the vaccine and elected officials mandating girls be vaccinated regardless of risks.

Advocates for HPV vaccination see the matter as a woman's health issue. The severe consequences for females who become infected with HPV has led a bipartisan group of female members of the US Congress to push for mandatory vaccination, for inclusion in state Medicaid programs, and for coverage by private health insurers.

Opponents to HPV vaccination come from diverse groups, including religious con-servatives, libertarians, and bioethicists. Vocal parents have objected to mandatory vac-cination on grounds of potentially deleterious side effects that won't emerge for years.

Several state legislatures allow religious and philosophical arguments against mandated vaccinations.

Public health concerns over the effect of exemptions to the vaccine note that a 2% to 4% exemption rate among school children places the rest of the students at risk for contracting communicable diseases. Another argument raised is that minors deserve to be protected against diseases for which vaccines have been developed. This latter argument discounts the rights of parents in the face of the needs of society at large. As an example, parental autonomy does not outweigh the need to protect children and society against outbreaks of smallpox, measles, and polio.

Educating adolescents about skin cancer. Malignant melanoma is one of the cancers most common to middle and later adolescents. We will look at two education programs aimed at informing adolescents about this type of cancer.

Program one. Medical practitioners in a London hospital's dermatology department developed a curriculum for adolescents between the ages of 12 and 16. The teaching methods involved "workbooks, pamphlets, a video, and interventional teaching" (Hughes, Altman, & Newton, 1993, p. 412). The focus of the curriculum was to impact cognitive and affective objectives, and the evaluation examined the effects of the program on students' knowledge, attitudes, and behavior.

The workbook informed readers about ultraviolet radiation and links to skin cancer, especially melanoma. The pamphlet presented information titled "Suncool" and not only attempted to make covering up from the sun desirable but also encouraged limiting sun exposure. In the video, also titled "Suncool," a well-known British television actress discussed with a class of children information about ultraviolet radiation and skin cancer. The program uses "active teaching" (p. 417) and offers examples of discussions teachers held with students about the material.

Five hundred and twelve children from a total of seven schools participated in the education program. Within each school, five classrooms were divided into five treatment conditions:

1. Group 1: Students who read the workbook and took home a pamphlet presenting the "suncool" ideas.
2. Group 2: Students in the same condition as Group 1 but who also watched the video.
3. Group 3: Students in the same condition as Group 1 but who were given homework to design posters about the material.
4. Group 4: Students in the same condition as Group 1 but who also engaged with teachers who led the students in "active teaching," that is, in discussion groups about the material.
5. Group 5: A control group given none of the educational materials.

The education program lasted for 2 months, and then the students twice answered questionnaires examining knowledge and attitudes: once in July immediately after completing the education program, and then in September upon return from the summer break. In September they also answered questions about behaviors engaged in over the summer break. The 33 knowledge questions were answered with a True–False format; a sample item is, "People who only go into the sun for 2 weeks a year are not likely to get skin cancer." The 15 attitude questions were answered with a Likert-type scale ranging from Strongly Disagree to Strongly Agree, and allowing for the possibility of "Can't Say." A sample item about attitudes is, "It is worth a lot of effort to get a sun tan." The questions about behavior were answered with a "Yes–No" format. A sample question is "Did you sunbathe during the summer holidays?"

Analysis of variance demonstrated significant differences in knowledge, attitudes, and behavior separating the four treatment groups from the group that did not receive the education program; the treatment groups showed gains over time in knowledge, attitudes, and behavior. There were no differences in knowledge and attitudes and behaviors of the four treatment groups. However, where families took their summer vacations influenced behavior. Namely, children who traveled abroad took precautions against sun exposure, but children who remained within England did not take seem to think such precautions were necessary. Correlations were noticed between overall scores on the attitudes questionnaire and such preventive behaviors as wearing sunscreen and covering up when in the sun.

Program two. This education program was presented to over 1,700 freshman and sophomore high school students in Chicago, Illinois. Nearly all the students were White. The education involved a 12-minute video focused on the dangers of skin cancer and a 33-minute class meeting in which (a) important points in the video were reviewed, (b) worksheets were completed assessing personal risks of damage due to sun exposure, and (c) the students discussed problems interfering with taking precautions against sun exposure.

Measures were taken before the intervention, once the intervention was completed a week later, and then 1 week later again to assess knowledge, attitudes, and behaviors. The adolescents confirmed what is known about adolescents in general: they spend a great deal of time in the sun during their summer vacations, consider a tan highly desirable, and take few precautions against the risks of sun exposure. The males in the study indicated they were much more at risk and less knowledgeable about sun exposure dangers than were the females.

Perceptions of vulnerability to dangers from sun exposure emerged as what most influenced adolescents to say they would take precautions. At the same time, perceptions of the benefits of being tan and of feeling good when in the sun worked strongly to influence attitudes against taking precautions. The evaluators pointed out the importance of assisting adolescents to gain knowledge about their personal vulnerability to sun damage if changes are to be made in use of precautions. They noted it will be a difficult goal to change adolescents' beliefs about the benefits of having a tan and of feeling good when outdoors in the sun.

Hospice and Prevention of Complicated Grief Disorder

Hospice is an umbrella term denoting (a) programs to help the terminally ill and their family members, (b) a holistic philosophy promoting quality of life for persons who are dying, and (c) facilities where such programs and philosophies play out. The starting point for hospice is the complete human person, and hospice considers the whole family to be the patient when one of its members enters hospice care. Services for the terminally ill individual run the gamut of the holistic template, covering such important needs as pain management, interpersonal relationships, and spiritual interests. Services for other family members involve support and education. The focus of this section of Chapter Ten is on hospice education that works to prevent complicated grief from developing once the terminally ill loved one dies.

Helping persons prepare for the death of a loved one has been linked to increasing their resiliency once the death occurs, and lack of preparation has been associated with symptoms of prolonged grief disorder 4 and 9 months following death to terminal illness. Very similar outcomes were found with a significant percentage of family members caring for dementia patients. Persons caring for a terminally ill loved one but not prepared for the death have a much greater likelihood to become depressed and experience complicated grief than caregivers who are prepared.

Nursing homes, assisted living facilities, and hospice all can contribute to preparing family members for the death of their loved one. Hospice in particular seems the most favorable arena within which to begin such a campaign for involvement with family members: The hospice philosophy embraces the family as the patient and the hospice is committed to bereavement care following the death. Hospice staff members often develop bonds of trust with family members that help promote family preparation for the death.

Preparing persons for the impending death can take various forms. For one, the actual act of enrolling in hospice early has been linked to reducing the risk of clinical depression during the first 6 months after the death. The mortality risks associated with complicated grief are greatly diminished in families that enroll in hospice. Trust levels forged between family members and hospice staff provide the opportunity to discuss the impending death and to encourage the family to address unsettled problems. Trust allows hospice staff to encourage persons to express their "appreciation, regrets, reassurances" (Zhang, El-Jawahri, & Prigerson, 2006, p. 1199), and to say goodbye.

A considerable roadblock to such desired results is the fact that a great proportion of persons who enter hospice do so with a week or so left to live. The average length of stay in hospice care in the 1970s was 70 days, but now half of all hospice patients are enrolled for less than a month, and over 30% for at most 7 days. It has been recommended that hospices and families need 2 to 3 months time for services to be maximally effective. In that time there is enough duration to prepare family members, assist the dying person to get things in order, to alleviate pain and distress, and to forge strong therapeutic relationships.

Benefits for the surviving family members favor those who choose early enrollment. The conclusion is to encourage health care professionals not to delay referring dying patients and their families to hospice. Early enrollments stem the patient's suffering, increase the possibilities for a good death, and prepare the family for the coming death.

College Programs Promoting Spiritual Development

College programs promoting spiritual development have emerged in the 21st century as a holistic response to education of the whole person. Some programs are embedded integrally into the duration of a student's undergraduate experience, and others are more time-limited. All the programs work from the premise that spirituality (a) is fundamental to human existence and (b) emerges from the human quest to find meaning, establish purpose, and make connections; these connections can be intellectual (as with scholarly investment in a field of study), interpersonal (as with forming friendships and building community), and transcendent (as with experiences of the divine).

Empirical data obtained from surveys and interviews with college students disclose that spiritual growth becomes increasingly important as students move from adolescence into young adulthood. Making meaning, establishing purpose, and forging connections are goals of fundamental significance to them; the irony is that the students typically keep these spiritual desires to themselves because faculty members resist talking with students about such aspirations.

Some campuses have directly faced this student quest for spirituality. Higher education leaders invested in promoting student spiritual development have seen the quest is linked fundamentally to core developmental transitions expected of young adults. The quest for spirituality is linked fundamentally to the core relationships that existential phenomenology has disclosed about human existence, and are inextricably linked to the developmental tasks of forming an autonomous identity, entering into intimate personal relationships, and choosing a career for engaging in the world.

One college response is the 4-year program that permeates an undergraduate's experience at St. John's University at Collegeville, Minnesota. Participation is voluntary. Here is a brief overview of this program taken from the book *Helping the Bereaved College Student* (Balk, 2011, pp. 231–232).

> The intentional program at St. John's University (Collegeville, MN) begins with the value of personal choice: students are invited to participate in a four-year small group exploration of their spirituality. The groups are limited to ten students, are facilitated by two adults, meet every 2 to 3 weeks for around an hour, and stress the utter expectation of confidentiality. Each meeting centers on one student's story about his personal spiritual journey. Time is set aside to allow other group members the opportunity to ask questions and share what the person's story has elicited in them. Themes shape the process through the four years. For instance, in year one the theme is to reflect on the statement "Who I am and what I believe." In the second year, the groups examine the theme of relationships, beliefs, and self-understanding. The third year theme is left to the group to pick; some themes that have been examined are authenticity and beauty. The fourth year involves reflecting on what the group experience has produced. External evaluators report very favorably on the effectiveness of this program in the growth and development of the participants and on how the groups are an integral part of the educational mission of St. John's.

Historical black colleges and universities (Morehouse and Fisk are examples) expressly see that their mission includes the character formation of the students matriculated in their programs of study. Spiritual development is a vital component in this character formation, and community involvement is integrally part of this growth into a person of character. Because spiritual development is part of the core mission of these historically black colleges and universities, students will find faculty responsive to the spiritual quest energizing them.

Wellesley College's program to foster spiritual growth was seen as a larger effort focused on acceptance of diversity. Wellesley grounded its program around emotional and relational expressions of self-identity. Spirituality was seen as a central aspect of growth in personal identity and fostering the spiritual development of students was identified as a core element in the college's purpose. When asked to share personal stories of meaning making that occurred within such an educational environment, narratives emerged of classroom experiences in which the students had been "awakened to a deeper understanding of themselves, of others around them, and of the world" (Kazanjian & Laurence, 2007, p. 4).

The role of meaning making in coping with life crises is a core assumption in this book, in the literature on coping, and in major models on recovery from bereavement. College efforts to nurture spiritual development as character formation serve a significant purpose by assisting students to achieve the affective educational objective of building a core set of beliefs, of achieving the existential impetus for extending oneself to the wider world, and of constructing a repertoire of skills for coping with adverse life situations, what Alexander Leighton called cross-sections of the moment.

Life Values Skill Building

Life values skill building is a unique, special approach to intervention aimed at holistic growth and embracing the values of spiritual development and character formation. One embodiment of life values skill building comes from decades of reflection and program development regarding career counseling. It is called the Life Values Inventory.

This primary prevention intervention works completely online and is free (www.lifevaluesinventory.org/). The intent of the Life Values Inventory is "to help individuals and organizations clarify their values and serve as a blueprint for effective decision-making and optimal functioning" (see the website). The 14 values that comprise the inventory are achievement, belonging, concern for the environment, concern for others, creativity, financial prosperity, health, humility, independence, interdependence, objective analysis, privacy, responsibility, and spirituality. The inventory is grounded in the history of career counseling within the profession of counseling psychology and is deeply influenced by the pioneering work of Donald Super and Milton Rokeach regarding the primary links between self-concept, values, and work.

The participant completes a series of steps whereby he or she identifies and puts in rank order those values that influence actions within relationships, the work setting, the community, and perhaps other situations. The end product is a values profile offering a discussion of values the person has ranked as holding high priority, values the person indicates are given too much attention, values given too little attention, and values with medium or low priority. For each value that has emerged, the values profile provides a brief discussion of what such a value means, how it fosters or hinders decision-making, and how it can be in conflict with other values. The values are seen to be in dynamic interaction and not simply exerting private, discrete influence in a person's life roles.

The Life Values Inventory provides a means to engage adolescent participants to reflect on matters promoting and hindering attainment of the developmental tasks they face. As an example, during later adolescence, the individual is expected to gain a coherent self-identity, enter into and maintain intimacy, and decide on how to make a living in the world. The Life Values Inventory exercise enables participants to explore their values and how they promote and hinder attaining these fundamental life objectives.

Statements testifying to the worth of the Life Values Inventory come from college students and from college professionals charged with the formation of young adults. Here are two quotes offered on the Life Values Inventory website. The first is from a university provost, and the second is from a person who founded Students Helping Honduras.

I've found the LVI to be an incredibly useful tool in my work with college students. We find that most students never really consider the importance of values in shaping their choices, even though our society sends young people a lot of messages about what they 'should' value. The LVI is the catalyst to a deliberate dialogue with our students about how values affect every part of their college experience and beyond. It gets them thinking about their goals and motivations in a brand new way.

The LVI helped me identify my life. For the first time, it gave me words to define my values and priorities in a clear, comprehensive way. After taking the inventory, I became more aware of the fact that most of the external conflicts in my life surfaced when my values and priorities were unbalanced. It was the best hour and a half I spent as an undergraduate. I learned how to study myself. I continue to apply the lessons that I learned from the inventory and workshop every day. I am a true believer of the LVI and would recommend anyone to go through this unforgettable experience.

Recently R. Kelly Crace, one of the founders of the Life Values Inventory, has turned his attention to "the dynamic relationship between values and fear and how (this dynamic relationship) is linked to both flourishing and languishing" (R. Kelly Crace, personal communication, February 28, 2013). A key notion is that fear of failure can be managed, that resiliency can be fostered, and that achieving balance in one's values promotes flourishing.

The task of achieving such balance is dynamic, and reminds me of the portrait Alexander Leighton has given of the constant experience of gaining and losing the essential striving sentiments. There are very clear links, at least on the surface and I suspect even deeper, between the 14 values in the Life Values Inventory and the essential striving sentiments. For instance, the value of belonging and the striving sentiment of being part of a definite group are closely allied. The value of creativity and the striving sentiment of expressing oneself creatively are linked. And for a third example, the values of responsibility, concern for others, and concern for the environment are embedded in the striving sentiment of being part of a moral order. Balance in the values in one's life roles would promote integrated, functional communities, a key factor in Leighton's sociocultural model on the factors promoting psychiatric health.

The final step in the Life Values Inventory provides keys for linking values to life roles and thereby promote flourishing and prevent languishing. Eight PDF documents offered in the Life Values Inventory examine such central topics as (a) values and relationships, (b) educational majors, (c) an occupations locator, and (d) managing life transitions.

- The PDF on values and relationships helps the person examine the interplay between sharing with others who endorse both similar and different values to one's own.
- The PDF on educational majors helps the person to identify college curricula that will satisfy the values they endorse.

- The PDF on locating occupations helps the person to identify occupations that are linked to the values the person endorses. There are instructions for consulting a valuable online resource produced by the federal government and titled the *Occupational Outlook Handbook.*
- The PDF on managing life transitions helps the person review the issues of uncertainty, fear of failure, and loss that often accompany making important changes in one's life; the PDF identifies strategies for actively coping with these issues and discusses assumptions that can militate against managing transitions well.

Public Service Announcements and Public Health Policy Decisions

Public service announcements and public health policy decisions afford two types of sweeping primary interventions aimed at the community and, by inference, at individuals at risk. Examples of public service announcement are the television spots showing the dangers of smoking, the risks of driving while under the influence or while texting, and the ongoing problems related to obesity. A public health policy decision is captured in the programmatic efforts of the Centers for Disease Control to prevent HIV infection in American adolescents.

Prevention of HIV infections among United States adolescents. Epidemiological studies in the United States indicate that a much higher proportion of adolescent females than males (61% versus 39%) contract the HIV virus. However, when extending the age span from 13 to 24, it is young African American males who account for a majority (56%) of all new cases of HIV infection.

The Centers for Disease Control (CDC) have developed guidelines for promoting HIV prevention with American youth. While the first guideline emphasizes early and clear parent–child conversations about sex, the CDC notes that successful prevention must take a community focus and include a diversity of activities. In particular, six strategies are identified. These strategies are:

1. *Effective school-based programs that reach youth before they begin to engage in risky sexual behavior.* The scope of these programs should extend from kindergarten through twelfth grade, reflect local control, be consistent with community and parental values, and examine a variety of behaviors such as drug use and sexual intercourse that place youth at risk of contracting HIV.
2. *Reach youth who do not attend local schools.* The CDC notes these youth may be runaways, juvenile offenders, homeless, or school dropouts. As early as 1993, for instance, surveys indicated on average 2.8% of incarcerated female adolescents were HIV positive.
3. *Sustain outreach efforts with gay and bisexual males.* Studies continue to show that HIV prevalence remains high with 15- to 22-year-old gay and bisexual males, in part because of their attraction to high-risk sexual behaviors. In particular, males from minority groups, especially African American and Hispanic, are at greater risk of infection than are White males.
4. *Link high-risk sexual behavior with drug-related behavior.* Youth who engage in high-risk sexual behaviors typically use drugs or alcohol simultaneously with their sexual

activities. Survey data from over two thirds of the states in the United States indicate that HIV infection for at least 50% of 13- to 24-year-olds infected occurred as a result of mixing sexual intercourse and drug activity.

5. *Focus attention on treating young people who have contracted a sexually transmitted disease (STD).* The CDC reported that persons infected with an STD are more vulnerable to become HIV-infected due to sexual exposure to the virus. The CDC also reported that partners of persons with STDs are at increased risk of becoming HIV-infected.

6. *Engage in continuous evaluation of behaviors placing youth at risk of HIV infection.* The wisdom here is to remain alert to changing patterns of behaviors that contribute to risk of infection.

Gun buy-back efforts. The link between easy access to fire arms and the homicide rate is obvious to proponents of tighter gun control measures. We will look (a) at efforts in Australia, Brazil, and Seattle, Washington to control firearms and (b) at the estimated impacts such efforts have on reducing homicides.

Australia's response. Between 1978 and 1996, there were 13 mass murders in Australia, all involving the use of semiautomatic rifles and pump action shotguns. The last straw was the mass murder in 1996 of 35 persons; 18 others were wounded. These events stimulated the Australian government in 1996 to pass legislation prohibiting semiautomatic and pump action rifles and shotguns. This legislation was called the National Firearms Agreement (NFA). The NFA mandated that gun owners (a) prove their need for a gun, (b) register firearms with a government licensing body, and (c) pass a test of firearm safety. The legislation mandated a 28-day waiting period and prohibited the private sale of firearms. Self-defense was ruled out as a compelling reason for owning a firearm.

The government sponsored a buy-back program to take these kinds of weapons out of circulation. Gun owners turned in 650,000 prohibited weapons as part of the buy-back program. Numerous evaluations have been conducted to examine the efficacy of the NFA. There are some uniform findings and some matters of controversy.

Program outcomes to signal success included measures of various forms of firearm-related deaths: mass murders, suicides, homicides, and accidents. Whereas there had been a mass murder nearly every 16 months prior to the implementation of NFA, no mass murders involving firearms have occurred since the implementation of the program.[3] Advocates of the NFA legislation question why evaluations of the legislation typically overlook the absence of mass murders since the passage of the firearms control law.

Evaluators agree that the number of firearm-related suicides noticeably declined following the passage of the NFA legislation. For instance, in 1995 and 1996 the number of suicides by firearms was 398 and 385, respectively. Between 1997 and 2004 the average number was 236. Of interest is that the number of suicides by other means than firearms also declined in that same 8-year period.

Evaluations conclude that the NFA legislation had no effect on the number of individual murders related to firearms. In the 4 years prior to passage of the legislation, the number of homicides averaged 66. Between 1997 and 2004 the average number was 51. The difference of 15 on average per year is not considered statistically significant. It is of interest that homicides by means other than firearms remained stable over the years following the passage of the NFA legislation.

Data regarding accidental deaths due to firearms puzzle the evaluators. The average number of such deaths annually in the 4 years preceding passage of the NFA legislation was 20. Between 1997 and 2004 the average number was 32. However, one set of evaluators drew attention to the wide swings in accidental deaths due to firearms from one year to the next (for instance, 44 in 2000, 17 in 2001, 31 in 2002) and cautioned that "any inference that the NFA 'caused' an increase in accidental firearm death would be extremely tenuous" (Baker & McPhedran, 2007, p. 461).

The summative conclusions about the efficacy of the NFA strike me as puzzling. Let me be clear on this point. It is not puzzling that evaluators conclude that the decline in mass murders coincided with the prohibition of certain types of firearms and with the buy-back program. The data indicate no puzzling conclusions about a decline in suicides by firearms, and can demonstrate no decline in firearm-related homicides or accidental deaths. What puzzles me is the conclusion by some evaluators that following the passage of the NFA legislation, the rate of firearm-related homicides and accidental deaths showed rapid declines. The conclusion from other evaluators about no effect on homicides or accidental deaths, as discomforting and counterintuitive as it may be, is more in line with the data.

Brazil's response. The homicide rate in Brazil is alarming. In 2002 the World Health Organization reported nearly 22 persons per 100,000 deaths due to firearms. In response to these alarming mortality statistics, the government of Brazil passed sweeping legislation that aimed to stem the movement of firearms into the country and make strict laws about gun ownership: (a) guns must be registered, (b) carrying firearms outside the home or one's business is illegal, (c) background checks are required to purchase guns, and (d) no one under the age of 25 may own a gun. In 2004 the government instituted a buy-back program. Local churches cooperated as sites for persons to bring guns in exchange for government vouchers that could be cashed at any bank in Brazil. The buy-back program resulted in the removal of over 450,000 firearms.

An evaluation of this program looked at its first year impact. Admittedly, that time frame is meager when it is the long-term effects that most matter. However, the first year data were encouraging. For instance, in the year following the passage of the legislation and implementation of the buy-back program, firearm-related murders declined 8% for the country as a whole and by 11% in urban centers, the sites where a plurality of homicides by firearm occur. Another decline was noted in the first year following the passage of the legislation and the implementation of the buy-back: hospitalizations due to firearm-related injuries declined nearly 5%. The evaluators estimated that the new policy toward firearms had prevented 5,563 deaths in the first year alone.

Seattle's response. The chapter on principal causes of death during adolescence highlighted the alarming statistic about homicide for 15- to 24-year-olds, particularly Black males living in large urban areas of the United States. Data in 2012 and 2013 about homicide rates in Chicago and Detroit do nothing to comfort us that the epidemic of firearm-related deaths is ebbing. The shock of the Newtown, Connecticut, massacre remains fresh in many persons' imaginations.

In 1992 some residents of Seattle, Washington, implemented a gun buy-back program in response to a weekend series of shootings in which two adolescents were murdered and one was seriously injured. Given the 2013 multiple homicides on weekends in Chicago, the two Seattle murders seem almost negligible; such a reaction no doubt discloses desensitization to such horrors.

The Seattle buy-back program was similar to others that had been tried in other American cities, among them Baltimore, Boston, and Rochester, New York. Seattle's program aimed to remove 2,000 weapons (primarily handguns) from use and give a $50 voucher for each firearm turned in.

The buy-back program obtained 1,772 firearms, and 93% were handguns. The average age of persons turning in a firearm was 44, and the majority of the participants in the program were male. Slightly less than 2% of the guns bought back were on a list of stolen weapons kept by the police.

Incentives for participating in the buy-back program varied. The great majority of persons cited the program offered a safe means to dispose of a gun no longer wanted. Younger persons said they needed the money. A bit more than one fifth of respondents (21%) said they wanted to get rid of the gun before someone in their homes was hurt. Some wanted to use the money to purchase a newer gun.

Following the implantation of the buy-back program, various 6-month indicators were checked. These indicators included (a) firearm-related assaults, robberies, and homicides, (b) trauma center admissions for firearm injuries, and (c) firearm-related suicides. There were no impacts on the incidence of assaults, robberies, or homicides that involved firearms. The number of homicides by firearm actually increased in the 6 months following the program, but not in a statistically significant manner. While there was a numerical decrease in trauma center admissions for firearm injuries, the decline was negligible. The small decline in firearm-related suicides was also not statistically significant.

Conclusions about the lack of impact of the Seattle gun buy-back program focused on the need to get a much larger number of guns off the street. The evaluators wrote that removing 10% of firearms is needed to reduce robberies and murders by 4%. As they wrote, "the effect of removing 1 percent of guns from the community on rates of firearm crimes is negligible" (Callahan, Rivara, & Koepsell, 1994, p. 476).

Gun buy-back programs in other cities have taken place since the Seattle experiment. The cities have included San Francisco, Camden, New Jersey, Los Angeles, Detroit, and Boston. Typically, what the cities have been willing to buy are handguns but more recently assault weapons as well. The incentive has been $100 to $200 per firearm. Each program does buy back firearms, but the small numbers obtained don't reach the 10% critical mass needed to impact a reduction in firearm-related crimes. Further, newer weapons that present a much greater risk of harm, such as high magazine assault weapons, don't get turned in.

Unlike other countries, the United States presents a distinct challenge regarding firearms. The United States Constitution specifies that gun ownership is a right. Prohibiting the sales of weapons has proven to be a formidable challenge. What gun buy-back programs in this country provide is voluntary choice, and they do not present an infringement on constitutional rights. Probably gun buy-back programs in this country would be formidably opposed if they had more than negligible impact in gun ownership.

Secondary Interventions

The notion of secondary prevention is to build resilience and resistance in the face of an already existing phenomenon that places persons at risk and could develop into greater difficulties if not handled properly. Examples of secondary prevention include crisis intervention support groups for children following divorce of their parents. Secondary interventions in thanatology include bereavement interventions targeting normal grief reactions and camp experiences for children and adolescents afflicted with life-threatening illnesses.

Grief Counseling

Before looking at some interventions with normally bereaved adolescents, it is incumbent on me to review the debate over the efficacy of grief counseling. Questioning the efficacy of grief counseling is one of the least popular stances a person can take in the field of thanatology. Questioning the value of grief counseling challenges an "uncritical acceptance of the assumption that help is beneficial" (Schut, Stroebe, van den Bout, & Terheggen, 2001, p. 705). Because good intentions are not sufficient to affect good outcomes, it is incumbent on bereavement practitioners and researchers to examine carefully whether interventions help persons who are grieving.

Recall that Sigmund Freud firmly ruled out that bereavement is a disorder requiring professional help. Although Erich Lindemann adopted much of what he termed Freud's "grief work theory," he devised a protocol for intervening professionally with bereaved individuals. Recent empirical studies have questioned not only whether the grief work theory works but also whether persons in normal bereavement respond positively to counseling. While critics of bereavement interventions are siding with Freud's argument against interference in cases of normal bereavement, at the same time they are voicing considerable skepticism over Freud's explanation that coping with bereavement requires (a) confronting the distress of the loss and (b) relinquishing emotional attachment to the person who died. No one questioning the grief work theory or the efficacy of grief counseling brings up the third part of Freud's explanation about recovery from bereavement, namely, the need to form a mental representation of the person who died.

Some studies claiming that grief counseling is basically without value have amalgamated published and unpublished reports of grief counseling and then subjected the studies to meta-analysis.[4] Meta-analysis is a sophisticated statistical means to synthesize results of several independent research studies. It increases the overall sample size by including results from participants in all the studies that are examined. Errors committed in one study are said to be moderated by bringing in data from other studies and, in effect, averaging out errors that have been committed in single studies. The main focus of the meta-analysis is a mathematical synthesis of what the studies as a whole mean. This meaning is presented in a statistical value, and the objectivity of this overall result is highly prized. Of course, meta-analysis cannot make up for poorly designed studies, and inclusion of poorly designed studies militates against the meaningfulness of the meta-analysis results.

The current debate over the efficacy of grief counseling emerged when meta-analysis was applied to grief counseling studies. These meta-analytic reviews have produced the controversial conclusion that grief counseling is of no benefit to persons in normal bereavement, and concluded further that a significant percentage of persons were worse off because of the treatment. Meta-analyses of interventions for complicated grief, however, endorse the efficacy of procedures used with persons whose acute grief has never lessened; these effective complicated grief interventions include a wide variety of procedures including psychoanalysis, systematic desensitization, hypnotherapy, and dynamic therapy.

The conclusion that grief counseling does not work for persons in normal bereavement has been challenged vigorously. The arguments raised look at the quality of the studies included in the meta-analyses. The prestigious bereavement research team at the University of Utrecht has wondered whether the quality of studies of grief counseling precludes conducting meta-analysis to determine efficacy of bereavement interventions.[5] A similar assessment occurred in a separate review: Lack of significant impact "may say more about the nature of the studies" than about the efficacy of bereavement intervention (Larson & Hoyt, 2007, p. 350).

Both the Utrecht scholars who agree that grief counseling lacks efficacy and the scholars in the United States who mistrust pessimistic conclusions about grief counseling noted that errors influencing results would come from including in treatment persons not motivated to seek counseling. "These research participants may not be typical of clients in actual practice settings" (Larson & Hoyt, 2007, p. 350).[6] Rather than being recruited for counseling, persons who want help seek it. This insight has led to formulating two questions to determine whether a normally bereaved person will profit from grief counseling: (a) Are you distressed by your bereavement? (b) Would you like help to cope with your bereavement?

It is imprudent to dismiss concerns whether grief counseling helps normally bereaved persons. Poorly designed interventions that stem from ignorance about bereavement, grief, and mourning won't help someone; for instance, treating bereavement as though it is depression or pushing a griever through Kubler-Ross's stages of grieving. It is also incautious to accept wholesale that bereavement interventions pose a scam or, at best, stem from misguided efforts. I trust the assessment of many bereavement counselors that interventions do help normally bereaved persons. An important issue is motivation to be in counseling. The two inclusion questions to assess motivation for counseling appeal to me intuitively; further, they address some of the questions raised in reviews of the meta-analyses of bereavement interventions.

Secondary Interventions with Bereaved Families

We will look at two well-researched interventions that rise to the level of evidence-based practices. One is the intervention Irwin Sandler and his colleagues developed at Arizona State University called the Family Bereavement Program. The other intervention is the work of the Australian psychiatrist, David Kissane, who works in hospitals with families that have a family member dying of cancer; Kissane calls his approach Family-Focused Grief Therapy.

The Family Bereavement Program. The Family Bereavement Program (FBP) is a model in procedures utilized to assess the efficacy of an intervention to assist bereaved children and adolescents following the death of a parent. This intervention meets all the norms established to call a practice evidence-based: it is grounded in a solid theory, it obtained repeated measures including pretest data, it randomly assigned participants to treatment or control groups, its authors published extensively in peer-reviewed sources, and a manual presents steps to take when conducting the intervention. Further, Sandler and his colleagues, early champions of bridging the gap separating practitioners and researchers, worked with a community agency to move the intervention to a real-world practice setting.

The construct of resiliency provides the theoretical underpinning for the intervention. The authors of the FBP refer to this theory as contextual resilience. Akin to Leighton's sociocultural theory explaining the interplay of individual and community factors in the development of healthy adaptation and in the development of psychiatric disorder, contextual resilience identifies several influences that "have important implications for the identification of risk and protective factors to target in intervention programs" (Sandler et al., 2008, p. 532). This grounding in contextual resilience led to three propositions guiding the intervention:

1. How well parentally bereaved children adjust to their environment following the death provides indicators accounting for how they function in response to distress. The theory of contextual resilience proposes that disruptions in the environment create problems for children to meet age-appropriate developmental tasks and threatens a child's sense of safety.
2. Functioning includes both positive influences, such as positive self-regard, and negative factors such as internalized and externalized problems. The theory of contextual resilience proposes an inverse relationship between self-regard and problems.
3. Resilience is the product of the cumulative effect of many risk and protective factors. The theory of contextual resilience, therefore, leads to the inference that to promote resilience in parentally bereaved children, an intervention needs to identify and target salient risk and protective factors that affect the functioning of children who are coping with a severe life crisis.

To accomplish its objective to promote the resiliency of parentally bereaved children (including adolescents), the FBP intervention focuses on (a) reinforcing positive interactions between the surviving parent and the children, (b) reducing the surviving parent's mental health problems, and (c) curtailing the children's involvement in distressing events. The intervention teaches parents to be affectionate and encouraging and to set limits for their children. Parents are taught to keep children from becoming embroiled in family issues, such as financial troubles, that are the province of an adult.

The intervention involves 12 group sessions with the children and parent, and two individual sessions. Five of the sessions involve "conjoint activities for the caregiver and youth" (Sandler et al., 2008, p. 537). To quote the FBP authors at length,

> The program focused on improving skills in coping and family interactions and promoted the use of these skills to accomplish personal goals that each caregiver and child identified at the beginning of the program. Active learning strategies were used to teach the program skills, and caregivers and children practiced the program skills at home after each session. Each session included a common structure, discussion of the home practice of program skills and progress toward achieving personal goals, teaching of a new program skill, and role play practice of the new skill.
>
> (Sandler et al., 2008, p. 537)

Activities to strengthen parent–child relationships involved taking time out to do things together and praising children for positive behavior. Attentive listening was also taught to the caregivers. Discipline was emphasized as an important component in strengthening parent–child relationships, and thus the intervention taught caregivers about consistency in discipline, clear explanation of expectations, and linking consequences to behavior. Other protective factors were taught parents such as setting personal goals, reassuring their children that the family would survive, and guarding against using children as though they were adults to confide in about problems.

Evaluation of the intervention is most promising. Families in the treatment condition showed gains in use of positive parenting, a decline in stressful events, an increase in joint parent–child activities, fewer mental health problems in parents, and an increase in active rather than passive coping; the families in the control groups did not show these gains. The mental health of children in the intervention improved such that internalizing and externalizing problems declined: examples of internalizing problems were anxiety and depression, and examples of externalizing problems were acting out and delinquent behaviors. These positive effects were seen in girls in the intervention, but not in girls in the control group; boys in both the intervention and in the control group showed a decline in internalizing and externalizing problems over time.[7] Long-term follow-up data gathered 6 years after the intervention confirmed that the FBP had lasting, positive effects confirmed both by the participants and by outside observers such as teachers.

A robust finding of the effects of the FBP involves the significant role of positive parenting in the resilient responses of bereaved children and adolescents. By positive parenting is meant affectionate interacting with children and consistent discipline. The intervention focused on more than teaching parenting skills; it also focused on promoting the parent's resilience in the face of the distress of bereavement and other stressors that impinge on the parent's mental health. A conclusion I have drawn is that if you want to make a difference in the lives of parentally bereaved youth and you have limited resources, focus on making a difference in the lives of the surviving parents.

Family-Focused Grief Therapy. Family-Focused Grief Therapy (FFGT) shares many of the indicators needed to be considered evidence-based practice. It is grounded in a definite theory, namely, family systems theory, and devised a set of procedures tested in randomized control trials at various sites. The procedures have been identified in a manual.

FFGT is used in palliative care/oncology settings; the intervention begins while the cancer-stricken family member is alive and includes all members of the family. In this regard, FFGT is responsive to Prigerson's conclusion that grieving families in hospice respond more positively to interventions when the family enters the hospice early and there is time to build a therapeutic alliance.

The point of the FFGT intervention is to assist a family grieving a death to adapt by means of making use of relational meaning. The FFGT innovators describe relational meaning is established in a family "through the active sharing of vulnerability, the fostering of tolerance and respect, the nurturance of generosity, and mutual care provision" (Kissane & Hooghe, 2011, p. 288). There are conceptual links with Nadeau's emphasis that meaning making is at the heart of family adjustment to adversity; there are also conceptual links to the idea of resilience and empowerment that have become current in psychology.

FFGT is designed for working with families "at risk of morbid psychological outcome as a result of how members relate together" (Kissane et al., 2006, p. 1208). I suspect that the notion of a morbid psychological outcome is a reference to complicated grief disorder, a condition that can be identified in individuals; I am not sure whether Kissane and his family therapy colleagues are suggesting that complicated grief can be identified as a family disorder.

FFGT starts with the designation of five types of families. These designations identify different interaction patterns and dynamics in a family according to how cohesive, emotionally expressive, and able to handle conflict the family is. Supportive families and conflict resolving families are considered to be functioning well and not in need of outside help to cope with bereavement over the death of a family member. However, there are three family types whose communication and cohesion are strained, and these families are considered at risk of responding poorly to the death of a family member.

The three types of families at risk are sullen families, hostile families, and intermediate families. Sullen families have strained communication patterns and little cohesion; the members stuff their anger and manifest high rates of depression. They are open to help, and respond to 8 to 12 sessions of FFGT over a 12- to 18-month duration. Hostile families have histories of open conflict that have left them fragmented; keeping away from each other emotionally has proven successful as a means for the survival of the family. These families seldom welcome the offer of outside help. The most that FFGT advocates suggest is possible with hostile families is setting modest goals and working with them in 12 to 16 sessions over 18 months. Intermediate families' interactions place them between the two functional family types and the two dysfunctional. Intermediate families are less troubled with conflict and problems communicating than found in sullen and hostile families, and they typically have histories of helping family members when in need. Intermediate families' cohesion and conflict resolution tend to crumble when faced with the distress of a family member's death. They are open to help, and 6 to 8 sessions of FFGT are said to prove effective in promoting relational meaning and preventing complicated grief.

FFGT uses a screening tool called the Family Relationships Index to identify families at risk. The screening tool is filled out by a family at the palliative care unit. The screening tool has been shown to have a very high degree of sensitivity to identify sullen, hostile, and intermediate families. Once at risk families are identified, the FFGT team invites the family to meet with a therapist.

The original description of the FFGT approach mentioned four to eight 90-minute sessions over a period of 9 to 18 months. It would appear from the differential use of the intervention with different types of families that the FFGT designers have modified the approach in response to clinical assessment and observation.

Statistical analyses of outcomes indicate the FFGT had the greatest positive impact on "the top 10% of family members with the most distress, depression, and poor social adjustment at baseline" (Kissane et al., 2006, p. 1214). This outcome can be argued to be all of a piece with the argument that bereavement interventions assist persons in the greatest distress. Overall, the members of treatment groups and control groups did not show any statistically significant differences in outcomes when measuring changes from pretest scores in terms of reductions in grief or in depression or in increases in social adjustment.

When outcomes were parceled out in terms of type of at-risk family, the FFGT clearly showed that sullen families benefited. "The most noteworthy improvements in distress and depression occurred in members of sullen families" (Kissane et al., 2006, p. 1214). The FFGT authors caution that these results were from a small subset of the overall research sample, namely, 22 families out of the 257 that took part in the study. While depression scores remain unchanged in hostile families in treatment, it is noteworthy that hostile families in the control group showed declines in depression. No explanation is given for this unanticipated finding.

Secondary Interventions with Bereaved College Students

Two interventions designed to assist bereaved college students are (a) a program designed by and for bereaved college students and (b) an intervention testing the efficacy of providing bereaved students social support and education about coping. The first program is the National Students of AMF and the second was a secondary prevention tested on the campus of Kansas State University.

National Students of AMF. National Students of AMF is a nonprofit organization started by college students that helps college students who are coping with the illness or death of a loved one. The impetus for the organization began at Georgetown University in 2004, due to the efforts of an undergraduate, David Fajgenbaum, whose mother had died of cancer the previous year; Fajgenbaum said starting a support group for grieving students was a promise he had made to his mother. In 2006 with the help of his friend Benjamin Chesson, a law student in North Carolina, Fajgenbaum filed papers to incorporate National Students of AMF as a 501(c)(3) nonprofit organization.

The officers of National Students of AMF work with students to help them start chapters on their own university campus. A college chapter offers two principal services: support groups and service groups. The student-led support groups meet to give grieving students a safe environment in which to listen to others and tell their own stories. Students of AMF make clear that the support groups are not in competition with the professional, official services available on campus. Chapters work with the official services and, when needed, refer students.

> Support group members, who may be enrolled undergraduate or graduate students, meet twice a month in an informal on-campus setting. Students discuss specific situations they've encountered, empathize with one another, and share coping techniques. The support group is not counseling, yet all students that can either provide or receive support are invited and encouraged to attend these meetings.
> (Retrieved April 11, 2013, from www.studentsofamf.org/campus-chapters/)

The chapter's service group is open to the entire campus and engages in projects for the benefit of the wider community. Examples of projects undertaken at various campus chapters include completing 10K walks for cancer, raising money for Ronald McDonald Houses, finding donors in a bone marrow drive, sponsoring a community walk to raise awareness about suicide prevention, and supporting a colon cancer awareness run. The service activities involve many more persons than the students who participate in the support groups, and include both grieving and nongrieving participants.

> The chapter Service Group, which is open to the entire campus community, encourages members to channel their grief towards championing (raising money and awareness for) causes that have impacted their own or their peers' lives. The Service Group provides a tangible and therapeutic benefit for the bereaved, a positive impact on the community at large, and an opportunity for friends of the bereaved to show their support. Each chapter service group is free to choose its own service projects; activities are often chosen in honor of a loved one or in support of a cause that has directly impacted the campus community.
>
> (Retrieved April 11, 2013, from www.studentsofamf.org/campus-chapters/)

Offering support and service groups promotes both the intuitive approaches to grieving and the instrumental. Persons can become involved in ways that matter to them. There is also a wisp of the Dual Process Model: the support group focuses participants on the loss orientation aspect to grieving and the service group focuses participants on the restoration aspect.

Students from over 170 separate colleges have worked with National Students of AMF. As of May 2013, chapters have been started and continue in operation at 50 campuses. The national office of Students of AMF produced well-thought out documents to help students start a chapter. There is a toolkit teaching how to make a chapter last. The national office of the organization pairs the interested campus leader with a young adult who has helped start and maintain his or her own chapter. National Students of AMF offers funding to support the chapter; this funding may be used "to pay for start-up and maintenance costs such as T-shirts/other promotional materials, flyers/other printing and copying needs, meeting space/travel to events, and food or drinks at meetings or receptions" (Retrieved April 11, 2013, from www.studentsofamf.org/campus-chapters/).

One form of support that the national office provides each chapter is a monthly conference call. The monthly call will have a specific topic, known in advance; the more veteran members, including officers from the national office, will discuss best practices and share experiences. The conference calls allow chapter leaders to be in touch with their peers at other campuses and to discuss matters that puzzle them.

Each August National Students of AMF sponsors a conference in Raleigh/Durham. The purpose is multifold: to bring together chapter leaders for face-to-face meetings, to sponsor presentations by leaders in mental health, bereavement research, and student counseling. The national office pays for all travel expenses for chapter leaders and helps offset costs for faculty advisors to chapters.

A Social Support Intervention with Bereaved College Students.   This intervention, funded by an NIMH grant, was examined on the Kansas State University campus. The intervention made use of the coping model developed by Rudolf Moos; eight sessions were organized around the five adaptive tasks and three domains of coping skills in the Moos model. The model is discussed in Chapter Four.

One hundred and eighty students were recruited to be part of the study. The bereaved students were randomly assigned to treatment or control group status. Multiple measures were collected at pretest, immediately after the intervention was completed, and 6 to 8 weeks after that. It was a repeated measures, randomized control group, pretest/posttest design. Members in the treatment group met eight separate times over a 4-week span. A serious mistake was not to have provided members of the control group any sort of plausible intervention; control group members were simply asked to fill out the data instruments on three separate occasions. The attrition rate, while minimal for the treatment group, was noticeable in members of the control group, raising a clear threat to the internal validity of the study.

The structure and content of the eight sessions merit consideration, but no claims can be made that the intervention has met the standard of evidence-based practice. The sessions are described next.

Overview of the sessions. Each social support group, comprised of four to eight students, was led by a facilitator, an advanced graduate student in the Marriage and Family Therapy program at Kansas State University. The facilitators were trained in the coping model, and each had experience in responding appropriately to persons in emotional distress. The facilitator's role involved creating a safe, nonjudgmental environment for discussions of death, grief, and mourning. The facilitators modeled attentive and empathic listening. The facilitators taught the basic elements of the Moos model. Facilitators acted on teachable moments when discussions indicated a group member, talking about responding to a death, was referring to a component of the Moos model.

Sessions lasted two hours at least, often more. The goal of each session was to support the group members "to talk about their experiences and then analyze them in terms of the Moos framework" (Balk, Tyson-Rawson, & Colletti-Wetzel, 1993, p. 433). As sessions progressed, participants made vicarious generalizations as they "connected the framework to their experiences and those of other group participants" (p. 433).

Session 1. The objectives in the first session are (a) to promote group trust and cohesion by getting participants to know one another and (b) to introduce the Moos model of coping with life crises. Specific attention is paid to presenting the adaptive task establishing meaning and personal understanding of the significance of the life crisis. Procedures involved six steps.

1. Place group participants in dyads. Each participant is to learn who his or her partner is, what occurred to lead them to be part of the intervention, concerns the person has about the support group meetings, and hopes for what will occur in the sessions.
2. After 30 minutes the dyads return to the larger group, and each person introduces his or her partner.
3. The facilitator identifies themes and topics presented by each dyad and writes them on large flip chart sheets of paper.
4. The facilitator gives an overview of the Moos model and the structure of the eight sessions.
5. Giving participants paper and pencils, the facilitator leads the group members in an exercise in which they write down what death means to them and whether the meaning changes according to who dies. The facilitator places the completed assignments in the middle of the group, reads aloud each paper, and encourages

discussion of what persons wrote (and heard). "This procedure should generate alternatives about establishing meaning and considering other ways in which death is viewed. The leader will facilitate group discussion about the meaning of the death for each participant by having the individuals discuss the relationship that was severed when the person died. One focus of the leader will be to provide feedback by giving positive comments and acknowledging how painful and difficult grieving is and to encourage participants to give feedback to each other" (Balk et al., 1993, p. 434).

6. The facilitator (a) provides specific information about establishing meaning and personal understanding of the significance of the life crisis and (b) leads discussion to assist participants to make connections with the adaptive task and what they have already talked about in the session.

Session 2. The objectives in the second session are to continue encouraging self-disclosure, attentive listening, empathic feedback, and making connections between the Moos model and participants' experiences. The material taught in session 2 is the adaptive task of confronting reality and responding to situational requirements. Procedures for session 2 involve five steps.

1. The facilitator asks persons to review what they recall about session 1.
2. The facilitator finds out what things have been like for participants since the first session.
3. The facilitator introduces a group exercise. Each participant is to write down five words that depict bereavement's pain. The discussion focuses on going around the group five times for each person to read one word and talk about it. These terms are placed on large flip chart paper. ""Participants can talk about the experiences that come to mind with those words and how some terms seem to overlap in terms of interpreting experiences" (p. 435).
4. Using the procedure mentioned in step 3, the facilitator has the participants engage in brainstorming about environmental demands that bereavement evokes. "The leader will facilitate a discussion of demands encountered, what the participants do when there are these demands, and what feelings accompany their experiencing such demands" (p. 435).
5. The facilitator (a) provides specific information about the Moos task of confronting reality and responding to situational demands and (b) leads discussion to assist participants to make connections with the adaptive task and what they have already talked about in this and the first session.

Session 3. The objectives in the third session are to continue the group dynamics established in sessions 1 and 2, to focus on making connections between experiences shared and the Moos model, and to teach about the task of sustaining interpersonal relationships. Procedures for session 3 involve four steps.

1. The facilitator asks persons to review what they recall about session 2.
2. The facilitator finds out what things have been like for participants since the second session.

3. The facilitator introduces a group exercise. Each participant is to write down the names of two persons: one individual the participant feels comfortable with on the topic of the death being grieved and an individual with whom the participant feels uncomfortable. "Participants will share the names, what the relationship with each person is like, and what the comfort/discomfort mean. The leader will facilitate discussion of what has happened in the relationships with those persons since the death—and how the relationships are maintained—and/or what has prevented any from being maintained" (p. 436).

4. The facilitator (a) provides specific information about the Moos task of sustaining interpersonal relationships and (b) leads discussion to assist participants to make connections with the adaptive task and what they have already talked about in this and the first two sessions.

Session 4. The objectives in the fourth session are to continue the group dynamics established in the first three sessions and to teach about the adaptive task of maintaining emotional balance. Procedures in session 4 involve four steps.

1. The facilitator asks persons to review what they recall about session 3.
2. The facilitator finds out what things have been like for participants since session 3.
3. The facilitator introduces a group exercise. The participants write down emotions that most illustrate their reactions to the death, how those emotions have changed over time, and how they have managed those emotions. The facilitator uses large flip chart pages to write down emotions the participants mention, and the facilitator solicits discussion about what participants mention. Here are some probes the facilitator is encouraged to use: "How did you deal with your emotions? Whom have you talked to? Have these feelings interfered with your life at times? At times do your emotions feel overwhelming and you'd prefer more sense of control? At times do you feel too much in control and would prefer to have an outlet? What emotions have you welcomed?" (p. 437).
4. The facilitator (a) provides specific information about the Moos task of maintaining emotional balance and (b) leads discussion to assist participants to make connections with the adaptive task and what they have already talked about in this and the other sessions.

Session 5. The objectives in the fifth session are to continue the group dynamics established in the first four sessions and to teach about the adaptive task of preserving a satisfactory self-image and maintaining a sense of self-efficacy. The fifth session starts 30 minutes earlier than the first four sessions so that participants may complete the Social Support Group Rating Scale. The facilitator reminds participants that four sessions remain. Procedures in session 5 involve four steps.

1. The facilitator asks persons to review what they recall about session 4.
2. The facilitator finds out what things have been like for participants since the fourth session.
3. The facilitator introduces a group exercise that uses the Jo-Hari window. The purpose is to facilitate discussion about perceptions of oneself. The Jo-Hari window

is a rectangular figure with four boxes in which to identify perceptions of self: (a) aspects known to oneself but not to others, (b) aspects known to others but not to oneself, (c) aspects known to others and to oneself, (d) aspects that remain hidden from everyone. Participants are instructed to draw their Jo-Hari window twice: once as it seems to be in reality and then as the person would prefer it. Discussion occurs as each participant talks about the personal significance of the actual and the ideal Jo-Hari windows that have been drawn. After this discussion of the Jo-Hari window drawings, the facilitator uses brainstorming to uncover what the participants have accomplished since the death occurred. The leader will use such probing questions as "Has this experience changed your sense of self? How has it changed your sense of competency? How has it changed your sense of what you can handle? Do you know more about yourself than you did before the death happened?" (p. 438). A task of the facilitator is to help participants integrate themes from other sessions and spot how matters discussed "illustrate ongoing issues and coping" (p. 438).

4. The facilitator (a) provides specific information about the Moos task of preserving a satisfactory self-image and maintaining self-efficacy and (b) leads discussion to assist participants to make connections with the adaptive task and what they have already talked about in this and other sessions.

Session 6. The objectives in the sixth session are to continue the group dynamics established in the first five sessions and to teach about the appraisal-focused coping skills of cognitive redefinition, logical analysis, and cognitive avoidance. Procedures for session 6 involve four steps.

1. The facilitator asks persons to review what they recall about session 5.
2. The facilitator finds out what things have been like for participants since the last session.
3. The facilitator teaches about appraisal-focused coping, offering definitions and examples that illustrate each appraisal-focused coping skill.
4. The facilitator leads a discussion about how participants can see they have used these skills—or how they could have used them—and how well the skills have helped the person to cope in some situations but not in others. The facilitator asks participants to recall discussions in sessions when the skills were mentioned. Some time will be used to discuss which appraisal-focused coping skills are easiest to use, which most difficult, and how participants can imagine using the skills in the future.

Session 7. The objectives in the seventh session are to continue the group dynamics established in the first six sessions and to teach about the problem-focused coping skills of taking action, seeking information and support, and identifying alternatives. Procedures for session 7 involve four steps.

1. The facilitator asks persons to review what they recall about session 6.
2. The facilitator finds out what things have been like for participants since the last session.
3. The facilitator teaches about problem-focused coping, offering definitions and examples that illustrate each problem-focused coping skill.

4. The facilitator leads a discussion about how participants can see they have used these skills—or how they could have used them—and how well the skills have helped the person to cope in some situations but not in others. The facilitator asks participants to recall discussions in sessions when the skills were mentioned. Some time will be used to discuss which problem-focused coping skills are easiest to use, which most difficult, and how participants can imagine using the skills in the future.

Session 8. The objectives in the eighth session are to continue the group dynamics established in the first seven sessions and to teach about the emotion-focused coping skills of emotional regulation, emotional discharge, and resigned acceptance. Procedures for session 8 involve four steps.

1. The facilitator asks persons to review what they recall about session 7.
2. The facilitator finds out what things have been like for participants since the last session.
3. The facilitator teaches about emotion-focused coping, offering definitions and examples that illustrate each emotion-focused coping skill.
4. The facilitator leads a discussion about how participants can see they have used these skills—or how they could have used them—and how well the skills have helped the person to cope in some situations but not in others. The facilitator asks participants to recall discussions in sessions when the skills were mentioned. Some time will be used to discuss which emotion-focused coping skills are easiest to use, which most difficult, and how participants can imagine using the skills in the future.

Intervention issues to keep in mind. Issues that emerged during the intervention deserve consideration. These issues are most likely issues one would anticipate. The presence of these etic issues, however, does not rule out the obligation of persons delivering the intervention to remain attentive to emic issues that may spring up unexpectedly and need to be addressed.

Some anticipated issues involve the students participating in the support group sessions, and others involve the group facilitators. First, we'll discuss the issues that involve the student participants.

The cohesion and trust that quickly emerges in the support group contrasts sharply with the participants' experience in the larger university community where they have learned to camouflage their grief because few understand what they are coping with. The openness and safety of the support group can actually become a distracter from the objective of the intervention. During group meetings persons may start sharing experiences not germane to the focus of the session. For instance, some participants began talking about issues important in themselves but not directly related to the intervention. Examples are concerns over a friend's problems with her boyfriend, difficulties with a class, strains with one's job, even the threat of domestic violence.

While openness is highly valued and without it the support group could not succeed, the facilitator has to weigh when the discussion is leading away from bereavement and the needs of the group as a whole. We determined the best advice was for the facilitator to assess the context and determine whether the discussion was tangential to the session.

We also determined "that there was a place in a 2 1/2–3 hour session for members to discuss their lives in a less formal manner" (p. 442).

Topics with potentially serious consequences, such as domestic violence to a participant, were discussed by the facilitator and group members. It would have been unethical to avoid discussing such issues; the structure of the intervention could not be rated more important than the safety of a group member. The facilitator identified referral sources for the person to contact and examined with her and other group members "strategic planning directed toward ensuring the safety of the member" (p. 442).

Facilitators were there to lead the group, not to run a therapy session. Sensitivity to therapy concerns may have been particularly relevant in this project because both group leaders were graduate students in marriage and family therapy. As such, both leaders could readily identify patterns indicative of preexisting problems. Their temptation was to transform the support group meeting into a therapy session focused on an individual in need. The issues that the leaders had become aware of included childhood physical or sexual abuse, substance abuse, and associations with dangerous people. The leaders felt torn between meeting the needs of the group and the pain and anguish of an individual member over matters outside the scope of the social support intervention.

We talked about these concerns and decided that to focus "on intensely and critically felt issues can create divisions in the group as time is monopolized by one member with matters that cannot be resolved in the support group setting" (p. 443). The balance we arrived at involved trusting the judgment of the facilitator in the moment. "Leaders resolved to provide attention to individual issues as long as such discussions could be time-limited, focused on the individual's need to take responsibility for obtaining assistance, and did not neglect the needs of other members" (p. 444).

Facilitator vulnerability to the distress of the group members is another issue meriting consideration. This phenomenon of vulnerability has become noted in the literature as an issue of vicarious trauma, in some sources called compassion fatigue. To keep the group working, the facilitator is not in a position to remain distant or aloof from the intensity of group discussions. "Indeed, for the group to operate effectively within the model, the leader must connect with each member in both cognitively and emotionally significant ways" (p. 444). Decompressing after a meeting was necessary for the leaders. One of the facilitators mentioned she could not just turn off the voices from the meeting once the session was completed and everyone had gone their separate ways. The leaders found their own strategies to cope with their emotional responses to a session. For instance, one strategy was to make sure there was free time after the group just to be by oneself "before moving on to other tasks" (p. 444). Another strategy used was weekly meetings between the facilitators and the project director where we discussed any difficulties and heard other perspectives. One outcome of these regular debriefing sessions was the "positive effect of sharing and giving support and having one's perspectives and responses validated by others with similar reactions" (p. 445).

Camps for Life-Threatened and Bereaved Adolescents

These camps have emerged throughout the United States and other countries. Some of the camps I know about are Camp Lloyd in Green Bay, Wisconsin; Camp Ānuenue in Hawaii; camps run by Calvary Hospital in New York City; Sky Camp in Amarillo, Texas;

Camp Solari in Las Vegas, Nevada; Family Bereavement Camp sponsored by Hospice Hawaii; and Camp Erin in Phoenix, Arizona. The Moyer Foundation sponsors a national bereavement camp conference to teach about organizing, running, and raising money for camps. I will present information on two camps, the Hole-in-the-Wall Gang and Comfort Free Zone.

Paul Newman and Joanne Woodward started the Hole-in-the-Wall Gang, a camp for youth stricken with serious diseases. Over a quarter of a century in existence, the Hole-in-the-Wall Gang Camp offers nine full week sessions a year, and up to 120 campers participate each session. Campers typically attend camp once a week for 3 years. The experiences offered encompass a legion of possibilities. For instance, camp sessions have allowed campers to "become naturalists and fishermen, athletes and actors, equestrians and hot air balloonists, potters and painters, poets and photographers, swimmers and singers, fly tiers and fly fishermen, outdoor campers and canoe paddlers, clowns and musicians, woodworkers and kite flyers" (www.holeinthewallgang.org/ retrieved May 23, 2013). The intent is more than to let the youth be distracted with unusual and interesting experiences; a fundamental purpose is to increase the camper's sense of competence and thus promote his or her trust in self and sense of resilience. In addition to the week-long camp sessions, programs include visits with hospitalized children, reunions, and family weekends. To promote ongoing connections following the week session, campers are given access to a website available only to Hole-in-the-Wall Gang participants.

Lynne Hughes started Comfort Free Zone as a safe haven for grieving children and adolescents. The camps are offered to offset the neglect grieving youth often experience following the death of a family member or friend. The camp offers free weekend bereavement camps throughout the year. There are camps located in California, Massachusetts, New Jersey, and Virginia. Travel expenses are picked up for children from families strapped for finances. The goal of the camps is to provide a safe, attentive environment for the camper to experience being noticed, listened to, and accepted. Each camper is paired with an adult volunteer. Pairing campers and volunteers occurs through a screening process conducted prior to the camper's arrival. "Matches are based on compatibility of personality, grief experience, hobbies and cultural backgrounds" (www.comfort zonecamp.org/about/lynnes-story, retrieved May 23, 2013).

Tertiary Interventions

The notion of tertiary prevention is to intervene with persons after severe problems have already occurred. Examples are physical rehabilitation following open-heart surgery and follow-up mental health services for persons with chronic psychiatric disorders such as schizophrenia. Tertiary interventions in thanatology encompass such phenomena as trauma and grief, complicated grief disorder, interventions aimed at adolescents surviving cancer, and palliative care for the terminally ill.

Tertiary Interventions Aimed at Trauma and Grief

We now have convincing evidence that brief cognitive-behavioral therapy is an effective means of preventing the onset of PTSD and of ameliorating ASD regardless of the age of the person afflicted. One issue yet to be determined is what is the optimal timing for these brief interventions to prevent PTSD. Preliminary evidence suggests that "better outcomes may be achieved if treatment is delayed for several months" (Friedman, Foa, & Charney, 2003, p. 766) rather than implemented on the heels of an acutely traumatizing event. An intervention now contraindicated for trauma victims is single session psychological debriefing. Initially, such debriefing sessions were thought to prevent the development of PTSD, but evidence indicates psychological debriefing has iatrogenic effects.

When persons are experiencing both trauma and bereavement, the rule-of-thumb is to focus first on the trauma so that the person may be freed to deal with the grief elicited by the loss. Excellent examples of intervention protocols developed to assist persons both traumatized and bereaved are the efforts designed for families following the terrorist attacks on the Twin Towers. One effort was the work of Grace Christ and her colleagues; another approach was the work of Elissa Brown, Michelle Pearlman, Robin Goodman, and their colleagues.

The work of Grace Christ and her colleagues. This trauma and grief intervention was modeled on successful efforts with families when a parent dies of cancer. The approach used a psychoeducational intervention carried out in each participating family's home. The study sample included 50 women, who ranged in age from 25 to 51, and 125 children, most who were between the ages of 6 and 9.

The initial intent to deliver the intervention to groups of families was scuttled when long round trips of 50 to 70 miles presented a major obstacle to participation. The intervention extended for 5 years. Impetus for the intervention came from the Counseling Service Unit (CSU) of the New York City Fire Department, which formed a partnership with bereavement specialists at Columbia University. The psychoeducational nature of the intervention met the desire of the CSU for "an intervention that would be responsive to the widows' pressing concerns" (Christ, Kane, & Horsley, 2011, p. 204); an important secondary goal was "to learn more about the trajectory of recovery for widows and children after a terrorist attack" (p. 204).

The intervention began with four assessment sessions extended over 8 weeks; the assessment of children also included a counseling component. These assessments included multiple standardized clinical instruments including the Child Behavior Checklist, the Expanded Grief Inventory, the Children's Depression Inventory, and the State Trait Anxiety Inventory. Children's teachers also gave reports of children in their classrooms.

Part of the educational component of the intervention was to give parents information about the assessments of their children. The detailed assessments, particularly of the children, were of considerable value for the participating mothers. The mothers expressed concern whether their children's reactions signified serious problems, and they were relieved when the assessment data indicated their children's responses "fell below the borderline or clinical range" (p. 214).

Extended interviews with family members were conducted in this early assessment period. Further, team members observed interactions and the home environment, and they discussed what they had seen and heard. These data from standardized instruments, observations, and interviews provided baseline information for the task of charting the paths recovery took for these family members.

Following the assessment and the initial counseling sessions with the children, the intervention team held monthly meetings in the family's home for the next 2 years, then three sessions per year, and with "more varied frequency as needed or requested in the third to fifth years" (p. 206). At least two team members went to each participating family's home, contingent on the number of children in the family. The nature of the intervention, in particular regular contact in the family's home, raised issues for the intervention team both of countertransference and of boundary setting. Responses to offset these issues involved (a) always visiting the family with another team member, (b) reviewing with the family each interview immediately after it was completed, (c) discussing with intervention partners the content of interviews, including nonverbals, and the family's dynamics, and (d) participating in weekly supervisory sessions to examine any problems or concerns and then to review a particular family in depth. These responses provided a means of attaining some distance and objectivity and offset the risk of becoming enmeshed with the families.

The psychoeducational meetings in the homes dealt with a diverse array of issues. Some stemmed from family members' initial mistrust of and hesitancy to interact with the team members. This resistance initially surprised the intervention teams, but upon reflection it became apparent that all these families' struggles "with intense anger, mistrust, and withdrawal were consistent with the responses described for families after other terrorist attacks" (p. 209). Further, numerous factors kept the trauma front and center, for instance, the constant TV coverage of the attack, commemorative events, and subsequent other losses such as unexpected deaths of friends. The team followed the treatment adage to focus first on the trauma before addressing the grief. "Priority had to be given to helping families cope with these (ongoing external trauma-inducing) events, to helping them achieve a sense of safety and calmness, and to building a 'protective shield'" (p. 209).

Significant effort with the mothers centered on helping them construct their own narrative of the event, of their grief, and of events since the attack on the Twin Towers. This approach forms part of the meaning making process that both Neimeyer and Nadeau emphasize is at the core of bereavement recovery. Framing these narratives paved the way for the mothers to cope proactively, "to engage in more adaptive thinking about what had occurred and would help them move forward" (Christ et al., 2011, p. 211), and thus uphold positive beliefs about one's ability to achieve desired outcomes.[8]

Another intervention goal that emerged as team members met with the families was to help the mothers accurately assess reactions to earlier losses in their lives and to losses that accumulated after the destruction of the Twin Towers. The psychoeducational component involved giving the women a frame of reference that allowed them to understand the power of these losses and "normalize" feelings of anxiety. Education about normal human reactions to ongoing stressors enabled the women to put their fears into perspective and "develop more realistic expectations about the intensity and complexity of the recovery process and the time required to complete it" (p. 213).

Practical matters such as problems with the schools and the need for financial advice were other issues that the team members helped resolve. A compelling example occurred when a school teacher put on her classroom wall a life-size picture of a firefighter; seeing the picture was so distressing to a boy whose father died in the Twin Towers attack that he became distraught. A team member met with the school teachers who "increased their sensitivity to the retraumatizing effects of such pictures" and "learned to prepare students ahead of time about imminent discussions on sensitive subjects" so that affected children could decide whether to take part or "engage in other activities, such as meeting with a school counselor" (p. 213).

A plausible explanation for the efficacy of the intervention involves the gentle persistence of the intervention team in the initial struggles to establish trust and rapport with family members resistant to the team members' presence. Another factor in the positive results is that the intervention enabled the families to remain engaged "with a secure community context" (p. 218) and helped the families gain entrée to varied resources.

As noted, this psychoeducational intervention ran for 5 years. In a presentation at the 2011 annual conference of the Association for Education and Counseling (ADEC), Grace Christ provided a synopsis of the 5-year outcomes. The following report is taken verbatim from an article that appeared in *The Forum*, ADEC's newsletter (see Balk, 2011).

> Year 1: The mothers sequestered their grief—delaying mourning somewhat—in order to fulfill new responsibilities of single parenting. Christ reported that grief and trauma reactions intertwined and were intense. As public events memorialized the attacks—including the killing of Osama Bin Laden 12 years after 9–11— the women and children re-experienced grief. The children's grief and trauma reactions diminished more quickly than did the widows'.
>
> Year 2: Grief reactions were more profound than in Year 1. "Public mourning seems to have delayed private grief." In Year 2, the children expressed distaste for being "9–11 kids." Widows who prior to 9–11 had effective emotional regulation fared better than women who had previous problems regulating affect.
>
> Years 3 and 4: The widows sometimes felt abandoned by their children who had put their bereavement behind them and wanted to be just normal kids. There was an ongoing need for widows and extended family members—particularly in-laws— to accept differences in grief intensity, timing of grief reactions, and duration of reactions. Widows' later needs for autonomy led to problems with in-laws over grief resolution and discrepancy in coping styles. Distribution of compensation also contributed to both anger and conflict between widows and in-laws. A subset of children, including those previously identified as resilient, began to manifest delayed reactions to the deaths of their fathers. Children continued to revisit the loss as their cognitive and emotional capabilities expanded.
>
> Years 4 and 5: Christ found that the widows demonstrated increasing self-confidence, confidence in single parenting, and capacity to engage in the world. They were re-defining themselves, planning new directions, and implementing their plans. Occasionally, waves of grief would overwhelm them (see Rosenblatt's comparable findings about grief and 19th century American pioneers). Widows felt relieved to view these later waves of grief as normative and part of the longer term process of integrating such a complex, traumatic, life changing loss rather than a failed mourning process.

Christ's longitudinal evidence supports the emergence of delayed grief—in contrast to Bonanno's conclusion that delayed grief has no empirical support. Christ speculated that the intertwining of trauma and grief—plus being a single parent to grieving children—provides a different set of circumstances than the sample of widows Bonanno studied, and these different circumstances promoted delayed or prolonged grieving.

Ambiguity plagued some widows when no remains of their husbands could be found. Initially women whose husbands' remains were not found had greater problems coming to terms with their loss than did other widows. However, discovering remains—perhaps years later—though helpful, did not produce closure.

The work of Elissa Brown, Michelle Pearlman, Robin Goodman, and their colleagues. Researchers and therapists at New York University and St. John's University also entered into an agreement with FDNY's Counseling Services Unit (CSU) to intervene with widows and children affected by the 9/11 terrorist attack. Their intervention, titled the Child and Family Recovery Program, included psychoeducation, assessment, and a cognitive-behavioral intervention aimed first at trauma and then at grief. They had in mind not only to assist the bereaved mothers and children but also to establish grounds for an evidence-based practice useful in cases of bereavement overlaid with trauma.

The outreach portion of the program, initiated 5 1/2 months after the fall of the Twin Towers, focused (a) on overcoming barriers widows and their children had toward participating and (b) on increasing use of the program. The outreach intent also was to document children's mental health needs. Phone calls, flyers, mailings, and large group meetings were used to inform the families about the program, to identify typical responses following a traumatic event, to normalize these responses, and briefly describe the support services being offered in conjunction with FDNY's CSU.

The assessment portion also was put into operation 5 1/2 months following the attack on the Twin Towers. Assessment packages were geared for different age groups: (a) 4- to 18-year-old children and adolescents, (b) 19- to 24-year-old young adults, and (c) the widows. For instance, adolescents were assessed regarding their trauma and bereavement histories, family functioning, coping, mental health issues, PTSD symptoms, and social support. Teacher reports were solicited. Parent functioning was assessed. The assessment data were obtained in one of three locations acceptable to the mother: a CSU site, a university office, or the family home. Nearly all the assessments occurred in family homes.

Following the collection of assessment information, the program directors invited widows and their children to be part of a 16 session intervention. Interventions were not provided in family homes, as were the interventions offered by Grace Christ and her colleagues, but at community-based offices near to where the mother and her children lived. The intervention involved two approaches: traumatic grief client-centered therapy (TG-CCT) and traumatic grief cognitive-behavioral therapy (TG-CBT). Families were randomly assigned to either the TG-CCT or TG-CBT intervention. Each intervention approach involved 16 sessions, the first 8 sessions focused on relieving trauma and the second eight sessions focused on grief. The intervention accepts that the starting point must be to address trauma before attention to bereavement will be fruitful.

The TG-CCT approach involved Rogerian client-centered therapy with its emphasis on reflecting the feeling and thoughts of clients. Client-centered therapy emphasizes (a) the inherent ability of persons to cope and (b) the healing power of a trusting relationship between the client and therapist. In the TG-CCT intervention children and parents set their own pace, and the therapist's role was to provide unconditional positive regard, accurately reflect thoughts and feelings of the mothers and children, and proceed without a preset agenda. At the same time, the TG-CCT intervention was divided into two sets of eight sessions: the first set to focus on trauma, and the second set to focus on grief.

The TG-CCT approach was considered a good fit "for families who had been functioning well prior to 9/11 and whose members could utilize the treatment's supportive context for addressing issues unrelated to the traumatic loss" (Cohen, Goodman, Brown, & Mannarino, 2004, p. 215). If families were assigned to treatment approaches based on assessment of risk, then the notion of random assignment to TG-CBT or TG-CCT actually had not occurred.

Reflecting on their risk-assessment approach to determine suitability of CCT versus CBT, the program designers acknowledged that troubled children in TG-CCT likely would need follow-up with symptom-focused interventions rather than continuance of CCT "in order to achieve further gains" (p. 215). Because no outcome results are reported for participants in TG-CCT, it is not clear what gains this approach produced.[9] The intervention team reported very promising results for families in the TG-CBT sessions, thereby implying that those sessions proved more effective than the TG-CCT sessions. Other publications focused on results obtained with the TG-CBT sessions; these results included improvements (a) in children's grief, anxiety, depression, PTSD, and behavioral problems and (b) in parents' PTSD and depression. The data supported the efficacy of initially focusing on trauma before intervening with grief.

The eight trauma-focused sessions in the TG-CBT offered information about traumatic grief, provided words to label responses, and taught stress-inoculation training[10] as well as relaxation procedures. Further, participants were taught how to reframe negative thoughts and to produce a personal narrative about the traumatic incident; this narrative incorporated emotional responses and various cues such as sights and sounds. The intent of producing these personal narratives is to reduce the distress that thinking about the trauma elicits.

The eight sessions focused on grief in the TG-CBT began with what we would recognize as the grief work theory, namely, confronting reminders of the death that elicit grief. Then the participant focused on memory-building, another aspect of the grief work theory, namely, constructing a mental representation of the deceased that is positive. Other sessions focused on the important adaptive coping tasks of (a) maintaining interpersonal relationships and (b) establishing the meaning and personal significance of the death. The final grief-focused session involved both the mother and her children talking about the father/husband who died and planning how to deal with upcoming, anticipated events that could prove problematic, such as the anniversary of the death.

Tertiary Interventions Aimed at Complicated Grief Disorder

Katherine Shear, a leading figure in outcome studies for treating complicated grief, has written about three treatment approaches: cognitive-behavioral therapy, meaning reconstruction, and complicated grief treatment. She examined the working assumptions of each approach, noted the strong commonalities they share, and concluded that they provided strong confirmation that expert opinions were converging on what helps persons overcome complicated grief.

In her own research program Shear has conducted randomized control trials of persons assigned either to 16 sessions of interpersonal psychotherapy (IP) or 16 sessions of complicated grief treatment (CGT). Each approach had introductory, middle, and ending phases. For instance, the introductory phase of the IP approach reviewed trauma and grief symptoms, examined role transitions, and focused on the difficulties for interpersonal relationships caused by one's grief; the middle IP phase examined more thoroughly these interpersonal difficulties, facilitated clients to assess the positive and negative features of their relationship with the deceased, and encouraged clients to reengage in the world; the ending phase focused on gains the clients had achieved, their plans for the future, and feelings about the end of the sessions.

The CGT introductory phase involved education about grief and about the dual process model. Following the dual process model, the CGT introductory phase had the clients examine losses associated with their bereavement and life goals to be achieved. One approach used by the CGT therapists was to ask the clients what would matter to them if their grief lessened. The middle phase of the CGT sessions were structured for clients to focus in more detail on the loss and restoration processes begun in the initial phase. During the ending phase of the CGT, clients reviewed treatment gains, plans for the future, and feelings about the end of the session.

In addition to its reliance on the dual process model, CGT differed from the IP approach in use of narrative and imaginal techniques so that clients would not only revisit the death but confront distressing situations they preferred avoiding; some of these situations involved distress created when yearning for the deceased and by "fears of losing the deceased forever" (Shear, Frank, Houck, & Reynolds, 2005, p. 2604). Links to the grief work theory and its emphasis on actively confronting what distresses the griever are easy to spot in this CGT approach. The CGT intervention also engages the griever in procedures promoting "a sense of connection to the deceased" (p. 2604). These procedures included engaging imaginally in a conversation with the person who died, and to respond in the role of the deceased.

While slightly over a quarter of the persons discontinued the IP and CGT sessions early, the percentages who left the program (26% and 27%, respectively) did not differ. Reasons given for leaving early did differ, but basically involved for the majority a perception that the sessions were not going to pay off. Most of the persons who left the CGT sessions did so because they found "the treatment too difficult and/or did not believe telling the highly painful story of the death could help them" (p. 2606). The majority of persons who left the IP sessions said they perceived the treatment was not working. For persons who stayed the full 16 sessions, the CGT completers had significantly better outcomes than IP completers on standardized measures of depression, complicated grief, and work and social adjustment. These results encouraged Shear and her colleagues that CGT is more effective than IP in resolving complicated grief, but they acknowledged their randomized clinical trial was a first step toward demonstrating CGT was an evidence-based practice.

Tertiary Interventions Aimed at Adolescents and Young Adults with Cancer

Treatment regimens for adolescents and young adults stricken with cancer aim at complete remission[11] and survival that is free of events such as bone pain, fractures, and reemergence of cancer. Achieving this dual goal is markedly elusive when the cancer is acute lymphoblastic leukemia (ALL) and the patient is in middle adolescence or young adulthood: persons between the ages of 16 and 20 have worse outcomes than do younger persons with ALL In addition, the incidence and prevalence of ALL is uncommon for middle and later adolescents; this rarity of the disease, particularly for young adults, leads to divergent treatment regimens: some of these stricken youth are placed in oncology programs for adults while some are placed in pediatric oncology programs.

Comparison of outcomes contingent on treatment in adult or pediatric oncology. The ALL approaches taken in adult oncology programs depart significantly from the approaches taken in pediatric programs. For instance, treatments in adult and pediatric ALL programs differ "in induction therapy, the intensity and duration of postremission therapy, the type and intensity of central nervous system (CNS) prophylaxis, and the duration of maintenance chemotherapy" (Stock et al., 2008, p. 1646). As an example, chemotherapy in adult ALL treatment regimens aims at being acceptable to persons ranging in age from 16 to 60. Once intensive chemotherapy achieves complete remission, adults receive both cranial irradiation and intensive chemotherapy injections into the spinal canal.[12]

Pediatric ALL treatment regimens separate patients according to risk for survival, and youth with greater risk of dying are given treatments more intensive and toxic than treatments given youth with greater likelihood of surviving. The goal in both adult and pediatric ALL treatment is to achieve complete remission, maintain remission with chemotherapy, and achieve survival free of deleterious events.

Knowing that ALL patients in middle adolescence and young adulthood can be treated in either pediatric or adult programs, a team of cancer researchers in the United States used causal-comparative approaches to determine whether outcomes differed according to which treatment regimen the adolescents and young adults had received. Here are some of the important findings.

- Complete remission was obtained for 90% of adolescents and young adults regardless which type of ALL treatment program they were in.
- Seventy-five percent of adolescents and young adults in pediatric ALL programs, "treated with more intensive postremission therapy" (p. 1646) than given in adult ALL trials, achieved 5-year event-free survival, as compared to 63% for youth in adult ALL programs.
- When measured over a 7-year survival trajectory, 63% of the adolescents and young adults in pediatric programs were event-free, as compared to 34% in adult programs.
- Relapse rates differed, with a noticeably higher reemergence of cancer in the central nervous system for patients treated in the adult oncology programs: in 7 years following treatment, 11% of the youth treated in adult programs showed central nervous system relapses as compared with 1% of the youth treated in pediatric programs.

Treatment adherence. A major issue when treating adolescents and young adults coping with cancer is getting patients to follow reliably the treatment regimen. Oncologists note with regret, for instance, the difficulties that these youth present over adhering to "self-administered treatments such as oral chemotherapy" (Kato, Cole, Bradlyn, & Pollock, 2008, p. 305). Increased adherence has been noted when these patients receive personal instruction. Of considerable importance is that survival rates have increased when treatment adherence also increased.

A video game called "Re-Mission." An intervention tested in multiple sites in randomized trials involved video-game-based learning to increase adherence to self-administered treatment regimens. The intervention built on documented success of video games to promote healthy outcomes in youth with such maladies as asthma, cystic fibrosis, and diabetes. Those various studies noted benefits in physiological indicators (for example, blood glucose levels), increased knowledge about specific illnesses, and behavioral changes (for example, self-care actions).

The video game built for this randomized trial is cleverly called Re-Mission, and it involves controlling a nanobot "within the bodies of young patients with cancers that commonly are diagnosed in AYA" (adolescents and young adults; p. 306). Among these cancers are acute lymphoblastic leukemia, non-Hodgkin's lymphoma, and brain tumors. The object of "Re-Mission" is to destroy cancer cells by using a host of actions including adherence to self-administered treatment regimens. "To win, players control the nanobot . . . to ensure strategically that virtual patients engage in positive self-care behaviors, such as taking oral chemotherapy" (p. 306).

The study was carried out in 34 medical centers in Canada, Australia, and the United States, and included 375 adolescent and young adult male and female research participants.[13] All the participants were in an initial diagnosis of cancer or had experienced a relapse. Following collection of baseline information, the participants were given minicomputers loaded with a commercial video game about Indiana Jones and then assigned randomly to the control group or video-game intervention. Persons in the intervention group also had loaded on their computer the video game "Re-Mission."

The study lasted 3 months. Participants were asked to play the video game(s) on their computers at least once a week for at least an hour. Many outcome measures were gathered 1 and 3 months following the collection of the baseline information. Outcomes included measures of treatment adherence, knowledge of the illness, and self-efficacy as well as measures of quality of life, levels of stress, and perceptions of control.

Overall treatment adherence did not differ between the "Re-Mission" video game players and the control group participants. For instance, participants in both groups reliably kept clinic appointments and did not differ in general adherence to medical treatments. There were no differences found in perceived stress, quality of life, or perceptions of control.

However, the intervention did produce some significant difference attributed to playing "Re-Mission." For instance, video game participants adhered to self-administered oral medication regimens significantly more than did control group participants. While both the intervention and the control groups showed increases in knowledge about their illnesses, the intervention group's increase in knowledge significantly surpassed the knowledge gain shown by the control group. Both groups showed increases in self-efficacy, but once again the video game participants significantly outstripped the control group in self-efficacy gains.

Tertiary Interventions Aimed at Palliative Care for the Terminally Ill

A constant in palliative care is management of pain. All patients, whether terminal or not, deserve to be as free as possible of pain; thus, palliative care applies in all medical settings, not just when treatment has been assessed to be futile. Thus, it is not only hospice where palliative care is practiced.

The purpose of palliative care within hospice is to insure quality of life without pain when someone is dying from a life-threatening condition. The holistic template provides one means to find indicators for what quality of life involves, whether at the end-of-life or other points along the life arc. At the end-of-life, unremitting, uncontrolled, agonizing pain prevents a person from dying on her own terms, prevents dying with dignity, and prevents attending to the various complex aspects that comprise human existence.

Fear of dying in uncontrollable, unremitting, agonizing pain is a prospect that troubles human beings. The holistic template highlights that pain can occur in one or more of the dimensions that comprise whole human existence: physical, behavioral, emotional, cognitive, interpersonal, and spiritual.

Here are some of the consequences of ongoing, unremitting physical pain:

1. Muscle tension
2. Increased blood clotting
3. Fluid retention
4. Impaired immune system functioning
5. Respiratory distress
6. Impaired gastric and bowel functioning

The other holistic dimensions—cognitive, emotional, behavioral, interpersonal, and spiritual—clearly intermingle and become influenced by unremitting physical pain. Just consider any experience you have had with severe physical pain—such as a piercing toothache or a migraine headache—and you will know that pain can overwhelm a person. Pain can include depression, utter despondency, hopelessness, wrenching isolation, guilt, and severe religious doubts. Hospice programs attend to "total pain," the suffering that encompasses multiple dimensions of a person's life. It is important to remember that pain may not be physical, and thus the need for multidisciplinary teams conversant with and expert in working with the whole person, not only the physical dimension to human existence.

Difficulties with anger offer a clear example of the cascading effects on the whole person. A dying adolescent who has been raised to suppress anger can find feelings of anger make him cognitively and physically uncomfortable. We know that anger produces rushes of adrenalin that can impact a dying person. And anger may foster interpersonal isolation and neglect as the person's anger induces others to stay away in order to avoid the person's irritability.

Best practices to manage pain. The World Health Organization (WHO) declared that palliative care programs are to assess pain 100% of the time and are to use practices that provide sufficient pain medication during medical procedures.

Best practices in palliative care are to carry out the following actions:

1. Review regularly the performance of clinicians in pain management and correct deficiencies.
2. Monitor side effects of pain medications and other pain management procedures.
3. Establish a 1–10 rating scale on which patients can report their level of pain and from which clinicians can rate conditions requiring action. Scores between 3 and 5 identify pain that requires intervention, and scores of 6 or higher are considered emergencies.

A rule of thumb among palliative care advocates is to tell patients that waiting until pain is severe and intense before informing a nurse or doctor is akin to waiting until a fever hits 106 degrees before consulting a physician. The concern is that delaying until pain is in the 6–10 rating scale increases the difficulty to control the pain.

Five guidelines to effect successful pain management. The WHO has identified five guidelines to insure greater success in controlling pain. These five guidelines are:

1. Codify and publish the rights and responsibilities of patients and of palliative care staff. These written statements increase patient and family trust in the organization as it becomes clear that the program expresses in clear language its commitment to manage pain. The written statements need to identify the steps that will be taken to bring pain under control and keep it from recurring.
2. Standardize pain assessment protocols. The first move in this direction is to adopt the 1–10 pain intensity scale. More than asking a patient how much it hurts on a scale of 1–10, a standardized pain assessment protocol requires asking such questions as, "Where does it hurt?", "What is the nature of the pain?", "When did the pain begin?", and "How have treatments affected the pain?" This second guideline is intended to empower patients to identify their own needs for pain control. A caution raised is that patients are likely to underestimate or underreport their pain.
3. Make pain the fifth vital sign. Nurses traditionally monitor four vital signs: temperature, pulse, blood pressure, and respiration. Anyone who has been a patient in a hospital recalls how frequently a nurse made readings of those four vital signs. Elevating pain to a person's vital signs makes managing pain a program priority. Staff objections to monitoring pain distill to these two observations: (a) I am overworked already with too many other things to monitor and (b) no reliable means exists to measure pain. The response to the first objection is that measuring and charting pain does not tax staff, and patients not in pain do not require follow-up work. The response to the second objection is that pain is very real to the person experiencing it. Assigning fixed numbers with universal meaning to all persons is less important than knowing whether a patient is disabled from pain and less important than knowing how levels of pain fluctuate during a 24-hour period.
4. Give the person a frame of reference to describe pain. A frame of reference allows the person to identify and talk about their pain. One widely adopted frame of reference is the 1–10 rating scale. Specifics for this rating scale indicate that
    *   1: no pain
    *   2–3: can carry on regular activities such as read a book or watch TV without being distracted by pain
    *   4–5: pain prevents the person from enjoying regular activities
    *   6 and above: the pain is severe or is on the verge of presenting a medical emergency

It is critical to use culturally appropriate methods to assess pain. Culturally appropriate methods are considered tied to local contexts. Culturally and ethnically diverse populations don't respond uniformly to the same method of assessing pain. Stoicism marks some cultural expectations, and persons tend to keep their pain private; it would go against self-concept and self-esteem to vocalize pain. Other cultures encourage open expression of pain, and persons learn that crying or groaning is expected when in pain. An important part of becoming aware of cultural influences on the experience of pain is to become aware of the cultural norms defining one's own awareness of pain.

Mary Curry Narayan, a nurse educator sensitive to transcultural issues, offers several questions to reflect on in order to promote awareness of the cultural influences on personal perception of pain and the expression of pain. Several questions focus on how the person was raised from childhood to regard pain. Two questions addressed to persons taking care of others in pain include, "Have you ever felt 'uncomfortable' with the way a patient was reacting (or not reacting) to pain?" and "Do you have 'feelings' (make value judgments) about patients in pain who behave more stoically or expressively than you would in a similar situation?" (Narayan, 2010, p. 40).

Concluding Comments

An important objective of this book is framed by the desire to find practical steps that assist life-threatened and grieving adolescents and young adults. I adhere to the position that solid, rational understanding of the phenomenology of adolescence, including developmental pressures and issues, and a grasp of information about life-threatening conditions and about bereavement must be the foundation for designing informed interventions. For several years I have been vocally promoting the value of theory as a guide to research and to intervention; I also have been denouncing the practice of practitioners who simply wing it from session to session with no informed plan or framework to guide their efforts.

This espousal of a needed and useful conceptual framework also extends to designing and delivering and evaluating interventions. I proposed as a starting point the tripartite model used in community mental health. It offers a means to organize interventions aimed at what are called primary, secondary, and tertiary levels. There are times when I suspect the boundaries between these levels become blurred and other times when assignment to a level is debatable. Cross-over from one level to another may strike some readers as another prospect.

What matters most is having a solid conceptual basis for an intervention, a clear sense of intervention goals, and a reasonable means to assess outcomes. I think these matters—when applied to life-threatened and grieving adolescents—start with addressing the overall theory that guides a person about promoting change to assist the adolescents at risk. And promoting desired changes must grasp both the field and ground not only of the back story of the adolescents but also what threatens them—and how to distinguish the salience of primary, secondary, and tertiary matters at stake when intervening in matters framed by life-threatening conditions or by bereavement.

Notes

1. Schut, Stroebe, van den Bout, & Terheggen (2001) classify primary, secondary, and tertiary interventions differently than do I. They consider primary prevention involves working with persons in normal bereavement, consider secondary prevention applies to working with

persons at high risk of developing complicated grief disorder, and restrict tertiary prevention to intervening with persons who are suffering from complicated grief.

2. Examination of high school courses in death, dying, and bereavement has uncovered a potpourri of topics or themes such as loss and change due to aging; children's understanding of death; definitions of death; the grief process; HIV/AIDS; the right to life and right to choose; funerals; suicide and suicide prevention; violence; ethics, mercy killing, and the right to die; and perspectives on grief across cultures and history.

3. In October of 2002 a student murdered two persons and injured five at Monash University.

4. This statistical procedure has been used with studies of psychotherapy overall and confirmed that psychotherapy does produce positive outcomes for clients.

5. The Utrecht researchers accept the conclusion that grief counseling is not effective with normally bereaved persons, except in the cases of interventions with bereaved children.

6. The Utrecht scholars noted that poor outcomes of interventions may have been due to recruiting volunteers rather than the real-world practice of programs "in which one waits for the bereaved person to initiate contact" (Schut et al., 2001, p. 731).

7. While not discussed as a possible explanation, the differential effects on male and female children may be attributed to instrumental and intuitive approaches to grieving; intuitive approaches to grieving that lead to persistent rumination have proven deleterious, and females engage in such practices much more than do males.

8. Links to cognitive coping models such as the one proposed by Moos are obvious in these outcomes that engage both problem-solving coping skills and the adaptive tasks of confronting the requirements of the situation and maintaining belief in one's efficacy.

9. Analyses comparing outcomes of TG-CBT and TG-CCT are said to be underway (cf. Cohen, Goodman, Brown, & Mannarino, 2004), but the only outcome studies I could find examined TG-CBT, and the researchers acknowledged those studies were preliminary at best.

10. Stress inoculation is a cognitive-behavioral procedure teaching persons how to recognize and cope with stress.

11. As an example, complete remission for ALL patients means a return to normal blood, with 5% or less blast cells in the bone marrow.

12. The term for such spinal canal injections is *intrathecal*.

13. Individuals were excluded if they had a history of seizures resulting from flashing lights; could not communicate in French, English, or Spanish; or demonstrated inability to follow directions.

Sources

Ayers, T. S., Kondo, C. C., & Sandler, I. N. (2011). Bridging the gap: Translating a research-based program into an agency-based service for bereaved children and families. In R. A. Neimeyer, D. L. Harris, W. R. Winokuer, & G. F. Thornton (Eds.), *Grief and bereavement in contemporary society: Bridging research and practice* (pp. 117–135). New York: Routledge.

Baker, J. & McPhedran, S. (2007). Gun laws and sudden death: Did the Australian firearms legislation of 1996 make a difference? *British Journal of Criminology*, 47, 455–469.

Balk, D. E. (2011). Bereavement of widows of firefighters killed in the World Trade Center attacks. *The Forum*, 37(4), 24.

Balk, D. E. (2013). Building a bridge to span the research-practice gap. *Grief Matters*, 16(1), 4–7.

Balk, D. E., Tyson-Rawson, K, & Colletti-Wetzel, J. (1993). Social support as an intervention with bereaved college students. *Death Studies*, 17, 427–450.

Bloom, B. S., Madaus, G. F., & Hastings, J. T. (1981). *Evaluation to improve learning*. New York: McGraw-Hill.

Bluebond-Langner, M. (1978). *The private worlds of dying children*. Princeton, NJ: Princeton University Press.

Bonanno, G. A. (2009). *The other side of sadness: What the new science of bereavement tells us about life after loss*. New York: Basic Books.

Breen, L. (2010–2011). Professionals' experiences of grief counseling: Implications for bridging the gap between research and practice. *Omega, 62*(3), 285–303.

Brown, D., Crace, R. K., & Almeida, L. (2006). A culturally sensitive, values-based approach to career counseling. In A. J. Palmo, W. J. Weikel, & D. P. Borsos (Eds.), *Foundations of mental health counseling* (3rd edition). (pp. 144–171). Springfield, IL: Charles C. Thomas.

Brown, E. J., Pearlman, M. Y., & Goodman, R. F. (2004). Facing fears and sadness: Cognitive-behavioral therapy for childhood traumatic grief. *Harvard Review of Psychiatry, 12*(4), 187–198.

Callahan, C. M., Rivara, F., & Koepsell, T. D. (1994). Money for guns: Evaluation of the Seattle gun buy-back program. *Public Health Reports, 109*(4), 472–477.

Chapman, S., Alpers, P., Agho, K., & Jones, M. (2006). Australia's 1996 gun law reforms: Faster falls in firearm deaths, firearm suicides, and a decade without mass shootings. *Injury Prevention, 12*, 365–372.

Christ, G. H. (2009). Children bereaved by the death of a parent. In C. A. Corr & D. E. Balk (Eds.), *Children's encounters with death, bereavement, and coping* (pp. 169–183). New York: Springer.

Christ, G. (2011). Bereavement of widows of firefighters who died on 9/11/01. A presentation at the Annual Conference of the Association for Death Education and Counseling, June 23, 2011, Miami, FL.

Christ, G., Kane, D., & Horsley, H. (2011). Grief after terrorism: Toward a family-focused intervention. In R. A. Neimeyer, D. L. Harris, H. R. Winokuer, & G. F. Thornton (Eds.), *Grief and bereavement in contemporary society Bridging research and practice* (pp. 203–219). New York: Routledge.

Christ, G., Raveis, V., Siegel, K, Karus, D., & Christ, A. (2005). Evaluation of a bereavement intervention. *Social Work in End-of-Life and Palliative Care, 1*, 57–81.

Cohen, J., Goodman, R. F., Brown, E. J., & Mannarino, A. (2004). Treatment of childhood traumatic grief contributing to a newly emerging condition in the wake of community trauma. *Harvard Review of Psychiatry, 12*(4), 213–216.

Cohen, J. A., Mannarino, A. P., & Knudsen, K. (2004). Treating childhood traumatic grief: A pilot study. *Journal of the American Academy of Child & Adolescent Psychiatry, 43*(10), 1225–1233.

Colgrove, J. (2006). The ethics and politics of compulsory HPV vaccination. *New England Journal of Medicine, 355*, 2389–2391.

Connor, S. R. (1998). *Hospice: Practice, pitfalls, and promise*. Washington, DC: Taylor & Francis.

Crace, R. K. & Brown, D. (1996). *Life values inventory*. Williamsburg, VA: Applied Psychology Resources.

Currier, J. M., Neimeyer, R. A., & Berman, J. S. (2008). The effectiveness of psychotherapeutic interventions for the bereaved: A comprehensive quantitative review. *Psychological Bulletin, 34*(5), 648–661.

De Souza, M., Macinko, J., Alencar, A. P., Malta, D.C., & Neto, O. (2007). Reductions in firearm-related mortality and hospitalizations in Brazil after gun control. *Health Affairs, 26*(2), 575–584.

Fajgenbaum, D., Chesson, B., & Lanzi, R. G. (2012). Building a network of grief support on college campuses: A national grassroots initiative. *Journal of College Student Psychotherapy, 26*(2), 99–120.

Friedman, M. J., Foa, E. B., & Charney, D. S. (2003). Toward evidence-based early intervention for acutely traumatized adults and children. *Biological Psychiatry, 53*, 765–768.

Goodman, R. F. & Brown, E. J. (2008). Service and science in times of crisis: Developing, planning, and implementing a clinical research program for children traumatically bereaved after 9/11. *Death Studies, 32*, 154–180.

Hagedon, H. J., Beck, K. J., Neubert, S. F., & Werlin, S. H. (1976). *Working manual of simple program evaluation techniques for community mental health centers.* Cambridge, MA: Arthur D. Little.

Hughes, B. R., Altman, D. G., & Newton, J. A. (1993). Melanoma and skin cancer: Evaluation of a health education programme for secondary schools. *British Journal of Dermatology,* **128,** 412–417.

Jordan, J. R. & Neimeyer, R. A. (2003). Does grief counseling work? *Death Studies,* 27, 763–786.

Kato, P. M., Cole, S. W., Bradlyn, A. S., & Pollock, B. H. (2008). A video game improves behavioral outcomes in adolescents and young adults with cancer: A randomized trial. *Pediatrics,* **122,** 305–317.

Kazanjian, V. & Laurence, P. (2007). The journey toward multi-faith community on campus: The religious and spiritual life program at Wellesley College. *Journal of College and Character,* 9(2), 1–12.

Kissane, D. W. & Hooghe, A. (2011). Family therapy for the bereaved. In R. A. Neimeyer, D. L. Harris, W. R. Winokuer, & G. F. Thornton (Eds.), *Grief and bereavement in contemporary society: Bridging research and practice* (pp. 287–302). New York: Routledge.

Kissane, D. W., McKenzie, M., Bloch, S., Moskowitz, C., McKenzie, D. P., & O'Neill, I. (2006). Family Focused Grief Therapy: A randomized, controlled trial in palliative care and bereavement. *American Journal of Psychiatry,* **163**(7), 1208–1218.

Larson, D. G. & Hoyt, W. T. (2007). What has become of grief counseling? An evaluation of the empirical foundation of the new pessimism. *Professional Psychology: Research and Practice,* **38**(4), 347–355.

Larson, D. G. & Hoyt, W. T. (2009). Grief counseling efficacy: What have we learned? *Bereavement Care,* 28(3), 14–19.

Lee, W. S. & Suardi, S. (2010). The Australian firearms buyback and its effect on gun deaths. *Contemporary Economic Policy,* 28(1), 65–79.

Mermelstein, R. J. & Riesenberg, L. A. (1992). Changing knowledge and attitudes about skin cancer risk factors in adolescents. *Health Psychology,* 11(6), 371–376.

Nadeau, J. W. (1998). *Families making sense of death.* Thousand Oaks, CA: Sage.

Narayan, M. C. (2010). Culture's effects on pain assessment and management: Cultural patterns influence nurses' and their patients' responses to pain. *American Journal of Nursing,* 111(4), 38–47.

Otis-Green, S. (Editor). (2013). Changing the change agents through palliative care education for psycho-oncology professionals. *Omega,* 67(1–2). Special issue.

Patten, M. L. (2009). *Understanding research methods: An overview of the essentials.* (7th edition). Los Angeles: Pyrczak.

Rokeach, M. (1973). *The nature of human values.* New York: The Free Press.

Rosenblatt, P. C. (1983). *Bitter, bitter tears: Nineteenth century diarists and twentieth century grief theories.* Minneapolis, MN: University of Minnesota Press.

Sandler, I. N., Ayers, T. S., Wolchik, S. A., Tein, J-Y., Kwok, O-M., Haine, R. A., Twohey-Jacobs, J., Suter, J., Lin, K., Padgett-Jones, S., & Weyer, J. L. (2003). The Family Bereavement Program: Efficacy evaluation of a theory-based prevention program for parentally bereaved children and adolescents. *Journal of Consulting and Clinical Psychology,* 71(5), 587–600.

Sandler, I. N, Wolchik, S. A., Ayers, T. S., Tein, J-Y., Coxe, S., & Chow, W. (2008). Linking theory and intervention to promote resilience in parentally bereaved children. In M. S. Stroebe, R. O. Hansson, H. Schut, & W. Stroebe (Eds.), *Handbook of bereavement research and practice: Advances in theory and intervention* (pp. 531–550). Washington, DC: American Psychological Association.

Schulberg, H. C. & Killilea, M. (Editors). (1982). *The modern practice of community mental health.* San Francisco: Jossey-Bass.

Schut, H., Stroebe, M. S., van den Bout, J., & Terheggen, M. (2001). The efficacy of bereavement interventions: Determining who benefits. In M. S. Stroebe, R. O. Hansson, W. Stroebe, & H.

Schut (Eds.), *Handbook of bereavement research: Consequences, coping, and care* (pp. 705–737). Washington, DC: American Psychological Association.

Shear, K., Boelen, P. A., & Neimeyer, R. A. (2011). Treating complicated grief: Converging approaches. In R. A. Neimeyer, Harris, D. L., Winokuer, H. R., & Thornton. G. F. (Eds.), *Grief and bereavement in contemporary society: Bridging research and practice* (pp. 139–162). New York: Routledge.

Shear, K., Frank, E., Houck, P. R., & Reynolds, C. F. (2005). Treatment of complicated grief: A randomized controlled trial, *JAMA, 293,* 2601–2608.

Stake, R. E. & Trumbull, D. J. (1982). Naturalistic generalizations. *Review Journal of Philosophy & Social Science,* VII(1 & 2), 1–7.

Stevens, M. M. & Dunsmore, J. C. (1996). Adolescents who are living with a life-threatening illness. In C. A. Corr & D. E. Balk (Eds.), *Handbook of adolescent death and bereavement* (pp. 107–155). New York: Springer.

Stevens, M. M., Dunsmore, J. C., Bennett, D. L., & Young, A. J. (2009). Adolescents living with life-threatening illness. In D. E. Balk & C. A. Corr (Eds.), *Adolescent encounters with death, bereavement, and coping* (pp. 115–140). New York: Springer.

Stevenson, R. G. (2009). Educating adolescents about death, bereavement, and coping. In D. E. Balk & C. A. Corr (Eds.), *Adolescent encounters with death, bereavement, and coping* (pp. 273–289). New York: Springer.

Stock, W., La, M., Sanford, B., Bloomfield, C. D., Vardiman, J. W., Gaynon, P., Larson, R. A., & Nachman, J. (2008). What determines the outcomes for adolescents and young adults with acute lymphoblastic leukemia treated on cooperative group protocols? A comparison of Children's Cancer Group and Cancer and Leukemia Group B studies. *Blood,* 112, 1646–1654.

Stroebe, M. (1992–1993). Coping with bereavement: A review of the grief work hypothesis. *Omega,* 26(1), 19–42.

Stroebe, W., Stroebe, M. S., & Schut, H. (2003). Does "grief work" work? *Bereavement Care,* 22(1), 3–5.

Super, D. E (1990). A life-span, life-space approach to career development. In D. Brown & L. Brooks (Eds.), *Career choice and development* (2nd ed.), (pp. 197–261). San Francisco: Jossey-Bass.

Wetzel, C., Tissot, A., Kollar, L. M., Hillard, P. A., Stone. R., & Kahn. J. A. (2007). Development of an HPV educational protocol for adolescents. *Journal of Pediatric and Adolescent Gynecology,* 20, 280–287.

Wogrin, C. (2013). Professional issues in thanatology. In D. K. Meagher & D. E. Balk (Eds.), *Handbook of thanatology: The essential body of knowledge for the study of death, dying, and bereavement* (pp. 395–409). New York: Routledge.

Zhang, B., El-Jawahri, E., & Prigerson, H. G. (2006). Update on bereavement research: Evidence-based guidelines for the diagnosis and treatment of complicated bereavement. *Journal of Palliative Medicine,* 9(5), 1188–1203.

11 Beyond Websites
The Relevance of the Internet and Technology for Adolescents Coping with Illness and Loss

Anne M. Smith and Corinne Cavuoti

All adolescents alive today were born into the digital age. Generation M is described as adolescents and young adults who are media savvy, multitaskers, and mobile. This generation embraces technology and has the capacity to adapt to the ever-changing technological environment. Much discussion has ensued regarding the impact of technology on the lives of adolescents, and most research to date has focused on the detrimental effects of media use, particularly the Internet. Limited research has been done to examine the positive impact of the Internet on adolescent development, socialization, and identity formation. Without a doubt, there are extensive changes and challenges to all aspects of human interaction as a result of the Internet and digital technology. New fields of study, such as cyberpsychology, have emerged to evaluate the impact of technology on human behavior and incorporate these changes into healthy living. Throughout the past decade, thanatologists have worked to understand and utilize technology as a means of support for life-threatened adolescents and bereaved adolescents. Technology is more than a modality we must learn to synthesize into practice and education—technology has transformed adolescent communication, socialization, education, and ability to obtain information. Technology is not something that affects adolescents—it is part of the reality of being adolescent.

Adolescent Development in the Digital Age

As adolescents navigate through the developmental process, they are faced with establishing a sense of self, consisting of personal identity and a sense of purpose in the world. A key factor to understanding and supporting adolescents will be the ability to adjust our view of some existing representations of the modern adolescent. The popular image of today's adolescent often contains negative stereotypes particularly regarding digital technology and online activity. Adolescents are often characterized as distracted, techno-crazed teenagers irresponsibly texting on smart phones while driving. These stereotypes detract from the ability to recognize the wealth of positive interactions and support that can be achieved through technology and the Internet.

In the postmodern, technological world, the definition and formation of self continue to evolve as we explore and acknowledge the embedded significance of the Internet and technology. Recent research exploring the transition from adolescence to adulthood has shown that not all adolescents face turmoil struggling to separate from their parents and develop a sense of identity. Many adolescents experience a smooth transition to adulthood while forming a healthy identity. Similarly, although technology is paramount in the lives of today's teenagers, many young people remain focused and directed on moving into adulthood, develop responsible behavior, and make contributions to society via the use of technology. As we review the impact of the technological era, we must realize the scope of technology and Internet usage in the lives of individual adolescents.

Historically, the concept of identity development has been redefined to incorporate changes in social construction, educational advancement, modern morality, and intellectual processes. In addition, there is need to rethink education based on technological advancement. Prensky (2001) noted, "Our students have changed radically. Today's students are no longer the people our educational system was designed to teach" (p. 1). Similarly, participation in virtual worlds, social networking, and the ability to be "always on" may expand opportunities for personal growth and development in addition to experiences in environments such as classrooms, playgrounds, and neighborhoods. Understanding how, when, and why adolescents utilize the multiple forums of technology and the Internet may offer further insight to online interaction, identity exploration and formation, adolescent coping techniques, and social awareness.

To meet the needs of Generation M, thanatologists must rethink and redefine how a developing adolescent may process and respond to illness and/or loss considering technology in the holistic sense. Along with Balk (2009) we propose viewing the complexities of adolescent encounters with death and bereavement through a combined conceptual focus using existential phenomenology and the holistic template. This "backstory" provides a basis to further our understanding of the individual response to grief as well as a means to identify coping skills geared toward resilient outcomes (pp. 3–17). Adding the reality of technological influence to all facets of self-formation and death-related experiences illuminates a gap in the understanding and support of adolescents.

How and Why Adolescents Use the Internet and Technology

The overwhelming majority (95%) of American teens have access to the Internet, and 93% have access through a computer or tablet at home. In addition, 78% of adolescents now own a cell phone, and almost half of those devices are smart phones (cell phones with high connectivity capabilities and high-tech applications) providing portable access to all media—24 hours a day. The rapid growth of cell phone use is attributed to the increase in inexpensive cell phone technology expanding use across socioeconomic lines. The current cohort of 8- to 18-year-olds spends an average of 7.5 hours a day utilizing media (TV, computers, video games, smart phones, music, and movies) and up to approximately 10.5 hours a day if you factor in multitasking (using two or more forms of media simultaneously). These youth have produced an "explosive" increase in media consumption via smart phones and the ability to multitask. An adolescent's link to social connectivity, information, and entertainment is often the cell phone—"the last thing they [adolescents] touch before falling asleep, and the first thing they reach for upon waking" (Rideout, Foehr, & Roberts, 2010, p. 2). When the 7.5 hours per day is broken down by type of media usage, the Internet (social networking sites, information retrieval, online surfing) makes up 1.3 hours per day and video gaming another 1.15 hours per day.

There has been extensive discussion on the pros and cons of online activity. Undoubtedly, there are concerns regarding digital dependence, cyberbullying, lack of privacy, and addictions that we address later in this chapter. However, many experts are now exploring the benefits of online activity—promoting positive social behavior, stress reduction, increased social awareness, and a means to promote self-esteem.

Current research focuses on adolescent time consumption excluding the emotional impact of Internet use. In 2009, MediaSnackers, a youth consultancy group in the United Kingdom, initiated a survey designed to explore how young people feel about the web and also the reasons behind the emotions. The survey, *How the Web Makes Me Feel (TWMMF Project)*, was administered to adolescents age 13 to 19. The primary focus of the survey was to expand understanding of adolescent use of the web beyond demographics, new technology, and time consumption to open a dialogue on the emotions that lead young people to embrace the Internet. Participating adolescents were given postcards and asked for one word describing how the web makes them feel. Approximately 450 postcards were returned citing over 140 emotions attributed to activity on the web. Of note, the top 10 words used by adolescents to describe how they feel included happy, connected, excited, free, and independent. Overall, 56% of respondents described positive emotional experiences in connection to interaction online; however, the number decreases in later years of adolescence suggesting shifts as youth move out of early and middle adolescence. These survey results provide a basis for further research to explore the emotional component to understanding the role of technology, the Internet, and "being connected" in the lives of today's adolescents.

The Internet is pervasive, affecting all facets of adolescent life; therefore, the assumption must be that an adolescent is utilizing some form of available media. When a counselor, caregiver, or helper is working with an adolescent, an initial assessment must be done exploring both the pros and cons related to the adolescent's individual use of digital technology and participation online. Important factors for consideration include an adolescent's media of choice, why the adolescent has chosen a particular forum, and the emotional impact of the online interaction.

For people born before 1982 (the advent of the Internet), digital technology may present challenges in communication, education, and the ability to support today's adolescent coping with illness and loss. Many areas of digital technology have been demonized and criticized over the past two decades citing infringement on privacy, corruption of education, and limiting face-to-face social connections. The history of technology includes similar debates and concerns as society adjusts and adapts to technological advancement. The original Kodak camera sparked legal and ethical questions surrounding privacy issues, and television ignited concerns about the impact of programming on childhood development and education. Undoubtedly, there are potential problems with digital technology and the Internet. There must be privacy controls, education, and regulation to ensure safety for using the Internet. For vulnerable adolescents dealing with loss, it is essential to also include monitoring of Internet practices. However, the key to moving forward will be to embrace and learn how to best utilize the technology within healthy parameters. First, how and why young people use media is central to understanding the impact on adolescent lives. In addition, understanding the pros and cons of media use is critical to defining and determining what is helpful and what is not.

Websites and Social Networking as Supportive Resources

Within the last 5 years, mobile phones and wireless handheld devices have transformed use of the Internet from stationary computers accessing websites to multitasking on mobile devices loaded with a variety of "apps" (abbreviation for software applications). Websites continue to be a fundamental resource for adolescents. Contrary to stereotypes, recent research exploring website use indicates that adolescents do not aimlessly surf the Internet wasting time—they are goal-oriented in their tasks online. Reasons cited for visiting websites include school assignments, information related to hobbies and special interests, entertainment, news, and shopping. Interestingly, many adolescents reported "boring" websites the worst encounter, but also "glitzy," cluttered, multimedia sites were negatively received. Interactive features were positive, but not in an overbearing environment. In fact, multimedia was described as having the power to "engage or enrage" teens.

Some website features are critical to capturing the adolescent audience—fast-loading, social-networking options, design for portable screens, and age-appropriate activities. Adolescents also reported that language used in a website is very important. They do not respond to condescending language or terms interpreted as childlike or babyish. Before making a website referral to an adolescent coping with illness or loss, it's best to visit websites and examine content and language to help identify sites well suited to the needs of the individual. As an example, Grouploop.org is a website designed for teens "touched by cancer." The site is simple but sophisticated, employing the tagline Teens. Talk. Cancer. Online. This site offers a place to talk, connections to Facebook, Twitter, multimedia resources, and referrals to other cancer-related websites. Similarly, Stupidcancer.org is a website designed to "empower young people affected by cancer by creating community, improving quality of life and providing meaningful survivorship" (stupidcancer.org/about). The website provides links to Facebook, Twitter, Instagram, YouTube, Pinterest, and LinkedIn—creating opportunities for adolescents to connect using their forum of choice. Of note, the website includes a tab inspiring visitors to "take action: get busy doing" and provides encouragement for involvement in a variety of different ways—connecting on social networks, joining advocacy groups, getting charitable, and participating locally. In addition this organization hosts an annual conference, OMG! Cancer Summit for Young Adults that fosters community, engagement, and development of age-appropriate programs for young people living with cancer. The 2013 OMG! Conference was held in Las Vegas, and was a multimedia event. Pictures, video, and comments from the event are displayed on the website and through Tumblr (a new blogging platform used to post texts, images, and links), empowering attendees and encouraging newcomers to join. The graphics are slick and appropriate without being overwhelming. Similarly, The Dougy Center at dougy.org directs bereaved adolescents to a help section on the website with information and support "for teens by teens." The language and graphics are appropriate and engaging, guiding adolescents to information such as "The Bill of Rights of Grieving Teens" and "How Should I Grieve?" These sites utilize Internet safety and security measures before allowing participation in discussion and blogging.

In February 2013, the Nielsen Norman Group conducted a study, *Teenage Usability: Designing Teen-Targeted Websites* to evaluate the expectations and performance of adolescents surfing the web. The study evaluated the positive and negative features associated with teen website use. A resounding theme through the report was that adolescents seeking specific information quickly become frustrated and "click out" of a website when it does not capture their attention or meet their needs. When seeking information related to illness or loss, adolescents respond best to succinct, clear, and age-appropriate content. Teens reacted positively to interactive websites citing online quizzes, games, features for sharing pictures and stories, message boards, and options to add content as positive features. Teens expressed the desire to "make their mark" and express themselves in a variety of different ways. For adolescents that are coping with illness and loss, the ability to share the experience returns us to the emotional component of online interaction.

What is the emotional benefit to online support? Stupid Cancer is an organization started by a young cancer patient to support adolescents and young adults affected by cancer. The foundation was started to acknowledge the unique needs of young people and provide supportive online venues that appeal to youth. On the home page of the Stupid Cancer website, the question appears: How can we help you? Following the question is a series of button options. The options include "I feel alone, I need a break, Am I fertile? I can't work." Throughout the website there are many options for adolescents to connect and bond supporting one another. The innovative approaches include the Stupid Cancer Show, a talk radio show billed as "the voice of young adults," and forums entitled "I Just Need to Vent" and "Off Topic: A place to discuss anything and everything" (stupidcancer.org). In addition, the promotion of group advocacy empowers young people to feel strength and control often contrary to their feelings upon initial diagnosis of an illness or when coping with death. Many adolescents utilize sites such as stupidcancer.org as a starting point to participate in social networking—a "jumping off" point for connection to peers with similar experiences. These unique venues build confidence and self-esteem that may be challenged as adolescents cope with illness and loss.

Social networking sites (SNSs) are an important means of communication and connection in the lives of adolescents. Seventy-three percent of online adolescents and emerging young adults use SNSs. The most successful social-networking site is Facebook. Started in 2004, Facebook has grown to a worldwide membership of approximately 955,000,000. Briefly, a Facebook page consists of a personal profile defined as a "summary of who you are, what you've been doing and your interests." A "friend" is someone connected to another through Facebook, usually an established friend or acquaintance outside of the SNS. Each Facebook user has a "wall" used to "post" comments, photos, or video clips. Friends can read and respond to all material posted through each other's walls. If desired, private messaging can be done through the user's profile as well. In addition to individual "walls," businesses or organizations have "pages," that also allow for interaction for those who are linked to the page through the "like" option. By using the privacy settings and "friend" approval settings within Facebook, an adolescent can monitor and control the level of exposure and support.

Facebook and other networks provide a forum for an adolescent to connect to existing friends or venture out to explore new relationships with other adolescents sharing similar experiences. An adolescent seeking support and/or information can connect to Facebook pages (user sites for organizations) such as Stupid Cancer directly from the website. In general these pages provide a forum to share experiences of loss, connect to educational articles and information, and create memorials for deceased friends and family. Some of these sites supplement general information with loss-specific and age-specific resources. In addition, there are Facebook pages such as Cancer Sucks! created by adolescents to unite and "sound off" about experiences with cancer and loss. This group describes themselves as "charity with ATTITUDE!" The diversity in websites and social networking opportunities provides adolescents with many different venues for education, expression, and connection according to self-identified need.

Social Networking: Applying the Dual Process Model of Coping

The dual process model of coping with grief acknowledges two integrated categories broadly defining the coping process—loss orientation and restoration orientation. Loss orientation may be defined as confrontation coping, and restoration orientation as avoidance coping. By "oscillating" between the adaptive processes of avoidance and confrontation, the bereaved navigate through the grieving process as they cope with and adjust to loss. Social networking and the Internet facilitate a means for an adolescent to maneuver through this model. An adolescent coping with loss may use social networking as a self-regulating coping tool as they oscillate from loss orientation to restoration orientation.[1]

In the loss orientation mode, an adolescent may visit grief support pages as a means to obtain information or share with other adolescents. These organizations or topic-specific pages provide access to a group sharing similar experiences. Adolescents can choose to participate or simply observe. Adolescents coping with sibling or friend bereavement will often post to the deceased's wall to express their loss and share those feelings with other adolescents. Mourning through this medium may create a sense of community helping the bereaved to process their grief. Privacy settings allow adolescents to regulate who can "see" the posts. Similarly, they can customize support by limiting access to friends authorized to view and comment as well as choosing when to connect and view support.

In the restoration orientation mode, a bereaved adolescent may return to his or her personal profile, or wall, and converse with friends and family in an attempt to "take a break" from grief. Reconnecting with friends may provide opportunity for the adolescent to "step out of their grief" and begin to reconstruct a new sense of identity. Social networking also provides adolescents with unprecedented access to possibilities for distraction. Within the social networking platform, there is also access to music, video, games, shopping, and so on. The social networks can be a powerful coping tool linking adolescents to diversions from grief, venues for new interests, and forums for support. Adolescents can determine when and how to engage in support and education best suited to their needs as they oscillate between loss and restoration orientations. The increasing use of smart phones allows seamless oscillation, as resources are available anytime, anywhere.

Online Gaming, Virtual Worlds, and Avatars

One of the most controversial aspects of adolescent Internet activity is online gaming and participation in online virtual worlds. Virtual worlds are defined as online environments created for interaction and socialization. Although virtual worlds may include or link to games, they are not stand-alone gaming platforms. Massively Multiplayer Online Role-Play Games (MMORPGs) are gaming platforms that include virtual worlds with thousands of online players. The various worlds may exist in different genres such as fantasy, science fiction, history, and reality.

Both virtual worlds and MMORPGs are accessed through the creation of an avatar (an online representation of the game user or character created in the game). Most virtual worlds and online games allow the user to customize an avatar's appearance and enhance the avatar with personal objects. The MMORPG game, World of Warcraft (WOW), is a popular multiplayer fantasy game. There are diverse options for development of an avatar. The character may be human, troll, orc (monster), or undead (zombie). Once the character type is chosen, additional options include race, gender, and physical features with some options for ornamentation.

Identity development is a fundamental task for adolescents. As adolescents strive to develop their identity, the ability to "try on" an identity through the use of an avatar may allow adolescents to explore different aspects of their developing identity. Through an avatar, an adolescent can experiment with an array of personal objects and traits that portray who they are and who they want to be. For adolescents coping with the physical changes resulting from medical treatment, trying on an avatar allows them to be strong and healthy in the virtual world, breaking away from their current status and empowering them to see their healthy "self" in the future.

Doctors at Tufts University, in Boston, Massachusetts, created a virtual world for adolescent transplant patients to communicate and interact with peers throughout the country sharing a similar experience. The adolescents responded positively to interacting within the web-based environment. Participating adolescents reported reduced feelings of isolation, increased normalcy, and an enhanced sense of self.

An adolescent coping with bereavement or illness can also escape to a world where the label of "bereaved" or "sick" is not a part of the interaction with peers. The game or virtual world may provide an outlet to step outside of their current reality and interact freely. The avatar may also offer an adolescent the ability to develop a post-loss identity and experiment with a new identity while interacting within the game or virtual world. In the WOW game, a player may also create or join a guild, a group of like-minded players that join together. The guild creator determines the criteria for membership. Some guilds are formed in relation to game ability, while other guilds are formed for personal reasons or motivations of the creator. For an adolescent coping with loss, membership in a guild may create a sense of belonging, support, and safety. Conversely, an adolescent may create a character that reflects the experience with illness or loss by emphasizing unhealthy appearance or interacting in a negative or aggressive manner. The creation of avatars in virtual worlds may provide a window to how an adolescent is coping in reality.

Virtual worlds and avatars provide tools to help adolescents coping with loss and illness as they reconstruct an identity. The environment may provide a safe forum for an adolescent to integrate changes to his or her vision of self. Often, these adolescents develop a greater sense of empathy as they integrate their loss experience. Interaction within the virtual world offers an opportunity to experiment with growing empathy. Helpers must be cautious not to stereotype and simplify adolescent online gaming and interaction in virtual worlds as merely a negative distraction from difficult situations in the adolescent's real world. Often, a helper's inexperience, lack of knowledge, and discomfort with the gaming medium overshadow the opportunity to gain insight into the adolescent's experience and offer significant support.

The most researched topic regarding video gaming is the effect of exposure to violence and aggression. Ongoing research exploring media violence shows correlations between exposure to violence, aggression, and antisocial behavior. MMORPGs and virtual worlds are often associated with developing compulsive, addictive behaviors and fostering aggression. The data offer valid reason for concern. The amount of violence portrayed in many online games is more intense than most violence on television, and the player is an active participant in the violent encounter. Research suggests that exposure to violent games may result in desensitization to violence over time. However, not all adolescents who are exposed to violent images on television or through video games will be negatively influenced outside of the game. It is important to assess and identify at-risk youth who may be vulnerable to negative aspects of violent gaming.

When assessing a bereaved adolescent's use of video and computer games, the nature of the loss and violence encountered in real life is an important factor. Research has shown that violent and traumatic deaths may hinder an adolescent's ability to make sense of a loss and process the grief due to traumatic imagery, fear of their own mortality, sense of injustice, and suddenness of the death. Participating in violent gaming may be detrimental to the grieving process. As an example, youths who have experienced gun-related deaths might exacerbate their grieving symptoms by engaging in violent online games that simulate comparable deaths. Similarly, a study examining media use by children and adolescents from New York City 6 months after the World Trade Center attack in 2001 suggests children and adolescents making intensive use of disaster-related media connections were likely to have been exposed to the disaster or have posttraumatic symptoms (Duarte et al., 2011). Exploration into an adolescent's use of online gaming, the Internet, and other forms of media will provide the opportunity to investigate the potential danger of engaging in unhealthy online interactions while coping with loss or post-traumatic stress disorder.

Despite the negative press and concerns regarding online gaming and Internet use, there are benefits and positive aspects of gaming and participation in virtual social interactions. Online gaming often provides stress relief for participants, an outlet for new friendships, and can improve psychological well-being and increase self-esteem. Being involved in a community online can also be therapeutic in removing an individual from real-life stressors and in providing the person a safe haven. A teenager may participate in gaming and online social networking limiting or alleviating involvement in risk-taking behavior such as substance abuse.

Internet Safety Practices

Adolescent safety in cyberspace remains a primary concern. Adolescents are sharing more personal information on social websites than they have in the past. Adolescents view the Internet as a private forum for them to express themselves through photos, video, blogging, and social interaction. Sixty percent of Facebook users now have their profile set to "private," limiting who can access their wall, view information, and respond to posts and comments. Twenty-five percent of adolescents set their profile to partially private settings, and 14% continue to leave their profile open to public viewing. Research exploring self-disclosure online revealed that people are more apt to self-disclose online than in physical face-to-face encounters. The ability to self-disclose is attributed to the unique lack of inhibition associated with online interaction. Adolescents who are coping with life-threatening illness, medical treatment, and loss often experience an increased sense of isolation and disconnection from peers contributing to their vulnerability in online encounters. Educating adolescents to be aware of the dangers and pitfalls of Internet use is critical to creating a safe environment.

Increasing media literacy is a promising strategy for mitigating harmful effects, but campaign messages must be carefully crafted to appeal to the target audience. Educating adolescents will prepare them to be less susceptible to unhealthy outcomes of Internet use. In addition, parents, educators, counselors, and caregivers must become informed about the many different media accessible to adolescents. Without a fundamental understanding of the online options and adolescent preferences, there is a tremendous gap in the capability of interacting with adolescents in a meaningful way. Recently a video, *Dumb Ways to Die*, appeared on YouTube. The video was created as a public service message by the Metro Trains in Melbourne, Australia, to warn adolescents of dangerous behavior around trains. The video is designed using stylish animation, black humor, sarcasm, and music appealing to adolescents. The video went "viral" on YouTube with over 47,000,000 "hits" (views). The advertisers who designed this video described their thought process as trying to "disguise a worthy safety message inside something that didn't feel like a safety message" (Nudd, 2012, p. 1). The video content attracts adolescents because it connects to their mode of communication, sense of humor, and intellect. An awareness to how, when, and why adolescents connect and communicate is the first step to education.

Monitoring an adolescent's activity is critical to building awareness. To monitor an adolescent's Internet use, parents and helpers often employ one of three different strategies. These strategies are an attempt to alleviate negative experiences online. Cocooning is parental effort to restrict exposure to negative influences. This strategy is more effective in younger children and linked with less aggressive behavior. Prearming encourages parent/child discussion regarding exposure to questionable content. The intention is to help an adolescent become a critical thinker and take an active role in understanding and evaluating online subject matter. Prearming has been linked to decreased physical aggression and decreased fear associated with violent events. Deference is often a parent's attempt to display trust for the adolescent by actively choosing to eliminate monitoring and is frequently used with older adolescents. Helpers monitoring bereaved adolescents may need to adjust their strategy depending on circumstances surrounding the loss, maturity of the adolescent, and available support. In addition to monitoring content, helpers must also be alert and monitor adolescents for unhealthy Internet activity.

Addictive and Compulsive Behaviors

Addiction and compulsive behavior are often associated with extensive use of the Internet. Although gaming and online addictions are prevalent topics in research and the media, current research suggests that specific aspects of the Internet may be more addictive than others. Communicative activities such as instant messaging and chatting are strongly associated with compulsive use of technology. Noncommunicative Internet use, such as surfing the web, information seeking, and gaming (exclusive of MMORPGs), were not strongly associated with problematic use. Adolescents coping with illness and loss often spend the majority of time on the Internet seeking information particularly in the early period following diagnosis or loss. This activity has been labeled the "Google stage of grief" and is often helpful for adolescents. The "google" activity is not linked to addictive Internet behavior; however, adolescents must be warned about the authenticity of websites and online information. Helpers need to identify the communicative and noncommunicative activities of an individual adolescent in order to assess risk for compulsive behaviors.

Cyberbullying and Coping with Loss

There are many positive aspects of adolescent culture that allow for self-expression and peer connection. Along with positive social attributes such as humor and language, negative aspects include psychological and physical aggression. Bullying is a dangerous characteristic of adolescent culture. Bullying is aggressive behavior described as repeated negative action to harm another person. The Centers for Disease Control (CDC) describes adolescent bullying as a form of youth violence occurring through physical, verbal, or psychological abuse. Adolescents engage in bullying for a variety of reasons— rites of passage, social position, power, popularity, and a desire to "fit in." The majority of bullying occurs in middle school to high school when adolescents form social alliances as they continue to construct a personal identity. The digital age elevates bullying to a new level. Cyberbullying is defined as bullying that uses Internet and electronic technology. Cyberbullying occurs using e-mail, chat rooms, instant messaging, texting, video, and online photos. A Pew Internet Report, *Cyberbullying 2010: What the Research Tells Us* states that 32% of adolescents online have experienced some form of online bullying or harassment. Bullying has been associated with school violence and suicide ideation. Bullied teens also have higher incidence of psychological problems, school avoidance, and substance abuse.

Adolescents coping with loss may be more vulnerable to bullying. As adolescents move through the developmental process, their peers become a major component in positive identity development. Part of that peer support is the connection to community and membership in a group. Online communication facilitates friendship formation among introverts and extroverts. Teens who are lonely, socially anxious, and depressed are more likely to use the Internet to communicate online. When adolescents lose a parent, sibling, or friend, they describe feeling like "outsiders," often embarrassed and anxious about the loss experience. Many adolescents withhold sharing their pain and emotions with peers because doing so will make them different. In addition, bereaved adolescents often lose support in the home as parents, siblings, and other family members struggle with their own grief experience. In response to grief, an adolescent may behave cautiously, become less social, and refrain from interaction. Peers may perceive the response as negative or become uncomfortable, and the situation may open the door to bullying.

As an adolescent there are many loss experiences often marginalized and overlooked by family, teachers, counselors, peers, and the community. Some of these losses may include loss of childhood as an adolescent enters college, loss of family as a result of parental divorce, and loss of a first love relationship. When losses do not receive recognition, options for appropriate support are limited creating a disenfranchised grief. Disenfranchised grief refers to losses that are not recognized, validated, or publicly mourned.

Having grief marginalized may leave the bereaved vulnerable for difficulty coping with loss contributing to "factors that may facilitate or impair grief resolution" (Doka, 2002, p. 18). Goldman and Livoti (2011) explore specific adolescent losses citing the "coming out" experience of GLBT (gay, lesbian, bisexual, transgender) adolescents as "both a literal and symbolic grieving process established and reinforced through the mechanisms of contemporary Western media" (p. 249). The marginalization of grief coupled with the existing stigma surrounding sexual orientation may further disenfranchise the grief felt by the adolescent.

The suicide of Tyler Clementi, a student at Rutgers University in New Jersey, highlights the many dangers associated with the Internet, cyberbullying, and loss. In 2010, Tyler and his roommate, Dharun Ravi, were both 18-year-old freshmen at Rutgers University. Both of these young men were adjusting to a new social environment acclimating to life on a college campus. As adolescents developing independent identities, they were exploring new social connections and relationships. Social renegotiation often creates an atmosphere conducive to bullying as adolescents jockey for social position. In addition, Tyler had recently shared his sexual orientation with family and close friends. Goldman and Livoti (2011) posit GLBT adolescents may "grieve the loss of being a part of a heteronormative social structure" (p. 254). The social pressures, environmental adjustments, and perhaps personal losses, may have created vulnerability for harassment and bullying.

Tyler's roommate secretly filmed Tyler's intimate encounter with another man. The video was "streamed" to the Internet exposing Tyler's sexual orientation online. The level of exposure available through the Internet exacerbated the repercussions from the incident. Tyler's suicide triggered legal action against the roommate as well as investigation and review of school policies. The tragic case of Tyler Clementi provides an example of the need to understand the impact of technology as part of the "backstory" of adolescent experiences with loss and death. Of note, the Internet and social media became a coping tool for those bereaved by Tyler's death. Many fellow students and friends created memorial sites on Facebook, supported one another online, and began an online dialogue to raise awareness of suicide and cyberbullying.

As a form of harassment, the Internet can quickly become a relentless means for torment. Before the Internet, most bullying was confined to a certain aspect of social interaction—camp, neighborhoods, or school. Cyberbullying makes it impossible to escape the harassment. There's no relief; in fact, the terror often grows as more "hits" and "comments" are added to the original "post." In addition, once pictures, videos, or texts are in cyberspace, complete retrieval is virtually impossible. The bullying can easily spiral out of control, leaving the victim feeling helpless and alone. The use of the Internet and electronic media, challenges of adolescent identity development, and the isolating nature of grief create a "perfect storm" for cyberbullying. Education designed to foster empathy building and Internet safety practices must become part of the curriculum for children prior to and throughout adolescence.

Connectivity, Empathy, and Social Awareness

On the reverse side, the Internet has the potential to affect adolescent empathy, raise social awareness, and encourage social activism. The Center for the Digital Future at the

University of Southern California reports that children and adolescents are using social networking platforms and media to voice opinions and take civil action. The modes of connectivity and information sharing are conducive to unite young people and raise awareness. The majority of young users report strong connections within online communities similar to feelings in real-world communities. The Pew Internet and American Life Project highlights the potential of media use to facilitate social engagement. Video game activities promote leadership qualities, team involvement, and foster community and global awareness. Activities within games often include guiding other players, making ethical decisions, and creating and planning communities. These activities have been called "civic gaming experiences" (Brown & Bobkowski, 2011, p. 96). A survey of 12- to 17-year-olds revealed that teens involved in gaming that have "civic gaming experiences" are more likely to be politically and civically engaged in the real world. The use of portable devices provides a wealth of possibilities for adolescents to actively engage in the social and political process. There is some controversy in the literature questioning the limitations of the Internet to truly motivate and inspire today's youth. Some cite the impersonal nature of the Internet as limiting attachment to the cause allowing young people to interact at only a surface level. Others promote the use of the Internet and social media as the new era of social activism connecting the world. Controversy aside, adolescents have chosen the Internet and digital technology as the form of connection and activism.

There are many examples of adolescents using digital media and social connectivity as a means to facilitate empathy and foster social support. Ava Lowery provides an example of an adolescent's ability to promote global awareness. In 2005, at the age of 15, Ava created animated short films in protest of the Iraq war. She went on to develop a multimedia website, peacetakescourage.com, promoting adolescent connection and activism through blogging, e-mail, LinkedIn, Facebook, and Vimeo (video-based sharing website). Today, Ava continues her activism and is currently at New York University pursuing an education in documentary production. Adolescents also use social networking as a platform for community involvement and support. In 2012, many adolescents used Facebook in the aftermath of Hurricane Sandy to provide emotional support, obtain and disseminate information, and participate in fundraising. Because electrical power was out in many areas limiting computer use, most of the support was provided through a network of cell phone users linked through social media, texting, e-mail, and websites. As needs were identified throughout the community, adolescents linked together to locate resources to fulfill these needs. Adolescents naturally used the Internet and social media to implement support, raise awareness, and promote activism.

Concluding Comments

The Internet and digital technology continue to shape and influence adolescent development. Technology in the lives of today's adolescents is far more than a source of communication, entertainment, or information—it defines the generation and adolescent culture. Eliminating negative stereotypes associated with adolescents and technology may help to bridge the gap in connecting with today's tech-savvy teenagers. In order to have a meaningful impact to guide or help an adolescent coping with loss, a helper must assess the pros and cons of an individual adolescent's Internet use and move beyond websites as the sole source of online support. Adolescent identity and self-concept are shaped by the pervasive influence of the Internet and media. Social networking, online gaming, texting, and other modes of connectivity are essential methods of adolescent communication. Being proficient in the diversity of options available to adolescents will enhance the ability to communicate effectively.

Helpers must also be able to navigate through digital technology to assess, evaluate, and provide support. In addition, adolescents need to be better prepared and informed of the dangers that exist on the Internet. Along with education for Internet safety practices, children must receive additional education to foster empathy and develop an understanding of loss. By implementing these types of educational programs, children will be better prepared to interact positively and support one another as they enter adolescence.

Note

1. We acknowledge that the restoration orientation also includes approach coping, not only avoidance coping, in the person's embrace of reengaging in the world.

Sources

Baird, D. E. (2009). Emotion, reason, & the web makes me feel. *Barking Robot*. Retrieved from www.debaird.net/blendededunet/2009/07/emotion-reason-the-web-the-web-makes-me-feel.html

Balk, D. E. (2009). Adolescent development: The backstory to adolescent encounters with death and bereavement. In D. E. Balk, & C. Corr (Eds.), *Adolescent encounters with death, bereavement, and coping* (pp. 3–20). New York: Springer.

Balk, D. E. (2011). *Helping the bereaved college student.* New York: Springer.

Barak, A. & Suler, J. (2008). Reflections on the psychology and social science of cyberspace. In A. Barak (Ed.), *Psychological aspects of cyberspace: Theory, research, applications* (pp. 1–12). Cambridge; New York: Cambridge University Press.

Beals, L. (2010). Content creation in virtual worlds to support adolescent identity development. *New Directions for Youth Development, 128*, 45–53.

Bers, M. U., Beals, L. M., Chau, C., Satoh, K., Blume, E. D., DeMaso, D. R., & Gonzalez-Heydrich, J. (2010). Use of a virtual community as a psychosocial support system in pediatric transplantation. *Pediatric Transplantation, 14*, 261–267.

Brown, J.D. & Bobkowski, P.S. (2011). Older and newer media: Patterns of use and effects on adolescents' health and well being. *Journal of Research on Adolescence., 21*(1), 95–113.

Cancer SUCKS! (2013). https://www.facebook.com/cancersucks

Centers for Disease Control and Prevention. (2012). *Understanding bullying.* Retrieved from www.cdc.gov/violenceprevention/pdf/bullyingfactsheet2012-a.pdf

Doka, K. J. (Editor). (2002). *Disenfranchised grief: new directions, challenges, and strategies for practice.* Champaign, IL: Research Press.

Dougy Center: The National Center for Grieving Children and Families. (2013). *Help for teens.* Retrieved from www.dougy.org/grief-resources/help-for-teens/

Duarte, C.S., Wu, P., Cheung, A., Mandell, D.J., Fan, B., Wicks, J., Musa, G.J., & Hoven, C.W. (2011, October). Media use by children and adolescents from New York city 6 Months after the WTC attack. *Journal of Traumatic Stress, 24*(5), 553–556.

Goddard, C. (2007, November-December). H8 @ skul: Cyber world bullying. *The Illinois School Board Journal*, 13–20.

Goldman, L. & Livoti, V. M. (2011). Grief in GLBT populations: Focus on gay and lesbian youth. In R. A. Neimeyer, D. L. Harris, H. Winokuer, & G. F. Thornton (Eds.), *Grief and bereavement in contemporary society: Bridging research and practice* (pp. 249–260). New York: Routledge.

Griffiths, M. (2010). Online video gaming: What should educational psychologists know? *Educational Psychology in Practice, 26*(1), 35–40.

Group Loop: Teens.Talk.Cancer.Online. (2013). Retrieved from www.grouploop.org.

Hadley, W. (2011, June). Can video gaming and virtual reality programming address clinical needs? *The Brown University Child and Adolescent Behavior Letter, 27*(6), 1 & 6.

Jarvis, J. (n.d.). Don't demonize technology. *Big Think*. Retrieved from http://bigthink.com/videos/dont-demonize-technology/

Madden, M., Lenhart, A., Cortesi, S., Gasser, U., & Smith, A. (2013). Teens, social media, and privacy. *Pew Internet & American Life Project*. Retrieved from www.pewinternet.org/Reports/2013/Teens-Social-Media-And-Privacy.aspx

Madden, M., Lenhart, A., Duggan, M., Cortesi, S., & Gasser, U. (2013). Teens and technology, 2013. *Pew Internet & American Life Project*. Retrieved from www.pewinternet.org/Reports/2013/Teens-and-Tech.aspx

MediaSnackers. (2010). How the web makes me feel project. Retrieved from http://thewebmakesmefeel.com/

Mescall, J. (Director), & Bradley, M. (Producer). (2012). *Dumb ways to die* [video]. Australia: McCann, Melbourne.

Mustacchi, J. (2009, March). R U Safe? *Educational Leadership, 66*(6), 78–82.

Nielsen, J. (2013). Teenage usability: Designing teen-targeted web sites. *Jakob Nielsen's Alertbox: February 4, 2013*. Retrieved from www.nngroup.com/articles/usability-of-websites-for-teenagers/

Noppe Cupit, I., Sofka, C. J., & Gilbert, K. R. (2012). Dying, death, and grief in a technological world: Implications for now and speculations about the future. In C. J. Sofka, I. Noppe Cupit, & K. R. Gilbert (Eds.) *Dying, death, and grief in an online universe* (pp. 47–60). New York: Springer.

Nudd, T. (2012). The spot: Angels of death. *Adweek*. Retrieved from www.adweek.com/news/advertising-branding/spot-angels-death-145668

Padilla-Walker, L. M. & Coyne, S. M. (2011). "Turn that thing off!" Parent and adolescent predictors of proactive media monitoring. *Journal of Adolescence, 34*, 705–715.

Patchin, J. W. & Sameer, H. (2010). Changes in adolescent online social networking behaviors from 2006 to 2009. *Computers in Human Behavior, 26*, 1818–1821.

Pomeroy, R. (2012). Video games or TV: Which is worse? *Real Clear Science*. Retrieved from www.realclearscience.com/blog/2012/07/video-games-or-tv-which-is-worse.html

Prensky, M. (2001). Digital natives, digital immigrants. *On the Horizon, 9*(5), 1–6.

Rideout, V. J., Foehr, U. G., & Roberts, D. F. (2010). Generation M2: Media in the lives of 8- to 18-year-olds. The Henry J. Kaiser Family Foundation. Retrieved from http://kaiserfamilyfoundation.files.wordpress.com/2013/01/8010.pdf

Seery, A. (2010). Education, the formation of self and the world of Web 2.0. *London Review of Economics, 8*(1), 63–73.

Smith, A. M. & Cavuoti, C. (2013). Thanatology in the digital age. In D. K. Meagher & D. E. Balk (Eds.). *Handbook of thanatology (2nd edition)* (pp. 429–439). New York: Routledge.

Sofka, C. J. (2009). Adolescents, technology, and the Internet: Coping with loss in the digital world. In D. E. Balk & C. Corr (Eds.). *Adolescent encounters with death, bereavement, and coping* (pp. 155–173). New York: Springer.

Sofka, C. J. (2012). The net generation: The special case of youth. In C. J. Sofka, I. Noppe Cupit, & K. R. Gilbert (Eds.) *Dying, death, and grief in an online universe* (pp. 47–60). New York: Springer.

Stroebe, M. S. & Schut, H. (2001). Models of coping with bereavement: A review. In M. S. Stroebe, R. O. Hansson, W. Stroebe, & H. Schut (Eds.). *Handbook of bereavement research: Consequences, coping, and care* (pp. 375–403). Washington, DC: American Psychological Association.

Strom, P. & Strom, R. (2012, October). The benefits and limitations of social networking. *The Education Digest.* www.eddigest.com.

Stupid Cancer. (2013). Retrieved from http://stupidcancer.org/

Walker, A. C. (2009). Adolescent bereavement and traumatic deaths. In D. E. Balk & C. Corr (Eds.). *Adolescent encounters with death, bereavement, and coping* (pp. 253–270). New York: Springer.

World of Warcraft [Computer software]. (2013). Irvine, CA: Blizzard Entertainment.

12 Some Final Thoughts

The title for this chapter, "Some Final Thoughts," may strike readers as draconian. I can imagine my wife saying, "If these thoughts are going to be the final ones you ever have, here's hoping you make them good." This last chapter offers the chance to profess my hopes in the new cohort of thanatology professionals (students, practitioners, researchers, teachers) who are finding interest in issues of thanatology and contributing to our understanding of dying and grieving during adolescence. Some of this new cohort will contribute to evidence-based interventions that target specific needs of dying or grieving adolescents. Some may team with the established generation of scholars and practitioners, and some may even solidify the span being built to bridge the gap separating bereavement researchers and practitioners. With this expression of hope in the contributions coming from the next generation of thanatology professionals, I have some specific ideas to offer for projects. Two of these projects are research studies, and one is an intervention combining creative arts expression and bereavement support. We will start with the intervention.

Using the Creative Arts[1]

The curricula of mental health counselors, student life professionals, and school psychologists (a) do not deal with assisting persons to cope with bereavement and grief and (b) do not focus on working with bereaved persons from varied cultures. A mandate for these professionals is to be sensitive to persons of various cultural backgrounds, to be attentive to the explicit and tacit messages they communicate, and to facilitate expression of what is difficult to put into words. Given the centrality of loss in the life experiences of children, adolescents, and adults, it is puzzling that counselors and psychologists and student life professionals are ill-equipped to work productively with persons for whom loss forms a significant influence in their lives.

The creative arts provide a dynamic means to bridge the training gap concerning loss and to extend the repertoire for interacting well with persons of varied cultures. Creative arts promote physical and psychological wholeness, foster expression, allow persons to give voice to their inner worlds, and provide means to communicate across cultures. The proposed project (a) will teach mental health counselors, student life professionals, and school psychologists the essentials about human bereavement and grief across cultures, (b) will teach them how to use the creative arts when working with persons who are bereaved, (c) will provide a supervised opportunity to apply this knowledge with bereaved families and individuals from the surrounding community and from the student body, and (d) will enable faculty and students to develop long-term collaborative efforts aimed at cross-cultural competencies centered on bereavement, grief, coping, and resiliency. This intervention will provide as well an outreach from the campus to the wider community.

Implementation Plan

The four-part project will occur on the campus in this manner:

Part 1. Experts in thanatology and the creative arts will run a 1-day educational workshop for campus professionals as well as mental health counseling, student life, and school psychology graduate students: (a) Two hours on the basics known about human bereavement and grief across cultures; (b) two hours on the basics of using the creative arts in counseling and psychology venues; (c) two hours of practice with various media (drawing, painting, sculpting, writing, music) to express experiences with loss; (d) one hour reflecting on the practice component, looking at themes, examining obstacles and roadblocks.

Part 2. The experts who conducted Part 1 will run a half-day refresher session for participants 1 week later reviewing the objectives of Part 1.

Part 3. Faculty and the participants from Parts 1 and 2 will sponsor on the campus a 1-day session for bereaved students and for families recruited from the larger community. They will be invited to come to a day focused on coping with loss via creative arts. Following introductions and an overview of the day's expectations, the project leaders will separate participants into three groups: the college students, the children, and the adults. Each group will be facilitated by participants from Parts 1 and 2 who will work with them on using creative arts to express loss. All persons will be brought back together to share with each other their creative arts projects. In small groups people will discuss what they experienced, what they learned, provide some links to what is known about human bereavement, and offer other observations.

Part 4. There will be a half-day evaluative reflection on the whole project. In this session workshop leaders, participants in Parts 1, 2, and 3, and the creative arts therapists can examine strengths and areas needing attention and discuss implications for the ongoing curricula in the programs.

Anticipated Benefits

Community residents and students will benefit from professionals who listen attentively to their narratives and who foster expression of their stories through the creative arts. The faculty and students will gain sensitivity and skill in communicating with people from diverse cultures, including listening attentively to one another. Lessons learned about multiculturalism and diversity will be taken back into the curriculum for further education of students on matters of bereavement, grief, coping, and resiliency.

Developing a Valid and Reliable Measure of Attachment Bonds

A key moderating influence on grief resolution is extent of attachment the person left to grieve feels for the person who died. In some research I have conducted I overlooked asking a simple question about how close the grieving adolescent was to the deceased. When researching adolescent responses to the death of friends, knowing vagaries in attachment would most likely have proven helpful in sorting out differences in grief and mourning. The statistically significant differences found about family coherency and sibling bereaved adolescents centered on matters of attachment: emotional closeness and self-disclosure. Among researchers and practitioners, the initially uncritical acceptance—even wholehearted endorsement—of continuing bonds has been tempered with the realization that ambivalent, disorganized, or anxious attachment bonds may need to be loosened rather than fostered and encouraged following a death.

A significant contribution to our understanding of adolescent bereavement will come from the development and validation of a self-report inventory measuring attachment and normed on early, middle, and later adolescents. A start at such an effort can be found in the chapter written about bereaved college students and attachment found in the book *Continuing Bonds: New Understandings of Grief.* Here is one form such a research project could take.

The Sample

Recruit adolescents who identify themselves as grieving the death of a family member or of a friend. Having learned the hard way that failure to establish time limits since a death occurred can create concerns about the meaning of bereavement data, I encourage advertising for adolescents whose bereavement is from 6 months to 2 years old. You'll need to obtain from the sample typical demographic data such as gender, racial/ethnic identity, date of birth (from which you can calculate an accurate age), religious preference, who died, when the death occurred, and the cause of death. For many of these data items it is possible to specify choices, and it is important to make sure that choices do comprise the full range of possibilities. For instance, religious preference and racial/ethnic identity have many options, and it is important to be as inclusive as possible.

Bereavement Data

Use an established self-report instrument that gathers data on the phenomena of adolescent bereavement. An instrument worth considering is the Hogan Grief Reaction Checklist. Use an established self-report instrument that identifies cases of prolonged grief disorder. The instrument of choice here is either Prigerson's Inventory of Traumatic Grief or the shorter version, the PG-13 inventory.

Attachment

Administer a self-report instrument that measures attachment to the person who died. The items for this instrument are presented in Table 12.1. They are items that proved helpful in differentiating grief responses of college students in terms of level of attachment the student had to the deceased. All of the items have the same scaled responses ranging from 1 to 5, specifically:

1. Not at all
2. Rarely, less than weekly
3. Some of the time, once a week
4. Often, 2 to 4 times a week
5. Almost all the time, 5 or more times a week

Items 1 through 15 and 18 through 28 begin with the stem "How often during the past month have you . . . ?" Items 16 and 17 begin with the stem "If you have thought about him or her . . ." Item 29 is presented as shown in the table with no lead-in stem. Higher scores indicate more attachment.

Table 12.1 Adolescent Attachment to the Person Who Died

---

1. Talked about him/her with other people.
2. Remembered things you did together, places where you and he/she had been.
3. Played his/her favorite songs or records.
4. Made a special effort to look at pictures, videotapes, or home movies of him/her.
5. Had everyday places remind you of him/her.
6. Made a special effort to visit places that remind you of him/her.
7. Thought of things you'll never get a chance to do with him/her.
8. Thought of things that he/she never had a chance to do with his/her life.
9. Worn or carried with you something that belonged to him/her.
10. Stored things that are reminders in a special place.
11. Gone to this special place to look at any of the items.
12. Asked questions to find out more about his/her life.
13. Thought about him/her when awake.
14. Pictured him/her in your mind.
15. Tried to recall how his/her voice sounded.
16. How often have your thoughts of him/her been comforting.
17. How often have your thoughts of him/her been distressing.
18. Thought about how he/she died.
19. Thought about other things going on that same day.
20. Thought about the last time you saw him/her.
21. Thought about the good times you shared together.
22. Thought about ways you wish you had behaved.
23. Done something to keep from thinking about him/her.
24. Done something to avoid having a conversation about him/her.
25. Avoided going to places that remind you of him/her.
26. Avoided doing something that reminds you of him/her.
27. Done something to keep from thinking about him/her.
28. Missed him/her.
29. How often do you think you will miss him/her during the coming months and years?

The primary goal is to establish the psychometric properties of the attachment inventory. There need to be solid measures of reliability and of validity. Measures of reliability will include calculating a Cronbach alpha coefficient to determine interitem consistency and, by use of repeated measures, calculating test-retest reliability. Cronbach alpha coefficient scores in the 0.80s or 0.90s will be obtained if the items hang together. To obtain test-retest reliability data, the inventory should be given to the same research participants about a month apart; the hypothesis that will be tested is that responses from the first administration and the second will positively correlate. The hope is for test-retest coefficient scores in the 0.80s or 0.90s.

Whether the inventory truly measures attachment needs to be established. Content validity can be obtained by having a panel of experts look at the instrument to determine that the items do gather data about attachment. Construct validity can be gathered by comparing responses to the attachment inventory with responses to the Offer Self-Image Questionnaire scales that measure peer relationships, family relationships, and superior adjustment. Concurrent validity can be determined by measuring responses to the attachment inventory and to the Reciprocal Attachment Questionnaire.

Measuring Transformation and Growth of Adolescents in Response to Loss

A life crisis possesses certain structural properties.

- The event poses a serious threat to your well-being and/or perhaps to the well-being of persons who matter to you.
- The event defies your current coping repertoire.
- The event will produce undesirable consequences if handled poorly.

However, in a paradoxical fashion, life crises contain within themselves the possibilities of growth and transformation. By growth and transformation I mean critical shifts in a person's understanding of self, the purpose of existence, and relationships with the world, with other persons, and with transcendent reality. I contend that life-threatening illnesses and bereavement are both life crises that can serve as transforming experiences promoting fundamentally new understandings of self, of the purpose of existence, and of relationships with the world, with other persons, and with transcendent reality. We need to examine whether, in what ways, and to which individuals such transformation occurs in the lives of dying and grieving adolescents. I have written what I consider to be constituent elements to consider when formulating such a research project with bereaved adolescents.

Key Indicators of This Transformation

Key indicators of this transformation are the emergence of empathy, altruism, compassion, and engagement with others as a consequence of coping with the threat to one's mortality and with the death of a loved one; in addition, transformation will manifest itself as new expressions of hope, faith, resilience, courage, and forgiveness.

The Confluence of Growth and Transformation with Developmental Tasks

Significant physical, emotional, cognitive, and interpersonal developments occur during adolescence and shape adolescents toward resolving three developmental tasks: selecting a career focus, becoming an independent person, and developing and maintaining lasting, intimate relationships. Terminal illness and grief can threaten the completion of these developmental tasks. Consider a college student whose illness or grief obstructs concentrating on studies, produces isolation from others, and leads to disinterest in planning for the future. However, certain responses to these serious circumstances can radically transform a person, leading to expressions of love manifested as empathy, altruism, compassion, and engagement with others. Such growth and transformation has links to identity formation and faith consciousness.

Love as Transforming

Love possesses transforming powers. Creativity is one of the chief manifestations of the power of love, and personality integration is the final outcome of a life transformed by love. The chief outward sign of love's creativity and integration is altruistic growth. A personality transformed by love is open to and marked by transcendence.

Empathy. This enables a person to understand what an experience means to someone else, to appreciate what another person feels, and to act out of a vicarious comprehension of someone else's situation. Empathy requires an individual to differentiate between his or her thoughts and feelings and another person's thoughts and feelings.

Altruism. The transition from empathic understanding to empathic communication, altruism involves actions taken on behalf of someone. We recognize the truly exceptional feats of altruism in public figures who devote their lives to the service of others (Mother Teresa provided a contemporary example) and in the extraordinary, singular acts of heroism performed by individuals who endanger their lives to save others (fire fighters, for instance). I contend that adolescents who are dying and those who are grieving develop behaviors that indicate a concern for the well-being of others. Examples could be an adolescent who offers an attentive ear to someone in emotional turmoil or an adolescent who talks to a friend about his at-risk behavior with drugs or sex and offers to help that person find a counselor. I have yet to meet an adolescent who has coped with bereavement who is afraid to be present to someone in emotional pain.

The Buddhist tradition emphasizes that *compassion* is inherent to human nature, that gentleness is the nature of humanity, and that selfless love is at the core of being human. "Compassion is a human emotional and cognitive experience that does not happen to a single individual in isolation, but as a response to another sentient being. It is a process of external and internal reorientation that softens our sense of individuality by bringing it into a felt relationship with the pain and needs of some other" (Harrington, 2002, p. 21). Evidence that "human beings are fundamentally compassionate is our natural ability to connect spontaneously and deeply with the suffering of others" (Dalai Lama, 2002, p. 73). Our "natural capacity to empathize with others' pain and suffering" indicates that we are "fundamentally self-giving, fundamentally generous" (Dalai Lama, 2002, p. 76).

Engagement with Others. Coping with bereavement leads some adolescents to reach out to others in distress, to lose their fear of others in pain, and to be present to them rather than to flee figuratively or literally when someone in anguish enters the room. I suspect the same possibility is true for adolescents with a life-threatening illness. Reaching out to others is a transformation that occurs as a positive response to coping with suffering; is a mark of empathy, altruism, and compassion; and indicates "this wonderful capacity to transcend the limitations of self-centeredness through acts of compassion and love" (Dalai Lama, 2002, p. 77).

We know that unresolved bereavement poses a serious health hazard. Adolescents are considered highly vulnerable to debilitating consequences following the death of a loved one because bereavement can seriously disrupt the developmental tasks and transitions adolescents are expected to complete. Poorly completed developmental tasks become in adulthood the source of chronic difficulties with self, the world of work, and interpersonal relations. It is not clear to me how to apply these same notions to life-threatened adolescents who may not live beyond their adolescence; however, I suspect that for some life-threatened adolescents there will be growth and transformation seen in empathy, compassion, altruism, and engagement with others, even if in highly restricted environments and constrained time frames.

Brammer presented a model describing how life crises lead to profound transformations. The fourfold process moves from disruption to incubation to transformation to action. Disruption means that the life crisis must profoundly unsettle our thinking and behavior; in other words the effects must present disruptive challenges to our assumptive world. Incubation involves a creative response to the crisis, and during this step ideas quietly simmer and people engage in detached reflection; the incubation process offers remarkable opportunities to consider new directions, new perspectives, new relationships, and new values. Transformation is the moment of insight wherein the world is seen differently; transformation is the critical point when the person is ready to grasp a new way of thinking or acting, a new awareness of being and of one's relationship to oneself, the world, other people, and transcendent reality. Action is the creative response to the crisis, and involves both an active letting go of old responses that inhibit change and taking hold of new responses that promote connections and continued development. Action produces altruism, empathy, and compassion.

The process of transformation emerging out of the life crisis, particularly out of the trauma of suffering, has been explained as a function of changed schemas. Such changed schemas involve examining anew the most fundamental relationships: our relationships to self, to other persons, to the greater world, and to transcendent reality. In short, these changed schemas occur when a person radically reexperiences and restructures these fundamental aspects of human existence.

Not all traumas produce changed schemas that are transformative. The distilled explanation is that transformative outcomes require certain changes to have occurred. First, the life crisis leads to a noticeable change in a person's perceptions of self and/or of the world. Second, this change in perceptions is seen to be a more profound understanding of reality than the individual previously had. Third, this more profound understanding opens the person to try new directions, new perspectives, new relationships, and new values. Fourth, the person is able to reframe what was lost and live now in relationships to self, the world, other persons, and transcendent reality more promising than had been considered before and during the threat the person faced. Fifth, changes that have occurred are now seen as central to responding to the crisis.

Some indicators of these transformative changes are: (a) allowing oneself to forgive others and to forgive oneself, (b) being energized by hope in one's future, (c) extending oneself empathetically to others in acts of altruism and compassion, (d) understanding God differently than one did before. Such changes point to a maturing of faith.

Faith Consciousness. James Fowler has constructed a theory about the development of faith consciousness across the life span. He makes clear that faith need not be religious in content or expression. Rather than a matter of religious commitment, faith denotes for Fowler the universal human quest to identify what is of ultimate value, what gives meaning to human existence, and what enables a person to be connected to others. He makes clear that relationships are important in the transitions that mark a person's changes over time in faith consciousness.

Fowler points to a stage of faith consciousness called "individuative-reflective," which emerges in late adolescence and early adulthood if certain factors are present. People reach individuative-reflective faith only when examining, evaluating, and restructuring their values and beliefs; making conscious, personal choices, rather than accepting unexamined commitments; and only after a period of crisis. Further, individuative-reflective faith depends on an important change in self-understanding: the person seeks foundations that underlie the roles and relationships in their lives. I am struck by the links between this quest for foundations, Attig's notion of relearning one's fundamental relationships, Neimeyer's ideas about meaning making, and the transformations that life crises can stimulate.

A Research Plan to Study Transformation and Growth

Here is a plan to use several researchers to examine transformation and growth of bereaved college students in terms of expressions of love manifested as empathy, altruism, compassion, and engagement with others. Such growth and transformation has links to identity formation and faith consciousness.[2] The research study addresses the question, "When does bereavement of late adolescent college students serve as a transforming experience promoting empathy, altruism, and compassion?"

Focus of the Research. At its heart this study will examine issues of hope, courage, altruism, compassion, and forgiveness as they emerge in bereaved college students' lives. The focus will be in-depth, longitudinal case studies of bereaved students' self-understandings, of their interpersonal relationships, of their relationships to the greater world, and of their relationship to a transcendent reality.

Methodology. The researchers will employ both quantitative and qualitative methods to study students whose responses to bereavement set them apart for resilience, compassion, and empathy. The researchers will gather in-depth, longitudinal case studies of bereaved students' self-understandings, of their interpersonal relationships, of their relationships to the greater world, and of their relationship to a transcendent reality. Strengths of the method include (a) the open use of triangulation by means of multiple methods, multiple data sources, and multiple researchers; (b) the means to obtain a complex synthesis indicating pathways leading bereaved students to extend love to others via empathy, altruism, and compassion; and (c) the production of rich, in-depth narratives enabling a vicarious understanding of the experiences of bereaved students.

Sample. The sample will come from (a) leaders of local chapters of the National Students of AMF and from (b) persons who know the students; this second group of participants will be key informants—typically adults on campus, but perhaps other students—who know the leaders of the AMF chapters. AMF chapter leaders will have been touched by death within the past 6 to 24 months. Contrast and comparison will be available by studying students from different campuses. Constructs to be examined include grief, meaning making, developmental tasks, cognitive development à la William Perry's categories, the inner representation of the deceased, social system interaction, and faith consciousness.

Data Collection. Standardized instruments, projective tools, participant journals, in-depth interviews, and longitudinal case study methods will be used to gather data. The standardized instruments will include the Hogan Grief Reaction Checklist, the Inventory of Traumatic Grief, the Attachment Inventory mentioned earlier in this chapter, and the Erikson Psychosocial Stage Inventory (EPSI). The Hogan Grief Reaction Checklist and the Inventory of Traumatic Grief were discussed in Chapter 8. The EPSI is a 72-item self-report inventory that assesses the extent of psychosocial maturity achieved by respondents. There are six scales, each 12 items long, that assess, respectively, trust, autonomy, initiative, industry, identity, and intimacy. Reliability and validity tests have been positive. Participants will complete the Life Values Inventory.

Qualitative data will be obtained in four ways: (a) administration of the Thematic Apperception Test (TAT), a projective technique used successfully with bereaved college students; (b) review of journals students keep on specific issues central to the study; (c) in-depth interviews regarding faith consciousness; and (d) interviews with key informants.

Ten cards from the 31 TAT assortment will be administered. Participants will be asked to write stories of at least 250 words about each of the cards. The instructions will be to write a description of what the card depicts, and then make up a story with these components: what happened before the scene in the picture, what is happening now, what are the people in the picture thinking and feeling, and how will things turn out. Responses will be analyzed for the presence of themes of death, loss, grief, altruism, empathy, and compassion.

Student participants will keep journals on specific issues central to the study: reflections on the meaning of death, on personal identity, on interpersonal relationships, and on career direction in life. We will examine the journals for preordinate as well as emergent, unexpected themes. The preordinate themes include expressions of hope, courage, altruism, resiliency, empathy, compassion, forgiveness, trusting in the predictability of events, gaining a sense of mastery and control, forging relationships marked by belonging, believing the world is fair and just, and developing self-confidence and self-efficacy.

In-depth interviews will include Fowler's faith stages interview, the Reflective Judgment Interview, and questions about the impact of the death on the student's social relationships, worldview, locus of authority, and other dimensions of meaning making. Rather than examine each stage in Fowler's faith consciousness theory, we will focus on individuative-reflective faith, the stage that typically emerges in late adolescence and early adulthood when certain factors are present, and the stage in faith consciousness preceding and following individuative-reflective faith. Persons reach individuative-reflective faith only when they engage in examining, evaluating, and restructuring their values and beliefs; and make conscious, personal choices rather than accepting unexamined commitments. The movement into this stage of faith consciousness occurs only after a period of crisis. Further, individuative-reflective faith depends on an important change in self-understanding: the person seeks foundations that underlie the roles and relationships in their lives. The links are striking between this quest for foundations and Attig's notion of relearning fundamental relationships.

Fowler used a four-part interview guide to examine development in faith consciousness. Part one is a life review and includes such questions as "Thinking about yourself at present, what gives your life meaning?" Part two focuses on life-shaping experiences and relationships and includes such questions as "Have you experienced losses, crises, or suffering that have changed or colored your life in special ways?" Part three examines present values and commitments and includes such questions as "What does death mean to you?" Part four looks at religion and includes such questions as "Where do you feel that you are changing, growing, struggling, or wrestling with doubt in your life at the present time?"

The Reflective Judgment Interview asks participants "to arrive at judgments about complex, ill-defined problems" such as "reconciling the beliefs of creationism with scientific evidence regarding evolution . . . or discussing the possibility that the pyramids were built with the assistance of visitors from other planets" (Pike, 2011, pp. 11–12). Measures of reliability and validity of the instrument are promising, suggesting this interview procedure does provide "accurate and appropriate information about how students (and others)" (p. 12) engage in various modes of what Perry called reflective judgment.

Interviews with the key informants will start with foreshadowing questions and be attentive to questions that need to be asked in response to answers given. Among foreshadowing questions to be asked of key informants are "What about this student makes him/her stand out from others who have experienced bereavement?", "Tell me of an incident in which this young adult reached out to others in pain," "How would you describe the way this youth deals with disappointment?", and "Where does this student go for support and encouragement when he/she needs it?"

Researchers will keep field notes. The field notes will be sources of information to craft vignettes and scenarios capturing what the researchers observed. Vignettes and scenarios will be shared with research participants for comments about credibility and fidelity to the overall cases being examined.

Concluding Comments

There is much work yet to complete to build our understanding of the realities that circumscribe dying and grieving during adolescence. Part of the effort needs to involve a great variety of research efforts that will disclose the complex phenomena impinging on adolescents who are faced with their own life-threatening illness or who are grieving the death of someone they love. Part of the effort needs to involve design and application of primary, secondary, and tertiary interventions responsive to specific needs.

Impressive strides have been made in both research and practice arenas, and some work even involves collaboration between practitioners and researchers. There is increasing awareness that adolescents' developmental pressures make them different than children and different than adults. There is increasing awareness that early, middle, and later adolescence present different possibilities, conflicts, and issues, and that these differences encompass backstories to the challenges adolescents and young adults face when dealing with bereavement or a life-threatening illness.

Persons interested in dying and grieving during adolescence are blessed to have had important contributors add to knowledge about life-threatened and bereaved adolescents. Many of these contributors remain active, and a new generation of practitioners and researchers is poised to make its mark. The future looks promising.

Notes

1. The material on using the creative arts appeared originally in *Helping the Bereaved College Student* (Balk, 2011, pp. 181–183).
2. Ideas for this research project were generated in stimulating discussions held over several weeks with Dennis Klass.

Sources

Balk, D. E. (1995). Attachment and the reactions of bereaved college students: A longitudinal study. In D. Klass, P. R. Silverman, & S. Nickman. (Eds.), *Continuing Bonds: New Understandings of Grief* (pp. 311–328). Washington, DC: Taylor & Francis.

Balk, D. E. (1999). Bereavement and spiritual change. *Death Studies, 23,* 485–493.

Balk, D. E. (2011). *Helping the bereaved college student.* New York: Springer.

Barnett, M.A., Thompson, M.A., & Pfeiffer, J.R. (1985). Perceived competence to help and the arousal of empathy. *Journal of Social Psychology, 125,* 679–680.

Brammer, L.M. (1992). Coping with life transitions. *International Journal for the Advancement of Counselling, 15,* 239–253.

Brammer, V. (1993). *The model of love: A study in philosophical theology.* Cambridge, UK: Cambridge University Press.

Calhoun, L.G. & Tedeschi, R.G. (2013). *Posttraumatic growth in clinical practice.* New York: Routledge.

Dalai Lama. (2002). Understanding our fundamental nature. In R. J. Davidson & A. Harrington (Eds.), *Visions of compassion: Western scientists and Tibetan Buddhists examine human nature* (pp. 66–80). New York: Oxford University Press.

Dana, R.H. (1986). Thematic Apperception Test used with adolescents. In A.I. Rabin (Ed.), *Projective techniques for adolescents and children* (pp. 14–36). New York: Springer.

Davidson, R. J. (2002). Toward a biology of positive affect and compassion. In R. J. Davidson & A. Harrington (Eds.), *Visions of compassion: Western scientists and Tibetan Buddhists examine human nature* (pp. 107–130). New York: Oxford University Press.

Fowler, J.A. (1981). *Stages of faith: The psychology of human development and the quest for meaning.* San Francisco: Harper & Row.

Harrington, A. (2002). A science of compassion or a compassionate science? What do we expect from a cross-cultural dialogue with Buddhism? In R. J. Davidson & A. Harrington (Eds.), *Visions of compassion: Western scientists and Tibetan Buddhists examine human nature* (pp.18–30). New York: Oxford University Press.

King, P.M. & Kitchener, K.S. (1994). *Developing reflective judgment: Understanding and promoting intellectual growth and critical thinking in adolescents and adults.* San Francisco: Jossey-Bass.

King, P.M. & Kitchener, K.S. (2002). The reflective judgment model: Twenty years of research on epistemicognition. In B.K. Hofer & P.R. Pintrich (Eds.), *Personal epistemology: The psychology of beliefs about knowledge and knowing* (pp. 37–61). Mahwah, NJ: Lawrence Erlbaum.

Pike, G.R. (2011). Assessment measures: The Reflective Judgment Interview. *Assessment Update,* 23(1), 11–12.

Prigerson, H.G. & Jacobs, S.C. (2001). Traumatic grief as a distinct disorder: A rationale, consensus criteria, and a preliminary empirical test. In M.S. Stroebe, R.O. Hansson, W. Stroebe, & H. Schut (Eds.), *Handbook of bereavement research: Consequences, coping, and care* (pp. 613–645). Washington, DC: American Psychological Association.

Prigerson, H.G., Maciejewski, P.K., Newsom, J., Reynolds, C.F., Frank, E., Bierhals, E.J., Miller, M., Fasiczka, A., Doman, J., & Houck, P.R. (1995). The Inventory of Complicated Grief: A scale to measure maladaptive symptoms of loss. *Psychiatry Research, 59,* 65–79.

Soble, A. (1960). *The structure of love.* New Haven, CT: Yale University Press.

Sorokin, P.A. (1954). *The ways and power of love: Types, factors, and techniques of moral transformation.* Boston: Beacon Press.

Sperling, M.B., Foelsch, P., & Grace, C. (1996). Measuring adult attachment: Are self-report instruments congruent? *Journal of Personality Assessment, 67,* 37–51.

Stake, R.E. (1995). *The art of case study research.* Thousand Oaks, CA: Sage.

Stake, R.E. (2010). *Qualitative research: Studying how things work.* New York: Guilford.

Tedeschi, R.G. & Calhoun, L.G. (1995). *Trauma and transformation: Growing in the aftermath of suffering.* Thousand Oaks, CA: Sage.

West, M., Sheldon, A., & Reiffer, L. (1987). An approach to the delineation of adult attachment: Scale development and reliability. *Journal of Nervous and Mental Disease, 175,* 738–741.

Appendix A

Syllabi for an Undergraduate College Course in Thanatology

CORC 3314—Human Encounters with Death and Bereavement (code: 2370)
Spring 2013, M & W 3:40–4:55 PM, 3413 Ingersoll
Dr. David E. Balk Office: 4110a N
Office Hours: Monday and Wednesday, 2:00–3:30 PM
Tuesday 2:30–5:00 PM
and by appointment
Office Phone: 718–951–5000 (x1232) E-Mail: dbalk@brooklyn.cuny.edu

Catalog Description: Individual and societal attitudes concerning death and life. How attitudes about death influence the quality of life and health. Impact of technology on the care of the dying. Medical concerns in the treatment of the terminally ill. The bereavement process.

Rationale: Experiences with death, dying, and bereavement are central to human existence. These three topics form areas of inquiry that concern numerous academic disciplines (literature, the classics, anthropology, sociology, philosophy, religious studies, and health and nutrition to name a few). This course examines major gains made in the 20th and 21st centuries to understand human responses to death, dying, and bereavement. Analysis of thanatological experiences has uncovered their holistic impact: these core experiences of human existence affect persons physically, cognitively, emotionally, behaviorally, interpersonally, and spiritually. The course looks at how medical research in league with technological advances and medical practice have extended the human life span and at the same time sequestered dying from normal experience. The course examines scientific criteria sharpened for determining when a human being is dead. Further, issues over assisted suicide are reviewed. The course underscores that advances in life-sustaining techniques place persons in ethical decision-making that persons were spared one or two generations ago. The course looks at the interdisciplinary efforts to assist the dying and the bereaved that have emerged in the latter half of the 20th century, and it explores cultural and ethnic differences in response to death, dying, and bereavement. The course is punctuated with examples illustrating the holistic dimensions of human encounters with death and bereavement.

Course Objectives: The students will

1. Identify the factors that influence personal attitudes toward death and dying.
2. Describe and analyze the various programs of care for the terminally ill.
3. Describe the process of bereavement and examine various models offered about bereavement.
4. Learn how adolescents and the elderly deal with death, dying, and bereavement.
4. Review and analyze three personal accounts about death, dying, and bereavement.
5. Engage in critical discussion of the personal accounts with a small group of students enrolled in the course.
6. Identify ways in which one may help a grieving family member or friend.
7. Critique the various arguments presented by proponents and opponents of the activities labeled as euthanasia.
8. Summarize and reflect on the feedback given to your written work.
9. Meet the due dates for assignments in the course.
10. Demonstrate willingness to listen to and understand points of view different than one's own.
11. Provide constructive critiques of others' written work, and accept constructive critiques from others about your own written work.
12. Complete a course project chosen from a variety of options listed in the syllabus.

Text: *Selected Chapters from Colleagues in the Field of Thanatology—To Be Provided to Students*

Course Outline
Part One: Weeks 1 thru 5: The Biomedical Model, Encounters with Death and Dying, and Dying on One's Own Terms. Read the course materials for Part One and Personal Account #1 ("The Courage to Face Death" by Cecil Neth).*

Thesis of Part One of the course: The biomedical model dominates experiences with and understandings of death and dying in developed, postindustrial countries.

Week 1—Introduction to course and review of the historical development of institutions for the dying
Week 2—Four themes about dying in 20th and 21st century secular cultures
Week 3—New forms of dying and definitions of death
Week 4—Review and discussion of the National Issues Forum "Dying on One's Own Terms"
Week 5—Group discussions of Personal Account #1

Exam Covering Materials for Part One, Lecture Notes, and Personal Account #1

Part Two: Weeks 6 thru 9: Coping with Death and Bereavement. Read the course materials for Part Two and Personal Account #2 ("Bereavement Experiences of Three College Students").*

Thesis of Part Two of the course: Encounters with death and bereavement are the paradigmatic life crises with which humans cope.

>   Week 6—Models for how humans cope with knowing they are dying; primary understandings of bereavement: Freud, Bowlby, Lindemann
>   Week 7—Bereavement seen as a stressful event
>   Week 8—Disenfranchised and complicated grief and major losses in the lives of college students
>   Week 9—Changes in expressions of mourning and group discussion of Personal Account #2

Exam Covering Materials for Part Two, Lecture Notes, and Personal Account #2

Part Three: Weeks 10 thru 14: Special Topics (Assisted Suicide, Caregivers and Burnout, and Health Care in an Aging Society). Read the materials for Part Three and Personal Account #3 ("Allowing the Debilitated to Die: Facing our Ethical Choices" by David Hilfiker).*

Thesis of Part Three of the course: More open discussion is called for regarding death, dying, and bereavement in contemporary society.

>   Weeks 10 and 11—The burden on caregivers for the chronically and terminally ill
>   Weeks 12 and 13—The international debate about and push for legalized assisted suicide
>   Week 14—Health care in an aging society and group discussion of Personal Account #3

Final Exam Covering Materials for Part Three, Lecture Notes, and Personal Account #3

*The professor will provide you copies of the personal accounts.

Grades will be based on the following point and percentage distribution:

Three exams: each worth 200 points	600
Three worksheets of group discussions: each worth 40 points	120
Three critical reviews of personal accounts: each worth 60 points	180
Course project	200
Present when attendance called (5 points each class)	140
Assessment forms turned in on time: each worth 10 points	30
Overall assessment from students of your group participation	46
Total	1316

A = 90–100% (1184–1316 points)
A = 1184–1222; A = 1223–1283; A+ = 1284–1316
B = 80–89% (1052–1183 points)
B– = 1052–1090; B = 1091–1151; B+ = 1152–1183

C = 70–79% (921–1051 points)
C– = 921–952; C = 953–1033; C+ = 1034–1051
D = 60–69% (789–920 points)
D– = 789–827; D = 828–888; D+ = 889–920
F = < 60% (0–788 points)

NOTE: All assignments are due on the date assigned. Ten points will be deducted for each day that an assignment is late. Ten points will not be added, however, for each day that an assignment is early. No assignment will be accepted after it is 4 days late.

Group Work on Personal Accounts

I will divide students into working groups of four to five members each. The tasks of the working groups are:

1. Each student will read the personal account, provide a 150- to 200-word summary of the personal account, and answer on a typed sheet the questions that have been indicated.
2. Bring to class enough printed copies of your answers to the questions for you, me, and each member of your group. Thus, if there are three persons plus you in your group, you will bring five copies. Do not use class time to make copies.
3. Each student will read aloud to the rest of the group his/her summary of the personal account and answers to the questions.
4. The group will discuss the summaries and identify what could be done to strengthen each student's review as a clear and reliable presentation of the personal account.
5. The group will discuss the questions and the various answers given to the personal account and alternate questions to consider that are pertinent to the account.
6. The group will complete a discussion worksheet (a) identifying points discussed about each student's review of the personal account, (b) mentioning personal experiences and observations of group members that confirm or call into question material in the personal account, (c) identifying areas on which people reach consensus and areas on which people disagree, and (d) identifying how the personal account could be strengthened as an introduction to one or more topics about this course.

Why am I structuring the class in this fashion? I have several reasons. One, I want to increase the likelihood that students will become engaged in the course. Becoming engaged in a course is more likely when the students are involved in active learning, connecting ideas from many sources, applying material to experiences, and applying their experiences to course material. The format I've chosen provides opportunities for active learning, for connecting ideas, and for applying experiences and material. Two, research with undergraduates indicates that they become most engaged in courses in which they work in small study groups and in which they regularly produce pieces of writing. Three, the written assignments provide an opportunity to extend your thinking. Regularly putting your thoughts into writing gives you an opportunity to clarify your thinking and stretch your communication skills. Four, college graduates emphasize writing well is the single most important professional skill they use every day. Undergraduates who share their writing with peers actually report their writing improves, if the peers and the instructor provide feedback. Five, I want students to grapple with the material in the course. The course materials can be more demanding than need be when the student does not interact actively with the material, that is, does not study actively. I no longer think it relevant to ask students, "Do you study?" Rather, the question I find relevant is, "How do you study?" This course requires active reading of the materials, working out ideas on paper, and discussing ideas with others. If used well, the format may promote actual dialogue about ideas and issues.

What should the written review of each personal account contain? It should provide adequate answers to the questions asked and issues raised about each personal account.

What should be the format of reviews of each personal account? See directly below.

Format for your review of each personal account:

1. Your name.
2. Title of the personal account.
3. Summary of what the personal account contains.
4. Answers to questions about the personal account.
5. One or two alternate questions you propose people consider and why the alternate questions strike you as important.
6. For the second and third reviews, a paragraph summarizing the feedback you have received and how you are responding to the feedback in your current review.

Remember: The work on these personal accounts must be your own. Do not copy someone else's work.

Attendance in Class: Students in this course are expected to show up on time for every class meeting and for every group meeting and to be in class for the whole period. Reliable and active participation as a group member is crucial for group interaction to prove beneficial to all group members. Students present when attendance is taken will earn five points. Don't negotiate for points if you come in after your name is called or if you leave class and are not present should attendance be taken before the class is dismissed. Students are expected to show common courtesy during the class and not get up to leave the room or wander around, text, or talk on cell phones.

Course Calendar for CORC 3314

Part One: January 28–March 6: Encounters with Death and Dying. Read the Part One reading materials.

January 28:	Introduction to course
January 30:	Lecture
February 4:	Lecture
February 6:	Lecture

February 11:	Lecture
February 12:	Lincoln's Birthday—College Closed
February 13:	Lecture (typed notice of project choices due)
February 18:	President's Day—College Closed
February 20:	Lecture (Conversion Day—Classes follow a Monday schedule)
February 25:	Group discussion of personal account #1
February 27:	Lecture
March 4:	Exam covering reading materials for Part One, lecture notes, and personal account #1

Part Two: March 6–April 5: Coping with Death and Bereavement. Read the Part Two reading materials.

March 6:	Lecture
March 11:	Lecture
March 13:	Lecture
March 18:	Lecture
March 20:	Lecture
Spring Recess:	March 25–April 2
April 3:	Lecture
April 8:	Group discussion of personal account #2
April 10:	Lecture
April 15:	Exam covering reading materials for Part Two, lecture notes, and personal account #2

Part Three: April 17 to end of course: Special Topics. Read the Part Three reading materials.

April 17:	Lecture
April 22:	Lecture
April 24:	Lecture—Course project due
April 29:	Lecture
May 1:	Lecture
May 6:	Lecture
May 8:	Group discussion of personal account #3
May 13:	Lecture
May 15:	Lecture

Final exam covering reading materials for Part Three, lecture notes, and personal account #3

Final exams are given May 18–24.

Exams in this course will be a combination of multiple choice items, short written answers, and essays.

Important Issue: This course is not intended as a means for a student to resolve losses in his/her life nor to provide therapy or counseling for persons bereaved over a death. Note that we take up topics that can solicit painful feelings for some individuals. In this

class we do not betray people by rescuing them from painful feelings but rather listen attentively and respectfully. If you sense the need to discuss painful feelings or thoughts with a professional counselor, please contact the Brooklyn College office of Personal Counseling in James Hall.

NOTE: RESPECT ME AND YOUR FELLOW STUDENTS. TURN OFF THE AUDIBLE RINGERS TO CELL PHONES AND PAGERS WHILE IN THIS CLASS. DON'T SEND TEXT MESSAGES WHILE WE ARE IN SESSION. DON'T TALK ON YOUR CELL PHONE WHILE WE ARE IN SESSION. DON'T TAKE OUT CELL PHONES TO LOOK AT, ADMIRE, SEND TEXT MESSAGES, CONDUCT CONVERSATIONS, OR WORSHIP AS SOME IDOL DURING CLASS SESSIONS.

Plagiarism and cheating are serious offenses and may be punished by failure on the exam, paper, or project; failure in the course; and/or expulsion from the university. Lest there be any confusion about what is meant by plagiarism, the term means *stealing or passing off as one's own the ideas or words of someone else*. A very common form of plagiarism seen on university campuses is verbatim copying from books and articles, without giving explicit credit to the real author. The dean of a college in Boston was removed from his job because he passed off as his work what others had written. A reporter for a newspaper in Fort Worth, Texas, was fired for using verbatim quotes from an article in *The Washington Post* without identifying the source.

You are expected when you quote someone else to place the words in quotation marks, identify explicitly the source, and give the page number(s) for the quote. When you use someone else's ideas but paraphrase them, you are expected to identify explicitly the source of your information.

Academic Accommodations for Disabled Students

Any student with a disability who needs an accommodation or other assistance in this course should make an appointment to speak with me as soon as possible and obtain official notice from the Office of Student Disability Services at Brooklyn College.

Worksheet for Use in Discussion of Personal Accounts

For each personal account that is discussed, review these questions and provide written responses documenting your group's discussion:

1. What are the strengths in **each person's summary** and what are some ways **each student** can improve his/her summary to provide a clear and reliable presentation of the personal account? (Give particulars about each group member's summary, not just a statement about the summaries in general.)
2. What were the strengths in **each person's** answers to the questions and what are some ways **each student** can improve his/her answers to the questions? (**Give particulars** about **each group member's answers,** not just a statement about the answers in general.)

3. What personal experiences and observations of group members were mentioned as experiences and observations that confirm or call into question material in the personal account? (**Give particulars** about **each group member's** experiences and observations, not just a statement about comments in general.)
4. What are areas on which people reach consensus? (**Give particulars.**)
5. What are areas on which people disagree? (**Give particulars.**)
6. How could the personal account be strengthened as an introduction to one or more topics about this course? (**Give particulars.**)

Synthesize the group's answers to the six items and turn in the worksheet with accompanying pages with summaries of the discussion. The summary is due at the end of the class in which the personal account is being discussed.

Take turns at each group meeting writing summaries to the items. Make sure each person in the group summarizes discussion about at least one item at the meeting. Be sure to give examples that illustrate what was discussed. Don't for instance simply say, "We agreed about everything." Give examples that verify or illustrate this agreement.

Title of personal account_____
Date of meeting: _____
Signatures of group members present:

Class Projects

Students will complete one of the following projects. The completed project is due April 24 at the start of class. All projects must be typed, double-spaced, with 1" margins all around, using New Times Roman or Old Bookman style and 11 or 12 point font. You must inform me by February 13 with an email message or a typed note of what project you intend to complete.

Choice 1: What do children between the ages of 6 and 10 know about death and grief? Select two books written especially for a child (ages 6 to 10) to read and for one of the child's parents to read as well. The book has to have at its basic theme an explanation of what death is or the dying or death of a person, or coping with loss due to the death of a person or of a pet. You must inform me by February 13 with a typed page (or in an email message) the titles of your books and explain how each book meets the criteria given in the sentences directly above.

Content of the project

1. Read and critique each book. Provide a brief overview of the story, and critique each book by applying information from the course materials, lecture notes, and any other sources based on scholarship.
2. Obtain permission from a parent to have his/her 6- to 10-year-old child read the books and for the parent to read the books also and discuss the books with their child once both have read them.

Table Appendix A Group Assessment Form for Discussion of Personal Accounts CORC 3314—
Spring 2013

Name: _____

Meeting Date:_____

Personal account # _____

Group Members: Give **both the first and last name** of each group member on the lines below. Don't evaluate your own participation

Names of Group Members					
1. Was the person present? (Yes/No) Yes = 2, No = 0					
2. Did the person arrive on time? (Yes/No) Yes = 2, No = 0					
3. Did the person stay the whole meeting? (Yes/No) Yes = 2, No = 0					
4. Rate their participation in the discussion. (0–10) 0 = poor 5 = fair 8 = good 10 = excellent					
5. Did the person come prepared? (0–10) 0 = poor 5 = fair 8 = good 10 = excellent					
6. Rate the person's knowledge of the material. (0–10) 0 = poor 5 = fair 8 = good 10 = excellent					
7. Rate the person's contribution to the work of the group. (0–10) 0 = poor 5 = fair 8 = good 10 = excellent					

Where on this line indicates the extent you are listened to in this group?

Not at all   Fully

Where on this line indicates the extent to which you are accepted as a full member of this group?

Not at all   Fully

3. Some questions for the parent to ask the child are
    a. What each book was about, including the main characters and the main theme(s) of the story
    b. What he/she thinks the author of each book wanted the reader to learn
    c. The important things about death each book taught
    d. If he/she enjoyed reading each book and why or why not
    e. How the story could be made even better in each book
    f. What feelings the child had from reading each book
    g. If the books are ones to recommend to other children and why or why not
4. Ask the parent his/her evaluation of the books, and what the parent learned about his/her child's understanding of death from discussing the books.

5. Ask the parent if he/she would recommend the books for other children of the same age as the child who read them.
6. Write a full report of the information obtained in items 3, 4, and 5.
7. Provide the name, address, and phone number of the parent (plus the name of the child).

Choice 2: Examine the role, content of, and actual rituals used in funerals conducted in three different religious traditions: for instance, in Protestantism (e.g., Lutheran, Pentecostal, Baptist, Methodist, Episcopalian), Catholicism (Roman, Orthodox), Judaism (Reformed, Orthodox, Conservative), Islam (e.g., Sunni, Shiite), Hinduism, Buddhism. Note: You will not be selecting three different religious traditions if you focus on three versions of Protestantism. You must inform me by February 13 if you intend to do choice 2.

1. Provide a clear explanation of the rituals followed for a funeral in the three religious traditions you select. Identify clearly the authoritative source for your information.
2. Interview a funeral director about funerals conducted within those three religious traditions.
3. Compare and contrast the funeral rituals in each tradition.
4. Interview a minister (priest, rabbi, cleric) in each of the three traditions about the purpose of funerals in that tradition.
5. Provide the name, address, and phone number of the funeral directors and of the ministers.

Choice 3: Conduct a survey of 20 college students between the ages of 18 and 25 and get their answers (yes or no) and their explanation of their answers to the 11 questions given below. The students CANNOT be persons enrolled in this course. Develop a consent sheet for each participant to sign. The consent sheet needs to tell the person clearly what you asking him/her to do, and provide a place to sign they have agreed to take part in the survey. Inform me by February 13 if you intend to do choice 3.

1. There are circumstances in which a person should be allowed to die.
2. People have the right to make their own decisions about receiving life-sustaining treatment.
3. Patients can count on doctors and nurses paying attention to instructions patients give about wanting or not wanting life-sustaining treatment.
4. When a terminally ill person is unable to communicate and has not made wishes known about continuing medical treatment, the closest family member should be allowed to make the decision.
5. In some circumstances it is permissible for a spouse to kill his/her partner suffering horrible pain from a terminal disease.
6. Most persons suffering from great physical pain or unable to carry out daily living functions would ask their physician to stop treatment rather than doing everything possible to continue their lives.
7. There should be legislation allowing medical treatment to be withdrawn or withheld if a terminally ill person so wishes.

8. Parents whose infant is born with a severe handicap have the right to refuse medical treatment.
9. If afflicted with an incurable disease, a person has the moral right to end his/her own life.
10. If a person's instructions to withhold life-sustaining treatment are ignored and the person survives but suffers a severe disability, the hospital or the physician should be held accountable.
11. A person whose illness is placing an extremely heavy burden on his/her family has the moral right to end his/her life.

Format for your completed project:

1. Describe in a summary paragraph your sample: gender, age, year in college, any experience with death of a friend or family member.
2. Summarize the responses of your sample to the 11 questions. Place in an appendix the actual responses of each person to the questions.
3. Discuss what themes you found in the responses and give quotes from respondents to the survey to illustrate the themes.
4. Examine these themes in light of information learned in this course.
5. Provide the signed consent sheet for each student who took part in your study.

Choice 4: Select a book written for educated adults and pertinent to the subject matter of this course. Turn into the instructor by February 13 two copies of a one-page typed paper (or an email message) identifying the book you have selected and giving your reason(s) for choosing this book. I will return one copy with my comments and retain the other copy in my files. Your job is to read the book critically and compose an 8- to 10-page review of the book. Your review should be typed, follow APA style guidelines, and be double-spaced.

The format of the review should be:

1. A **brief synopsis** of the contents of the book, (1–1 1/2 pages)
2. **Critical analysis** of the book (5–7 pages) (critical analysis will come from applying information from the course materials, from this course, from your personal observations and experiences,[1] and from the rest of your college coursework
3. An assessment of the value of the book for persons interested in thanatology (1 1/2–2 pages) (give reasons to support your assessment)

Some examples of books that are written for educated adults and pertinent to the subject matter of this course:

Attig, T. (1996). *How we grieve; Relearning the world.* New York: Oxford University Press.
Bayer, R. & Oppenheimer, G. M. (2000). *AIDS doctors: Voices from the epidemic.* New York: Oxford University Press.

Bluebond-Langner, M. A. (1996). *In the shadow of illness: Parents and siblings of the chronically ill child.* Princeton, NJ: Princeton University Press.

Bonanno, G. A. (2009). *The other side of sadness: What the new science of bereavement tells us about life after loss.* New York: Basic Books.

Davies, B. (1995). *Fading away: The experience of transition in families with terminal illness.* Amityville, NY: Baywood.

Kushner, H. S. (1983). *When bad things happen to good people.* New York: Avon.

Nuland, S. B. (1994). *How we die: Reflections of life's final chapter.* New York: Knopf.

An excellent source to consult regarding book reviews is *Contemporary Psychology.* Another good source is *Death Studies.* Consulting these journals will give you an idea of how professionals organize a book review. Remember: This assignment is NOT a book report in which you merely summarize the book but a review in which you critically analyze the book.

Choice 5: Analyze how eight songs in popular music handle topics of death, dying, and bereavement. Inform me by February 13 if you have selected this project. Your analysis should examine themes pertinent to this course that you find expressed in each song. It is not necessary that the same theme(s) be expressed in each song although such similarity could give your project clear focus. Your analysis needs to do more than summarize the words of the song and the theme(s) such words express. You need to explain the themes by examining what literature (the course materials and at least two other written sources) has to say about the themes, and you need to examine and assess how well (if at all) the songs present these themes.

The format of the analysis should be:

1. **A brief synopsis** of each song including the title and artist (3–4 pages)
2. **Critical analysis** of thanatology themes the songs express and how the songs express those themes (5–7 pages)
3. **Assessment of the value of these songs** as vehicles to present ideas important to thanatology (1–2 pages) (give reasons to support your assessment)

Choice 6: Analyze how four movies handle topics of death, dying, and bereavement. Inform me by February 13 if you have selected this project. Your analysis should examine themes pertinent to this course that you find expressed in each movie. It is not necessary that the same theme(s) be expressed in each movie although such similarity could give your project clear focus. Your analysis needs to do more than summarize each film and the theme(s) the film presents. You need to explain the themes by examining what literature (the course materials and at least two other written sources) has to say about the themes, and you need to examine and assess how well (if at all) the movies present these themes.

The format of the analysis should be:

1. **A brief synopsis** of the movies (3–4 pages)
2. **Critical analysis** of thanatology themes the films express and how the films express those themes (5–7 pages)
3. **Assessment of the value of the these movies** as vehicles to present ideas important to thanatology (1–2 pages) (give reasons to support your assessment)

Choice 7: Analyze how one fiction and one nonfiction book written for adolescents handle topics of death, dying, and bereavement. Inform me by February 13 if you have selected this project. Your analysis should examine themes pertinent to this course that you find expressed in each book. It is not necessary that the same theme(s) be expressed in each book although such similarity could give your project clear focus. Your analysis needs to do more than summarize each book and the theme(s) the book presents. You need to explain the themes by examining what literature (the course materials and at least two other written sources) has to say about the themes, and you need to examine and assess how well (if at all) the books present these themes.

The format of the analysis should be:

1. **A brief synopsis** of the books (3–4 pages)
2. **Critical analysis** of thanatology themes the books express and how the books express those themes (5–7 pages)
3. **Assessment of the value of the these books** as vehicles to present ideas important to thanatology (1–2 pages) (give reasons to support your assessment)

See the caution given earlier about not simply writing a book report.

Use of Correct English in Papers

I expect your papers to use written English correctly, and to follow APA rules for citations, headers, reference lists, and page numbers. Papers with presentation mistakes—such as typos, poor organization, and run-on sentences—lose credibility with readers. Obviously, content is crucial; poor presentation of good content makes for a bad report, however. Turn in credible reports.

Composition Mistakes

Common composition mistakes I see regularly are given below. This list is not exhaustive. I fully trust students are capable of making other mistakes than those I am listing here.

Run-on sentences: For instance, "The author used few references in his work, the lack of such references is a weakness." Another example is "There was general agreement that he would end up either a rich man or hanged, his family disowned him."

Sentence fragments (sometimes called "incomplete sentences"): For instance, "Which goes a long way to demonstrate the author's position."

Typos and misspelled words: I am not going to try to give you examples. Students here are very creative.

Incorrect use of words: For instance, "there" for "their" as in this example "There mortgage payments were getting too much to bear." For instance, "it's" for the possessive form of the pronoun *it*. "It's" = "it is." The possessive form of the pronoun is *its,* as in this example: "Its circumference was 20 inches." For instance, "your" for "you're", as in this example: "Your glad to see that question on the exam."

Use of the word *this* with no clear reference to what *this* denotes: For instance, "This led to an emotional breakdown." I expect you to indicate specifically what "this" denotes and not to use the word *this* in isolation. For instance, consider this example: "This traumatic experience led to an emotional breakdown."

Challenge yourself to be clear and specific.

NOTE: In papers written after the first assignment, I expect you to indicate in a beginning paragraph what you have done to incorporate feedback about improving your writing. Within the paper place in *italics* or in **bold font** examples of your responding to feedback about your writing. I expect to find evidence in your paper of what you claim you are doing in your beginning paragraph.

Posting Grades (Copy for Student)

Some students like to have periodic reminders of how they are doing in a course. I need your written permission to post grades, and I must insure that confidentiality is protected in any posting of grades. To insure confidentiality, I will post grades according to five-digit numbers that students assign themselves. If two or more students select the same five-digit number, then they will have to choose new numbers. Students who select to have their grades posted can withdraw that permission later. Students who select NOT to have their grades posted can select to have them posted later. All such decisions must be given in writing. Posted grades will be sent in email attachments.

Select one of these two options (I suspect you realize you are not to select each one):

1. **I give permission to Dr. David Balk to post my grades periodically for CORC 3314: Human Encounters with Death and Bereavement.**
    Name_____   Signature_____   Date_____
    5-digit # _____
2. **I do NOT give permission to Dr. David Balk to post my grades periodically for CORC 3314: Human Encounters with Death and Bereavement.**
    Name_____   Signature_____   Date_____
    My preferred email address is _____

Posting Grades (Copy to Give the Professor)

Some students like to have periodic reminders of how they are doing in a course. I need your written permission to post grades, and I must insure that confidentiality is protected in any posting of grades. To insure confidentiality, I will post grades according to five-digit numbers that students assign themselves. If two or more students select the same five-digit number, then they will have to choose new numbers. Students who select to have their grades posted can withdraw that permission later. Students who select NOT to have their grades posted can select to have them posted later. All such decisions must be given in writing. Posted grades will be sent in email attachments.

Select one of these two options (I suspect you realize you are not to select each one):

1. I give permission to Dr. David Balk to post my grades periodically for CORC 3314: Human Encounters with Death and Bereavement.
   Name_____   Signature_____   Date_____
   5-digit # _____
2. I do NOT give permission to Dr. David Balk to post my grades periodically for CORC 3314: Human Encounters with Death and Bereavement.
   Name_____   Signature_____   Date_____
   My preferred email address is _____

Note

1. While I expect you to use your observations and experiences as one source of information to analyze the book, do NOT use personal experiences and observations as the sole or main source of your critical analysis.

Index